FUNDAMENTALS OF REASONING

A Logic Book

Fourth Edition

Robert M. Johnson

CASTLETON STATE COLLEGE

WADSWORTH

THOMSON LEARNING ™

Australia • Canada • Mexico • Singapore • Spain • United Kingdom • United States

WADSWORTH

THOMSON LEARNING

Publisher: Eve Howard
Philosophy Editor: Peter Adams
Assistant Editor: Kara Kindstrom
Editorial Assistant: Chalida Anusasananan
Development Consultant: Jake Warde
Marketing Manager: Dave Garrison
Marketing Assistant: Adam Hofmann

Print/Media Buyer: Barbara Britton
Production Service: Matrix Productions
Permissions Editor: Bob Kauser
Copy Editor: Chuck Cox
Cover Designer: Bill Stanton
Compositor: G&S Typesetters, Inc.
Cover and Text Printer: Webcom Limited

For permission to use material from this text, contact us by **Web:** http://www.thomsonrights.com
Fax: 1-800-730-2215   **Phone:** 1-800-730-2214

ISBN 0-534-56108-X

For more information, contact
Wadsworth / Thomson Learning
10 Davis Drive
Belmont, CA 94002-3098
USA
For more information about our products, contact us:
Thomson Learning Academic Resource Center
1-800-423-0563
http://www.wadsworth.com

International Headquarters
Thomson Learning
International Division
290 Harbor Drive, 2nd Floor
Stamford, CT 06902-7477
USA

UK/Europe/Middle East/South Africa
Thomson Learning
Berkshire House
168-173 High Holborn
London WC1V 7AA
United Kingdom

Asia
Thomson Learning
60 Albert Complex, #15-01
Singapore 189969

Canada
Nelson Thomson Learning
1120 Birchmount Rd.
Toronto, Ontario M1K 5G4
Canada

Library of Congress Cataloging-in-Publication Data
Johnson, Robert M.
  Fundamentals of reasoning : a logic book / Robert M. Johnson.— 4th ed.
   p. cm.
  Rev. ed. of: A logic book. 3rd ed. c1999.
  Includes index.
  ISBN 0-534-56108-X
   1. Logic. I. Title: Logic book. II. Johnson, Robert M. Logic book.
  III. Title.
BC71.J48 2002
160—dc21   2001035358

Contents

CHAPTER 2

Good Argument, Deductive Validity, and Inductive Strength   29

CHAPTER 3

Categorical Logic Part I   50

CHAPTER 7

Formal Deduction   180

CHAPTER 8

Inductive Logic   206

CHAPTER 9

Informal Fallacies   263

Preface

While the title has changed from *A Logic Book* to *Fundamentals of Reasoning,* this is still the same "user-friendly" textbook designed for a first course in logic. It is also suitable as a supplementary text for courses in critical thinking or rhetoric or as an introduction for the reader who seeks a clear and concise survey of logic. This book presupposes no previous study in logic but goes to great pains to make logic understandable and useful.

Fundamentals of Reasoning covers the traditional subjects of logic: deductive and inductive reasoning and informal fallacies. The book is designed so that professors may select from the topics or present all in one semester. For example, Chapters 1 and 2 introduce basic concepts—specifically, argument and inferential strength—and should be read first. Then professors will probably want to introduce students to deductive reasoning. Two different theories of deductive reasoning are presented: categorical logic and truth-functional logic. Since the presentations of categorical and truth-functional logic are independent, professors may teach one or both. (I prefer to teach categorical logic one semester and truth-functional the next.)

Professors who teach truth-functional logic, Chapters 5 and 6, may continue into Chapter 7 on formal deduction. It is possible to teach Chapter 7 without Chapters 5 and 6 first but professors would probably want students to study at least Sections 5.4 "The Symbols and Their Uses," 5.5 "Grouping and the Scope of Operators," 5.7 "The Truth-functions," and 5.8 "Constructing Truth Tables."

After treating deductive reasoning, most courses in logic will turn to inductive reasoning. Chapter 8 provides a clear and comprehensive presentation of inductive generalization, causal reasoning, and analogical reasoning, a standard classification of types of inductive argument. Then professors may want to teach informal fallacies, Chapter 9. For those professors who prefer, Chapter 9 "Informal Fallacies" can be taught right after Chapters 1 and 2 and before deductive reasoning. The treatment of the informal fallacies in *Fundamentals of Reasoning* does not presuppose an understanding of either deductive or inductive reasoning.

The final chapter, "Evaluating Arguments," returns to and expands upon recognizing arguments, exclusively from real sources, enthymemes, and exposing arguments in long passages. It provides a wealth of real examples showing students how they may paraphrase and rewrite arguments. It also demonstrates evaluating arguments using concepts from throughout the book. It is possible to study Chapter 10 without having studied deductive or inductive reasoning. The chapter is designed to work independently. However, for those who have studied one of the deductive theories, inductive reasoning, and the fallacies, Chapter 10 is perfect for applying the tools of logic to real arguments.

In terms of depth, reading level, and pedagogic approach *Fundamentals of Reasoning* is designed for a typical one-semester (fifteen-week), introductory college course. It is written in clear, straightforward language and employs a number of "user-friendly" features.

- Each chapter opens with a brief summary of the major concepts or skills presented. New terms and concepts are printed in italic type.
- Each chapter includes an abundance of examples, explanatory charts and diagrams, and sample problems.
- Each chapter is divided into sections with exercise sets.
- Exercises range in difficulty from simple problems designed solely to help students acquire the relevant skills to more complex examples from magazines, newspapers, and literature that will give students practice in the everyday application of the concepts.
- Solutions to the odd-numbered exercises are provided in the back of the book so that students may test their understanding and may study on their own.
- Several chapters end with discussion questions designed for classroom discussions or writing assignments.
- Review questions at the end of each chapter focus attention on central concepts and encourage students to explain them in their own words.

The New Edition

Below is a list of notable changes in this new edition. But two additions, in particular, are worth your attention. New to this edition is a "Glossary of Important Terms." What a welcomed suggestion coming from one of the book's reviewers! Second, I have added INFOTRAC assignments to Chapters 1, 2, 8, and 10. Students get online, use the password that comes with the book, and access INFOTRAC. What they find is a wealth of essays, articles, and abstracts from popular and scholarly publications. Here they can search for arguments, find premises for their own arguments, and read essays on subjects in logic. This is an exciting resource for the study of real arguments.

Now for the list of changes:

- A "Glossary of Important Terms" is at the end.

- INFOTRAC assignments are added to the end of Chapters 1, 2, 8, and 10.

- Chapter 1. Section 1.2 on "Statements" has been revised, though with no conceptual change.

- New Exercise 1.4B "Composing Arguments." Students are given subject statements and asked to offer reasons for or against them.

- In Section 1.5 on "Diagramming Arguments," the explanation of the difference between Joint Support and Independent Support has been clarified and illustrated.

- Chapter 2. Minor revisions to Section 2.1 "Good Arguments."

- Exercise 2.3 "Does the Conclusion Follow?" has been divided into two sets: Ex. 2.3A "Deductive Validity: Does the Conclusion Follow Necessarily?" and Ex. 2.3B "Inductive Strength: Does the Conclusion Follow Probably?"

- Chapter 3. My own teaching experience has shown me that learning how to examine inferences on the Square of Opposition is one of the more complex and difficult tasks in the study of Categorical Logic. Therefore, I have broken down the presentation. New is Section 3.5 "Recognizing Simple Inferences," a brief introduction to spotting categorical statements in reasoning. It is followed by a new set of problems, Exercise 3.5 "Recognizing Simple Inferences."

- Continuing the revised presentation of the Square of Opposition is a general introduction to the Squares, Section 3.6 "The Squares of Opposition."

- The previous edition's exercises on evaluating inferences on the Traditional Square have been revised into three sets of problems of increasing difficulty. Exercise 3.6A "Inferences on the Traditional Square of Opposition" consists of easier problems and does not require the use of Venn Diagrams. Exercise 3.6B "More Inferences" requires Venn diagrams in the demonstrations, and Exercise 3.6C "Quick Check on the Square" requires short answers to questions about simple inferences.

- Exercise 3.7B "What Operation?" is a new exercise requiring students to identify the operation by looking closely at the changes that have occurred.

- Exercise 3.7D "Simplifying with Operations" is an exercise in rewriting statements into logically equivalent forms by using the relevant operation.

- Chapter Eight. Section 8.2 on "Inductive Generalization" has been expanded to include a discussion of the question of sample size and inductive strength. An argument is presented—Three Reasons Why Size Is Not What Matters Most!—to challenge the common misconception that sample size is what determines the strength of an inductive generalization.

- Exercise 8.2 "Inductive Generalizations" has been divided into two sets of problems. Exercise 8.2A "Inductive Generalizations" is a new set of problems in which students are asked to write the arguments in Argument Form. Exercise 8.2B "More Inductive Generalizations" is a more difficult set of problems—many from the previous edition—in which students write the argument in Argument Form, identify the concepts of a generalization, and describe the strength of the argument.

- Exercise 8.5 "Identifying Types of Arguments" has been divided into two sets: Exercise 8.5A "Identifying Types of Arguments" and Exercise 8.5B "Identifying More Difficult Arguments." The problems in 8.5A are new; those in 8.5B are substantially unchanged from the previous edition.

- Chapter Nine. Exercise 9.1C "Composing Fallacies" is new. Students are given conclusions and asked to commit a fallacy in defense! A great way to learn the fallacies is to learn how to commit them.

Many thanks to all those people whose comments were so helpful with the previous editions: Raymond Frey, Centenary College; Michael McMahon, College of the Canyons; Paul Shepard, El Camino College; Ted Stolze, California State Polytechnic University, Pomona; F. J. O'Toole, California Polytechnic State University, San Luis Obispo; Drew Christie, University of New Hampshire; John E. Clifford, University of Missouri–St. Louis; Richard Lambert, Carroll College; Ned W. Schillow, LeHigh Carbon Community College; and my friend Wendell Stephenson, Fresno Community College. For helpful advice on the present edition, I thank the following professors: Susan Bachman, Concordia University; Elizabeth Hodge, Gavilan College; John King, University of North Carolina–Greensboro; and Tom Morrow, Richland Community College.

Many thanks to all my students at Castleton State College. May the labor of this book be partial payment for all the pleasure they bring me. Love and gratitude to my wife Kit, my cat Alice, my sister Sherry, my parents Adelaide and Myles, my late Aunt Panda, and friends Bob and Jorinda Gershon.

CHAPTER ONE
Logic and Argument

The purpose of this chapter is to introduce the subject of logic and certain basic concepts and techniques. We learn to recognize *arguments*, two techniques for *exposing arguments*—writing them in
argument form and *diagramming* them—and we are
introduced to supplying *missing parts*.

1.1 Logic Defined

Logic can be defined as *the study of the principles of good reasoning.* Its purpose is to
develop a science of reasoning involving the fundamental concepts of *argument, inference,
truth, falsity,* and *validity,* among others. Logic is enormously important in all areas of human knowledge. It clarifies our thinking and helps us evaluate the reasoning behind the
claims people make and the beliefs and theories that we encounter in life. Logic helps
us to understand what our beliefs mean, how to express them clearly, and how they may
be supported.

Logic, then, is about reasoning, and reasoning is a kind of thinking. It is a kind
of thinking in which we try to solve a problem, make a decision, or determine what is
true. *Reasoning is thinking with a purpose,* as opposed to daydreaming or speculating. We
may define reasoning as *thinking that aims at a conclusion.* No doubt we reason countless

times a day, and if some reasoning takes place subconsciously, as some philosophers and psychologists believe, then we are often not looking carefully at how well we reason. Hence, we make errors. We believe or choose what we should not. Therefore, as we will see, one advantage of studying logic is the increased awareness of our own reasoning that we gain. Another advantage is, of course, that it enables us to recognize errors of reasoning and to avoid making them.

Reasoning is studied not just in logic but in psychology as well. However, the two disciplines are different in important ways. Psychologists studying reasoning are concerned with how people do, in fact, reason. They observe people, either individually or in groups, and seek to describe patterns of thinking. Logicians, on the other hand, are concerned not with how people *do* reason but with the *principles* of reasoning, independent of any individual or group. Logic, unlike psychology, is not dependent upon observations of what people actually do. Its purpose is largely to formulate the principles of correct reasoning and to distinguish good from bad reasoning.

Here is an illustration of some simple logical principles concerning this introduction. Logic is defined as the study of reasoning, and reasoning is defined as thinking that aims at a conclusion. Your sense of logic should already tell you that logic must therefore be the study of thinking that aims at a conclusion. Logic is defined in terms of reasoning, and reasoning in terms of thinking. Therefore, logic may also be defined in terms of thinking. The principle at work here is called *transitivity*. Formally, transitivity may be expressed in the following schema: 'If A is B and B is C, then A is C.' Transitivity is one example of a principle of logic.

As a second example, notice that reasoning is defined as a kind of thinking. The definition asserts, in other words, that all reasoning is thinking. Suppose we switch the terms 'reasoning' and 'thinking' to form the new statement 'all thinking is reasoning.' (Switching the terms is called *conversion* and results in a new statement called the *converse* of the original statement.) Does the statement 'all reasoning is thinking' imply the converse, 'all thinking is reasoning'? We can establish that it does not, simply by using a common logical technique.

Suppose we graphically represent the statement 'all reasoning is thinking.' Let a circle be drawn to represent all thinking. Then let another circle representing reasoning be placed so as to show what the statement asserts about their relation. Since the statement asserts that *all* reasoning is thinking, the circle representing reasoning should be placed fully inside the circle representing thinking. But the statement does not assert that reasoning is the same as thinking. Thus, the "reasoning" circle will not be coextensive with the "thinking" circle; it will be a smaller circle inside, as shown here.

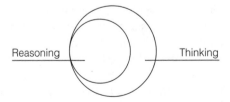

The diagram shows what the statement implies. The area outside the "reasoning" circle represents types of thinking that are not reasoning, such as daydreaming.

The above example illustrates the logical principle that any statement of the form 'all A is B' does not imply its converse, 'all B is A.' Make up some examples to test this principle for yourself.

1.2 Statements

A basic element in reasoning is the statement. *A statement is an assertion that something is or is not the case.* This assertion could be true or it could be false. In logic, whenever something can be true or false, we say that it has *truth-value.* (All that means is that it is the kind of thing that can be true or false. It does not mean that we know what its truth-value is.) Statements can be true or false; therefore, statements have truth-value. Look at these examples.

Example 1	*Logic is the study of the principles of correct reasoning.*
Example 2	*At least twelve different species of hummingbirds can be found in the United States.*
Example 3	*Being a president is like riding a tiger.* (Harry S. Truman, *Memoirs*)
Example 4	*Charles Dickens wrote* Romeo and Juliet.
Example 5	*That's my book.*

Each of those examples is an assertion that something is the case. Each is a statement and each has truth-value. Now it so happens that Examples 1 and 2 are true. Example 3 is arguably true; Example 4 is false, and Example 5 is true depending on the context in which it occurs.

Not all sentences are statements because not all sentences make assertions. For example, these sentences do not have truth-value.

Example 6	*Will you help me?*
Example 7	*Sit down and behave!*
Example 8	*Ouch!*
Example 9	*Let's take the earlier history course.*

In general, questions, commands, requests, and exclamations are not statements. Usually when people express commands, make requests, or ask questions, they are not making assertions that something is the case. But sometimes we can infer an assertion from what they say. For example, spoken truthfully, people who say "Ouch!" are feeling pain, and people who make requests want something. So a natural way of thinking about such examples is to distinguish between the words or sentences themselves and what we may *infer* from them. Thus, while "Ouch!" is not a statement, we can reasonably infer a statement from it: 'I feel pain.'

Consider the case of commands. *Commands are sentences in which a speaker tells someone what to do.* They are often expressed in sentences that do not have truth-value: "Vote for Smith!" "Shut the door." Those are not statements. Yet, statements are easily inferred from them: 'You should vote for Smith,' 'You should shut the door,' or 'I want you to shut the door.' In general, we can say that questions, exclamations, commands, requests, and the like are not statements but may be the occasion for inferring, or often may be rewritten as, statements, as we will see in Chapter 10.

Thus far we have seen that statements are sentences that have truth-value. Not all sentences are statements, however. So, we can distinguish between sentences that make assertions and those that do not.

Next, notice that a sentence may contain more than one assertion, thus more than one statement.

Example 10   *Soccer is one of the fastest growing sports, and nearly every college sponsors teams for men's and women's soccer.*

Example 11   *Officials denied reports of a gas leak, but they encouraged workers to be cautious.*

Examples 10 and 11 contain two simpler statements and assert that both are the case.

Similarly, a sentence containing more than one statement may assert that one *or* the other is the case. For example:

Example 12   *Your pain may be caused by inflammation of the surrounding tissue or by the displaced cartilage.*

Third, a sentence containing more than one statement may *assert a relationship between the two,* that one bears on the other in some way.

Example 13   *Max doesn't trust Smith because Smith lied to him.*

Example 14   *American youth do not appreciate the seriousness of war because they have forgotten the trauma of Vietnam.*

Each of those examples is a complex consisting of three assertions. For instance, Example 13 asserts that (1) Max doesn't trust Smith, that (2) Smith lied to Max, and that (3) statement (1) is so because of (2). Thus, a complex statement may assert or deny that two or more things are the case, and that one's being so bears on the other. In other words, a statement may assert a relationship between other statements.

Consider now a special type of statement called the *conditional. A conditional is a statement asserting that if a certain condition is met, then something else will be so.* For example:

Example 15   *If it rains, then my car is wet.*

Example 16   *If Smith lied to Max, then Max doesn't trust him.*

Example 17   *If America's young people forget Vietnam, then they will not appreciate the seriousness of war.*

According to Example 15, my car is wet on the condition that it rains. Hence, the name *conditional*. But notice something important. In each example, only the relationship is being asserted; the individual parts of the sentence are not. For example, 15 does not assert that it is raining; neither does it assert that my car is wet. Rather, 15 asserts a relationship: that one statement is true, given the other. Similarly, Example 16 does not assert that Smith lied. Rather it asserts that Max doesn't trust Smith *if* Smith lied to him. As we will see, conditionals are among the most important types of statements in logic, for they are statements that capture the idea of reasoning from one statement to another. In logic, the word we have for that is the word *inference* or *inferring*. More on that later.

Summary

- A *statement* is an assertion that something is or is not the case.
- A statement has *truth-value*, which means that it can be true or false.
- A statement may contain two or more simpler statements.
- A statement may assert that something is (or is not) the case *because* something else is (or is not) the case.
- A *conditional* statement asserts that something is (or is not) the case *if* something else is (or is not) the case.

Exercise 1.2   Identifying Statements   Read the sentences and determine which are *statements*, that is, which have truth-value. Make a special note of those you believe to be *conditional* statements.

1. If you require a broker only to place, buy and sell orders, you can save on commissions by using a discount broker. (J. K. Lasser, *Smart Money Management*)
2. Don't criticize imaginative writing until you fully appreciate what the author has tried to make you experience. (Mortimer Adler, *How to Read a Book*)
3. Deep in the heart of the mountains of Guerrero lies the picturesque village of Olinala. (Chloe Sayer, *The Crafts of Mexico*)

4. It is absurd to divide people into good and bad. People are either charming or tedious. (Oscar Wilde, *Lady Windermere's Fan*)

5. Lead me from the unreal to the real! (The Upanishads)

6. East is east; and west is west . . .

7. The Simiadae then branched off into two great stems, the New World and Old World monkeys; and from the latter at a remote period, man, the wonder and glory of the universe, proceeded. (Charles Darwin, *The Descent of Man*)

8. A man is rich in proportion to the number of things which he can afford to let alone. (Henry David Thoreau, *Walden*)

9. There are two cardinal sins from which all the others spring: impatience and laziness. (Franz Kafka, *Reflections*)

10. O True Believers, take your necessary precautions against your enemies, and either go forth to war in separate parties or go forth all together in a body. (The Koran)

11. Fight for the religion of God. (The Koran)

12. If I am mad then I'm not mad, and if I'm not mad then I'm mad.

13. Let us eat and drink; for tomorrow we shall die. (Isaiah 22:13)

14. No freeman shall be taken, or imprisoned, or outlawed, or exiled, or in any way harmed . . . (The Magna Carta, clause 39)

15. At two hours after midnight appeared the land, at a distance of two leagues. (Christopher Columbus, *Journal 1492*)

16. The foxes have holes, and the birds of the air have nests; but the Son of Man hath not where to lay his head. (Matthew 8:20)

17. Your eyes shall be opened, and ye shall be as gods, knowing good and evil. (Genesis 3:5)

18. The one means that wins the easiest victory over reason: terror and force. (Adolf Hitler, *Mein Kampf*)

19. Rose is a rose is a rose is a rose. (Gertrude Stein, *Sacred Emily*)

20. Let every nation know, whether it wishes us well or ill, that we shall pay any price, bear any burden, meet any hardship, support any friend, oppose any foe to assure the survival and the success of liberty. (John F. Kennedy, 1961 Inaugural Address)

21. Neither a borrower nor a lender be; for loan oft loses both itself and friend . . . (Shakespeare, *Hamlet*)

22. I want to be left alone. (Attributed to Greta Garbo)

23. Nice guys finish last. (Attributed to Leo Durocher)

24. Nonviolence is the answer to the crucial political and moral questions of our time. (Martin Luther King, Jr., Nobel Prize address)

25. Macbeth does murder sleep! the innocent sleep, sleep that knits up the ravel'd sleave of care . . . (Shakespeare, *Macbeth*)

1.3 Argument Defined

Astronomy is the study of the stars. Biology is the study of living things. *Logic is the study of arguments.* Arguments are the subject matter of logic because they are specific instances of reasoning. In logic we study the types of arguments, the meanings or logical implications of arguments, and, most importantly, the criteria for distinguishing good arguments from bad. Ultimately we want to decide which arguments we should accept and which we should reject.

In logic an argument is not a quarrel or fight, although people who are quarreling may use logical arguments. Rather, *in logic an argument is an identifiable piece of reasoning in which a point is expressed and reasons are offered for that point.* In that sense, whenever someone tries to persuade you to believe something and offers reasons for the belief, that person is giving an argument. Politicians give you reasons why you should vote for them. Salespersons try to convince you to buy their product. Friends offer advice about what you should do. All of these are occasions for arguments. Let us have an example and a precise definition of the term 'argument.'

> **Example 18**   *All humans are mortal. Socrates is a human. Therefore, Socrates is mortal.*

This well-worn example is an argument. A claim is made and reasons are offered for it. It has the defining elements of an argument. Here is our definition.

> argument   *A group of statements, one of which is claimed to follow from the others.*

In our example, we have a group of statements, and one of them—'Socrates is mortal'—is claimed to follow from the other two. That statement, which is claimed to follow, is called the *conclusion* of the argument. By definition, every argument has a conclusion. As well, every argument has at least one statement supporting the conclusion. A statement that provides a reason for the conclusion is called a *premise*. There may be one premise or several. Example 18 has two premises. According to the definition then, *every argument has one conclusion and at least one premise, from which the conclusion is claimed to follow.*

Why do we say that the conclusion *is claimed to follow?* The reason is that not all arguments succeed. The definition must reflect the fact that although all arguments *claim* that a statement follows from the others, only some arguments successfully establish that claim.

As can be seen in the definition, the statements of an argument are in a special relationship. That special relationship, in which one or more statements provide reason for another, is called an *inferential relationship*. We say that there is an *inference* from the premises to the conclusion, or the conclusion is *inferred* from the premises. Thus, an earmark of an argument is the presence of that inferential relationship.

Exposing the Argument   To expose an argument is to pick out the conclusion and the premise or premises. This can be difficult, so you have to read the argument carefully and think about what the words mean. With experience your sensitivity to the language and your skill at recognizing the logic of words will improve. Here are some tips for exposing arguments. *Usually it is easier to pick out the conclusion first.* To do so, read the argument and ask yourself, "What does the speaker want to persuade me to believe? What is the main point?" That should help you to identify the conclusion. To identify the premises, ask, "What reasons does the speaker give to persuade me?" Thus, to expose an argument, you look for the speaker's main point and his or her reasons.

There are clues one can use to pick out the conclusion and premises of an argument. Certain words in our language may be used to signal conclusions or premises, such as the following:

Conclusion Clue Words

therefore, thus, hence, it follows that, it must be that, we may conclude that, we may infer that, implies that, entails that, consequently, so

Notice how any one of the above *conclusion clues* could fill the blank in this argument:

All humans are mortal, Socrates is a human, _____ Socrates is mortal.

Premises, on the other hand, may be signaled by words such as these:

Premise Clue Words

since, because, for, for the reason that, in that, due to the fact that, given that, may be concluded from

Try each of the above *premise clues* in the blank below.

Socrates is mortal, _____ all humans are mortal, and Socrates is a human.

Be aware of the words that typically introduce conclusions and premises, and use them as clues to exposing the argument.

Argument Form When we examine an argument in logic, we can see it more clearly if we write it out in *argument form*. In this format, the premises are listed first, followed by a solid line separating them from the conclusion, listed at the bottom. Each statement is numbered. The form is as follows:

Premise 1 . . .
Premise 2 . . .

.
.
.

Premise n . . .

_____

Conclusion n + 1 . . .

Thus, Example 18 is written in argument form as follows:

1. *All humans are mortal.*
2. *Socrates is a human.*

_____

3. *Therefore, Socrates is mortal.*

Premises are listed in any order and separated by a solid line; all statements are numbered. Consider a more challenging argument.

Example 19

God does not exist because if he did, there would be no suffering and evil in the world; but obviously suffering and evil do exist. Thus, there is no God.

Clearly, the conclusion is 'Thus, there is no God.' But notice that the conclusion is also stated in the opening sentence: 'God does not exist. . . .' It is common for writers to state their conclusion upfront, offer reasons, and then restate the conclusion upon completion. Yet, in logical analysis we will write the conclusion only once, at the end of the form. Notice also, that in writing the argument in argument form, we break out and provide a line for each premise, including the premise introduced by *because* in the opening sentence.

Exposed and written in argument form, it appears as

1. *If God existed, there would be no suffering and evil in the world.*
2. *But obviously suffering and evil do exist.*

_____

3. *Thus, there is no God.*

So, be aware that conclusions may occur at any place in a passage: at the beginning, middle, or end. Second, be aware that conclusions or premises may need to be taken out of a larger sentence.

When an argument is written in *argument form,* we see exactly what the argument claims. Its structure is clarified, the premises and conclusion have been identified, and the argument is prepared for evaluation. Exposing an argument by writing it in argument form is an extremely valuable tool in the overall procedure of analyzing arguments.

Exercise 1.3   Argument Form   Read the exercises carefully and determine which express arguments and which do not. Draw a circle around any *premise clue words* or *conclusion clue words*. Write those that are arguments in the format called *argument form*, as described above, numbering the premises and conclusions.

Sample

If each man had a definite set of rules of conduct by which he regulated his life, he would be no better than a machine. But there are no such rules, so men cannot be machines. (A.M. Turing, 1950)

> 1. *If each man had a definite set of rules of conduct by which he regulated his life he would be no better than a machine.*
>
> 2. *But there are no such rules.*
>
> ---
>
> 3. *Men cannot be machines.*

1. Every literature major must take a course in Shakespeare. John has taken the Shakespeare course; therefore, he must be a literature major.

2. All the finalists were flown to Houston. From there they went to Galveston for the banquet and presentation of awards. Jay was a finalist, so he must have gone to Galveston.

3. A time-honored policeman's adage has it that with homicides, if you haven't nailed your killer inside a week, your chances of ever doing so divide by half for every subsequent week that passes. (Archer Mayor, *The Skeleton's Knee*)

4. Any professional can outplay any amateur. Jones is a professional, but he cannot outplay Meyers. It follows that Meyers is not an amateur.

5. If the president dies in office, then the first lady becomes the new president. Since Laura Bush is the first lady, she will take over if President Bush dies in office.

6. For reasons we don't quite understand, artists are frequently neurotic individuals. The incidence of artistic creativity in conjunction with neurosis is so remarkably high that it is probable that neurosis is a symptom of artistic creativity.

7. If the creationists are right, then the universe was created and has a beginning in time. Now, whatever has a beginning must also have an end. Therefore, if the creationists are right, the universe must have an end as well.

8. Some fruits are sweet. Honey is sweet; so it must be a fruit.

9. A person can't be a marine and a sailor both. Since Max is a sailor, it must be that he is not a marine.

10. If the fever continues into tomorrow, give me a call and I'll drop by on my way home. Now don't hesitate to call.

11. There is freedom in the sense of being able to move as one pleases, freedom in the sense of being able to do and speak as one pleases, and freedom in the sense of being able to think for oneself. This last type makes the others possible. Consequently, it is our most important freedom.

12. Because there has been such an increase in costs and because the potential hazards have not been eliminated, the only sensible thing to do is to defeat the proposal for a nuclear plant in our county.

13. The Mennonites are members of a Protestant sect that originated in Zurich, Switzerland, in about 1525 under the direction of Menno Simons. They first came to the United States in 1663 and are currently found in small communities throughout the Midwest and parts of the East.

14. It is better not to marry for love. Marriage is supposed to last a lifetime, but love never does. And once love is gone you'll need some lasting reason for the marriage. It is therefore better not to marry for love.

15. Computers do not have feelings for the reasons that only living things can have feelings and computers are not living things.

16. You cannot teach people to love something. Philosophy is the love of wisdom; hence, you cannot teach philosophy.

17. You cannot hold a person liable for something he or she did not know about. But you have not shown that your client did not know about the faulty wiring in the house he sold. We can conclude then that your client cannot be excused for damages.

18. We have a duty to protect citizens from crime. Punishment protects society by deterring criminals. Thus, we have a duty to punish criminals.

19. House builders work awfully hard. The workday is often more than eight hours long; there's heavy lifting to do, the possibility of injury, and cranky supervisors; and the weather doesn't always cooperate.

20. Beat an egg and add cornstarch. Heat milk and sugar in saucepan; gradually add egg mixture. Stir until thick. Add vanilla. Top with graham cracker crumbs and chill. Serves six.

21. The mind directly perceives only ideas. Material objects are not ideas. These facts entail that the mind does not directly perceive material objects.

22. Because friendships are so ill defined, we often don't know a reasonable expectation from an inappropriate one. As a result, the morality of friendship is murky as well. (Joshua Halberstam, *Everyday Ethics*)

23. Kids should not be put behind bars with adults. Being in jail is frightening enough for kids, but locking them up with adults is inviting tragedy.

24. Dollar for dollar the new Victory is the best car on the road. If you want comfort and economy, make the Victory your family car.

25. Since mice are just smallish rats, it would seem to follow that housecats are just smallish tigers.

26. Every month with thirty-one days except July and December is followed by a month with fewer days. Since August follows July, August does not have fewer than thirty-one days.

27. Why fear death? If there is no afterlife, then at the moment of death we are nothing. If there *is* an afterlife, then at the moment of death we are born into a new life.

28. The big bang was *not* an explosion that hurled matter into pre-existing space. On the contrary, the big bang was an event that took place *everywhere*. (Richard Morris, *The Edges of Science*)

29. The most common large woodpecker in our area is the red-headed woodpecker. What I saw was a large woodpecker, so, even though I did not see its head, it probably was a red-headed woodpecker.

30. In the event of a tornado the sirens blast, the police drive their cars through the neighborhoods giving warning, and everyone is urged to seek shelter immediately.

1.4 Diagramming Arguments

Another way to expose an argument is to diagram it. A brief introduction will be helpful for now. For more on diagramming, see Chapter 10.

To diagram an argument, first read it through and number each statement in sequence. For example,

Example 20 ① *Webb was promoted to vice-president; therefore,* ② *she will move to Pittsburgh.*

Then draw an arrow from the statement number of the premise to the number for the conclusion as follows.

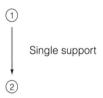

The diagram shows that statement ① is the only support offered for the conclusion, statement ②. We will call this *single support*.

Example 21 ① *If Webb is promoted to vice-president, then she will move to Pittsburgh.* ② *She's bound to be promoted.* ③ *So, she will be moving to Pittsburgh.*

This argument offers two premises for concluding that ③ 'She will be moving to Pittsburgh.' Notice that statement ① is a conditional asserting that *if* she is promoted, *then* she will move. It does not assert that she *is* promoted; neither does it assert that she *will* move. Rather, as a conditional, it counts as one statement. Second, notice that the premises operate together in support of the conclusion. Premise ① does not provide a reason for ③ without being joined with ②. We will call this kind of support *joint support* and indicate their dependence with the sign '+'.

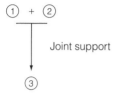

On the other hand, consider the structure of this argument.

Example 22   ① *Cats make good pets because*
                  ② *they are affectionate.* ③ *They are*
                  clean. ④ *They are entertaining, and*
                  ⑤ *they do well in apartments.*

The conclusion is statement ①. Notice that four distinct premises are offered in support. Further, notice that the premises do not need one another to provide support. We will call this *independent support* and indicate the separate inferential support by an arrow from each premise to the conclusion.

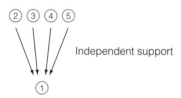

How can we tell whether premises offer joint or independent support? *Joint premises pass support to a conclusion only when taken together.* Remove one of them, and the other is weakened. Look at this example.

Example 23   ① *All birds migrate.* ② *Ravens are*
                  birds. ③ *Therefore, ravens migrate.*

Remove premise ①, and the inference from statement ② to ③ is weakened. The same holds if we imagine only ① supporting ③. Taken together, ① and ② provide a strong inference; separate, they do not. Independent premises, on the other hand, are unaffected by the removal of a companion premise. In example 22 above, premise ② is not weakened by the removal of ③, ④, or ⑤. None is affected by the removal of the others.

When we see that to be the case, we judge the premise to be independent and give it its own arrow to the conclusion.

Now consider a structure in which an argument has, in effect, two conclusions. For example,

Example 24   ① *Cats make good pets because* ② *they are affectionate.* ③ *They are clean.* ④ *They are entertaining, and* ⑤ *they do well in apartments. So,* ⑥ *if you want a good pet, you should get a cat.*

Premises ② through ⑤ support the conclusion ① that cats make good pets. From that conclusion it is further concluded that ⑥ if you want a good pet, you should get a cat.

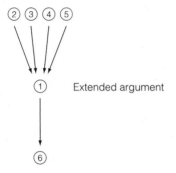

Extended argument

We will call this an *extended argument* because it contains an argument within an argument. Here is another example.

Example 25   ① *Cats make good pets and* ② *cats make good anatomical subjects. Therefore,* ③ *some good pets make good anatomical subjects. Since* ④ *good anatomical subjects are in high demand in medical schools, it follows* ⑤ *that some good pets are in high demand in medical schools.*

Here we see that premises ① and ② support ③. Statement ③ is then combined with ④ to support the conclusion ⑤.

Summary

1. On your first pass through an argument, number the statements sequentially.

2. Write down the number of the conclusion first.

3. Above the conclusion number write the statement numbers that support it.

4. Indicate independent support by drawing an arrow from each independent premise to the conclusion.

5. Indicate joint support by linking premises with a + and an arrow to the conclusion.

6. An arrow indicates that an inference is being drawn from a statement or statements to a conclusion. An arrow *from* a conclusion to another conclusion indicates an extended argument.

Exercise 1.4A Diagramming Arguments Diagram the following arguments and identify any of the particular structures we have studied: single support, joint support, independent support, or extended argument.

1. All humans are mortal. Socrates is a human. Therefore, Socrates is mortal.

2. Since history is a required subject, you should take the course now.

3. House builders work awfully hard. The workday is often more than eight hours long; there's heavy lifting to do, the possibility of injury, and cranky supervisors; and the weather doesn't always cooperate.

4. If interest rates continue to rise, then loans will be harder to obtain. If loans are harder to obtain, then sales will fall. And if sales fall, there will be a production slowdown. Therefore, if interest rates continue to rise, there will be a production slowdown.

5. There is no reason for fearing death because either we survive death or we do not. If we do not survive death, then at the moment of death we are nothing. If we do survive death, then we are born into new life.

6. Research is a requirement for tenure and is generally more lucrative and often more exciting than teaching. As a result, research has gradually displaced teaching as the principal concern of many faculty members. (Don Wycliff, *New York Times*)

7. Parents are principally responsible for the education and upbringing of their children and are, therefore, the most qualified persons to select the formal schooling for their children. (Letter to the editor)

8. Under the GI Bill we enabled over 9 million people to go to college. The GI Bill is gone now; therefore, a college education is out of the reach of most young people.

9. The United States spends nearly $2000 per year per capita on health care. Yet the indicators of national health show that we are getting less for our dollars than countries that spend less per capita. This is the reason why we need to thoroughly reexamine our health-care system in the United States.

10. There is no system of health-care delivery in the United States. The word 'system' implies organization and uniformity. What we have is a disorganized and varied complex of competing parties: the federal government, state governments, Medicaid, Medicare, HMOs, various insurers, private organizations, and so on.

11. If people want good roads, then they must pay for them. That is the reason why you should support increased highway taxes.

12. In an infinite universe, every point can be regarded as the center, because every point has an infinite number of stars on each side of it. (Stephen Hawking, *A Brief History of Time*)

13. Whenever a solid is heated, its color changes from red to orange, yellow, and then bluish white. Since this change is the same for all solids, it seems that it could be explained without having to know much about the actual structure of any particular solid. Furthermore, it seems reasonable to conclude that there could be a unified theory of radiant energy.

14. Big-time college athletics has nothing to do with education; it is entertainment pure and simple. In our society people who entertain are paid for it. It is about time we began paying college athletes for the entertainment they provide and stop fooling them and ourselves by calling it education.

15. In general the child from a large family makes a better team player. Such a child develops better interpersonal skills because he or she learns to cooperate with others, to share responsibilities, and to see things from the other's viewpoint.

Exercise 1.4B   Composing Arguments   Practice composing arguments by providing reasons either for or against the following propositions.

1. *Cats make better pets than dogs.*

2. *Christmas is getting much too commercial.*

3. *Capital punishment, or the death penalty, should not be permitted, no matter how savage the crime.*

4. *A high school student who is convicted of a crime should not be allowed to participate on any athletic team.*

5. *Cheating is not a big deal! Everyone has times when he or she has to "borrow" a paper from a friend.*

6. *There is nothing that cannot be dreamt.*

7. *Computers can think!*

8. *A parent should never, ever raise his or her hand to a child. No spanking, ever!*

9. *The preservation of endangered species is important but never more important than the rights of citizens to decent jobs and natural resources.*

10. *The rule that says that lying is always wrong is not practical. In some circumstances lying is the right thing to do.*

1.5 Supplying Missing Parts: Enthymemes

In logic we have a name for arguments that are missing a premise or conclusion. Such arguments are called *enthymemes.* In everyday conversation, speakers will leave out what they know their listeners will fill in. It is not necessary to say everything to our listeners; some ideas can be taken for granted. Thus, we find arguments in which a premise or even a conclusion is missing. In logic we need to supply these missing parts, thus making the reasoning explicit. Here is an example of an enthymeme in which a premise is left unstated:

Example 26   *All chemists are scientists, so*
Mrs. Merk must be a scientist.

As stated, the argument is incomplete. Clearly it assumes that the premise 'Mrs. Merk is a chemist' will be understood. Supplying the missing premise (marked here with an asterisk) makes the argument explicit.

　 1. All chemists are scientists.
* *2. Mrs. Merk is a chemist.*
_____

　 3. Mrs. Merk is a scientist.

You may think of supplying missing premises as making explicit what the argument, as given, seems to assume. Consider another example of an incomplete argument:

Example 27

1. God created the world.
_____

3. The world is good.

To make explicit the reasoning of this argument, we supply a premise such as 'Whatever God creates is good.'

1. God created the world.

*   *2. Whatever God creates is good.*

___

3. The world is good.

Less common are arguments with a *missing conclusion*. For example, one might argue as follows:

Example 28

You're not 21, and you have to be 21 to drink in this state.

The premises point to the conclusion 'You can't drink in this state,' but the speaker chooses not to express it. Deliberately leaving out the conclusion invites the speaker to participate in the reasoning.

As another example, consider Dr. Richard Barth's argument in defense of the purchase of a $400,000 diagnostic machine called a CT scanner, as reported in the newspaper:

Example 29

A hospital that's going to be in business and trying to deliver care . . . is going to have to have access to a certain degree of basic services. CT is really a basic service now.
(Letter to the editor, *Rutland Herald*)

Barth's argument leaves it to the reader to draw the conclusion that a viable hospital has to have a CT scanner.

1. *A hospital that's going to be in business and trying to deliver care . . . is going to have to have access to a certain degree of basic services.*

2. *The CT scanner is a basic service.*

___

*   3. *A viable hospital has to have a CT scanner.*

One further example illustrates how we may have to rephrase an argument as well as supply missing parts. Consider this reply:

Example 30

What? Did you ask if we were going home now? Well, this is just the intermission, and there are two more acts.

The point the speaker is making is that "we are not going home now." Fully exposed the argument would read:

1. *We won't go home until the play is over.*

2. *This is just the intermission, and there are two more acts.*

---

3. *We are not going home now.*

Exercise 1.5 Enthymemes: Missing Premises and Conclusions Write out the following arguments in *argument form,* supplying the necessary premise or conclusion. Indicate a supplied statement with an asterisk (*).

1. You can't vote; you haven't registered.

2. Whales must bear their young alive because all mammals do.

3. Most scientists are liberals, so Professor Pipes must be a liberal.

4. You should vote for Congressman Smith. He's the kind of representative who cares about his people.

5. Abortion kills the fetus. It's murder.

6. Most major religions include a belief in a god. So, Confucianism must also.

7. We are certain that she feels no pain and has no sensations whatsoever because all mental life—feelings, thoughts, sensations—cease when the brain is dead.

8. John Hinckley should not be punished for his attempt to assassinate the president. He's mentally ill.

9. By the age of eighty, most people's eyes show some significant macular degeneration, a deterioration of the retina that is the leading cause of loss of vision. Hence, the problem is that we are living longer than our eyes.

10. People enjoy imitations; hence, they enjoy looking at photographs.

11. If the theory of evolution were correct, then the fossil record would show a continuous sequence of fossils connecting the simplest organisms with the higher life-forms. But the fact is that there are large gaps, for example, between invertebrates and vertebrates, between reptiles and mammals, and between the apes and man. (Adapted from *Science and Unreason* by Daisie Radner and Michael Radner)

12. A minimum of 70 points is required to pass this exam, Mr. Fluke. You scored 68. You know what that means.

13. Vehicles that run on methanol rather than gasoline could hit the market as soon as 2001. Assuming that happens, it is certain that we won't be vulnerable to Persian Gulf politics then.

14. The Japanese economy is characterized by a relatively free-market system and private ownership of the means of production. It is therefore a capitalistic economy.

15. Apes cannot reason! They don't have language.

16. As I write this, in November 1971, people are dying in East Bengal from lack of food, shelter, and medical care. The suffering and death that are occurring there

now are not inevitable, not unavoidable in any fatalistic sense of the term. It is not beyond the capacity of the richer nations to give enough assistance to reduce any further suffering to very small proportions.

I begin with the assumption that suffering and death from lack of food, shelter, and medical care are bad. My next point is this: if it is in our power to prevent something bad from happening, without thereby sacrificing anything of comparable moral importance, we ought morally to do it. (Peter Singer, "Famine, Affluence, and Morality")

17. The salient reason there are so few species here [the Arctic Circle] is that so few have metabolic processes or patterns of growth that can adapt to so little light. (Barry Lopez, *Arctic Dreams*)

18. Each of the following inferences is missing a premise.

- *Don't fall in love for beauty. Looks don't last.*
- *Don't fall in love for money. Money comes and goes.*
- *Don't fall in love for brains. You want a lover, not a conversational partner.*
- *Don't fall in love for social status. They won't accept you anyway.*

(Joshua Halberstam, *Everyday Ethics* © 1993 by Joshua Halberstam. Used by permission of Viking Penguin, a division of Penguin Putnam Inc.)

1.6 Recognizing Real Arguments

Real arguments are arguments found outside of logic class. They appear in essays, letters to the editor, speeches, discussions, and any context in which people reason to a conclusion. Some of the exercises you've had already in this chapter are real arguments, as can be seen by the attributions in parentheses. Real arguments may be simple and easy to follow, difficult and ambiguous, or brilliant pieces of fine reasoning, which are a joy to experience. They are the arguments of real people and as such can exhibit all the richness of people doing the work of logic. In this section let's practice recognizing real arguments of moderate difficulty. In Chapter 10 we will study longer, more challenging pieces.

First, a brief review of what we've learned about recognizing arguments thus far. An argument *presents reasons* for a point. Arguing for a point is more than merely stating a point, describing an event, or explaining how something is done. Arguments may do all those things, but what distinguishes an argument from—for example, merely stating a point—is that an argument has reasons for a conclusion. It states, in effect, "Believe this and here's *why* you should!" Therefore, we ask, "Does this passage assert a point and offer reasons for it?" To help with that question, we look for *clue words*. Recall the list of conclusion clue words and premise clue words earlier (p. 8). Any such words should be circled; they are your evidence of an inference.

Let's begin by comparing a couple of passages.

Example 31

I am more concerned with the microcosm than the macrocosm; I am more interested in how a man lives than how a star dies; how a woman makes her way in the world than how a comet streaks across the heavens. If there is a God, He is present as much in the creation of each of us as He was at the creation of the earth. The human condition is the mystery that engages my fascination, not the condition of the cosmos. (Sherwin Nuland, *How We Die*)

Example 32

For myself, I like a universe that includes much that is unknown and, at the same time, much that is knowable. A universe in which everything is known would be static and dull, as boring as the heaven of some weak-minded theologians. A universe that is unknowable is no fit place for a thinking being. The ideal universe for us is one very much like the universe we inhabit. And I would guess that this is not really much of a coincidence. (Carl Sagan, "Can We Know the Universe?" in *The Sacred Beetle*)

Both writers, Nuland and Sagan, are stating a point. For Nuland, human issues are more important than cosmic ones. He says this in different ways, comparing the life of a man and a star, the path of a woman and a comet. If there is a God, he says, then each kind of issue is an occasion for God's presence; each is a mystery. Yet, Nuland does not offer reasons for preferring the human to the cosmic. Rather he states in so many ways what that preference is. How different it would be had he explained why human issues are more important.

Sagan, on the other hand, presents an argument for his preference for a partly unknown yet knowable universe. To paraphrase his reasons, they are that (1) a fully known universe would be dull and (2) an unknowable universe is not suitable for thinking beings. Therefore, (3) 'the ideal universe for us is one very much like the universe we inhabit,' so he likes a universe open to inquiry. His is an argument. You may look at his reasons, ask whether they are true, and whether his conclusion follows.

Consider another example.

Example 33

Perhaps the most valuable product of a good education is the development of a critical attitude. In this context, critical *does not mean negative or hostile. From the Greek root* kritikes, *meaning "to judge" or "to discern," a critical attitude is one that does not take things at face value, and that demands reasonable proof before accepting or rejecting claims.*

> *The heart of a critical attitude is sophisticated, ra-*
> *tional analysis of truth claims, whether they occur in for-*
> *mal philosophical arguments, political speeches, sermons,*
> *commercials, or in everyday conversation.* (Douglas J.
> Soccio, *How to Get the Most Out of Philosophy*)

This writer is clearly stating a point: a critical attitude is a valued goal of education. He clarifies what that is but he does *not* offer reasons for his assertion that it is 'Perhaps the most valuable product of a good education. . . .' Neither does he offer reasons why we should strive to achieve a critical attitude, except to say that it is most valuable. We have here perhaps the beginning of an argument, but, as it is, there is no inference present.

Now, another example.

Example 34

> *On Halloween, the eve of Mexico's two-day-long* Dia de
> los Muertos *(Day of the Dead), gangs of face-painted*
> *and black-painted children rove the streets trick-or-treat-*
> *ing.* Dia de los Muertos *is one of the most important*
> *holidays in Mexico. Children accompany parents to ceme-*
> *teries, clean tombstones, play special games, and offer gifts*
> *to their dead relatives.*
>   *Mexicans commune with the dead, not in the*
> *Christian sense of the hereafter so much as in the cultural*
> *belief that the past is not dead. They have a different con-*
> *cept of time; Mexicans tend to the past and let the fates*
> *shepherd the future.* (Jonathan Waterman, *Kayaking*
> *the Vermilion Sea*)

Here the writer describes an event and briefly explains its cultural significance. In so do-ing, he makes some general statements: 'Mexicans commune with the dead . . . in the cultural belief that the past is not dead' and 'They have a different concept of time. . . .' Are those statements conclusions to an argument? Is the first paragraph a set of prem-ises? This is not a clear case; it appears to be a matter of judgment. Let's consider how to handle this example.

First, try reading Example 34 as an argument and, therefore, see the first paragraph as presenting premises. We have his description of the Day of the Dead celebration, and we conclude, *therefore,* 'Mexicans commune with the dead . . . and have a different con-cept of time. . . .' Is that what the writer is saying? Consider how you would diagram it as an argument.

On the other hand, read the passage not as an argument but as an illustration clar-ifying an idea. (Sometimes illustrations provide reasons; see Chapter 10.) On this inter-pretation, the writer is not arguing *for* the claim that Mexicans commune with the dead but illustrating it, helping us see what that means. The description of the celebration clarifies the cultural beliefs but does not support their truth-value.

So, which is it? Is this passage an argument or not? The issue hinges on whether you think this passage is best read as *attempting to persuade you* to believe the claims about

Mexican culture or is *explaining* what they mean. The evidence is not clear. I would judge it not an argument, but then I must admit that interpreting it as one is not out of the question. The problem this case raises is an important one, however.

What do we do when a passage seems ambiguous as regards argument? Here is the protocol: First, if the author is available, ask him or her. *Are you making an argument here?* Second, if the author is unavailable, apply the principle of charity, which is to say, give the author the benefit of the doubt. Let's examine this idea.

Interpretation and the Principle of Charity

Accept at the very beginning the fact that people do not write and speak as clearly as we and the logicians would like. Their words may be gray where we would prefer black and white. So, it is not uncommon in logic to have to interpret, paraphrase, rewrite, or otherwise analyze the meaning of sentences and passages. If a person's words are not clear, we may have to interpret what we are given, and *to interpret is to risk interpreting incorrectly.* How then do we avoid mistakes? There is no hard and fast rule here; there is rather a useful principle to follow. It is that you ought to stay as close as possible to the person's own words and apply the most plausible interpretation to them. In logic we call this the principle of charity.

> principle of charity   *Given two or more possible interpretations, apply the most plausible.*

And what is meant by "the most plausible interpretation?" In a nutshell, whenever you see that one interpretation is stronger or makes more sense than another, then that is the one you ought to choose. As you learn more logic—in particular, as you master the chapters in this book—you will be able to recognize and demonstrate, in many cases, the most plausible interpretation. That, after all, is one of the major objectives of the study of logic. You will have occasion to apply the principle of charity in many of the exercises throughout this book.

Practicing the principle of charity is one of the characteristics of doing logic well, one of the virtues of the good logician. It is worth pausing to consider *why* one should be charitable with one's opponent. Why should we choose the interpretation that is stronger? Isn't the purpose of studying logic to help us win arguments? The answer is no. *We study logic to learn to reason well,* not to win at all costs. There are at least two good reasons in support of charity in the use of logic. First, *failure to show charity in logic is a waste of time.* Interpreting a person's words or reasoning unfavorably simply means that the more plausible interpretation is not being addressed. Sooner or later, you will face the issue again.

Second, *failure to show charity is unethical.* It is morally objectionable to take advantage of an opponent's lack of skill in reasoning or communicating. Unfortunately, we all know people who do exactly that, and it is probable that your study of logic will enable you to join them, if you choose. But it is an ill-gotten victory that comes by way of "logic-chopping" bullying or deception. Thus, reasoning well is not just reasoning astutely or efficiently; it is reasoning with fairness and good will. (For more on interpretation, see Section 10.3.)

Exercise 1.6 Recognizing Real Arguments The following passages come from newspapers, magazines, and books. Read each passage and decide whether an argument is present. For those you believe contain arguments, number the statements and expose the arguments by drawing a diagram.

1. If two events happen in different places, you cannot say, as was formerly supposed, that they are separated by so many miles and minutes, because different observers, all equally careful, will make different estimates of the miles and minutes, all equally legitimate. (Bertrand Russell, "The Greatness of Albert Einstein")

2. Our ears project auditory information to *both* hemispheres, not just the "contralateral" one (i.e., the one on the opposite side). Therefore, "sealing off" the right ear by using the right thumb does very little with regard to eliminating the passage of information to the left hemisphere and does not substantially enhance the flow of information to the right hemisphere. (Letter to the editor)

3. [Under present law] federal regulations do not require the use of anesthesia if the experimenter says it will interfere with the results of the study. In 1982, more than 130,000 painful experiments were carried out on animals without anesthesia, and drugs were commonly administered which do not relieve pain but which do paralyze the animal so that it is unable to move or cry out, permitting the experimenter to carry out an experiment involving considerable pain without having to face the animal's agony. . . . As moral beings, we have the responsibility to do everything in our power to grant the unfortunate creatures forced to submit to experimentation by humans every possible comfort in their misery. (Letter to the editor)

4. To imagine that God is pleased because children pray in a classroom borders on the naive. To think that such action by pupils in a public school will inspire faith is questionable. Many pupils will have no other contact with religion and will see prayer as a kind of starting gun for the day's activities. Meanwhile, religion in which God is served by more than words is lost from sight. (Newspaper article)

5. I am an eighteen-year-old Sikh. I strongly adhere to my religion and want to be free to practice it. I believe that if my government does not provide me with the freedom to practice my religion, and deprives me of my basic human rights, then I have the right to choose another government or have my own, which will provide the freedom that I and my kind need. (Letter to the editor)

6. STATEMENT ON AMA [American Medical Association] ENDORSEMENTS: The AMA is a professional organization, not a trade association, and it should avoid involvement in the marketing or advertising of particular products or services through endorsements or other arrangements. Such activities inevitably blur the

distinction between professional and business objectives, and diminish respect for the AMA and the profession it represents. The AMA cannot speak with moral authority in defense of professional values if it sells endorsements, regardless of how the gains may be used. (Dr. Arnold Relman for the AMA)

7. Has it ever occurred to critics what would happen with the smaller states during an election if it weren't for the Electoral College? All a candidate would have to do is work on the big states like New York, California, etc., win there and forget about the smaller states because of lower population. The Electoral College [in which each state gets one vote for each representative and senator] give the smaller states something they need in an election—a real vote. (Letter to the editor)

8. My response to the welfare recipient featured in your article who says, "I just don't always want to work," is: "Fine. If you don't work, you don't eat." The idea that those who do nothing are entitled to receive money, medical benefits, child care and other types of support at the expense of those who work is nothing short of morally wrong. (Letter to the editor, *New York Times*)

9. *Is our current sexual morality satisfactory?* I submit that the state of our sexual life is a mess. Our culture has us in a perpetual moral muddle. Traditional morality expects sexual moderation, while popular morality urges a more casual experimental sex life. For teenagers in our society these contradictory messages become an excruciating vise—damned if they do, damned if they don't. When it comes to sexual morality, most people proceed in varying stages of moral confusion. (Joshua Halberstam, *Everyday Ethics*)

10. The TWA plane hijack is another in a long line of events that show the U.S. has become the target of spies and terrorists. Unfortunately, we lack the national will to retaliate. Turning the other cheek only invites further terrorism. Our government needs more guts. (Letter to the editor)

11. "There are a lot of reasons why letting a coach run everything is a bad idea, with the main one being you just can't develop an organization that way," Young said. "Coaches come and go. What happens when a coach gets fired? All of his people go, then the next guy comes in and brings all his people. The organization suffers." (Mike Freeman, "They Answer to Themselves," *New York Times*)

12. Broadcast television imposes limits, strict but self-enforced limits, on explicit sex. Why not on explicit terror? There is no reason why all the news of a terrorist event, like news of a rape, cannot be transmitted in some form. But in the interest of decency, diplomacy and our own self-respect, it need not be live melodrama. (Charles Krauthammer, *Time*)

13. When, in ordinary life, we speak of *the* colour of the table, we only mean the sort of colour which it will seem to have to a normal spectator from an ordinary point of view under usual condition of light. But the other colours which appear under other conditions have just as good a right to be considered real; and therefore, to avoid favouritism, we are compelled to deny that, in itself, the table has any one particular colour. (Bertrand Russell, *The Problems of Philosophy*)

14. When the deer hunter sits down he sits where he can see ahead, and with his back to something. The duck hunter sits where he can see overhead, and behind something. The non-hunter sits where he is comfortable. None of these watches the dog. The bird hunter watches only the dog, and always knows

where the dog is, whether or not visible at the moment. The dog's nose is the bird hunter's eye. (Aldo Leopold, *A Sand County Almanac*)

15. It's easy to forget that this is *your* education. Customize it. Work at it. *You are invited to participate in "the great conversation."* Socrates guided others out of the cave of ignorance, but they provided the effort. I offer you a map to help you on your way to wisdom. The next step is yours. (Douglas J. Soccio, *How to Get the Most Out of Philosophy*)

16. But if life has an aim, it is clear that it ought to come to an end when that aim is reached . . . if the aim of humanity is goodness, righteousness, love—call it what you will—if it is what the prophets have said, that all mankind should be united together in love, that the spears should be beaten into pruning-hooks and so forth, what is it that hinders the attainment of this aim? The passions hinder it. Of all the passions the strongest, cruellest, and most stubborn is the sex-passion, physical love; and therefore if the passions are destroyed, including the strongest of them—physical love—the prophecies will be fulfilled, mankind will be brought into unity, the aim of human existence will be attained, and there will be nothing further to live for. (Leo Tolstoy, "The Kreutzer Sonata")

17. The idea of solidity is that of two objects, which being impell'd by the utmost force, cannot penetrate each other; but still maintain a separate and distinct existence. Solidity, therefore, is perfectly incomprehensible alone, and without the conception of some bodies, which are solid, and maintain this separate and distinct existence. (David Hume, *Treatise on Human Nature*)

18. The capacity for suffering and enjoying things is a prerequisite for having interests at all. . . . A stone does not have interests because it cannot suffer. Nothing that we can do to it could possibly make any difference to its welfare. A mouse, on the other hand, does have an interest in not being tormented, because it will suffer if it is. (Peter Singer, *Practical Ethics*)

19. If we leave selection of public art to residents of a community . . . we will end up with an aesthetic common denominator of sterile, benign and conventional art that will neither offend nor stimulate. A community, no matter how enlightened, will rarely, if ever, embrace innovation at first glance. Selection, therefore, cannot be left to a popular vote. Only a panel of recognized art experts . . . can properly choose the high caliber of public art that justifies the expenditure of public money. (Alvin S. Lane, newspaper article)

20. As for the terms *good and bad,* they indicate no positive quality in things regarded in themselves, but are merely modes of thinking, or notions which we form from the comparison of things one with another. Thus one and the same thing can be at the same time good, bad, and indifferent. For instance, music is good for him that is melancholy, bad for him that mourns; for him that is deaf, it is neither good nor bad. (Benedict Spinoza, *The Ethics*)

Summary

This chapter has covered some of the most important basic concepts in logic. We defined *logic* as the study of the principles of correct reasoning. An *argument* is a group of statements, one of which is claimed to follow from the others. *Statements* are sentences that have truth-value. In the context of an argument, the statement that is claimed to follow is called the *conclusion*, and the statement or statements that provide support are called *premises*. The relationship between premises and conclusion is called *inferential*; thus, drawing a conclusion from premises is making an *inference*. We learned two ways to expose or make explicit the structure of an argument: writing it in *argument form* and drawing an *argument diagram*. We were introduced to the *enthymeme*, or incomplete, argument; and lastly, we began studying the identification of real arguments, those outside logic class.

Review Questions

1. What is logic? What is its purpose?

2. What is reasoning?

3. How do logic and psychology differ in their treatment of reasoning?

4. Name several words in our language that often indicate a premise.

5. What is a statement?

6. Define the term 'argument' and explain the parts of an argument.

7. What is a conditional statement?

8. The following passage contains commands. Rewrite the passage in the form of a conditional statement.

   Do not seek to have events happen as you want them to,
   but instead want them to happen as they do happen, and
   your life will go well. (Epictetus)

9. Read this passage. List each assertion made in this passage.

   If economic growth slows down, if income gaps increase,
   if the corruption continues to erode the reputation of the
   leadership, or if there is a new, internationally televised
   movement for greater freedom similar to the 1989 student
   demonstrations, the regime will wrap itself in the flag.
   (Richard Bernstein and Ross H. Munro, *The Com-*
   ing Conflict with China © 1997 by Richard Bernstein and Ross H. Munro. Reprinted by permission
   of Alfred A. Knopf, Inc.)

10. In the definition of 'argument,' why do we say that the conclusion "is *claimed* to follow" rather than saying simply that the conclusion "follows" from the premises?

True or False?

1. Every argument has a conclusion and two premises.

2. To say that a statement has a truth-value means that it is a true statement.

3. The premise of one argument may be a conclusion of another.

4. In the statement 'the welders are on strike because their benefits are inadequate,' it is being asserted that the welders are on strike.

5. In diagramming arguments, if a premise provides support without requiring another premise, then we call it independent support.

6. According to the principle of charity, it is always best to let your opponent win the argument.

7. An argument is a group of statements, one of which follows from the others.

8. An enthymeme is an argument that has no conclusion.

9. Not all statements have truth-value.

10. In diagramming, the arrow shows the "direction" of an inference just as does the word 'therefore,' for example.

Discussion Questions

1. When it comes to showing the structure of an argument, what differences do you notice between writing it in argument form and diagramming it? Choose an example from the exercises in this chapter to illustrate your points.

2. Argue for or against the claim that 'Ethics has nothing to do with logic.' Consider the arguments in the text to the effect that 'Failure to show charity in logic is a waste of time' and 'Failure to show charity is unethical.'

 ## INFOTRAC Assignments

1. Using INFOTRAC look up the subject word *LOGIC* and follow to *Encyclopedia excerpts* and *Periodical references*. Compose a list of eight articles dealing with logic.

2. Using INFOTRAC look up any of the following subject words:

   STUDENT ETHICS

   COLLEGE SPORTS

   MUSIC

   LAUGHTER

   ENDANGERED SPECIES

   Locate an essay in which you find an argument. Write the argument in argument form.

CHAPTER TWO
Good Argument, Deductive Validity, and Inductive Strength

In this chapter we examine the concept of a good argument and, relatedly, deductive validity and inductive strength. We learn several valid and invalid logical forms, and we examine the relationship between validity and truth.

2.1 Good Arguments

In this section we examine the complex notion of a *good argument*. Identifying good arguments is one of the most important objectives of logic and is, in large part, what the rest of this book is about.

We know that not all arguments are good; some are better than others, and some are not to be believed at all. But how do we tell the difference between good arguments and weak arguments? As a beginning, recall the definition of an argument: *a group of statements one of which is claimed to follow from the others*. One of those statements is a conclusion and at least one other is a premise offered for the conclusion. An argument is a good one if the conclusion *does* indeed follow from the premises and the premises are *true*.

There are, in other words, two conditions that an argument must meet in order to be good: (1) The conclusion *follows from* the premises and (2) the premises are *true*.

It is easy to see that if either one of these conditions is not the case, the argument has failed to establish its conclusion. For example, if a premise is false, as in the example below,

Example 1

1. *Cats are invertebrates.*
2. *Invertebrates are cuddly.*

---

3. *Therefore, cats are cuddly.*

then the premise has no actual support to pass to the conclusion. On the other hand, if the conclusion does not follow, then whether or not the premises are true, they do not support the conclusion drawn. For example,

Example 2

1. *All physicists are good at mathematics.*
2. *All engineers are good at mathematics.*

---

3. *Therefore, all physicists are engineers.*

Examples 1 and 2 are not good arguments for different reasons. Example 1 has a false premise. Example 2, however, has true premises but the conclusion does not follow.

> good argument   *(1) The conclusion follows from the premises, and (2) the premises are true.*

Now, not only are there two requirements for a good argument, but these two requirements are **logically separable,** as we will see. Requirement 1 has to do with the logical relationship between the premises and the conclusion, in other words, the inference; requirement 2 has to do with the actual truth of the premises. An argument may meet one condition but not the other. We return to this very important point in Section 2.5; for the present, let's focus on requirement 1: whether, given the premises, the conclusion follows.

2.2 Inferential Support: Does the Conclusion Follow?

What does it mean to say that "the conclusion follows from the premises?" In logic this means one of two things: Either the conclusion follows *necessarily* or the conclusion follows *probably*. This gives us two different notions of strong inferential support. The first we call *deductive validity* and the second we call *inductive strength*. Each of these important concepts is developed thoroughly in later chapters, but let's become familiar with them now. Consider these two arguments:

Example 3

1. *All snakes are poisonous.*
2. *The coachwhip is a snake.*

---

3. *Therefore, the coachwhip is poisonous.*

Example 4

1. *Most snakes are poisonous.*
2. *The coachwhip is a snake.*

---

3. *Therefore, the coachwhip is poisonous.*

These arguments are alike except for their first premises. Notice the difference it makes to reason from '*Most* snakes are poisonous' rather than '*All* snakes are poisonous.' For instance, in Example 3, if we are given as premises that *all* snakes are poisonous and that the coachwhip is a snake, it *must* follow that the coachwhip is poisonous. The conclusion follows *necessarily*. On the other hand, if it is that *most* snakes are poisonous, then the coachwhip, a snake, is *likely to be* poisonous, *but is not necessarily*. The conclusion in Example 4 follows *probably*.

Examples 3 and 4 illustrate two different senses of "follows from" in the definition of a good argument. In Example 3, the conclusion follows necessarily; in Example 4, the conclusion follows probably. The inferential support in Example 4 is weaker than in 3. Yet notice that the support in Example 4 is not to be dismissed; after all, if *most* snakes are poisonous, then isn't it likely that the coachwhip is, too?

Comparing Examples 3 and 4 with a third, we see an additional point about inference:

Example 5

1. *Few snakes are poisonous.*
2. *The coachwhip is a snake.*

---

3. *The coachwhip is poisonous.*

The conclusion in Example 5 certainly does not *necessarily* follow; furthermore, it does not follow *probably*. Example 5 provides less support for the conclusion than does Example 4: Given that *few* snakes are poisonous, it is even less likely that the coachwhip is poisonous. We say that the conclusion in Example 5 *does not follow*.

Looking at all three examples and focusing just on the relationships of support, we can see that they compare differently on the *degree* of support each offers the conclusion.

On the one hand, there is Example 3, an inference that could be no stronger. Given its premises, it is certain that the coachwhip is poisonous. On the other, there is Example 5 that, given its premises, offers very little reason for the conclusion. Example 4 sits in between, providing more reason than 5 but slightly less than 3.

As another example, consider the argument in Example 2:

1. *All physicists are good at mathematics.*

2. *All engineers are good at mathematics.*

---

3. *Therefore, all physicists are engineers.*

Here we have premises that are as strongly worded as one could want. Yet, if those premises are true, would it follow that physicists are engineers? Would it follow necessarily? Would it follow even probably? The answers are *no*. There is no more reason to conclude that physicists are engineers from those premises than that tomatoes are onions because both are vegetables!

Whenever we have an argument in which, given the premises, the conclusion follows necessarily, we will say that it is a *deductively valid* argument. Whenever we have an argument in which, given the premises, the conclusion follows probably, we will say that it is *inductively strong*. And when we have an argument in which, given the premises, the conclusion is not even probable, we will say that it is *inductively weak*, or in other words, that it *does not follow*. An argument in which the conclusion does not follow cannot be a good argument.

If we think of inferential support as a descending scale of strength from the strongest possible to the weakest, we can see that the examples we've discussed rest at different places on that scale ranging from logical certainty—as is the case with deductive validity—through degrees of inductive strength to inductive weakness.

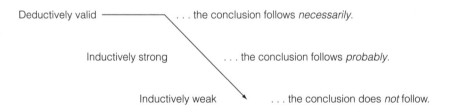

Given the premises . . .

Deductively valid ——————— . . . the conclusion follows *necessarily.*

Inductively strong   . . . the conclusion follows *probably.*

Inductively weak   . . . the conclusion does *not* follow.

We are now in a position to be more precise in our account of a good argument and to appreciate some of the complexity of that concept. A good argument, we said, is one in which the premises are true and the conclusion follows from them. We have seen, however, that premises vary in the degree of support they provide for their conclusion. In a good argument the conclusion may follow from the premises with necessity—that is, deductive validity—or with probability—that is, inductive strength. Thus, here is a better definition of a good argument:

good argument   *(1) The conclusion follows from the premises either necessarily (deductive validity) or probably (inductive strength); and (2) the premises are true.*

Conversely, an argument may be bad for either of two reasons: (1) it is neither deductively valid nor inductively strong, or (2) at least one premise is false. Therefore, we can conclude that the inferences of arguments are either deductively valid, inductively strong, or inductively weak. In Chapter 8 we return to examine the concept of inductive strength. In Section 2.3 we examine the concept of deductive validity more closely.

The points in this section can be summarized as follows:

1. A good argument is one in which (1) the conclusion follows from the premises and (2) the premises are true.

2. Since the conclusion may follow from the premises with deductive validity or with a degree of inductive strength, it follows that

3. *A good argument* is one in which (1) the conclusion follows from the premises either with deductive validity or with inductive strength and (2) the premises are true.

4. A conclusion follows with *deductive validity* if, given the premises, the conclusion follows necessarily.

5. Otherwise, a conclusion follows with *inductive strength* if, given the premises, the conclusion follows probably. The degree of support premises lend to an inductive conclusion varies from little or none to very strong.

2.3 Deductive Validity Defined

> . . . if the Ugly Sisters are older than Cinderella,
> it is (in an iron and awful sense) necessary that
> Cinderella is younger than the Ugly Sisters. There
> is no getting out of it. If Jack is the son of a miller,
> a miller is the father of Jack. Cold reason decrees it
> from her awful throne. . . .
> (G. K. Chesterton, "The Logic of Elfland")

An argument is deductively valid if and only if, given the premises, the conclusion necessarily follows.

Another way to say it is this: If you assume the premises are true, then it must follow that the conclusion is true; the conclusion *cannot* be false. That is what is meant by saying that the conclusion *necessarily* follows from the premises. "Cold reason decrees it from her awful throne. . . ." Consider what happens if we attempt to deny this necessity:

Example 6a

  1. *Max is taller than Fred.*

  2. *Fred is taller than Steve.*

  _____

  3a. Therefore, Max is taller than Steve.

To see how *cold reason* logically forces you to accept the conclusion, try to affirm the premises yet deny the conclusion, as we see in this modification of Example 6a:

Example 6b

  1. *Max is taller than Fred.*

  2. *Fred is taller than Steve.*

  _____

  3b. Max is not taller than Steve.

Statement 3b is the denial of "Max is taller than Steve." When you try to assert all three statements together, you encounter a contradiction. If premises 1 and 2 are true, then 3b must be false. Or if 1 and 3b are true, then 2 must be false, and so on. Thus, what the argument in Example 6b asserts is logically impossible. It is like asserting that the Ugly Sisters are older than Cinderella but that she is *not* younger than they! What we are noticing is a logical fact about deductively valid arguments: namely, *a valid argument will yield a logical contradiction if you assert the premises and deny the conclusion.* This is why we say that, given the premises, the conclusion must follow. It cannot fail to follow on pain of logical nonsense!

On the other hand, an *invalid* argument does *not* logically compel acceptance of the conclusion. For example,

Example 7

  1. *If Myles is a Frenchman, then he speaks French.*

  2. *Myles speaks French.*

  _____

  3. Therefore, Myles is a Frenchman.

Given premises 1 and 2, the conclusion does not have to be true. In this example it is easy to assume the premises are true yet deny that Myles is a Frenchman. For example, assume it is true that *if* he were a Frenchman he'd speak French. Assume also that he *does* speak French, having studied it in school, perhaps. But he happens not to be a Frenchman. No contradiction results. Why is this? Notice that premise 1 states that if he's a Frenchman he'll speak French. It does not state that *only* Frenchmen speak French. The logical difference between those words makes the difference in this case between an invalid and a valid argument.

Example 8

1. *If you study, you will pass the test.*
2. *You do not study.*

---

3. *Therefore, you do not pass the test.*

Is it conceivable that if you study, you will pass, and you do not study, yet you *do pass* the test? Surely we can imagine this. Here is a counterexample: You got a copy of the test questions in advance and passed not by studying but by copying the answers. So, given the premises, the conclusion does not necessarily follow; its denial is possible.

Exercise 2.3A   Deductive Validity. Does the Conclusion Follow Necessarily?   With each exercise below, assume the premises are true and ask: *Given the premises, does the conclusion follow necessarily?* If you believe it does, then you will judge the argument to be deductively valid. If not, you will judge it to be invalid. Give a brief explanation for your judgment.

1. Every chemistry major must take one year of organic chemistry. Max is a chemistry major, so he must take a year of organic chem.
2. All life requires water. There is no water on the planet Venus. Therefore, no life is possible on Venus.
3. Drinking coffee stunts your growth. Max's growth is stunted. Therefore, Max drinks coffee.
4. If you speed, then you will get a ticket. But you do not speed; therefore, you do not get a ticket.
5. Patients who take their medicine almost always get better. Since you've been taking your medicine, you will get better.
6. After the cabinet members met, the choices before the president were to escalate the economic boycott of South Africa or veto the pacification plan. He will not choose to veto; therefore, he will escalate the boycott.
7. Only movie stars live in Hollywood. Robert Redford is a movie star. Therefore, he lives in Hollywood.
8. All movie stars live in Hollywood. Robert Redford is a movie star. Therefore, he lives in Hollywood.
9. All movie stars live in Hollywood. Robert Redford lives in Hollywood. Therefore, he is a movie star.
10. There are 367 students in my history class. I reason that at least two of them have birthdays on the same day of the year.
11. You are right to be suspicious of someone who does not think that he needs to abide by the rules that apply to everyone else. Harold Thrower routinely violates traffic laws, saying while doing so that because he is a superior driver, he does not need to slow down for curves or stop for lights. Therefore, you are right to be suspicious of him!

12. There are no excuses for late papers. Well, there are excuses but no *legitimate* excuses! What makes an excuse legitimate, you ask? Simple. An excusing event is legitimate if it is an act of God! Since there are no acts of God, it follows that there are no legitimate excuses for late papers.

13. The right to life, which every person possesses, does not give one the right to whatever one needs in order to live. So, even though a person dying of, say, kidney disease has a right to life, that person does not thereby have a right to use another's kidneys.

14. The superior forms of art are those that capture reality and display it for us. Film is one art form that most successfully captures reality and displays it; thus, film is a superior art form.

15. The human mind has no weight, no shape, and no size. The human brain has weight, shape, and size. Two or more things are identical only if they have all the same properties. Therefore, the mind and the brain are not identical.

Exercise 2.3B   Inductive Strength. Does the Conclusion Follow Probably?   With each exercise below, assume the premises are true and ask: *Given the premises, does the conclusion follow probably though not necessarily?* If you believe it does, then you will judge the argument to be inductively strong. If not, you will judge it to be weak. Give a brief explanation for your judgment.

1. Most religions include a belief in a god. Buddhism is a religion, therefore, it contains a belief in god.

2. Some students prefer take-home exams. So, if you give students what they prefer, then you should always give them take-home exams.

3. Lauren bought a new American Motors 4-door Galaxy with sunroof and within a year she had to have the transmission replaced. Therefore, do not buy a 4-door Galaxy.

4. Most federal employees have managed-care plans because all federal employees were given a choice of type of plan and managed-care plans have better benefits.

5. The incidence of infection due to cat bites is very high; therefore, if you do not take an antibiotic, you probably will get an infection.

6. The incidence of infection due to insect bites is quite low. Therefore, even if you do not take an antibiotic, you probably will not get an infection.

7. Tax cuts are not likely to cause a reduction in the deficit, but they will encourage consumer spending. And increased consumer spending can counteract the negative effects of an inflated national debt. Therefore, tax cuts are a good thing for the economy.

8. If you need a lawyer and don't have one, then there's a very good chance that a judge will reject your case. You don't have a lawyer and do need one; therefore, you will probably have your case rejected by the judge.

9. There are 350 students in my philosophy class. I reason that at least two of them have birthdays on the same day of the year.

10. For punishment to effectively deter potential criminals several conditions must exist. First, people must believe that they will very likely be caught, convicted, and punished. Second, people must be able to control their conduct according to that belief. But most potential lawbreakers think they will not get caught and surely not punished. Furthermore, many crimes are committed impulsively by people who are temporarily so upset they are unable to discipline themselves. Thus, punishment is not an effective deterrent of crime.

11. Large doses of vitamin C can prevent the onset of colds, according to chemist Linus Pauling. His own laboratory came up with the finding that high doses of the vitamin could reduce the average number of symptomatic days per cold from 7.8 to 7.1. Is his conclusion inductively strong?

12. For the past twenty years researchers have been training chimpanzees to use sign language. Washoe, the first chimp to communicate with sign language, recently began teaching a ten-month-old chimp named Loulis to use signs. She even went so far as to mold Loulis' hands to form signs. Thus far, Loulis has learned fifty-five words. This evidence is good reason for concluding that animals other than humans can learn languages.

13. Most people who major in the humanities go on to teach the humanities. People who teach the humanities are happy because the humanities are always exciting and fun, and they are about things of human importance. Work that keeps you focused on being human is hardly work at all. It comes to be a labor of love. Therefore, people who major in the humanities love their work.

14. "My own conclusion is that feed [not freshness] is the chief influence on flavor [in eggs], followed by the condition of the 'layers,' as hens are known in the trade. Small-farm eggs taste better than big-farm ones. . . . Free-range chickens, allowed to forage for food to supplement their feed, generally produce better-tasting eggs than hens confined to a henhouse, and "cage-free" hens, allowed to roam around a henhouse, produce better eggs than hens cooped up . . ." (Corby Kummer, "A Better Egg," *Atlantic Monthly*)

15. Why is getting an infection in a hospital so much more dangerous than getting one outside of a hospital? Biologist Paul Ewald reasons: "Antibiotic-resistant *Staphylococcus aureus*, for example, is particularly lethal in hospitals. Much of the damage is attributable to the compromised defenses of the patients . . . . But staph outbreaks also appear to cause more overt diseases in nurses than one would expect from studies of the outside community . . . . The available information supports the idea that cycling in hospitals makes pathogens more harmful . . . . The longer the strains had been circulating in the hospital environment, the more lethal the outbreak. . . ." (Paul W. Ewald, *Plague Time*)

2.4 Validity and Logical Form

Let us develop our understanding of deductive validity by a brief examination of validity and *logical form*. In this section we learn about the concept of logical form and several recognizable forms, some deductively valid, some invalid. To begin with, consider these two important rules we will employ.

Rule 1   Any argument with a valid logical form is a valid argument.

Rule 2   Any argument with an invalid logical form is an invalid argument.

Let us begin by illustrating logical form. Consider the following example.

Example 9

1. *All cows are ruminating animals.*
2. *All ruminating animals are docile.*

---

3. *All cows are docile.*

Now compare Example 9 with the example below.

Example 10

1. *All A are B.*
2. *All B are C.*

---

3. *Therefore, all A are C.*

Letting the letters A, B, and C stand for 'cows,' 'ruminating animals,' and 'docile,' respectively, we see that Example 10 is *the underlying form* of Example 9. We will say that Example 10 is the logical form of 9 and that Example 9 is a *substitution instance* of that form.

Example 9	**Example 10**
1. *All cows are ruminating animals.*	1. *All A are B.*
2. *All ruminating animals are docile.*	2. *All B are C.*
3. *All cows are docile.*	3. *All A are C.*

Example 10 is a well-recognized example of a valid logical form called "Barbara" (a mnemonic device by which medieval logicians could remember the forms of the statements and their exact order in an argument). Since Example 10 is a valid logical form and since Example 9 is a substitution instance of 10, Example 9 is a valid argument. To put it differently, Example 9 is an argument with a valid logical form; therefore, it is valid by rule 1 above.

1. *All A are B.*   VALID LOGICAL FORM

2. *All B are C.*   BARBARA

---

3. *Therefore, all A are C.*

Just as Example 9 is an exact substitution of the form Barbara, so other arguments may also have that valid logical form. They, too, will be valid under rule 1, which states that any argument with a valid logical form is a valid argument.

Let's consider other examples and introduce several other valid logical forms.

Example 11	VALID LOGICAL FORM DISJUNCTIVE SYLLOGISM
1. *Max wears glasses or contact lenses.*	1. *A or B*
2. *Max does not wear glasses.*	2. *Not A*
3. *Max wears contact lenses.*	3. *B*

The *disjunctive syllogism* is a valid logical form according to which, if we are given that A *or* B is the case, and that A is *not* the case, then it must follow that B *is* the case. Since Example 11 has that form, it is a valid argument. It can be demonstrated, as we will see in Chapter 7, that the logical form

1. *A or B*
2. *Not B*
3. *A*

is also an instance of disjunctive syllogism: a disjunction, the denial of one part, and the inference to the other. Disjunctive syllogism derives its name from the fact that it consists of three statements (hence, "syllogism"): an 'or' statement called a disjunction, the denial of one part of the disjunction, and an inference to the other part.

Here is a third valid logical form.

Example 12	VALID LOGICAL FORM MODUS PONENS
1. *If it rains, then your car is wet.*	1. *If A then B*
2. *It rains.*	2. *A*
3. *Your car is wet.*	3. *B*

Briefly consider the form of *modus ponens*. Given that if A then B, and that A obtains, it must follow that B obtains. Notice that Example 12 is of the form *modus ponens*. Therefore, it is a valid argument.

A fourth valid logical form is *modus tollens*.

Example 13	VALID LOGICAL FORM MODUS TOLLENS
1. *If it rains, then your car is wet.*	1. *If A then B*
2. *Your car is not wet.*	2. *Not B*
3. *It does not rain.*	3. *Not A*

We can intuitively convince ourselves of the validity of *modus tollens* by considering what it asserts: Statement 1 says that if A occurs, then B occurs; 2 states that B does not occur. It must follow then that A does not occur, since if 3 were false, then by 1, statement 2 would be false. Thus, given 1 and 2, conclusion 3 must follow. Since *modus tollens* is a valid form and since Example 13 is one of its instances, Example 13 is a valid argument.

Let's consider three *invalid* logical forms. First, the fallacy of *denying the antecedent,* illustrated in this example.

Example 14	FALLACY OF DENYING THE ANTECEDENT
1. If you study, then you pass.	*1. If A then B*
2. You do not study.	*2. Not A*
3. You do not pass.	*3. Not B*

As the name suggests, the fallacy of denying the antecedent involves a premise, here premise 2, that denies the *antecedent,* or first part, of a conditional statement, here premise 1. Conclusion 3 does not necessarily follow, since both 1 and 2 may be true yet 3 false as we saw when we examined Example 8.

A second invalid logical form involving the conditional is the fallacy of *affirming the consequent:*

Example 15	FALLACY OF AFFIRMING THE CONSEQUENT
1. If you study, then you pass.	*1. If A then B*
2. You pass.	*2. B*
3. You study.	*3. A*

Here the *consequent,* the second part of the conditional, is asserted, as in premise 2; the argument concludes that 3, the antecedent of the conditional, must follow. But this argument form is invalid, since, for example, that you studied does not follow from the premises that if you study, you pass, and you did pass. Again, in our discussion of Example 8 we saw that a counterexample is conceivable: namely, you pass by means other than studying, yet it may still be true of you that if you study, you will pass.

A third invalid logical form is the fallacy of *undistributed middle:*

Example 16	FALLACY OF UNDISTRIBUTED MIDDLE
1. All ants are insects.	*1. All A are B.*
2. All beetles are insects.	*2. All C are B.*
3. All beetles are ants.	*3. All C are A.*

Notice that the term B in the form (as its counterpart 'insects' in the example) is the term common to the other two terms, A and C. Yet being common to A and C does not entail that A and C are related as conclusion 3 asserts. The problem is that neither premise attributes being an A or being a C to every B. In the example neither premise attributes being an ant or being a beetle to all insects. In technical language, the middle term, B, is not *distributed over* at least one of the other terms. Hence the name *fallacy of undistributed middle*.

VALID LOGICAL FORMS

BARBARA	DISJUNCTIVE SYLLOGISM
1. All A are B.	*1. A or B*
2. All B are C.	*2. Not A*
3. All A are C.	*3. B*

MODUS PONENS	MODUS TOLLENS
1. If A then B	*1. If A then B*
2. A	*2. Not B*
3. B	*3. Not A*

INVALID LOGICAL FORMS

FALLACY OF DENYING THE ANTECEDENT	FALLACY OF AFFIRMING THE CONSEQUENT
1. If A then B	*1. If A then B*
2. Not A	*2. B*
3. Not B	*3. A*

FALLACY OF
UNDISTRIBUTED MIDDLE

1. All A are B.
2. All C are B.

3. All C are A.

We have reviewed four valid forms of arguments and three invalid forms. We have illustrated how an argument may be understood as having a form and, thus, how two or more arguments may be said to have the same form. We have also illustrated these two important rules about validity: (1) a substitution instance of a valid logical form is a valid argument; and (2) a substitution instance of an invalid logical form is an invalid argument. Perhaps the most important point to emerge from this discussion is that validity is a matter of the logical form or structure of an argument, less a matter of its content.

This review also raises important questions. How do we determine the form of an argument? What counts as form and what counts as content? How do we know that valid forms are indeed valid? Are there ways to prove validity and invalidity? These are questions answered by a study of the two logical systems we will take up. We will see that there are techniques for supplying the form of an argument and procedures for proving validity and invalidity.

Exercise 2.4A Validity and Logical Form. State which logical form the argument exhibits and whether it is a valid or invalid argument.

1. If Webb is promoted, then Walters is transferred. Webb is promoted; therefore, Walters is transferred.

2. There will be either sunshine or rain. It will not rain; therefore, there will be sunshine.

3. Every fire official came to the conference and, since all who came to the conference enjoyed the dinner, all the fire officials enjoyed the dinner.

4. If she doesn't have a fever, then she doesn't have the flu. She doesn't have a fever. So she doesn't have the flu.

5. All logicians have good manners and all physicians have good manners. Therefore, all logicians are physicians.

6. All Chinook winds have the fohn effect, and the fohn effect can raise air temperatures by as much as 40° F. So all Chinook winds are capable of raising the temperature as much as 40° F.

7. There is no need for surgery because if there is a tumor, then there is need for surgery, but there is no tumor.

8. If her argument is good, then all her premises are true. But it's not the case that all her premises are true; thus, her argument is not good.

9. If Shakespeare's works are histories, then they are not science fiction. Shakespeare's works are histories; therefore, they are not science fiction.

10. If Shakespeare's works are histories, then they are not science fiction. They are science fiction. Therefore, they are not histories.

11. If there is a tumor, then there is need for surgery. There is need for surgery; therefore, there is a tumor.

12. Either the emergence of democracy is a cause for hope, or environmental problems will overshadow any promise of a bright future. Since environmental problems will not overshadow any promise of a bright future, it follows that the emergence of democracy is a cause for hope.

13. If it is possible to keep people alive indefinitely, then we face serious questions about the purpose and quality of such life. Therefore, since it is not possible to keep people alive indefinitely, we do not have to face those serious questions.

14. Every pediatrician is an M.D., and so is every podiatrist. Hence every pediatrician is a podiatrist.

15. If all elementary and secondary schools across the country are re-examining their educational objectives, then major educational reform will be a national goal. Since such re-examination is the case, so is the national goal of educational reform.

Exercise 2.4B   More Logical Form.   What logical form do you see at work in the following passages? If necessary, write the argument in argument form to reveal the pattern.

1. *Cats like to gaze at the moon.*
   Animals that gaze at the moon are untrustworthy.
   Untrustworthy animals are predators.
   Predators are wily and unpredictable.
   Wily and unpredictable animals make poor house pets.
   Poor house pets are good only as laboratory test animals.
   Therefore, cats are good only as laboratory test animals.

2. If any journalists learn about the invasion, then the newspapers will print the news. And if the newspapers print the news, then the invasion will not be a secret. If the invasion is not a secret, then our troops will not have the advantage of surprise. If we do not have the advantage of surprise, then the enemy will be prepared. And if the enemy is prepared, then we are likely to suffer higher casualties. But no journalists learn about the invasion. Therefore, we are not likely to suffer higher casualties.

3. To function as a citizen, you need to know a little bit about a lot of different sciences—a little biology, a little geology, a little physics, and so on. But universities (and, by extension, primary and secondary schools) are set up to teach one science at a time. Thus, a fundamental mismatch exists between the kinds of knowledge educational institutions are equipped to impart and the kind of knowledge the citizen needs. (Robert M. Hazen and James Trefil, *Science Matters: Achieving Scientific Literacy*)
   Hint: Rewrite the first premise to read this way:

   If people get what they need to function as citizens, then they would be taught a little bit about a lot of different sciences.

4. In fact, there can be no such thing as a perfectly rigid body in nature. If a golf ball were that rigid, and the entire ball began moving at once, then the shock wave would have to travel through the ball at an infinite velocity. This is forbidden by Einstein's special theory of relativity, which states that no signal or causal influence can travel at a velocity greater than that of light. Thus it appears that if we accept the strictures of relativity—which is one of the best-confirmed theories in physics—then we must conclude that . . . no thing in nature can be perfectly rigid. (Richard Morris, *The Edges of Science*)

5. When a bone is damaged, as part of Mr. Fuller's spine was by the same bullet, it undergoes a series of sequential changes before stabilizing, much as the skin does

when it scars over. But the process with the skin occurs rapidly, whereas the bone takes its time, five years generally, from start to finish. Technically, all I could say is that since Mr. Fuller's bone-tissue exhibits having gone through this entire process, his wound is at least five years old. (Archer Mayor, *The Skeleton's Knee*)

6. How does one determine when a law is just or unjust? A just law is a man-made code that squares with the moral law of God. An unjust law is a code that is out of harmony with the moral law. To put it in the terms of Saint Thomas Aquinas, an unjust law is a human law that is not rooted in eternal and natural law. <u>Any law that uplifts human personality is just. Any law that degrades human personality is unjust. All segregation statutes are unjust because segregation distorts the soul and damages the personality. It gives the segregator a false sense of superiority, and the segregated a false sense of inferiority.</u> (Martin Luther King, Jr., "Letter from Birmingham Jail")

   Hint: Focus on the inference that is underlined. Write it in argument form and judge which logical form it most exemplifies.

2.5 Truth, Validity, and Good Argument

The strongest inferential relationship is deductive validity. Recall that a deductively valid inference is one in which, given the premises, the conclusion must follow. That property of an argument—being deductively valid—is about the relationship between premises and conclusion; it is about, to put it roughly, the reasoning in the argument. What does it have to do with truth? Furthermore, what does it have to do with whether the argument is a good one? These are the issues we will discuss. Let us study a number of points about validity, truth, and good arguments.

1. Truth is a property of statements. Validity is a property of arguments and inferences.

Truth-value refers to a property of statements, including premises and conclusions. They, along with beliefs, opinions, and judgments, are the kinds of things that are either true or false. Arguments and inferences, on the other hand, are either deductively valid or invalid, inductively weak or strong. Therefore, statements are not valid! Arguments are not true!

2. An argument may be deductively valid yet have one or more false premises.

Example 17

1. *Smoking makes you stronger.*

2. *Being stronger makes you happier.*

---

3. *Therefore, smoking makes you happier.*

Example 17 has at least one false premise yet it is deductively valid. Therefore, deductively validity does not entail true premises.

3. An argument may be deductively valid yet not a good argument.

Example 17 is deductively valid yet not a good argument because it does not have all true premises. Do not think that an argument is good and should be accepted merely because it is valid. Validity is only part of the concept of a good argument.

4. All the statements of an argument may be true yet it is not deductively valid.

Example 18	*Example 19*
1. 5 is greater than 3	1. Mozart was a musician.
2. 4 is greater than 3	2. Composers are musicians.
3. Thus, 5 is greater than 4	3. Mozart was a composer.

True premises and conclusion do not make an argument valid. Examples 18 and 19 exhibit the form we call the fallacy of undistributed middle.

5. If the premises of a deductively valid argument are true, then the conclusion is true.

Given that an argument is deductively valid and the premises are true, then it must follow that the conclusion is true. As we have seen, to deny the conclusion entails asserting either that the argument is not deductively valid or that at least one premise is not true.

Example 20

1. All robins are thrushes.

2. All thrushes are passerines (perching birds).

3. All robins are passerines (perching birds).

6. If the conclusion of a deductively valid argument is false, then at least one premise is false.

Example 21

1. The only justification for a military invasion of another country is self-defense.

2. It is self-defense only if a nation faces imminent danger at its borders.

3. The United States was not threatened by imminent danger at its borders before or during the military invasion of Iraq.

4. *Therefore, the United States was not acting in self-defense in the military invasion of Iraq.*

5. *Therefore, the United States was not justified in the military invasion of Iraq.*

Example 21 is a deductively valid argument; it exemplifies the valid logical form *modus tollens*. Many would argue that the conclusion of this valid argument, statement 5, is false. We were justified in invading Iraq, they say. Therefore, since the argument is valid and 5 is denied, it follows that at least one premise must be denied. This illustrates a useful strategy in criticism: *If you see that an argument is deductively valid and yet you deny the conclusion, then at least one premise must be denied.* Locating such a premise and showing that it is false is, of course, to show that the argument is not a good one.

There is perhaps no more important point in logic than the point we have been discussing here from different angles. *Validity has to do with the logical connection between premises and conclusion, not with the actual truth or falsity of the premises.* So do not confuse what you may know about the *actual* truth or falsity of the premises with asking whether a particular argument is or is not valid. To determine validity, *always assume the premises are true* and ask, "Must the conclusion follow?"

Second, validity does not indicate a good argument. As we have seen, an argument may be deductively valid yet not good. Similarly, an argument may be good yet not deductively valid, as is the case with inductively strong arguments.

Exercise 2.5   What, if Anything, Is Wrong with This Argument?   The following exercises test your understanding of the concepts we have studied in this section, the relationship between truth and validity. Read the passage and, using the concepts of truth and validity, discuss the argument.

Address three questions in particular: (a) To the best of your knowledge, are the statements true? (b) Is the argument deductively valid? If not, why not? (c) Is the argument good? If not, how does the argument fail?

1. 1. *All fish are swimmers.*

    2. *All trout are swimmers.*

    ---

    3. *All trout are fish.*

2. 1. *Health care costs are declining.*

    2. *If health care costs are declining, then the federal deficit will decrease.*

    ---

    3. *Therefore, the deficit will decrease.*

3. 1. *If something is dangerous, then people should avoid it.*

    2. *People should avoid hang gliding.*

    ---

    3. *Therefore, hang gliding is dangerous.*

4. *1. All composers are artists.*

   2. Elton John is an artist.

   ---

   3. Elton John is a composer.

5. *1. Abortion is the act of killing the fetus.*

   2. The fetus is a person.

   3. Killing a person is morally wrong.

   ---

   4. Therefore, abortion is morally wrong.

6. The predominant language in the United States is very difficult to learn. That is because the predominant language is German, and German is difficult to learn.

7. Crows are birds because birds have feathers and crows have feathers.

8. For this exercise, read Derek Gjertsen's comment on a deductive argument written by the philosopher Spinoza. Given the concepts we have studied in this chapter, how would you describe Gjertsen's analysis of Spinoza's argument?

   Commenting on a deductive argument written by Spinoza, Derek Gjertsen writes,

   Thus, from the two axioms:

   Axiom 4.   The knowledge of an effect depends on and involves the knowledge of a cause.

   Axiom 5.   Things which have nothing in common cannot be understood, the one by means of the other,

   Spinoza tries to deduce:

   Proposition 3.   Things which have nothing in common cannot one be the cause of the other.

   The proof itself is obvious. Assume two things which have nothing in common. Then, by Axiom 5, we cannot understand one in terms of the other. Consequently, by Axiom 4, neither can be the cause of the other. Therefore, we have proved Proposition 3.

   But the proof depends upon the soundness of the axioms. However impeccable the rigour of the logic employed, if the axioms are at all doubtful, then the system itself will be suspect. In this Spinoza has fared no better than many another system-builder. Is, for example, the already quoted Axiom 4 really acceptable? To have some knowledge of an effect do I really need to have knowledge of the cause? I know Newton had a breakdown in 1693, and I also know that Vesalius died in mysterious circumstances in 1564. The causes of these events are unknown to me and, I fear, anyone else. Many things are known about past catastrophes and present diseases without their causes having yet been identified. (Derek Gjertsen, *Science and Philosophy: Past and Present*)

Summary

In this chapter we have examined the concept of a good argument. We saw that good arguments have both true premises and strong inferential support. Inferential support may be one of deductive validity or inductive strength. We were introduced to the ideas of logical form and valid and invalid logical forms, in particular. Next, we examined the very important distinction between truth and validity. We saw that the validity of an argument is independent of the truth-value of the premises.

Since assessing inferential support is a central objective of logic, in the chapters to follow we will concentrate on systematic techniques for determining inferential support. We will study two systems of logic in Chapters 3 through 6, categorical logic and truth-functional logic. Each system provides, among other things, a framework for examining arguments for deductive validity. Then in Chapter 8 we will explore methods for assessing inductive support. In Chapter 9 we will look at failures in good reasoning called informal fallacies. Finally, Chapter 10 outlines an overall strategy for analyzing arguments and applying the techniques we have learned.

Review Questions

1. What is a good argument?
2. According to the text, what is the definition of a deductively valid argument?
3. According to the text, what is the definition of an inductively strong argument?
4. Make up examples illustrating all those valid logical forms we've studied that employ a conditional as a premise.
5. In what ways might an argument fail to be a good one?
6. Why is it that true premises do not make an argument deductively valid?
7. If you were a chemist, you would be a scientist. But you aren't a scientist. What can we validly conclude from those premises?
8. If an argument is deductively valid and yet the conclusion is false, why must there be at least one false premise?
9. What does it mean to say that the validity of an argument is logically independent of the truth-value of the premises? Explain that idea.
10. In your own words, explain the claim of this text that *statements are not valid and arguments are not true.* Why is that?

True or False?

1. If an argument is not valid, then it is not a good argument.
2. If an argument is valid and you believe the conclusion is false, then you must conclude that at least one premise is false.

3. If the conclusion of an argument does not necessarily follow from the premises, then it must be an inductive argument.

4. Deductive validity is only part and not a necessary part of a good argument.

5. A statement may be valid or invalid depending on who judges it.

6. If the premises are false, then the argument is not valid.

7. If you assume the premises are true and get a contradiction when you deny the conclusion, then the argument must be valid.

8. Two arguments can have the same logical form yet one is valid and the other invalid.

9. The antecedent is the first part of a conditional statement.

10. Of the logical forms we studied, only *Barbara* employs an "or" statement.

Discussion Questions

1. In describing the logical power of deductive validity G. K. Chesterton writes the following:

   If Jack is the son of a miller, a miller is the father of Jack.
   Cold reason decrees it from her awful throne. . . .

   Why does Chesterton refer to reason as a cold ruler on an awful throne? Is reason cold and awful, lacking in heart? It has that reputation. Do you think it is well deserved? Argue for or against the claim that logic makes us cold and unfeeling.

2. Imagine two possibilities for yourself. One is that you have great skill at constructing strong arguments but lack knowledge. The other is that you have knowledge but not ability to reason well with it. In the first case, all your arguments are deductively valid only; in the second, all your arguments have true premises but nothing else. Supposing that between knowledge and logical ability, you could have only one, which would you choose for yourself? Why?

INFOTRAC Assignments

1. Using INFOTRAC look up the subject word *LOGIC* and follow to Encyclopedia excerpts and Periodical references. Look for articles on any of the following subject words:

   DEDUCTION   *DEDUCTIVE REASONING*
   INDUCTION   *INDUCTIVE REASONING*

CHAPTER THREE
Categorical Logic
Part I

In this chapter we begin our survey of categorical logic. We learn the categorical forms of statements, use Venn diagrams, and learn how to draw inferences by means of the square of opposition. We also examine how the traditional operations are performed on the categorical forms.

3.1 Introduction

The Practical Use of Logical Systems   Imagine that you are a farmer living in the previous century. You would want to know the condition of the soil on your farmland, as all farmers do. You might not know about soil acidity and alkalinity, but you would probably have your own terms, handed down through the generations, for describing and evaluating the soil. You would check the soil by looking at it, smelling it, tasting it, squeezing it between your fingers, and seeing how well it held water. Using your senses and applying what you'd learned from your ancestors, you would reach a judgment about the quality of the soil. Such a method works fairly well, but it is not accurate or wholly reliable, and it might vary from person to person. Today, farmers have their own soil-testing kits, developed by chemists specializing in soil composition, so that they can evaluate the condition of their soil. The analysis is accurate, objective, and certain.

Prior to learning a system of logic, the thinker is in much the same position as the old-time farmers relying on their senses and experience. For instance, in the previous chapter you were relying on your intuition to tell whether an argument was valid. You really had no way yet of checking your judgment other than by appealing to what seemed to "make sense." Suppose you and a friend disagree about the validity of an argument. You know the argument cannot be both valid and invalid, but how do you tell who is correct? It would be useful at such a time to have a "testing kit" for evaluating arguments. With an accurate test not only could you determine which judgment is correct, but you could do so with certainty and objectivity. This is precisely what the system of categorical logic is designed to do. *In general, the purpose of a system of logic is to provide an objective procedure for (1) clarifying language, (2) revealing its logical structure, (3) defining the concepts of logic, and (4) evaluating arguments for their validity.* An objective procedure is desirable because it is easy to apply, it gives the same results no matter who uses it, and it is free of the human errors associated with intuitions. So, in short, a system of logic provides methods of testing our reasoning.

Categorical logic originated with the Greek philosopher Aristotle (384–322 BCE). Thus, much of what we will learn in this survey is over two thousand years old. From fragments of their writings we know that philosophers living as early as 700 BCE had an understanding of good argument and used reasoning to draw abstract conclusions, but Aristotle was the first person to develop a logical system. His comprehensive theory includes precise definitions, principles of reasoning, a system for exposing arguments, and rules for evaluating reasoning. Most of our common notions of reasoning—inference, argument, affirmation, denial, contradiction, tautology, validity, and so on—were deliberately and systematically studied and refined by Aristotle. Categorical logic is not the whole of Aristotle's work in logic, but it is one of his most important contributions and provides an excellent example of a deductive system.

Before we begin this survey of categorical logic, let us briefly preview what will be covered. Categorical logic is a system for analyzing deductive arguments, or what Aristotle called *syllogisms*. (A syllogism, as we see in Chapter 4, is a precisely defined format for expressing certain deductive arguments.) One of the requirements of categorical logic is that statements be in a certain form, called *categorical form*. These statements are *categorical statements*, and they assert a relationship between one group of things and another. In this chapter we learn about categorical statements and how they are logically related to each other. In the next chapter we learn how to translate many ordinary sentences into categorical statements. We then apply our knowledge of the relations among categorical statements to the task of evaluating arguments expressed in categorical form. We use a nineteenth-century technique called Venn diagramming to represent statements and arguments graphically. In these chapters you learn a systematic way of translating sentences and arguments into a form that makes them clear and easy to evaluate. The technique of Venn diagramming gives you a graphic way of showing the implications of statements and the validity or invalidity of arguments.

3.2 Categories and Reasoning

Categorical logic is a deductive logical system. It makes certain important basic assumptions about deductive reasoning, which we discuss in this section.

(1) Categories are classes or groups of things. The words and phrases we use in our language to refer to or name categories will be called *terms*. Here are some examples of terms that name categories:

red things	humans	metals
silverfish	living things	nonmetals
guitar players	soft things	senators
biting insects	people who are athletic	

The membership of a category or class is relative to our interests and needs. We could conceivably categorize or "break things up into categories" any way we wished, but such categorizing might not be useful or sensible. Look around your room and categorize things into 'all wooden things', 'all living things', or 'all things requiring oxygen'. As you can see, many things are members of more than one group. You, for instance, belong to the classes of living things, things requiring oxygen, fleshy things, thinking things, and so on. You are not a member of the class of wooden things. (Are you classifiable into any of these categories: Democrats, athletes, chess players, chocolate lovers, science fiction buffs, rednecks, stamp collectors, card sharks, sun worshippers, or car owners?) Describing yourself may be thought of as a matter of finding the categories that correctly apply to you. (Is there a list of categories that applies to you and you alone for all eternity? That is, do you possess a unique classification?)

The notions of categories and categorizing extend beyond logic and involve a number of thought-provoking philosophical questions. For instance, are there any limits to the ways we can classify reality? Some argue that there are no limits; others argue that there are, at the very least, those limits imposed by the character of reality itself. Is thought possible without categorizing? Could we think if we did not have the ability to think in terms of groups of things? Many philosophers believe that the concept of the category is so fundamental to thinking that without it we could not have developed science, probably could not have learned to communicate beyond grunts and groans, and would very likely not experience the world and ourselves as we do. Aristotle's great genius is evident in his recognition of the immense importance of the notion of the category.

(2) Statements in categorical logic assert a relationship between one category and another. Whenever we form a statement, we pick out something and we think something about it. Suppose you are thinking right now that these desks are hard. What you have picked out to think about is 'these desks'; the subject of your statement is 'these desks'. Every statement must have a subject. What you are thinking about these desks is that they 'are hard'; this second part of the statement is called the predicate. Your statement 'these desks are hard' can be seen as asserting a relationship between the *subject category,* named by the words 'these desks', and the *predicate category,* named by the words 'hard things'. In effect, you are saying that these desks belong to the category of hard things.

Example 1

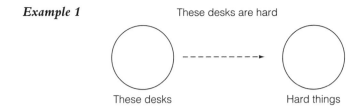

These desks are hard

These desks   Hard things

It is almost as though you were rounding up all the desks you are thinking about and moving them into a pigeonhole in your mind labeled 'hard things'. Think of statements as assertions about such relationships of groups of things.

Aristotle's system is based on the idea that almost all statements can be expressed in terms of categories and the assertion of a relationship between categories. Here are some examples of how ordinary statements can be understood as making assertions about categories.

	ORDINARY STATEMENT	CATEGORICAL INTERPRETATION
Example 2	*Some dogs bark.*	*At least one member of the class of dogs is a member of the class of things that bark.*
Example 3	*All spiders have eight legs.*	*All members of the class of spiders are members of the class of things having eight legs.*
Example 4	*No bankers favor the withholding of interest on savings accounts.*	*No members of the class of bankers are members of the class of persons favoring withholding interest on savings accounts.*
Example 5	*The Syrians deported Yassar Arafat.*	*All things identical to the government of Syria are members of the class of things deporting Yassar Arafat.*

Such categorical interpretations as these may strike you as unnecessarily wordy, but the advantages of treating statements as assertions about categories will become clear to you soon. In Chapter 4 we will learn how to translate ordinary statements into categorical form, which, you will see, need not be as wordy as Examples 2–5.

(3) All reasoning in categorical logic is reasoning about categories. This is merely an application to arguments of what we have seen about statements. Here is a simple example of an argument:

Example 6

1. Artists are humans.

2. Humans are mortal.

---

3. Therefore, artists are mortal.

We may analyze this reasoning as follows: Premise 1 asserts that all artists belong to the category of humans. Premise 2 asserts that all humans belong to the category of mortal things. Now, since all artists are part of the group of humans, and all humans are part of the group of mortal things, 3 must follow: All artists are part of the group of mortal things as well. We see that the conclusion of the argument follows from the relationships expressed in the premises. The example above relates categories in this pattern:

1. *All As are Bs.*
2. *All Bs are Cs.*

----

3. *Therefore, All As are Cs.*

Looking over the form or pattern of this argument, we can see that other possible arguments exemplify that form also. For example, these arguments both have the same form as the example above:

Example 7

1. *All Soviet agents are communists.*
2. *All communists are Marxists.*

----

3. *Therefore, all Soviet agents are Marxists.*

Example 8

1. *All mothers are Democrats.*
2. *All Democrats are liberals.*

----

3. *Therefore, all mothers are liberals.*

The arguments may not have true premises, but they all have the same form. This fact means that if the form above is a valid argument form—and it happens that it is—then so are all arguments having that form. This appeal to valid forms enormously simplifies the business of checking for validity, for *if an argument conforms to a valid argument form, then it is a valid argument.* We will be using Venn diagrams to help us discover valid argument forms.

3.3 The Four Categorical Forms

Every statement asserts a relationship between categories. Given a statement with 'artists' as its subject and 'humans' as its predicate, categorical logic specifies four basic forms that such a statement can take. In other words, there are four relationships between those two categories, as exemplified in these statements:

All artists *are* humans.

No artists *are* humans.

Some artists *are* humans.

Some artists *are not* humans.

Either all artists belong to the group of humans, none do, some do, or some do not. We can represent the form of those statements by letting the letter 'S' stand for the subject and the letter 'P' stand for the predicate.

EXAMPLES	THE FOUR CATEGORICAL FORMS
All artists are humans.	All S are P.
No artists are humans.	No S are P.
Some artists are humans.	Some S are P.
Some artists are not humans.	Some S are not P.

Every statement in categorical logic can be represented according to one of these four forms, which comprise the core of categorical logic. We will be studying these forms very carefully, so for convenience we name them as follows:

CATEGORICAL FORM NAME	CATEGORICAL FORM
A	All S are P.
E	No S are P.
I	Some S are P.
O	Some S are not P.

Now let's look at how each form will be understood—that is, what it is logically asserting.

Form A: 'All S are P' asserts that the predicate *is affirmed of all members* of S, the subject category.

Form E: 'No S are P' asserts that the predicate *is denied of all members* of S.

Form I: 'Some S are P' asserts that *there is at least one member* of S and the predicate *is affirmed of it.*

Form O: 'Some S are not P' asserts that *there is at least one member* of S and the predicate *is denied of it.*

Notice that forms A and E are about all members of the subject group. Form A says that they are *all* Ps; form E says that *none* of them is a P. Because they are statements about all of the subject group, they are called *universal.* Universality is their *logical quantity.* Logical quantity has to do with how much of the subject class is referred to in the statement.

Figure 3.1

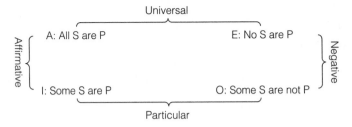

Forms I and O, on the other hand, are not about all members of the subject class, nor can one tell from the statement form how many Ss are referred to. But there must be at least one S for the statement form to be true. Logically speaking, we must understand the statement forms as referring to at least one member of the S group. There may, of course, be more Ss that are or are not Ps, but we cannot conclude that without further information. Thus, the statement form 'Some S are P' asserts that *there is at least one S* and it is a P; whereas, 'Some S are not P' asserts that *there is at least one S* and it is not a P. These two forms are said to be *particular* in *quantity* because they refer to at least one S.

Now notice that both forms A and I are affirmative. They assert that the predicate *does* belong to the subject; they are said to be *affirmative in quality.* The quality of a statement refers to its affirmation or denial of the predicate of the subject class. Forms E and O both deny that the predicate belongs to the subject, so they are said to be *negative* in *quality.*

To summarize at this point, we can say that the four categorical forms named A, E, I, and O are the core of categorical logic. In this system almost all statements and therefore almost all arguments can be expressed in terms of these forms. The four forms may be distinguished by quantity and quality. Quantity refers to how much of the subject group is referred to: either all or some. Quality refers to whether the predicate is affirmed or denied of the subject. Thus, regarding quantity, A and E are universal, whereas I and O are particular. Regarding quality, A and I are affirmative, whereas E and O are negative. All that we have learned thus far can be seen represented in the diagram shown in Figure 3.1.

Exercise 3.3A   Categorical Forms   For each of the statements listed below, (1) identify the subject and the predicate; (2) identify the categorical form: A, E, I, or O; (3) determine its quality; and (4) determine its quantity.

1. All astronomers are trained in mathematics.

2. Some Dachshunds are dogs with back problems.

3. All past presidents are invited to a luncheon on Friday.

4. No students are protesters.

5. Some traffic monitors are not well-trained people.

6. Some dermatologists are bald.

7. All football fans are fanatics.

8. No careless drivers are licensed drivers in Idaho.

9. Some members of the Kiwanis Club are active supporters of the right-to-life movement.

10. Some photographers who develop their own film are not professionals.

Exercise 3.3B   Change the Quality   For each statement listed below, change the quality to its opposite. For example, the affirmative A-form statement 'All humans are mortals' would change to the negative E-form statement 'No humans are mortals'. Be sure not to change the quantity.

1. All piranhas are vicious fish.

2. No small land birds are nonmigratory birds.

3. Some sailboats are equipped with outboard motors.

4. Some passengers on the airplane are traveling to Los Angeles.

5. All good investments are tax-free investments.

6. Some logicians are not musically inclined.

7. All bartenders in this state are licensed.

8. No red-headed woodpeckers are here during the winter.

9. Some wheelwrights are still in business.

10. Some pastors are not Methodists.

Exercise 3.3C   Change the Quantity   If a statement is universal, change its quantity to particular. If it is particular, change it to universal. Do not change the quality at the same time.

1. All happy people are happy in the same way.

2. All unhappy people are unhappy in their own solitary way.

3. No specimens from the site are ready for examination.

4. Some sun worshipers are not permitted on the beach.

5. Some vicious fish are piranhas.

6. Some logicians are not musically inclined.

7. No bartenders are licensed in this state.

8. All philosophers are frustrated actors.

9. Some chess players are not grand masters.

10. No popular vocalists are poor.

3.4 Venn Diagrams

The *Venn diagram,* developed by the logician John Venn (1834–1923), is a very useful tool for representing graphically the logical meaning of a statement. It provides a simple method for testing inferences and arguments for their validity, among other things. The Venn diagram will be our main tool in this survey of categorical logic. We use it to represent statements in this chapter and arguments in the next chapter.

The Venn diagram uses circles to represent categories. To begin with a very simple diagram, suppose the circle below stands for the category 'meat eaters'.

Example 9

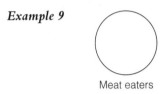

Meat eaters

The area within the circle represents meat eaters, and the area outside the circle stands for everything that is not a meat eater. With this one circle we have thus represented pictorially a "logical" distinction between meat eaters and non–meat eaters.

Now by using an X to stand for the existence of something, we can represent logically different statements. An X within the circle represents the statement 'something is a meat eater'. An X outside the circle represents 'something is not a meat eater'.

Example 10

Something is a meat eater   Something is not a meat eater

By using shading as illustrated in the next diagram, we can show that an area has nothing in it. Thus, this diagram represents the statement 'nothing is a meat eater' or 'there are no meat eaters'. The shading marks close off an area and indicate that nothing exists there.

Example 11

Nothing is a meat eater

On the other hand, we can say that all things are meat eaters by crossing out the area outside the circle:

Example 12

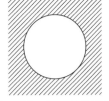

Everything is a meat eater
(or There are no non-–meat eaters)

Diagramming with Two Categories

Now let us use the Venn diagram technique to represent categorical statements. To do this we need two circles, one for each of the categories of a statement. The circles overlap so the diagram can represent all possible relationships between the two categories. The diagram therefore has four distinct "logical" areas, as shown below. Suppose we use the categories 'people' and 'athletes'.

Example 13

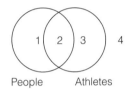

People   Athletes

Notice the meanings of the four areas. Area 1 would represent members of the category 'people who are not athletes'. Area 2 would represent 'things that are both people and athletes'. Something in that area would be a person and an athlete. Area 3 would represent 'things that are athletes but not people'. And the area outside both circles, area 4, would represent 'things that are neither people nor athletes'. (Where, for instance, would you place Mel Gibson? Where would you place Tiger Woods, Santa Claus, and your logic book?)

To diagram categorical statements, we let one circle represent the subject category and the other the predicate category. Then by using either an X or the shading marks, we can show what the relationship is. Let us consider each categorical statement form.

The A-form says that 'All S are P'. We first draw two overlapping circles. We let the left-hand circle represent the subject category and the right-hand circle represent the predicate category. We label them S and P, respectively. Now we want to show that *all* Ss are members of the P circle. We do this by closing out that area where no Ss should be:

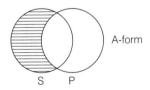

A-form

S   P

Think of it this way. In the A-form statement, 'All S are P', you are talking about Ss, so you want to show in your diagram how *they* are related to Ps. Thus, you must put shading inside area 1 to indicate that there are no Ss there. Doing so "locates" all the Ss inside area 2, the area representing things that are Ss and also Ps.

The E-form says that 'No S are P'; thus, you want the diagram to indicate that Ss are completely separated from Ps. By shading in area 2 you indicate that that area contains nothing. Thus, there are no Ss that are Ps. All Ss are represented as being in area 1, as the diagram for the E-form shows:

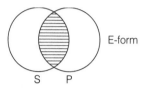

The I-form says that 'Some S are P'. The O-form says that 'Some S are not P'. The symbol X is traditionally used to represent the meaning 'some' or 'at least one'. To depict the I- and O-forms, simply place the X in the proper place, as shown below:

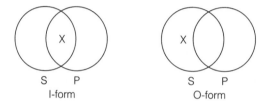

Remember that with a 'some' statement (that is, I or O), you must put the X in the appropriate place. In the statement 'Some S are P', you see that you are talking about Ss, so you must place an X somewhere *within* the S circle because only an X within the S circle can represent 'Some Ss'. Then you see that it must also be placed inside the P circle. Following are some examples of ordinary categorical statements and the Venn diagrams representing them.

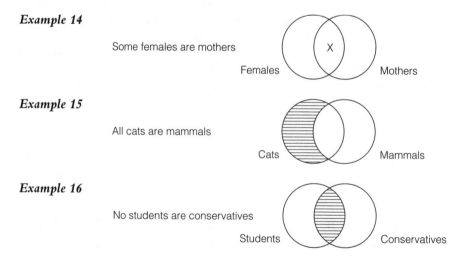

Example 14

Some females are mothers

Females   Mothers

Example 15

All cats are mammals

Cats   Mammals

Example 16

No students are conservatives

Students   Conservatives

Example 17

Some Parisians are not French

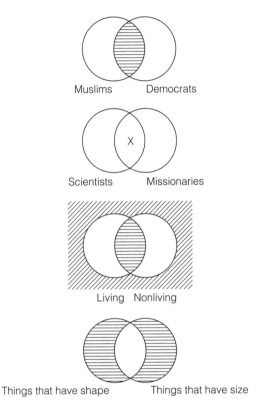

Parisians   French

Now try your hand at "reading" some Venn diagrams. What do you think the following diagrams depict?

Muslims   Democrats

Scientists   Missionaries

Living   Nonliving

Things that have shape   Things that have size

The first diagram says that no Muslims are Democrats. It also says that no Democrats are Muslims. The second diagram says that some scientists are missionaries. It also says that some missionaries are scientists. The third one tells us that everything is living or nonliving but not both. And the fourth one indicates that everything that has shape also has size, and vice versa.

Exercise 3.4A   Drawing Venn Diagrams   For each statement, identify the form, the quality, and the quantity and then draw a Venn diagram.

1. No eucalyptus trees are natives of California.
2. All scientists are humanitarians.

3. All machines are the products of intelligent beings.

4. Some animals are not predators.

5. Some lawyers are people whom we can respect.

6. No doctors who are not trained in neurophysiology are brain surgeons.

7. No person wants to be harmed.

8. Some sailcats do not reproduce.

9. All logicians love Venn diagrams.

10. Some students are registered voters.

11. No male vocalists are sopranos at the Met.

12. Some Western historians are historians who oppose the Marxist interpretation of the American Revolution.

13. All members of the student council must maintain at least a 3.0 grade-point average.

14. Some of the professors I have had are excellent teachers.

15. No computers are capable of thought.

16. All dogs must have their day.

17. All animal lovers will appreciate the efforts of the Humane Society.

18. (a) No things are free. (b) Nothing is free.

19. Some teas contain caffeine.

20. Some psychologists are not Freudians.

Exercise 3.4B   Reading Venn Diagrams   Write the categorical statements represented by the following Venn diagrams.

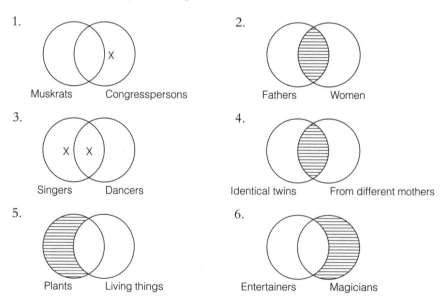

1.

Muskrats   Congresspersons

2.

Fathers   Women

3.

Singers   Dancers

4.

Identical twins   From different mothers

5.

Plants   Living things

6.

Entertainers   Magicians

3.5 Recognizing Simple Inferences

Some common inferences are easily recognizable as inferences from one categorical statement to another. For example, from the premise that *all snakes are poisonous,* we might infer that *some snakes are poisonous.* That would be to reason from an A-statement to an I. Further, we might infer that, since the A-statement is true, then the E-statement—*No snakes are poisonous*—is false. Setting aside the question whether such inferences are valid, it is often fairly easy to spot inferences between categorical statements. Look at the following illustrations of such inferences. Notice how we indicate the truth-values of the categorical statements.

Example 18

Since no astronauts have landed on Mars,	TRUE E
it follows that some astronauts have not landed on Mars.	TRUE O

Example 19

Some swans are not white; therefore,	TRUE O
it is false that all swans are white.	FALSE A

Example 20

O'Riley: It's not true that some opiates are not addictive.	FALSE O
Murphy: Okay, so all opiates are addictive.	TRUE A

Exercise 3.5   Recognizing Simple Inferences   Write the following arguments in Argument Form, showing the premise and conclusion, the Cat Form name, and the truth-value of the statements. Unless explicitly stated otherwise, you may assume a statement is true. Follow this example.

SAMPLE	*All estate agents are licensed. Therefore, it is false that no estate agents are licensed.*

1. All estate agents are licensed.	TRUE A
2. Thus, it's false that no estate agents are licensed.	FALSE E

1. No modern sculptors are better than Henry Moore. So it's false that some are better than Moore.

2. It's not true that every religion includes a belief in immortality; so some religions do not include such a belief.

3. There is at least one senator who voted for the tax cut. Therefore, it cannot be that no one voted for it.

4. Some art historians are employed. It follows therefore that some art historians are not employed.

5. It is false that all great chess players are foreigners. So none are foreigners.

6. Brown: Some players are not playing by the rules.
   Smith: I guess it follows from what you say that not all are playing by the rules.

7. Adelaide: It's not true that all people like logic.
   Myles: Then no one likes logic.

8. It is false that some philanthropists are not wealthy benefactors because all philanthropists are wealthy benefactors.

9. Annie: All logicians are cold and heartless.
   Wendell: Therefore, it can't be true that none are.

10. Betty: Some men are interested only in sex.
    Maxine: So you mean that not all men are interested in sex.

3.6 The Squares of Opposition

Introduction to the Squares of Opposition. What logical relations exist among the four categorical forms? If we know, for example, that some statement of the form 'All S are P' is true, what, if anything, can we infer about the truth or falsity of the other categorical statements? Interestingly enough, the answer depends on whether we make what is called an *existential assumption,* that is, whether we assume there are Ss in existence or whether we do not.

In this and the next section we will study the logical relationships among the categorical statements. Those relationships are organized in the manner of a square having as its corners the four categorical statement forms. It is called the *Square of Opposition.* There are two presentations of the Square or, in other words, two Squares. One, called the *Traditional Square of Opposition,* is the classical theory of the statement forms and their logical relations, and it is attributed to Aristotle. The other is called the *Modern Square of Opposition,* and it provides a different set of logical relations. But let's begin by discussing the reason for two versions of the Square.

Why two different Squares of Opposition? The simple reason why there are two versions of the Square of Opposition is that there are two different ways to interpret the universal statement forms, A and E. One way is to interpret them as *asserting the existence of the things they are about.* That is called an *existential* interpretation. The Traditional Square makes just that assertion; the Modern interpretation does not. It represents the second way of interpreting a universal statement. Here is an explanation of the difference.

Consider this A-form statement: *All Confucian scholars are Beijing University graduates.* A natural way to interpret this is that it says that *there are Confucian scholars* and that *all of them are Beijing University graduates.* In other words, the statement asserts the existence of Confucian scholars—*there are Confucian scholars*—and then goes on to say something about them. On this interpretation, the statement makes an existential assertion. Similarly, an E-form statement such as *No neutrinos have mass* can be interpreted as asserting that *neutrinos exist* and that *none have mass.* Once again, an existential assertion is understood as part of the meaning of the statement. Generally speaking, then, an A-form statement is taken to mean "There is at least one S and all S are P" and an E-form statement is taken to mean "There is at least one S and no S are P." This is the **Traditional interpretation** and, as we will see, it invokes a distinct set of logical relationships.

However, according to the **Modern interpretation,** the universal statements do not make an existential assertion. Rather, they are interpreted *hypothetically:* that is, *If the subject exists, then . . . .* For example, the statement *No measuring devices are perfectly accurate* is taken to mean "If anything is a measuring device, then none is perfectly accurate."

For some statements, the Modern interpretation is preferable to the Traditional. Consider these three true statements:

All passenger pigeons are extinct.

No isolated magnetic poles are possible in nature.

All bodies at rest remain at rest.

Each is true but it is odd, if not false, to interpret them existentially. For example, it is odd to say "There are passenger pigeons, and all are extinct." And, since there can be no isolated magnetic poles and no bodies at rest, it is false to assert their existence as in "There are isolated magnetic poles, and none are possible in nature" and "There is at least one body at rest and all bodies at rest remain at rest." Rather, these examples are best interpreted hypothetically.

The Traditional Square of Opposition. According to the Traditional version of the Square of Opposition, the statement 'All Martians are intelligent' asserts that there are Martians in existence. Similarly, the statement 'No Martians are intelligent' also asserts that there are Martians. Looking at examples of the A and E forms, this is how we will interpret them:

Example 21

All Martians are intelligent.   *No Martians are intelligent.*

are taken to mean

> *There is at least one Martian,*   *There is at least one Martian,*
> *and all are intelligent.*   *and no Martians are intelligent.*

Notice the existential claim—'there is at least one . . .' taken to be part of the meaning of the universal statements. Now, to show the existential assumption, we place an X in the diagrams for the A- and E-forms, just as we do for the I- and O-forms (see Figure 3.2).

Figure 3.2   The Four Forms with Existential Assumption

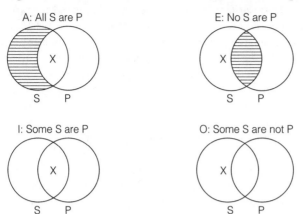

What logical relations hold among these four forms? The description of the logical relations among the four categorical forms is represented in the Traditional Square of Opposition. Let's develop it systematically.

1. *A and E are* superalternates *relative to I and O, respectively.* Superalternation is that relationship in which one statement implies, but is not implied by, another. For example: A implies I, but I does not imply A. Consider first what follows from the truth of a universal statement.

   If A is true, then I is true. Given the traditional interpretation, if it is true that all Martians are intelligent, then it must be true that some Martians are intelligent. In fact, we can see that the I-diagram is "contained within" the A-diagram. Thus, 'All Martians are intelligent' implies 'Some Martians are intelligent'.

   If E is true, then O is true. Similarly, if it is true that no Martians are intelligent, then it must be true that some Martians are not intelligent. The O-diagram is contained within the E-diagram. 'No Martians are intelligent' implies 'Some Martians are not intelligent'.

   Notice, however, that the reverse is not valid. *I does not imply A; O does not imply E.* Thus, 'Some Martians are intelligent' does not entail that 'All Martians are intelligent', and the fact that some Martians are not intelligent does not imply that none are.

   To summarize, both of the universal statements E and A imply their corresponding particular statements, but a valid inference cannot be made from the truth of the particular to the truth of the universal. Those relationships are called *superalternation,* and A and E are said to be *superalternates* relative to I and O.

2. *I and O are* subalternates *relative to A and E, respectively.* Subalternation is that relationship in which the falsity of one statement implies, but is not implied by, the falsity of another. For example: a false I implies a false O, but not the reverse. Consider.

   If I is false, then A is false. If O is false, then E is false. If it is not true that some Martians are intelligent, then it cannot be true that all Martians are intelligent:

If I is false, then A is false. If it is not true that some Martians are not intelligent, then it cannot be true that no Martians are intelligent: *If O is false, then E is false.*

However, the reverse is not true: the falsity of the universal does not imply the falsity of the particular. So, for example, that 'All Martians are intelligent' is false does not imply that 'Some Martians are intelligent' is false.

These relationships—that between the false I and A and that between the false O and E—are called *subalternation.* I is the *subalternate* of A, and O is the subalternate of E.

3. *A and E are* contraries. Statements are contraries, relative to each other, just in case they cannot both be true but can both be false. A and E have precisely that relationship.

Start with either one as true. If it is true that all Martians are intelligent, for example, then it must be false that no Martians are intelligent. The A-diagram indicates that all Martians are in area 2, whereas the E-diagram indicates that no Martians are in area 2. Thus, if A is true, then E must be false, and if E is true, then A must be false.

However, both A and E can be false. For example, if it turns out that some Martians are intelligent and some Martians are not intelligent, then both A and E are false.

To summarize, since A and E cannot both be true, it follows that if one is true, the other must be false. However, given one false, we cannot infer anything about the truth-value of the other. If 'All Martians are intelligent' is false, 'No Martians are intelligent' could be either true or false.

4. *I and O are* subcontraries. Subcontraries are statements that, relative to each other, cannot both be false but can both be true. In other words, if one is false, the other must be true, but not the reverse.

I and O cannot both be false. Assume either one to be false, and it must follow that the other is true. For example, if it is false that some Martians are intelligent, then it is true that some Martians are not intelligent. The same conclusion holds if we begin with the O-form as false. If I is false, then O is true; if O is false, then I is true. I and O are called *subcontraries* because they cannot both be false, but they can both be true. They can both be true if, for instance, it turns out that some Martians are intelligent and some are not.

5. *A and O are* contradictories, *and E and I are* contradictories. Contradictories have exactly opposite truth-values. If A is true, then O is false, and vice versa. If I is true, then E is false, and vice versa. Consider what each pair asserts. A asserts, for example, that all Martians are intelligent, and O asserts that some Martians are not intelligent. They are exact opposites. The same applies for I and E. In Figure 3.2, the Venn diagrams diagonally opposite each other are contradictories. Thus, whatever truth-value E has, I has the opposite; and whatever A has, O has the opposite.

Now we can graphically represent the Traditional Square of Opposition depicting the logical relations in detail (Figure 3.3). Note the relationships of the contraries and the subcontraries and also note the contradictories. Then notice how each universal form is related to its particular form.

Figure 3.3   Traditional Square of Opposition

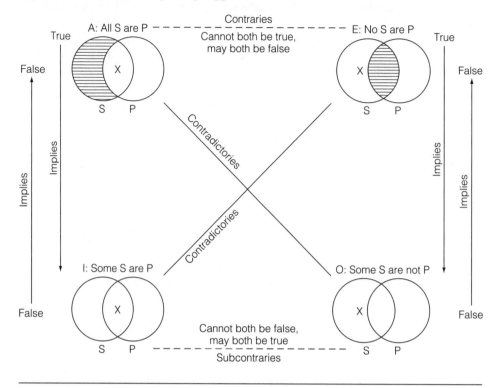

Summary

1. *Superalternation*
   A implies I. I does not imply A.
   E implies O. O does not imply E.

   "Truth goes down."

2. *Subalternation*
   The falsity of I implies the falsity of A, but not the reverse.
   The falsity of O implies the falsity of E, but not the reverse.

   "Falsehood goes up."

3. *A and E are contraries.*

   "Cannot both be true, may both be false."

4. *I and O are subcontraries.*

   "Cannot both be false, may both be true."

5. *A and O are contradictories.*
   I and E are contradictories.

   "They have exactly opposite truth-value."

Inferences on the Traditional Square   By using Venn diagrams and the Square of Opposition, we can evaluate common inferences made between any two of the four categorical forms. For example, if someone asserts that all snakes are poisonous and then concludes that it is false that some snakes are not poisonous, we can see from the Venn diagram and the Square that this inference is valid. Let us work through several examples of such evaluations. In these exercises we are working with the Traditional Square and are therefore adopting the existential assumption that members of the subject category do exist. Remember that the Venn diagrams for the A- and E-forms reflect that assumption, with an X in the circle representing the subject category.

Example 22

Some mushrooms are poisonous.
Therefore, it is false that no mushrooms are poisonous.

To determine whether this is a valid inference, we first identify the categorical forms. We have an inference from '*some mushrooms are poisonous*' to 'it is false that *no mushrooms are poisonous*'—that is, from the truth of an I to the falsity of an E. We now look at the Square and the diagrams of the relevant forms (refer to Figure 3.3). What can we tell about the relationship between the I and the E?

In the Venn diagram of the I-form statement, we see an X in the area representing mushrooms that are poisonous. In the diagram of the E-form statement, we observe that same logical area to be empty. The Venn diagrams show us that if I is true, then E is false. Recall also that I and E are contradictories and thus have opposite truth-values. We therefore conclude that it is a valid inference from the truth of I to the falsehood of E.

Example 23

No Buddhists are Catholics.
Therefore, some Buddhists are not Catholics.

Is this inference—from E to O—a valid one?

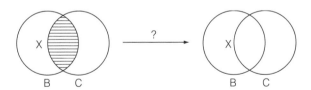

The diagrams show that O is implied by E; thus, it is a valid inference.

Example 24

Some senators are not communists.
Therefore, some senators are communists.

Is this a valid inference? From the fact that some are not, does it follow that some are?

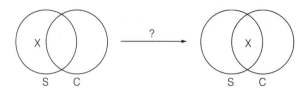

We see that this inference from O to I is not valid. Given that some senators are not communists, we do not have to conclude that some *are*. Some may be communists, but perhaps none are.

The inference from O to I is a very common mistake. Remember that I does not imply O and O does not imply I. If we know that some marines are tough, for example, we cannot conclude from that alone that some marines are not tough. All we know from the premise is that some are. It may turn out that *all* are, in which case the O statement would not be true. Thus, strictly speaking, it is invalid to reason from the truth of I to O and, as we saw, from the truth of O to I.

Now, in everyday conversation the context may provide more information than is provided by statements of the form 'Some S are P' or 'Some S are not P'. From other things a speaker says we may be able to conclude that, for example, some marines are not tough. Imagine a researcher reports, "I have examined all marines, and I can now say that *some* marines are tough." Given that all marines were examined, we would expect the researcher to say something about all of them. That he says "some are tough" in this context conversationally implies that some are not. However, we are not entitled to that inference from the categorical statement alone; we can infer it only if there are additional unstated premises. Despite contexts that might warrant our adding a missing premise, the point remains: The categorical statement forms I and O do not imply one another.

Example 25

Given that a statement of the A-form is true, what, if anything, can you conclude about: (a) the I-form? (b) the O-form? (c) the E-form?

Answers: If A is true, then (a) I is true; (b) O is false; and (c) E is false.

Example 26

Given that the I-form is true, what, if anything, can you infer about (a) the A-form? (b) the O-form? (c) the E-form?

Answers: If I is true, then (a) no inference can be made about A; (b) no inference can be made about O; and (c) E is false.

Example 27

Given that the O-form is false, what, if anything, can you infer about (a) the A-form? (b) the E-form? (c) the I-form?

Answers: If O is false, then (a) A is true; (b) E is false; and (c) I is true.

Example 28

Given that the E-form is false, what, if anything,
can you infer about (a) the A-form? (b) the I-form?
(c) the O-form?

Answers: If E is false, then (a) no inference can be made about A; (b) I is true;
(c) no inference can be made about O.

For the following group of examples, determine whether the arguments are valid or invalid, using Venn diagrams. Then check your answers with those given below.

Example 29   *It is false that no mechanics are on
                 duty today; therefore, some are on
                 duty today.*

Example 30   *Some lawyers are politicians; there-
                 fore, some lawyers are not politicians.*

Example 31   *All the people at the fair are from out
                 of town; therefore, it is false that none
                 are from out of town.*

Example 32   *It is not true that some political parties
                 are revolutionary; therefore, none are.*

Answers:

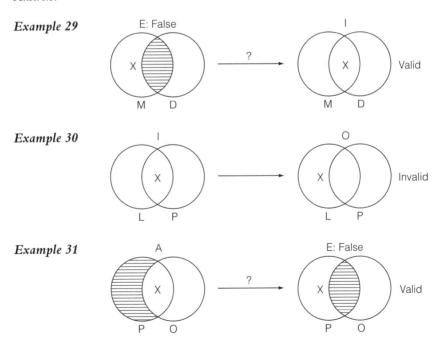

Example 32

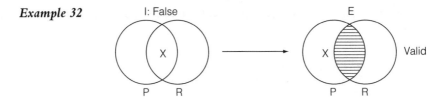

The logical relations shown in the Square of Opposition probably seem like common sense to you. The Square of Opposition is really just a convenient tool for organizing the kinds of inferences you make every day. More than this, however, the diagrams in the Square provide you with a simple method for demonstrating those logical relations and the inferences they allow you to make.

Exercise 3.6A   Inferences on the Traditional Square of Opposition
Use Venn diagrams and the Traditional Square to determine whether the following arguments are valid or invalid. Remember to include the existential assumption in your diagrams. Show your work as illustrated in **Examples 29–32.**

1. All sea kayakers are amateur athletes. Therefore, some sea kayakers are amateur athletes.
2. All classical musicians are trained by European teachers. Therefore, some classical musicians are trained by European teachers.
3. All residential students are on the meal plan; therefore, it's false that no residential students are on the meal plan.
4. Some defects of memory are defects of perception. Therefore, it is not true that no defects of memory are defects of perception.
5. Some words elicit visual images. Thus, all words elicit visual images.
6. It is false that all plumbing problems are expensive to repair. Hence, it is false that some plumbing problems are expensive to repair.
7. Some microwave ovens will not burn food, since no microwave ovens will burn food.
8. Some police officers are underpaid. Therefore, some are not underpaid.
9. No proposals from the transportation committee are over budget. Therefore, it is false that some proposals from the transportation committee are over budget.
10. All figure skaters are exciting to watch because it is just not true that no figure skaters are exciting to watch.
11. Some TV commercials are really mini-dramas. The reason I say this is that it is not true that all TV commercials are mini-dramas.
12. Since every modern business economist is a system builder, it follows that it is not true that some modern business economists are not system builders.
13. Some woodstoves are not airtight. Therefore, no woodstoves are airtight.
14. All western states are water-hungry. It follows that some western states are water-hungry.

15. Since some species of birds are not toxic, it follows that some species of birds are toxic.

Exercise 3.6B   More Inferences   Use Venn diagrams and the Traditional Square to answer the following questions. Show your work as illustrated in Examples 29–32.

1. Is Smith's inference valid?
   Brown: Some players are not playing by the rules.
   Smith: I guess it follows from what you say that not all are playing by the rules.

2. Is Myles' inference valid?
   Adelaide: It's not true that all people like logic.
   Myles: Then no one likes logic.

3. There is at least one senator who voted for the tax cut. Therefore, it cannot be that no one voted for it.

4. It is false that all great chess players are foreigners. So none are foreigners.

5. No modern sculptors are better than Henry Moore. So it's false that some are better than Moore.

6. Some art historians are employed. It therefore follows that some art historians are not employed.

7. It is false that some philanthropists are not wealthy benefactors because all philanthropists are wealthy benefactors.

8. Is Wendell's inference valid?
   Annie: All logicians are cold and heartless.
   Wendell: Therefore, it can't be true that none are.

9. Is Maxine's inference valid?
   Betty: Some men are interested only in sex.
   Maxine: So you mean that not all men are interested in sex.

10. It's not true that every religion includes a belief in immortality; so some religions do not include such a belief.

Exercise 3.6C   Quick Check on the Square   Assuming the Traditional Square, answer the following questions about simple inferences.

1. Given that the E-form is true, what, if anything, can you infer about (a) the A-form? (b) the I-form? (c) the O-form?

2. Given that the I-form is true, what, if anything, can you infer about (a) the A-form? (b) the O-form? (c) the E-form?

3. If some bats are deaf, then what, if anything, can you infer about the claim that all bats are deaf?

4. If it's not true that all snakes are poisonous, then what about the claim that no snakes are poisonous?

5. If some people are not afraid of heights, then what can you infer about the claim that some people are afraid of heights?

6. Some humans are mortal. What can you infer about the claim that all humans are mortal?

7. Some humans are mortal. What can you infer about the claim that some humans are not mortal?

8. All houseplants need sunlight and water. What can you infer about the claim that it's false that some houseplants do not need sunlight and water?

9. If it's false that some Latin Americans do not speak Spanish, then what can you infer about the claim that all Latin Americans speak Spanish?

10. No great novelists are also great pianists. What can you infer about the claim that some great novelists are not great pianists?

The Modern Square of Opposition. You will recall that according to the traditional interpretation of universal statements, an existential assumption is made. In other words, we read this example of an A–form statement:

Example 33   *All terriers are short-tailed.*

to mean that 'There is at least one terrier, and all are short-tailed'. The E-form is interpreted to mean, 'There is at least one terrier, and none are short-tailed'. The existential claim is expressed in the phrase 'There is at least one terrier'. On the Modern interpretation of universal statements, *no existential assertion is made.* Neither A nor E asserts that any members of the subject class exist. Thus, when we state that, for example, 'All Martians are intelligent', we are not asserting that any Martians exist; neither are we asserting that none exist. We make no commitment at all about their existence. Rather, the universal statements are interpreted *hypothetically,* not existentially. For example, the A-form statement

Example 34   *All raptors are carnivorous.*

is taken to mean, 'If anything is a raptor, then it is carnivorous'. The E-form means, 'If anything is a raptor, then it is not carnivorous'. Notice the conditional character of the statements, that the existence of raptors is hypothetical, and compare the following two interpretations.

Example 35   *All pochards are migratory.*

TRADITIONAL	MODERN
There is at least one pochard, and all pochards are migratory.	*If anything is a pochard, then it is migratory.*

On the other hand, the Modern and the Traditional versions treat the particular statements, I and O, exactly alike. On both versions they are taken to assert the existence of members of the subject class. I, for example, states that 'There is at least one S, and it is a P'. The O-form, while asserting the existence of Ss, denies the predicate of them. So, the Modern and the Traditional differ only in their interpretations of the universal statements A and E.

Why would we use the Modern, and what difference does it make? First, notice this beginning point. On the Traditional interpretation, the universal statements are true *only if* members of the subject class exist. Let us return to

Example 35   *All pochards are migratory*

which is taken to mean that the statement 'There is at least one pochard, and all are migratory', is false if there are no pochards. Yet so also is the E-statement, 'No pochards are migratory'. If pochards do not exist, then both statements are false. To put it differently, at least one of the particular statements must be true on the traditional interpretation; otherwise, all four forms are false. Logicians regard this as limiting. What, for example, shall we do with statements about hypotheticals, ideal entities, theoretical entities, or fictional entities? For example, many people would say that the following statements are true.

Example 36

A circle is a closed figure whose points are all equidistant from its center.

Example 37

Happiness is . . . that which makes life desirable and lacking in nothing. (Aristotle)

Example 38

Every body continues in its state of rest, or of uniform motion in a straight line, unless it is compelled to change that state by forces impressed upon it. (Newton's first law of motion)

Yet we do not thereby believe that there are in existence things that actually meet the conditions described. For example, one might agree that Example 36 is true yet deny that in reality there exists an entity whose points are truly equidistant from its center. Similarly, one may affirm Example 37 yet deny that anyone has or ever has had happiness as defined. Neither must we assume the existence of bodies at rest or in straight and uniform motion in order to accept Example 38 as true. What there are, we might agree, are things that come close to those descriptions. Nevertheless, the statements are arguably true independently of our reluctance to affirm the existence of the things described.

What, furthermore, is to be done with this kind of statement?

Figure 3.4   The Modern Square of Opposition

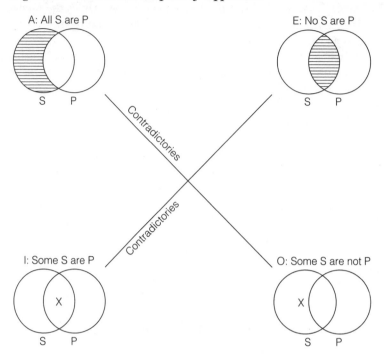

A: All S are P

E: No S are P

I: Some S are P

O: Some S are not P

Contradictories

Contradictories

S   P

S   P

S   P

S   P

X

X

Example 39

All shoplifters are prosecuted to the full extent of the law.

That statement is true just in case no shoplifter goes unprosecuted. Curiously, if it is effective as a deterrent, there are no shoplifters, and the statement is true. The truth of the statement does not depend on there being shoplifters in existence. It does not presuppose the existence of shoplifters. It is the Modern Square with its hypothetical interpretation that is most useful in handling cases such as the examples we have seen above.

To see what difference it makes when we interpret the universals hypothetically, let us develop the Modern version of the Square of Opposition (Figure 3.4), showing the logical relations among the four categorical forms without an existential assumption. Note that we do not place an X in the diagrams for A and E because we are not making an existential assumption.

1. *A and O are contradictories. E and I are contradictories.* 'All shoplifters are prosecuted' asserts just what 'Some shoplifters are not prosecuted' denies. If A is true, then O is false, and vice versa. Similarly, if A is false—if it is not true that all shoplifters are prosecuted—then it is true that some shoplifters are not prosecuted. The E- and I-forms are related in exactly the same way. If it is true that no shoplifters are prosecuted, then it is false that some shoplifters are prosecuted, and vice versa. The Modern version preserves the relationships of the contradictories, as the diagrams of the pairs on the diagonals show. Consider the A- and

E-diagrams and notice that what they depict is exactly opposite. Thus, if one is true, the other is false.

All shoplifters are prosecuted

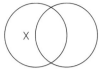

Some shoplifters are not prosecuted

2. *A and E are not contraries.* It would seem that 'All shoplifters are prosecuted' and 'No shoplifters are prosecuted' cannot both be true, but this is not so. Recall that A and E assert that 'if anything is a shoplifter, then . . .'. *If there are no shoplifters, then both statements are true.* If there are no shoplifters, then no shoplifters are not prosecuted—A is true—and no shoplifters are prosecuted—E is true. Notice how the diagram below shows that there are no shoplifters and, thus, both A and E are true. Thus, if you are given that A is true, you cannot infer that E is false.

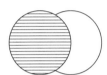

Shoplifters   Persons prosecuted

3. *I and O are not subcontraries.* I and O may both be true, and I and O may also both be false, which means that on the Modern version they are not subcontraries. Recall that subcontraries cannot both be false. I says there is at least one shoplifter and that shoplifter is prosecuted, and O says that there is at least one shoplifter and that shoplifter is not prosecuted. Yet *if there are no shoplifters at all, then each statement is false.* Thus, these two are not subcontraries.

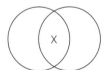

Some shoplifters are prosecuted

Some shoplifters are not prosecuted

4. *A does not imply I; E does not imply O.* These pairs no longer exhibit superalternation. We saw in the Traditional version that A implies I and E implies O, but this is not so in the Modern version. Given that 'If there is a shoplifter, then all shoplifters are prosecuted'—which is what the A-statement means—it does not follow that 'There is at least one shoplifter, and it is prosecuted'—the I statement—is true. Likewise, E may be true, yet it does not entail the existence of a shoplifter who is prosecuted. In fact, in just the case that there are no shoplifters, A is true and I is false. So also, E is true and O is false.

An example should help you see this. We say that 'All mermaids have tails' is true, yet it is false that 'Some mermaids have tails'—that is, false that there is at least one mermaid and she has a tail. Thus, A does not imply I, and for similar reasoning, E does not imply O. What makes this so, as you can see, is that A and

E do not carry an existential commitment. But I and O do, for each asserts that 'There is at least one S'. And, of course, if there are no Ss, then I and O are false because of that assertion.

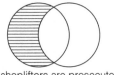

All shoplifters are prosecuted

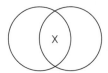

Some shoplifters are prosecuted

5. *The falsity of I does not imply the falsity of A; the falsity of O does not imply the falsity of E.* These pairs no longer exhibit subalternation. If there are no shoplifters, then both I and O are false. However, that does not make A or E false. Consider, for example, that I may be false and A is true. That would be the case if there are no shoplifters who are prosecuted; yet, it is still the case that *if* there are shoplifters, all will be prosecuted. Thus, the falsity of I does not imply that A is false, and likewise for O and E.

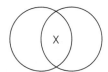

Some shoplifters are prosecuted

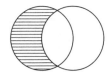

All shoplifters are prosecuted

We can see from this examination that the only inferences preserved on the Modern version of the Square are the inferences of the contradictories. It is evident that the existential assumption makes an important logical difference in the relationships among the four categorical forms.

Exercise 3.6D   Inferences on the Modern Square of Opposition   Use Venn diagrams and the Modern Square to determine whether the following inferences are valid. Recall that on the Modern Square you do not assume the existence of members of the subject category. Show your work.

1. All mermaids are lovely creatures; therefore, some mermaids are lovely creatures.

2. Some Cheshire cats are big smilers, so it's false that no Cheshire cats are big smilers.

3. No spirits are material; therefore, it's false that all spirits are material.

4. Some subatomic particles are not theoretical entities; therefore, it's true that some *are* theoretical entities.

5. All serious music lovers are people who read music because it's false that some serious music lovers are not people who read music.

6. It's not true that some uranium mines are hazardous, so it must be that some are not hazardous.

7. It's false that all precocious children are gifted because it's false that some precocious children are gifted.

8. No atheists are Christians; therefore, some atheists are not Christians.

9. All golden mountains are fictitious, so it follows that some golden mountains are fictitious.

10. Since no intelligent television comedies are successful, it follows that 'Some intelligent television comedies are successful' is false.

3.7 The Operations

Operations are defined procedures for manipulating statements. With the four types of categorical statements described above, we can perform three important operations: conversion, obversion, and contraposition. These operations yield several valid inferences and in some cases provide different ways of saying the same thing while preserving logical meaning. Hence, they indicate certain ways of logically extending our knowledge.

An important concept in the study of the operations is that of logical equivalence. In logic we say that two statements are *logically equivalent* if and only if they necessarily have the same truth conditions. That is, if one statement is true (or false), then necessarily the other statement is true (or false). We mean the same thing in daily life when we say that two sentences "have the same meaning" or "are just two different ways of saying the same thing." Logically equivalent statements are typically interchangeable. When two statements are logically equivalent, we can validly infer from the truth (or falsity) of one to the truth (or falsity) of the other. We can recognize logically equivalent statements by the fact that their Venn diagrams are identical.

In this section we learn how to (1) perform each operation, (2) diagram the resulting statement, and (3) tell whether the resulting statement is logically equivalent to the original. Finally, we learn how to (4) evaluate inferences made between a statement and its converse, obverse, and contrapositive. *Valid inferences made from the operations do not require an existential assumption.* That is, we do not need to assume that members of the subject category exist in order to assess these inferences. Let's begin with conversion and see how it applies to each of the four forms.

Conversion: Switch Subject and Predicate Terms

To perform this operation, we simply switch the subject and predicate of the statement. The resulting statement is called the *converse*. Here are the four forms and their converses:

STATEMENT FORM		CONVERSE
A: *All S are P.*	becomes	*All P are S.*
E: *No S are P.*	becomes	*No P are S.*
I: *Some S are P.*	becomes	*Some P are S.*
O: *Some S are not P.*	becomes	*Some P are not S.*

Here are some examples:

	STATEMENT	CONVERSE
Example 40	All tomatoes are vegetables.	All vegetables are tomatoes.
Example 41	No snails are pretty.	No pretty things are snails.
Example 42	Some records are hits.	Some hits are records.
Example 43	Some dogs are not attackers.	Some attackers are not dogs.

Venn diagrams provide a convenient way to determine the logical relation between a statement and its converse. Done correctly, they show us whether the statement resulting from an operation is logically equivalent to the original statement. When you are diagramming a statement formed from an operation, it is very important to *label the circles exactly as they are labeled in the diagram of the original statement.* Even though the positions of subject and predicate may change, the circles must be labeled the same if you are to see the effect of the operation on the original statement. Notice how the statements are labeled in the illustration of the A-form below:

Example 44

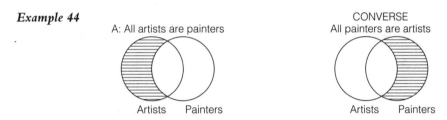

The diagram of the A-form and its converse are different; they are, in fact, mirror images of one another. This indicates that the A-form statement and its converse do not mean the same thing, or rather that converting an A-form statement does not produce just another way of saying the same thing. *The A and its converse are not logically equivalent.* Thus, no valid inference should be made from the A to its converse. For example, given that 'All artists are painters', it does not follow that 'All painters are artists'. From 'All biologists are scientists', you cannot validly infer that 'All scientists are biologists'. In sum, *the truth (or falsity) of the A-form does not imply the truth (or falsity) of its converse.*

Let us consider the E-form and its converse:

Example 45

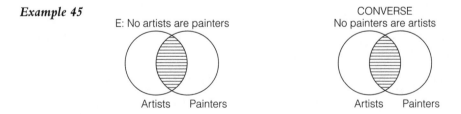

The diagrams are identical, so the converse of an E-form statement is logically equivalent to the original. Common sense also tells us that if no artists are painters, then no painters are artists. *We can validly infer from the truth (or falsity) of the E-form to the truth (or falsity) of its converse.* The diagrams indicate this by showing that the statements carry the same information.

Now consider the I-form:

Example 46

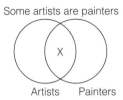

Some artists are painters

CONVERSE
Some painters are artists

The diagrams are the same, indicating that the statements 'Some artists are painters' and 'Some painters are artists' are logically equivalent. If we know that one is true (or false), we can infer that the other is true (or false). *The I-form and its converse are logically equivalent, and therefore valid inferences can be made between them.*

Consider the O-form:

Example 47

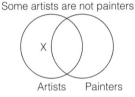

Some artists are not painters

CONVERSE
Some painters are not artists

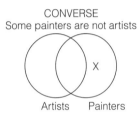

The O-form statement is not the same as its converse. Hence, you cannot infer that 'some painters are not artists' from the fact that 'some artists are not painters'. Suppose you know that some vegetables are not tomatoes. The converse, 'Some tomatoes are not vegetables', surely does not follow. *The O-form and its converse are not equivalent, and therefore inferences cannot be validly made between them.*

In sum, conversion switches the subject and predicate. Statements of forms A and O are not logically equivalent to their converses, and statements of forms E and I *are* logically equivalent to their converses.

Obversion: Change the Quality and Negate the Predicate

We form the *obverse* of a statement in two steps. First, we change the quality, from affirmative to negative or from negative to affirmative. Changing the quality of 'Some cats are runners' yields 'Some cats are not runners'. Changing the quality of 'All cats are runners' yields 'No cats are runners'. We change the quality of a statement by "moving horizontally across the square." The second step is to negate the predicate, which we do by adding the prefix *non* to it. Negating the terms 'mice', 'hermits', and 'combatants' yields 'nonmice', 'nonhermits', and 'noncombatants'. Here are some examples of this two-step procedure for forming the obverse:

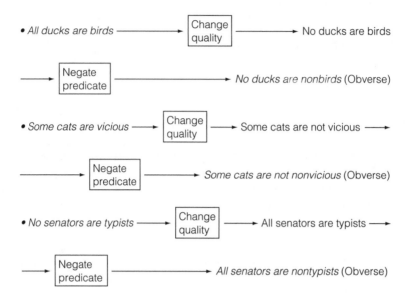

The four forms and their obverses are as follows:

STATEMENT FORM		OBVERSE
A: *All S are P.*	becomes	*No S are non-P.*
E: *No S are P.*	becomes	*All S are non-P.*
I: *Some S are P.*	becomes	*Some S are not non-P.*
O: *Some S are not P.*	becomes	*Some S are non-P.*

What logical relations do you expect between the four forms and their obverses? If you know that all ducks are birds, can you infer that no ducks are nonbirds? If some cats are vicious, does it follow that some cats are not nonvicious? Diagramming the forms reveals that all four of them are logically equivalent to their obverses. Hence, valid inferences can be made between each form and its obverse. Here is the A-form and its obverse:

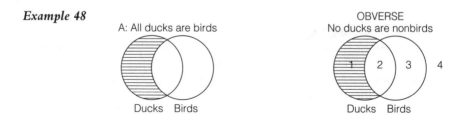

Example 48

A: All ducks are birds

Ducks Birds

OBVERSE
No ducks are nonbirds

Ducks Birds

To draw the diagram of the obverse of this statement, we must indicate something about its subject, ducks, with the circle representing ducks. We are saying that no ducks are nonbirds, and nonbirds would be anywhere *outside* the birds circle in this diagram, that is, either area 1 or area 4. We therefore cross out that area within the ducks circle that is outside the birds circle. The shading in area 1 shows that there are no ducks that are nonbirds. Notice that the resulting diagram is identical to the original, indicating that the inference is valid. If all ducks are birds, it validly follows that no ducks are nonbirds.

Consider the E-form.

Example 49

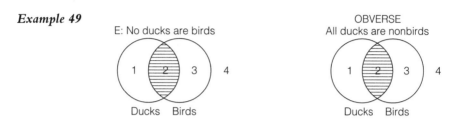

The obverse of E states that all ducks are nonbirds. To depict this statement, we want to show that all ducks are only in that part of the ducks circle in which they are nonbirds, that is, the area outside the birds circle, area 1. We therefore empty out area 2, and we obtain a diagram identical to the original.

Now consider the I-form and its obverse:

Example 50

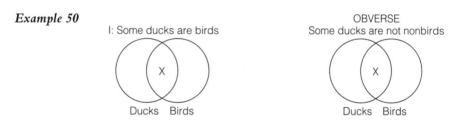

To say that some ducks are *not nonbirds* is the same as saying that some ducks are *not outside* the birds circle; they are inside it. We can see that the phrase 'not non-P' really amounts to the phrase 'P'.

Now look at the O-form and its obverse:

Example 51

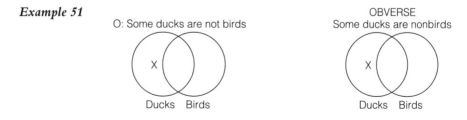

The two diagrams are the same because the phrase 'are nonbirds' is logically equivalent to the phrase 'are not birds'. If ducks are nonbirds, then they are represented *outside* the birds circle.

In sum, *every categorical statement is equivalent to its obverse. Obversion always yields a logically equivalent statement.*

Contraposition: Switch Subject and Predicate, Then Negate Both

We also form the *contrapositive* of a statement in two steps. First, we switch the subject and predicate terms of the statement. Then, we negate each term by adding *non*. The four forms and their contrapositives are as follows:

STATEMENT FORM		CONTRAPOSITIVE
A: *All S are P.*	becomes	*All non-P are non-S.*
E: *No S are P.*	becomes	*No non-P are non-S.*
I: *Some S are P.*	becomes	*Some non-P are non-S.*
O: *Some S are not P.*	becomes	*Some non-P are not non-S.*

The A-form and its contrapositive are diagrammed as follows:

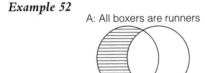

Example 52

A: All boxers are runners

CONTRAPOSITIVE
All nonrunners are nonboxers

Boxers Runners

Boxers Runners

As always, the circles must be labeled just as they were in the original statement. In the contrapositive the new subject of the statement is 'nonrunners', and these are represented as being *anywhere outside* the runners circle. The predicate states that they are all nonboxers; that is, that they are all *outside* the boxers circle. Hence, we want to show that everything outside the runners circle is also outside the boxers circle. Thus, the area where there are nonrunners who are boxers is crossed out to show that all nonrunners are nonboxers. Try going through this with an example of your own. We see that *the A-form and its contrapositive are logically equivalent, and therefore we can validly infer from one to the other.*

Let us look at the contrapositive of the E-form:

Example 53

E: No boxers are runners

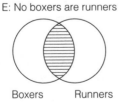

Boxers Runners

CONTRAPOSITIVE
No nonrunners are nonboxers

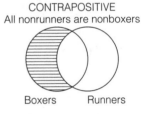

Boxers Runners

The contrapositive of the E-form is an interesting one to diagram. The subject of the statement 'No nonrunners are nonboxers' is nonrunners, which is everything outside the runners circle. About nonrunners we are saying that none of them is a nonboxer, that is, that none of them is outside the boxers circle. No things outside the runners circle are outside the boxers circle. Thus, we shade area 4, the area outside both circles. The two diagrams are not the same, indicating that *the E-form and its contrapositive are not equivalent*.

The I-form and its contrapositive are as follows:

Example 54

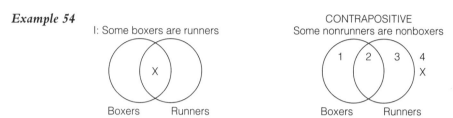

The contrapositive of the I in our example states that some nonrunners are nonboxers. We must place an X representing nonrunners somewhere *outside* the runners circle. That leaves only two places: area 1, where nonrunners and boxers are, or area 4, where nonrunners and nonboxers are. Clearly, the X should go in area 4, thus showing that there are some nonrunners who are also nonboxers. The diagram is not identical to the original, indicating that *the I-form and its contrapositive are not equivalent*.

Consider now the contrapositive of the O-form:

Example 55

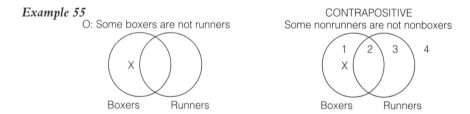

The contrapositive states that some nonrunners are not nonboxers. We can understand this as saying that some things outside the runners circle are not outside the boxers circle; they are inside the boxers circle. Thus, an X representing nonrunners must be placed outside the runners circle and inside the boxers circle, in area 1. The resulting diagram is identical to the original, showing that *the O form is logically equivalent to its contrapositive*.

Table 3.1 summarizes the operations and shows which yield logically equivalent statements, and a summary of the diagrams of the operations is provided in Figure 3.5. The symbol '≡' indicates logical equivalence. The symbol '≢' indicates no logical equivalence. Valid inferences can be made between logically equivalent pairs.

Table 3.1 The Operations: Equivalences

CONVERSION: Switch Subject and Predicate Terms

A:	All S are P	$\neq$	All P are S
E:	No S are P	$\equiv$	No P are S
I:	Some S are P	$\equiv$	Some P are S
O:	Some S are not P	$\neq$	Some P are not S

OBVERSION: Change the Quality and Negate the Predicate

A:	All S are P	$\equiv$	No S are non-P
E:	No S are P	$\equiv$	All S are non-P
I:	Some S are P	$\equiv$	Some S are not non-P
O:	Some S are not P	$\equiv$	Some S are non-P

CONTRAPOSITION: Switch Subject and Predicate. Then Negate Both

A:	All S are P	$\equiv$	All non-P are non-S
E:	No S are P	$\neq$	No non-P are non-S
I:	Some S are P	$\neq$	Some non-P are non-S
O:	Some S are not P	$\equiv$	Some non-P are not non-S

Notice that obversion yields equivalences on all forms. Conversion yields equivalences only on E and I. Contraposition yields equivalences on the other two forms. A and O—a surprising symmetry.

Negating Terms: Contradictories and Contraries

Both obversion and contraposition involve negating terms. Our rule for convenience has been that a term is negated by adding *non* as a prefix. When we add *non* as a prefix, we change a term to its exact opposite, its *contradictory*. If one is true of a subject, then the other is false, and vice versa. When we negate a term for the purpose of the operations, we want to form a contradictory. Frequently, the resulting negated term is awkward and would not be encountered in ordinary speech, as for example, 'nonbirds' and 'nontail'.

However, some terms in our language have a recognized and common term that is a negation but *may not* be a contradictory. For example, the term 'happy' has a common negation in our language, the term 'unhappy'. But 'unhappy' is *not* the contradictory; it is the *contrary*. Notice the difference between these pairs.

Figure 3.5 Diagrams of the Operations

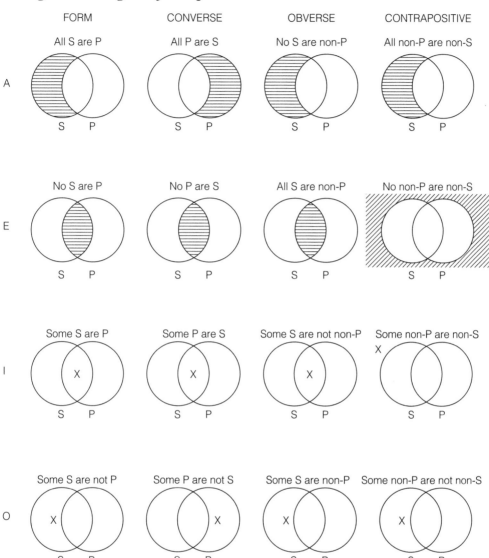

FORM   CONVERSE   OBVERSE   CONTRAPOSITIVE

A   All S are P   All P are S   No S are non-P   All non-P are non-S

E   No S are P   No P are S   All S are non-P   No non-P are non-S

I   Some S are P   Some P are S   Some S are not non-P   Some non-P are non-S

O   Some S are not P   Some P are not S   Some S are non-P   Some non-P are not non-S

87

Contradictories:

1. *Mary is happy.*   *Mary is nonhappy.*

Contraries:

2. *Mary is happy.*   *Mary is unhappy.*

The pairs in 1 cannot both be true and cannot both be false. The pairs in 2 cannot both be true but can both be false. Imagine that Mary is neither happy nor unhappy; she's simply "blah" today. We all know that feeling. Unhappiness is an opposite of happiness, but not the contradictory. It is the contrary. Therefore, 'unhappy' is not the same as the negated term 'nonhappy' and should not substitute for it.

Some terms have negations that are contraries. They are not equivalent to the term negated by adding *non*. The contrary of a term is not a suitable negation to use in forming the obverse or contrapositive because, as we have seen, the contradictory and the contrary are logically very different. Consider now this list of terms with contradictories and, I would argue, contraries.

TERM	CONTRADICTORY	CONTRARY
good	nongood	bad
happy	nonhappy	unhappy/sad
wealthy	nonwealthy	poor
healthy	nonhealthy	unhealthy/sick/ill
tall	nontall	short
violent	nonviolent	peaceful/pacifist
moral	nonmoral	amoral/immoral
communicative	noncommunicative	incommunicative
responsible	nonresponsible	irresponsible
living	nonliving	dead
caring	noncaring	uncaring
warm	nonwarm	cool

Looking over this list, do you agree that the terms in the contradictory and contrary columns are not the same in meaning? Would you agree, for example, that nonwealthy is different from poor? Would you say the same about the others on the list? In those cases in which the right-hand term is not the equivalent of the negation by adding *non*, the term is a different predicate altogether and would not be a suitable term for an operation.

On the other hand are terms that, it is arguable, are the same in meaning as the negation with *non*. For example, are these not the same?

TERM	CONTRADICTORY	EQUIVALENT
friendly	nonfriendly	unfriendly
aggressive	nonaggressive	unaggressive

competitive	noncompetitive	uncompetitive
colored	noncolored	uncolored
musical	nonmusical	unmusical
athletic	nonathletic	unathletic
productive	nonproductive	unproductive

If you believe that the more common term (the right-hand column) is equivalent to the contradictory, then it is a logically suitable substitute. If not, then it belongs in the list of contraries. In applying the logic of the operations, we may use any term that is logically equivalent to the negation formed by adding *non*. I would say that the right-column terms above are such terms. Would you?

Examples of Inferences

Now let's consider how the operations may yield valid inferences. In the following examples we determine what operation or operations are being performed and whether the inferences made are valid or invalid.

Example 56

Some capitalists are not materialists.
Therefore, some capitalists are nonmaterialists.

To determine what operation is involved, ask yourself what changes have been made from the original statement to the resulting statement. We see that the quality has changed and the predicate has been negated, indicating obversion. Venn diagrams of the premises and conclusion are identical; thus, the inference is valid.

Example 57

No welders are union members.
Therefore, no nonunion members are nonwelders.

In this example the subject and predicate have switched places, and each has been negated, indicating contraposition. The diagrams reveal that the inference is invalid.

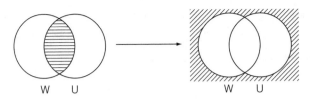

Example 58

Some people are cooperative.
Therefore, some people are not uncooperative.

The quality has changed, and the predicate has been negated, indicating obversion. The diagrams show that it is a valid inference:

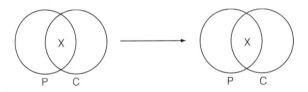

Example 59

Some nonviolent people are not dangerous.
Therefore, some nondangerous people are not violent.

The subject and predicate terms have changed places, and both terms have been negated. The subject term 'nonviolent people' appears in the predicate position, changed to 'violent people', and the predicate term is similarly changed, indicating contraposition. The diagrams below show that the inference is valid:

Example 60

Some aggressive people are comedians.
Therefore, some comedians are not nonaggressive people.

Look closely at this example. The subject and predicate terms have changed places, but the quality has changed, too. Since no single operation has such results, this argument may employ more than one operation. Examining it we see that the terms have switched places, the quality has changed, and the term 'aggressive people' has been negated. The operation of obversion must be involved, since it is the only one that changes the quality of a statement; obversion also accounts for the negation of the term 'aggressive people'. To account for the switching of the terms, we consider conversion and contraposition, and we eliminate contraposition because it negates *both* terms. Thus, the conclusion results from the operation of conversion and then obversion. Writing this all out and drawing the diagrams makes it quite clear:

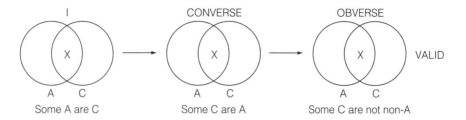

And since each of these operations yields a logically equivalent statement, it follows that the inference is valid.

Exercise 3.7A   Operations   For each statement perform the operation indicated in parentheses, and then draw Venn diagrams for both the original and the resulting statement.

1. All scientists are researchers.

    (Converse) _____

2. Some capitalists are not materialists.

    (Obverse) _____

3. No artists are wealthy.

    (Contrapositive) _____

4. No filmmakers are independent artists.

    (Contrapositive) _____

5. All trees are plants.

    (Obverse) _____

6. Some mutts are mixed breeds.

    (Converse) _____

7. Some buyers are market managers.

    (Contrapositive) _____

8. Some cats type fifty words per minute.

    (Converse) _____

9. No gypsies are loiterers.

    (Obverse) _____

10. No planets in our solar system other than Earth are suitable for life.

(Obverse) _____

11. Some citrus growers are not nonunion supporters.

(Obverse) _____

12. No educated people are nongraduates.

(Obverse) _____

13. Some retired service people are nonbeneficiaries.

(Converse) _____

14. All third-world countries are presently nonindustrialized.

(Contrapositive) _____

15. Some sociopaths are not nonmoral people.

(Obverse) _____

Exercise 3.7B   What Operation?   Determine what operation has been performed on the first statement by examining what changes have taken place.

SAMPLE

All estate agents are licensed.
No estate agents are nonlicensed.

Obversion. The quality has been changed and the predicate has been changed to its opposite by adding *non*.

1. Some capitalists are materialists.
   Some capitalists are not nonmaterialists.

2. No welders are union members.
   All welders are nonunion members.

3. Some cashiers are friendly.
   Some friendly people are cashiers.

4. All violent people are dangerous.
   All nondangerous people are nonviolent.

5. All unenlightened people are uneducated.
   All educated people are enlightened.

6. No alien spaceships are unidentified flying objects.
   All alien spaceships are identified flying objects.

7. Some aggressive people are comedians.
   Some comedians are not nonaggressive people.

8. No sopranos are contraltos.
   All sopranos are noncontraltos.

9. Some publishers are nonconformists.
   Some nonconformists are publishers.

10. No hawks are vegetarians.
    No nonvegetarians are nonhawks.

11. All spiders are predators.
    No spiders are nonpredators.

12. Some actors are not nonunion employees.
    Some nonunion employees are not actors.

13. Some actors are not nonunion employees.
    Some actors are non-nonunion employees.

14. No comatose patients are conscious.
    No conscious patients are comatose.

15. All intelligent people are rational.
    All nonrational people are nonintelligent.

Exercise 3.7C Valid or Invalid? Use Venn diagrams to determine whether the inference is valid in each of the following statements. Identify the operation or operations involved. Show your work as illustrated in Examples 56–60.

1. No patriots are traitors. Therefore, all patriots are nontraitors.
2. Some sales are not refundable sales. Therefore, some refundable sales are not sales.
3. All revolutionaries are radicals. So no revolutionaries are nonradicals.
4. Some noncombatants are not neutrals. Hence, some nonneutrals are not combatants.
5. Some people are not friendly, so some people are unfriendly.
6. All members of the faculty are recognized geniuses, because no members of the faculty are unrecognized geniuses.
7. Some metals are liquids. Therefore, some liquids are not nonmetals.
8. All Muslims are non-Buddhists, because no Muslims are Buddhists.
9. No senators are infants. Therefore, no noninfants are nonsenators.
10. All souls are immortal. Thus, no souls are mortal.

Exercise 3.7D Simplifying with Operations Let's say that one statement is simpler than another if it contains fewer negated terms (i.e., fewer negated subject and predicate terms like "nontall"). Thus, **All militant protestors are violent protestors** is simpler than **All nonviolent protestors are nonmilitant protestors.** Simplify the following statements by rewriting each in logically equivalent forms using one or more operation.

Sample

All poodles are nongood with children.
No poodles are good with children. By Obversion

1. Some comatose patients are not unconscious.
2. Some machinists are not nonunion employees.
3. Some amoral people are not nonprofessors.
4. All nonrational people are unambitious.
5. No alien spaceships are unidentified flying objects.
6. Some actors are not nonunion guild members.
7. All unenlightened persons are uneducated persons.
8. All smokers are unhealthy.
9. Some amoral people are not nonbusiness people.
10. No ducks are nonmigratory.

Review Questions

1. What is the purpose of a logical system? Explain in your own words why a mechanical and objective procedure is desirable.
2. What are categories?
3. In your opinion, is it conceivable that we could categorize reality in any way whatsoever? If so, describe a way. If not, what limitations are there?
4. What are the four categorical forms? What is meant by 'quantity' and 'quality'? Compare the four forms in terms of quantity and quality.
5. Explain what Venn diagrams are and what purpose they serve.
6. Is the statement "Your birthday is unforgettable" the contradictory or the contrary of "Your birthday is forgettable?" Explain your answer.
7. Briefly explain how the two versions of the Square of Opposition differ.
8. Which forms are the contraries? Explain what that means.
9. Which forms are the subcontraries? Explain what that means.
10. Which forms are the contradictories? Explain what that means.
11. Explain how each of these operations is performed: (a) conversion, (b) obversion, and (c) contraposition.
12. What things can be learned from the operations?
13. What is the law of double negation? What does it permit one to do?
14. What is logical equivalence? How can you tell that two or more statements are logically equivalent by using Venn diagrams? What is useful about knowing that two or more statements are logically equivalent?

15. Which of the categorical forms yield logical equivalences when converted? When obverted? When contraposed?

True or False?

1. 'Some chemists are good mathematicians' is the contradictory of 'No chemists are good mathematicians'.
2. If two statements are logically equivalent, then they have the same truth conditions.
3. Every categorical statement is equivalent to its converse.
4. The A-form statement is particular, affirmative.
5. If two statements are contraries, then they can both be true, but they cannot both be false.
6. If you obvert 'No human beings are immortal', you get 'All human beings are mortal'.
7. A statement of the form 'Some S are P' asserts that there is at least one S and it is a P. Thus, it asserts the existence of at least one S, and if there are no Ss, then it is a false statement.
8. If A is true, then E is false only if you assume the existence of members of the subject category.
9. If one of the subcontraries is true, then the other must be false.
10. Inferences made between a statement and its converse, obverse, or contrapositive are valid only if one is making an existential assumption.

Discussion Questions

1. After explaining what an existential assumption is, do you think that in everyday conversations we always or most often assume the existence of the things we talk about? In what circumstances do we not? Explain your answer.
2. Compose a list of terms. Write the contradicatory of each by adding *non*. Now for each term, think of a common, everyday term in our language that is (a) a contradictory or (b) a contrary? (For some terms this may not be possible.) To get you started:

TERM	CONTRADICTORY	COMMON CONTRADICTORY	CONTRARY
small	nonsmall	large	big
friendly	nonfriendly	unfriendly	rude
intelligent	nonintelligent	unintelligent	dumb

fast	nonfast	slow
mammal	nonmammal	
vertebrate	nonvertebrate	invertebrate
vegetarian	nonvegetarian	carnivore

3. What is your judgment of the following notorious puzzle called the Raven paradox?

The students in Terry's natural science class were given cameras and told to collect as many confirming instances of the statement 'All ravens are black' as they could find. "A prize for the student with the most confirmations," the professor said. Monday morning Terry came in with the most. She had photos of green frogs, red leaves, orange butterflies, yellow caterpillars, blue flowers, and, of course, black ravens. Terry, a sharp logic student, reasoned that all those things confirm the statement 'All nonblack things are nonravens', the contrapositive and equivalent of 'All ravens are black'! Does she win the prize?

CHAPTER FOUR
Categorical Logic
Part II

In this chapter we apply the principles of categorical logic to the evaluation of deductive arguments. We learn how to translate sentences in ordinary language into proper categorical form and how to write arguments in the form we call the categorical syllogism. Finally, we learn to use Venn diagrams to evaluate syllogisms and chains of syllogisms called sorites.

4.1 Translating into Categorical Form

As we know, everyday writing and speaking do not usually come already expressed in the forms of categorical logic. The statements of ordinary language are typically much richer. Nevertheless, logical clarity may be gained, and applying the techniques of categorical logic is made possible by rendering statements into categorical form. Therefore, to use categorical logic on everyday language, we have to translate statements into their proper form. This task varies in difficulty. Many ordinary-language statements are easily translated; others are not. Some guidelines for handling the more difficult constructions are helpful and will be presented in this chapter. The basic idea, however, is not difficult to grasp: We identify the *categories* that are the subject and predicate of the statement, and then we determine how much of the subject is being referred to—all, none, or some. Once we have translated into categorical form, we usually have a much clearer understanding of what the statement asserts, for categorical logic shows the relationship between categories, whether an affirmation or denial, and prepares the statement for further analysis.

To be in categorical form, a statement must, strictly speaking, have three features:

1. A standard quantifier: 'all', 'no', or 'some'
2. A copula: 'are' (or 'are not' in the case of the O-form)
3. Subject and predicate terms that refer to categories

These requirements make explicit what we saw in Chapter 3: Categorical statements must have a standard quantifier, 'all', 'no', or 'some'; they must have a linking verb, called the *copula,* either 'are' or (in the case of the O-form statement) 'are not'; and their subject and predicate terms should be *group terms,* that is, terms referring to categories or groups of things.

A statement in categorical form can be schematized as follows:

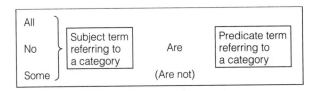

The sentences below are not in categorical form:

Not all magicians use mirrors.

The cat swallowed the bird.

There's a rusty car in the ditch.

No men are allowed.

Jane kissed Tom.

Only chemists are excluded.

Everyone except the graduating seniors is dismissed.

But each of these sentences can be translated into proper categorical form, and we turn now to a discussion of guidelines for such translations.

4.2 Translating Guide

1. Supplying Group Terms   Many words or phrases in ordinary language do not explicitly refer to a group or category. For example, in 'Some roses are red' the predicate term 'red' does not name a group of things. But we can easily supply it. The sentence says, in effect, that some roses belong to the category of red things. We can therefore rewrite it as 'Some roses are red things' or '. . . red flowers', if we are sure it refers only to flowers. When we supply group terms, we rewrite the subject or predicate terms so they name groups of things. In the following examples the words or phrases supplied to achieve proper categorical form are underlined.

Example 1	*All bachelors are unmarried.*	*All bachelors are unmarried <u>males.</u>*
Example 2	*Some letter carriers are tired.*	*Some letter carriers are tired <u>persons.</u>*
Example 3	*No dancers are ready for the performance.*	*No dancers are <u>persons who are</u> ready for the performance.*
Example 4	*Some of the platoon are infantrymen.*	*Some <u>members</u> of the platoon are infantrymen.*

2. Supplying a Copula   Translating sentences using verbs other than 'are' and 'are not' usually requires placing the original verb "inside" the predicate phrase. In the following examples, notice how the verbs are translated, especially verbs in the past tense. The phrases supplied are underlined.

Example 5	*No seagulls like pelicans.*	*No seagulls <u>are</u> <u>birds that</u> like pelicans.*
Example 6	*Some dogs would rather bite than bark.*	*Some dogs <u>are</u> <u>dogs that</u> would rather bite than bark.*
Example 7	*All dieters eat vegetables.*	*All dieters <u>are</u> <u>persons who</u> eat vegetables.*
Example 8	*Some players were not present.*	*Some players <u>are</u> <u>persons who</u> were not present.*

3. Proper Names and Singular Expressions   *Proper names* are names of persons, countries, brands of products, and so on. *Singular expressions* are expressions that refer to a particular person or thing, such as 'this house', 'that car', or 'the man in the trenchcoat'. Both proper names and singular expressions refer to particular things rather than to groups of things. Here are some examples:

Socrates is a man.

This firefighter is due for a raise.

Venezuela is an oil-rich country.

John kissed Mary.

Today is my birthday.

This type of sentence presents a special problem in categorical logic because it is not a statement about a *group* of things. You might be tempted to translate 'Socrates is a man', for example, as 'All Socrates are men' (or, even worse, 'Some Socrates are men'). That not only sounds odd but suggests that 'Socrates' names a group of things (in this case, a group of men), and surely it does not.

How then do we handle statements about individuals in a system designed for statements about groups? The solution is wordy but clever. We introduce a group that necessarily has only one member in it. The term 'persons identical to Socrates' names a group, but it is a group that can have only one member in it, since only one thing in existence is identical to Socrates, namely, Socrates himself. (This special expression 'identical to' is understood to mean *'one and the same as'*. It does not mean 'another one the same as', as in the sentence 'Your car is identical to my car'.) The examples given above can be translated into categorical statements using this special expression as follows:

Example 9	*Socrates is a man.*	<u>All persons identical to</u> *Socrates are men.*
Example 10	*This fire-fighter is due for a raise.*	<u>All persons identical to</u> *this fire-fighter are* <u>persons due for a raise.</u>
Example 11	*Venezuela is an oil-rich country.*	<u>All countries identical to</u> *Venezuela are oil-rich countries.*
Example 12	*John kissed Mary.*	<u>All persons identical to</u> *John* <u>are persons who</u> *kissed Mary.*
Example 13	*Today is my birthday.*	<u>All days identical to</u> *today are* <u>days identical to</u> *my birthday.*

4. Supplying Quantifiers   In some cases the quantifier of a statement is left unstated. You must determine how much of the subject is being referred to and whether it is meant to affirm or deny the predicate of the subject. Consider these examples:

Example 14	*Roses are red.*	<u>All</u> *roses are red flowers.*

Example 15	The ox is a strong beast.	<u>All</u> oxen are strong beasts.
Example 16	Emeralds are not cheap.	<u>No</u> emeralds are cheap.
Example 17	The soul is not immortal.	<u>No</u> souls are immortal.

Some uses of the articles 'a' and 'the' are ambiguous. In some sentences they may be used to refer to all members of a class—as in 'The whale is an enormous mammal'—and in others they refer to a single individual—as in 'The whale is on the beach'. When the article is ambiguous, ask yourself: In this sentence are we talking about all members of the subject class, some of them, or a single individual? Read the following examples carefully and notice how the same phrase may refer to a group in one context and to an individual in another.

Example 18	The police officer is our friend.	<u>All</u> police officers are our friends.
Example 19	The police officer is at the door.	<u>All persons iden-tical to</u> this police officer are <u>persons</u> at the door.
Example 20	Police officers are our friends.	<u>All</u> police officers are our friends.
Example 21	Police officers are at our door.	<u>Some</u> police offi-cers are <u>persons</u> at our door.
Example 22	An apricot is not a vegetable.	<u>No</u> apricots are vegetables.
Example 23	A fish is on the line.	<u>All things identical</u> to this fish are <u>things</u> on the line.

5. Other Quantifiers and Quantifying Expressions   Our language contains many other quantifiers besides 'all', 'no', and 'some'; some important ones are 'few', 'many', and 'most'. There is a standard way to translate sentences using these and other, similar quantifiers. Sentences using 'few', 'many', 'most', and so on clearly refer to some—rather than all—of the subject class, but they also carry more information than the 'some' categorical statements. For example, 'Few people came to the game' implies that some came to the game *and* some did not. Unlike the I- and O-form statements, these sentences carry the implication that some are something and some are not. If you are able to say that 'few people came', then you imply those two categorical assertions.

Thus, to translate such sentences, we rewrite them as *two categorical statements,* as these examples illustrate:

Example 24	*Few people came to the game.*	<u>Some people are</u> people who came to the game. <u>Some people are</u> <u>not</u> people who came to the game.
Example 25	*Most cattle are breeders.*	<u>Some</u> cattle <u>are</u> breeders. <u>Some</u> cattle <u>are not</u> breeders.
Example 26	*Many voters are registered.*	<u>Some</u> voters <u>are</u> registered voters. <u>Some</u> voters <u>are</u> <u>not</u> registered voters.

To diagram a sentence that has been translated into two categorical statements, draw the two interlocking circles as usual, label them according to the two categories involved, and then simply diagram each statement, combining the information from both into one diagram. For example, consider the diagram for Example 26, 'Some voters are registered voters. Some voters are not registered voters':

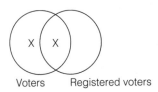

Voters   Registered voters

Notice that when you translate the quantifiers 'few', 'many', and 'most' into two categorical statements, forms I and O, you lose the distinctions among them. All three are translated in the same way! You could not infer from the translations themselves that, for example, the number of people who came to the game was *few.* Thus, some precision is lost in this particular rule of translation. What is gained, however, is that we have captured the logical inference contained in those quantifiers, namely, that "some . . . are . . ." and "some . . . are not. . . ." For more on this issue, see Discussion Question 1 at the end of the chapter.

Another quantifying expression in our language is 'all . . . are not', which almost always means 'none are', as indicated in these examples:

Example 27	*All toads are not frogs.*	No toads are frogs.
Example 28	*All Picassos are not cheap.*	No Picassos are cheap things.

However, the phrase 'all . . . are not' is occasionally used to give emphasis to a denial of an A-form statement ('All S are P'). For example, if someone says, 'All citizens are eligible to become president', you might deny this by saying, 'All citizens are *not* eligible to become president'. You would not be saying that no citizens are eligible; you would be saying that the statement 'All citizens are eligible to become president' is false. Your statement would be translated, 'Some citizens are not persons eligible to become president'. Examine the examples below and compare them to each other:

Example 29	*All recruits are not on leave.*	<u>*No*</u> *recruits are persons on leave.*
Example 30	*All recruits are not on leave.*	<u>*Some*</u> *recruits* <u>*are*</u> <u>*not*</u> *persons on leave.*

The second statement gives emphasis to a denial of an A-form statement. The first usage is the more likely, but you will have to consider the context to decide which is the better translation.

The phrase 'not all . . . are' is the denial of the A-form statement. 'Not all humans are mortals' means that it is not true that all humans are mortals. It is translated as 'Some humans are not mortals'.

Example 31	*Not all Democrats are voters.*	*Some Democrats are not voters.*

6. Adverbs of Place and Time   Occasionally you will want to translate a statement in such a way that it refers to a time or place. Use the word 'places' in both the subject and predicate terms to translate such adverbs of place as the following:

where

wherever

everywhere

somewhere

nowhere

Here are some examples:

Example 32	*Checkered squirrels are found nowhere.*	*No* <u>*places*</u> *are* <u>*places where*</u> *checkered squirrels are found.*
Example 33	*Somewhere I lost my wallet.*	*Some* <u>*places*</u> *are* <u>*places where*</u> *I lost my wallet.*

| *Example 34* | *Wherever she goes, he goes.* | *All <u>places</u> where she goes are <u>places</u> where he goes.* |

Use the word 'times' in both the subject and predicate to translate adverbs of time like these:

always whenever
never   sometimes
when   every time

Some examples of this method follow:

Example 35	*The team never loses.*	*No <u>times</u> are <u>times</u> the team loses.*
Example 36	*When they sing we laugh.*	*All <u>times</u> they sing are <u>times</u> we laugh.*
Example 37	*Sometimes it rains.*	*Some <u>times</u> are <u>times</u> it rains.*
Example 38	*Every time I begin to work the phone rings.*	*All <u>times</u> I begin to work are <u>times</u> the phone rings.*

7. Conditionals 'If . . . then', 'only if', and 'if and only if' are some of the more important phrases in our language that express conditionals. *A conditional statement asserts that something is the case if a certain condition is met.* For example, 'If it rains, then the streets will be wet' asserts that the streets will be wet given the condition that it rains. To translate statements expressing conditionals, you use either the A-form or the E-form, depending upon whether the statement is best rendered as affirmative or negative. Here are some examples of 'if . . . then' and 'only if' statements:

Example 39	*If a man is a bachelor, then he is unmarried.*	*<u>All</u> bachelors are unmarried men.*
Example 40	*If it rains, then the streets will be wet.*	*<u>All</u> times it rains are times the streets will be wet.*
Example 41	*If this bird eats seeds, then it is not a flycatcher.*	*<u>No</u> birds that eat seeds are flycatchers.*

Example 42	*A man is a bachelor only if he is unmarried.*	<u>*All*</u> *bachelors are unmarried men.*
Example 43	*Your house is safe only if it is locked tightly.*	<u>*All*</u> *safe houses are houses that are locked tightly.*

The phrase 'if and only if' is a "two-way" conditional; that is, it asserts an 'if . . . then' relationship in both directions. For example, 'A man is a bachelor if and only if he is an unmarried male' asserts that *if* a man is a bachelor, then he is an unmarried male, *and if* a man is an unmarried male, then he is a bachelor. 'If and only if' asserts that each is a condition of the other or, in other words, if either one is true, then the other is also true. Notice in the examples that these "double conditionals" must be translated using two categorical statements.

Example 44	*A man is a bachelor if and only if he is unmarried.*	*All bachelors are unmarried men. All unmarried men are bachelors.*
Example 45	*It's a sound argument if and only if it is a good argument.*	*All sound arguments are good arguments. All good arguments are sound arguments.*

To diagram the two categorical statements required to translate an 'if and only if' sentence, combine the information from both statements into one diagram, thus representing exactly what the original sentence asserts. For example, the categorical statements 'All bachelors are unmarried men. All unmarried men are bachelors' would be diagrammed as follows:

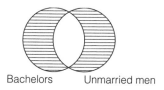

Bachelors   Unmarried men

8. Logical Groups   'Only', 'the only', 'all and only', and 'all except' are words and phrases in our language that are used to group things together or to separate things logically. To translate these words, you must consider carefully just what they do logically. The following guidelines show how the major logical grouping words work.

(a) 'Only' and 'none but'   The words 'only' and 'none but' are frequently misunderstood. What does the statement 'Only humans use reason' really mean? Does it mean

that *all* humans use reason? No, for you can sensibly say, 'Only humans use reason, but not all of them do'. What it does mean is that all things that use reason are humans. The statement form 'Only X are Y' really means 'All Y are X'. Similarly, the statement 'None but the coaches have keys' says that all who have keys are coaches, but it does not say that *all* coaches have keys. As a general rule, the phrase immediately following 'only' or 'none but' is the *predicate* of the categorical statement, not the subject. Here are some examples:

Example 46	Only dogs bark.	All who bark are dogs.
Example 47	Only citizens can vote.	All who can vote are citizens.
Example 48	None but logicians love logic.	All who love logic are logicians.

(b) *'The only'* This phrase operates differently than 'only'. If we say, 'The only owl here is the barred owl', we mean not that all barred owls are here but that all owls here are barred owls. As a general rule, the phrase immediately following 'the only' is the *subject* of the categorical statement. Consider these examples:

Example 49	The only people with keys are the coaches.	All people with keys are the coaches.
Example 50	The seniors are the only students allowed to leave.	All students allowed to leave are seniors.

(c) *'All and only'* 'All and only logicians love logic' states that all logicians love logic *and* all who love logic are logicians. The phrase 'all and only' is a combination of 'All S are P' and 'Only S are P'. Therefore, it must be translated into two categorical statements, as shown below:

Example 51	All and only logicians love logic.	All logicians are lovers of logic. All lovers of logic are logicians.
Example 52	All and only predators are meat eaters.	All predators are meat eaters. All meat eaters are predators.

Because the complete translation of 'all and only' statements requires two categorical statements, their diagrams resemble those of 'if and only if' statements. Here is a diagram representing the translation of Example 51, 'All and only logicians love logic':

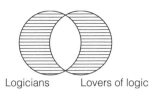

Logicians   Lovers of logic

(d) 'All except'   Statements using the phrase 'all except' are also translated with two categorical statements. A statement of the form 'All except X are Y' is asserting two things: 'All non-X are Y' and 'No X are Y', as in these examples:

Example 53	*All except the musicians are salaried.*	*All <u>nonmusicians</u> are salaried persons. No <u>musicians</u> are salaried persons.*
Example 54	*All except the judges must leave the room.*	*All <u>nonjudges</u> are people who must leave the room. No <u>judges</u> are people who must leave the room.*

Follow this formula for treating sentences with 'all except':

> *All except X are Y ≡ All non-X are Y*
>   *No X are Y*

To diagram the translations of 'all except' sentences, you again need two circles for the two categories. Be careful to diagram the statement about 'non-Xs' correctly. Here is the diagram of Example 53, 'All nonmusicians are salaried persons. No musicians are salaried persons':

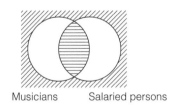

Musicians   Salaried persons

(e) 'All . . . except'   A variation on 'All except X are Y' is the form 'All Z except X are Y'—for example, 'All seniors except the transfers are routine graduates'. This statement has three categories—seniors, transfers, and routine graduates—and it asserts two things: 'All nontransfer seniors are routine graduates' and 'No transfers are routine graduates'. Follow this formula when you translate 'all . . . except' sentences:

> *All Z except X are Y ≡ All non-X Z are Y*
>   *No X are Y*

The diagram of this type of sentence *requires three circles,* because the statements *involve three categories.* (A detailed explanation of diagramming with three categories is given in Section 4.4.) First, draw three circles as shown below and label them. Then diagram each statement.

Example 55   *All seniors ex-   All nontransfer
                  cept the transfers   seniors are rou-
                  are routine   tine graduates.
                  graduates.   No transfers are
                                       routine
                                       graduates.*

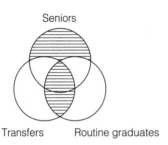

Seniors

Transfers   Routine graduates

Exercise 4.2A   Translating   Translate the following sentences into proper categorical form.

1. Some phones are off the hook.
2. The firefighter is a civil servant.
3. It always rains whenever we have a picnic.
4. Tolstoy is the most important of all the Russian novelists.
5. Most historians are good writers.
6. If a patient has good skin color, then it can't be jaundice the patient has.
7. Only the young go to war.
8. All and only sound arguments are good arguments.
9. All faculty are not permitted to cancel classes.
10. Few people stayed to clean up.
11. Logic develops only the mind.
12. Only the wealthy go to France.
13. Where there's smoke there's fire.
14. Not all people are happy with their jobs.
15. Aristotle developed the doctrine of the golden mean.
16. A person is not morally responsible for acts that he or she cannot control.

17. Every major African religion contains the idea of a supreme god.

18. There's never a police officer around when you need one.

19. If consumer spending increases, then interest rates will decline.

20. Tonight is a special night.

21. Everyone needs regular exercise.

22. Where the drink goes in, there the wit goes out. (George Herbert)

23. The whole of science is nothing more than a refinement of everyday thinking. (Albert Einstein)

24. The mass of men lead lives of quiet desperation. (Henry David Thoreau)

25. Religion is an illusion. (Sigmund Freud)

Exercise 4.2B   Translating   Translate the following sentences into proper categorical form. Then draw Venn diagrams representing them.

1. All and only sound arguments are good arguments.

2. All except freshmen must take the makeup exams.

3. Few singers are successful.

4. Only the doctors are permitted in the pathology lab.

5. A person is a medical doctor if and only if he or she has earned an M.D. degree.

6. The only isolated virus is the BK12 virus.

7. All North American geese except the emperor goose are regular visitors to Missouri.

8. None but the good die young.

9. You can order a drink here only if you are at least twenty-one.

10. Wherever we go, we look for good, authentic Mexican food.

4.3 The Categorical Syllogism

The major argument form in categorical logic is the syllogism. A *categorical syllogism* is a deductive argument having the following three features:

1. There are three categorical statements: two premises and a conclusion.

2. There are exactly three different terms or category names.

3. Each term occurs exactly twice in the argument.

Here is an example of a categorical syllogism:

Example 56

1. *All successful businesspersons are good writers.*

2. *All good writers are college graduates.*

_____

3. *Therefore, all successful businesspersons are college
   graduates.*

Notice how the example meets the three requirements of the syllogism form: Each
statement is in proper categorical form, there are three terms, and each term occurs exactly twice. Expressed in this form the argument is very clear. A great advantage of the
syllogism form is that it enables us easily to use Venn diagrams to determine an argument's validity.

4.4 Testing Validity with Venn Diagrams

Using Venn diagrams to check validity requires that you learn only two new procedures: using three circles in diagramming and using the symbol '___', called the *bar.*
  We have to use three circles in diagramming because we need one circle for each
of the three terms in the syllogism. Begin by drawing three interlocking circles as shown
below.

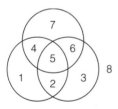

The circles must interlock to create exactly eight areas. This provides for every possible combination of relationships among the three categories. We will work with Example 56:

1. *All successful businesspersons are good writers.*

2. *All good writers are college graduates.*

_____

3. *Therefore, all successful businesspersons are college
   graduates.*

To label the circles, let the *subject of the conclusion* be represented by the bottom–left
circle, the *predicate of the conclusion* by the bottom–right circle, and the *remaining category*

name by the top circle. (This format ensures that your diagrams are oriented the same as everyone else's. It does not affect the results of the testing technique.) Thus, the circles are labeled as follows:

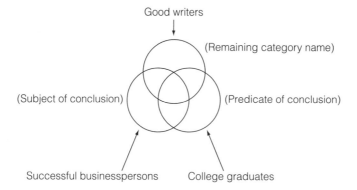

The procedure for checking validity consists of two steps:

1. Diagram the premises.

    a. If a premise is a universal statement, diagram it first.

    b. Make explicit in your diagram any necessary existential assumptions (more on this later).

Do not diagram the conclusion!

2. Check to see if the resulting diagram depicts the conclusion.

    a. If it does, the argument is *valid*.

    b. If it does not, the argument is *invalid*.

Let's go through this procedure with our example. First, we diagram the premises. If an argument has a universal premise, it simplifies matters to diagram it first. (In our example both premises are universals, so we can diagram either one first.) We diagram the first premise just as though we were dealing with only two circles. We must represent what the premise says completely, so we fill in the entire area, extending the shading into the third circle. The first premise—'All successful businesspersons are good writers'—is depicted correctly in the diagram on the left below and incorrectly in the one on the right.

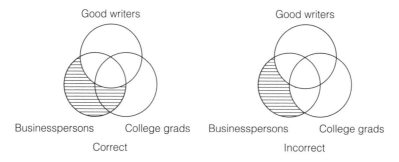

The diagram on the right leaves open the possibility that successful businesspersons are not good writers and so does not properly represent the premise.

After diagramming the first premise, we diagram the remaining one—'All good writers are college graduates'—using the circles just as though there were only two of them:

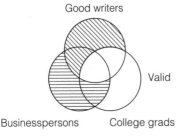

Good writers

Valid

Businesspersons   College grads

Proceeding to the second step, we examine the resulting diagram to see if it depicts the conclusion. If the conclusion is already represented in the diagram, the argument is valid, for the premises taken together contain the information that the conclusion asserts. We can see that the conclusion 'All successful businesspersons are college graduates' is depicted in the diagram above. Thus, the argument is valid.

Let us consider another example:

Example 57

1. *All viceroys are kingsmen.*

2. *No dukes are viceroys.*

_____

3. *Therefore, no dukes are kingsmen.*

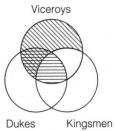

Viceroys

Dukes   Kingsmen

The Venn diagram *does not* show that no dukes are kingsmen. The diagram leaves open the possibility that there are dukes who are kingsmen. Thus, the conclusion does not validly follow, and the argument is invalid.

Consider a third example:

Example 58

1. *No congresspersons are novelists.*

2. *Some lawyers are congresspersons.*

_____

3. *Therefore, some lawyers are not novelists.*

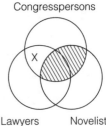

Congresspersons

Lawyers   Novelists

The Venn diagram has an X in the area representing some lawyers who are not novelists. Thus, it does correctly depict the conclusion, indicating that the argument is valid.

The Bar

The next example introduces a new device, the bar, symbolized '━'.

Example 59

1. *All hunters are conservationists.*
2. *Some conservationists are not protesters.*

---

3. *Therefore, some hunters are not protesters.*

The diagram below shows the first premise represented. As we diagram the second premise, we see that there are two places where, it seems, we could place the X representing the second premise, 'Some conservationists are not protesters':

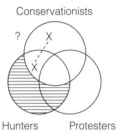

We want to show that some conservationists are not protesters, but by placing the X in area 7 we are also "saying" that those conservationists are *not* hunters. On the other hand, if we place the X in area 4, we are saying that those conservationists *are* hunters. Either way we would be symbolizing more than what the premise says and, hence, misrepresenting the premise. The only way to represent precisely what the premise says *and no more* is to indicate that those conservationists who are not protesters could be in either area. To do so, we use a bar running across the two areas where the X might be considered to be. The bar is understood to mean that the X could be in either area and that the premise alone does not specify which. Completing the diagram, we see that the conclusion is not represented, for the diagram does not reveal that there is at least one hunter who is not a protester. The diagram shows that there could be hunters who are not protesters—the possibility indicated by the bar extending into the hunter circle—but not that there *must* be some hunters who are not protesters. Thus, this argument is invalid.

the bar *The bar is always and only used when a premise does not specify in which of two areas the X should be placed. The bar indicates that some (that is, at least one) members of the subject category are "in" one of the two areas into which it extends.*

Here is another example requiring a bar:

Example 60

1. *Some animals are trainable animals.*

2. *Some animals are vicious animals.*

3. *Therefore, some vicious animals are trainable animals.*

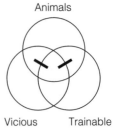

You can see that the argument fails to establish its conclusion. *An argument whose diagram shows two bars will always be invalid.* Make up some examples of your own to illustrate this point.

Making an Existential Assumption

The validity of some arguments can be demonstrated using Venn diagrams *only if* an existential assumption is made, that is, only if a premise is interpreted according to the traditional version (see Section 3.6). Others, such as those valid arguments illustrated above, can be shown to be valid with or without an existential assumption. We know which arguments require an existential assumption to show their validity: *syllogisms whose premises are both universal statements and whose conclusion is a particular statement.* It stands to reason. Arguments with universal premises have no X in their Venn diagram. Then, if the conclusion is a particular statement, there will be no X representing that conclusion. Consider this argument:

Example 61

1. *No computers are thinkers.*

2. *All humans are thinkers.*

3. *Therefore, some humans are not computers.*

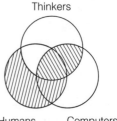

If we diagrammed this argument without making an existential assumption, there would be no X in the completed diagram, indicating that some humans are not computers, and it would therefore be an invalid argument. However, if we assume that members of the category of humans do exist, then we can place an X in the humans circle to express that assumption. (Recall that an existential assumption is permitted with the universal statements A or E and that we indicate it by placing an X within the circle representing the subject category.)

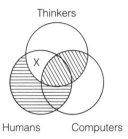

We can now see that the argument is valid. To generalize, we can say that if an argument with universal premises and a particular conclusion is valid, then we must make the existential assumption to show its validity with the Venn diagram method.

Exercise 4.4A   Diagramming with Three Circles   The following statements are not arguments but exercises in constructing Venn diagrams with three circles. Practice diagramming the pair of statements as though they were the premises of an argument.

1. No members of the all-star team are professionals. All athletes with high salaries are professionals.

2. Some Indians are Hindus. All Hindus believe in Brahma.

3. No valid syllogisms are arguments with four premises. No valid syllogisms are unprovable by Venn diagrams.

4. All government bonds are good investments. Some good investments are not commodities.

5. All reptiles are cold-blooded creatures. Some cold-blooded creatures are good pets.

6. All whales are mammals. Some mammals are not carnivores.

7. Some chess players are grand masters. No grand masters are good checkers players.

8. All corporate executives are members of the board. All members of the board are civic leaders.

9. No Palestinians are elected officials. Some Palestinians are freedom fighters.

10. Some fast-food diners are purveyors of unsavory food. All fast-food diners are money-making operations.

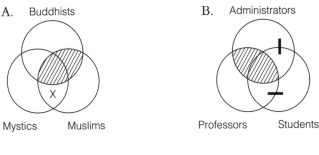

A.   Buddhists

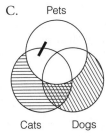

Mystics   Muslims

B.   Administrators

Professors   Students

C.   Pets

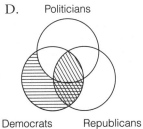

Cats   Dogs

D.   Politicians

Democrats   Republicans

1. Does A show that no Buddhists are Muslims?

2. Does A show that some mystics are not Buddhists?

3. Does A show that some mystics are Muslims?

4. According to B, are some professors students? Could there be some professors who are students?

5. Does B show that some administrators are students?

6. Does B show that some administrators are not professors?

7. Does B show that some students are not adminstrators?

8. Does C show that some pets are not dogs?

9. Does C show that no cats are dogs?

10. Are all dogs pets according to C?

11. Does D show that there are Democrats who are politicians?

12. Does D show that no Republicans are Democrats?

Exercise 4.4C   Testing Validity with Venn Diagrams   Use Venn diagrams to determine whether the following arguments are valid or invalid. Some arguments may be valid only if you make an existential assumption. Show your work.

1. All dancers are vegetarians. No dentists are dancers. Hence, no dentists are vegetarians.

2. No soldiers are comedians. Some Americans are soldiers; therefore, some Americans are not comedians.

3. No conservationists are advocates of nuclear energy. All farmers are conservationists. So no farmers are advocates of nuclear energy.

4. All spiders are things having eight legs. All black widows are spiders; therefore, all black widows are things having eight legs.

5. All books are books worth reading. Some books are novels. Therefore, some novels are books worth reading.

6. No pelicans are predators. All pelicans are birds. Therefore, no birds are predators.

7. Some females are not women. All mothers are females. So, some mothers are not women.

8. Some books are books worth reading. Some novels are books. Hence, some novels are books worth reading.

9. All Egyptians are North Africans. No Egyptians are Asians. Therefore, some North Africans are not Asians.

10. All New Mexico chilis are the hottest chilis. All the hottest chilis are chilis with the most vitamin C. Therefore, some chilis with the most vitamin C are New Mexico chilis. [For interest, make an existential assumption for the premises as you diagram them.]

11. Some emotions are sensations caused by thought. Some sensations caused by thought are neurotic states. Therefore, some emotions are neurotic states.

12. All anthropologists are gentlemen. Some politicians are gentlemen. So some politicians are anthropologists.

13. All cameramen are photographers. Some photographers are not artists. Therefore, some cameramen are not artists.

14. All modern recordings are things made of vinyl. Some recordings are not things made of vinyl. Therefore, some recordings are not modern recordings.

15. Some Japanese watches are digital watches. No analog watches are digital watches. Therefore, some analog watches are not Japanese watches.

4.5 Special Cases for the Syllogism

Almost all deductive arguments need some revision before they fit into the proper syllogistic form required for Venn diagramming. Recall that proper syllogistic form has three features: (1) The argument must have three categorical statements—two premises and a conclusion; (2) there must be exactly three terms or category names; and (3) each term must occur exactly twice in the argument. There are several ways of analyzing arguments that are not already in syllogistic form: (1) using the operations to reduce the number of terms; (2) diagramming arguments with three terms but also three premises; and (3) constructing *sorites,* or chains of syllogisms, by breaking up arguments with more than three terms and premises. Such arguments can be rewritten so that they fit into syllogistic form or at least so that the three-circle technique of Venn diagramming can be applied to them. Let's consider each of these methods in turn.

1. Using the Operations to Reduce Terms   In the third chapter we saw how applying some of the operations to some of the categorical forms produces logically equivalent statements. The operations can be used to simplify arguments with too many terms if one or more terms occur in both an affirmative and a negative form. Consider this example:

Example 62

1. *Some senators are noncommunists.*

2. *All communists are nonliberals.*

_____

3. *Therefore, some liberals are not senators.*

Strictly speaking, this argument has two terms too many: 'senators', 'noncommunists', 'communists', 'nonliberals', and 'liberals'. We can check such an argument with Venn diagrams without revision, for Venn diagramming is sufficient to represent terms and their negations, but usually diagramming is simplified if we can *reduce the number of terms* to just three. In Example 62, two of the terms occur in both affirmative and negative forms: 'communists' and 'noncommunists' and 'liberals' and 'nonliberals'. Arguments with such paired terms can almost always be rewritten with fewer terms. However, *a premise can be replaced only with a logically equivalent statement.* Thus, only an operation that results in a logically equivalent expression is permitted. We can use obversion to rewrite our example as follows:

1′. *Some senators are not communists.* (1 by obversion)

2′. *No communists are liberals.* (2 by obversion)

_____

3. *Some liberals are not senators.*

The new premises are logically equivalent to the old ones because, as you recall, obversion always yields a statement that is logically equivalent to the original. The rewritten argument is in proper syllogistic form and can be diagrammed more easily.

Here is another example:

Example 63

1. *All combatants are nonneutrals.*

2. *All volunteer advisors are neutrals.*

_____

3. *Therefore, all volunteer advisors are noncombatants.*

The categories are 'combatants', 'noncombatants', 'nonneutrals', 'neutrals', and 'volunteer advisors'. There are at least two ways to reduce the number of terms in this argument. We could use obversion on statements (1) and (3) as follows:

1′. *No combatants are neutrals.* (1 by obversion)

2. *All volunteer advisors are neutrals.*

―――――――――――――――――――

3′. *Therefore, no volunteer advisors are combatants.*
   (3 by obversion)

The argument can now be diagrammed easily. However, an even simpler approach is to use contraposition on statement (1). Contraposition switches the subject and predicate terms in the first premise and negates both, producing this result:

1′. *All neutrals are noncombatants.* (1 by contraposition)

No other changes are needed because the argument now contains only three categories. Diagramming the argument will reveal whether it is valid or invalid.

   In sum, if an argument contains too many terms because one or more occur in both an affirmative and a negative form, the number of terms can probably be reduced to three by substituting logically equivalent statements obtained by using the operations.

2. Diagramming Arguments with Three Terms and Three Premises
We saw earlier that it required *two* categorical statements to express some statements in categorical form. Such a translation may give us an argument with three premises—which is, strictly speaking, not in syllogistic form—yet still with only three terms, that is, three categories. As long as the argument contains only three terms, the Venn diagram technique can be used. We simply have to diagram three premises rather than the usual two. Here is an example:

Example 64

1. *Many African art objects are religious objects.*

2. *Religious objects are beautiful.*

―――――――――――――――――――

3. *Thus, some African art objects are beautiful.*

To translate the first premise into categorical form, we rewrite it using two categorical statements, as follows:

1. *Some African art objects are religious objects.*

2. *Some African art objects are not religious objects.*

3. *All religious objects are things that are beautiful.*

―――――――――――――――――――

4. *Thus, some African art objects are things that are beautiful.*

The argument is still not in proper syllogistic form, but since only three categories are involved, we can use the three-circle Venn diagram to determine whether it is valid.

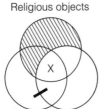

Religious objects

African art objects   Things that are beautiful

Here is another example:

Example 65

1. *All except the surveyors are government employees.*
2. *All government employees have retirement plans.*

---

3. *Therefore, no surveyors have retirement plans.*

Rewriting the statements as categorical statements yields this:

1. *All nonsurveyors are government employees.*
2. *No surveyors are government employees.*
3. *All government employees are persons with retirement plans.*

---

4. *Therefore, no surveyors are persons with retirement plans.*

The argument could be diagrammed now without further revision. (And you should try to do so to appreciate how reducing the terms to three simplifies matters.) However, by using the operations—both conversion and obversion on statements (2) and (4)—we can reduce the number of different terms to three:

1. *All nonsurveyors are government employees.*
2′. *All government employees are nonsurveyors.* (2 by conversion and then obversion)
3. *All government employees are persons with retirement plans.*

4′. *Therefore, all persons with retirement plans are non-surveyors.* (4 by conversion and then obversion)

3. Constructing Sorites Many arguments have more than two premises. Techniques like those described above may be used to reduce the number of terms, but another approach is to break up the argument into smaller arguments, each of which is a syllogism. A chain of such syllogisms is called a *sorites* (pronounced "so-RI-teez"). The rationale behind breaking up an argument—that is, constructing a sorites—is that the original argument is valid if each syllogism it contains is valid. If any syllogism in the chain is invalid, then so is the original argument. To construct a sorites, follow these four rules:

RULES FOR THE SORITES

1. Each statement must be in categorical form.
2. Each term must occur twice.
3. The first premise must contain the subject or predicate term of the conclusion.
4. Each premise (except the first) must have a term in common with the premise preceding it.

Consider this example of an argument form:

Example 66

All A are B.
All B are C.
All C are D.
—————————————————————————————
Thus, all A are D.

First, we see whether the argument meets the four requirements for the sorites. Each statement is in categorical form; each term occurs twice; the first premise contains a term that also occurs in the conclusion; and each premise except the first has a term in common with the one above it. Thus, it does meet the requirements. If an argument cannot be brought into proper sorites form, then it cannot be evaluated as a chain of syllogisms.

Once the argument is in proper sorites form, then the procedure for evaluating the sorites is as follows:

Step 1 Construct a Venn diagram using the first two premises.

Step 2 Determine from that diagram what conclusion, if any, can be validly deduced.

Step 3 Take that intermediate conclusion together with the next premise and construct another Venn diagram.

Repeat steps 2 and 3 Repeat until the conclusion of the original argument is reached or no valid conclusion can be deduced.

Let us go over the procedure slowly, using Example 66.

Step 1 Diagram the first two premises:

All A are B.
All B are C.

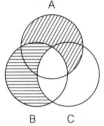

Thus, all A are C.

Step 2 The diagram allows you to draw the intermediate conclusion that 'All A are C'.

Step 3 Take the intermediate conclusion together with the next premise and construct another Venn diagram:

All A are C.
All C are D.

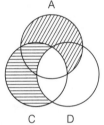

Thus, all A are D.

Repeat step 2 The diagram allows you to draw the conclusion that 'All A are D', which is the conclusion of the sorites. Each syllogism in the chain is valid; thus, the whole sorites or chain of syllogisms is valid.

Now consider another example of an argument form:

Example 67

No T are Q.
All S are T.
No Q are R.

Thus, no S are R.

Notice that this argument does not conform to the rules for proper sorites form—the first premise does not contain a term in common with the conclusion. However, the second premise does, so the argument can be rearranged as follows:

All S are T.
No T are Q.
No Q are R.

Thus, no S are R.

Step 1 Construct a Venn diagram with the first two premises:

All S are T.
No T are Q.

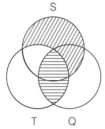

Thus, no S are Q.

Step 2 You can draw the intermediate conclusion that 'No S are Q'.

Step 3 Take the intermediate conclusion and construct a diagram with it and the next premise, which in this case is 'No Q are R'.

No S are Q.
No Q are R.

Repeat step 2 The diagram shows that the conclusion of the sorites does not follow. Thus, this argument is invalid.

Here is another example:

Example 68

All Methodists are Protestants.
No Jews are Protestants.
All Hassidim are Jews.
All Catholics are Hassidim.

Thus, no Methodists are Catholics.

Does the argument conform to the four rules? It does. Proceed then to

Step 1.

All Methodists are Protestants.
No Jews are Protestants.

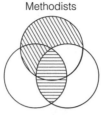

Methodists

Jews   Protestants

Thus, no Methodists are Jews.

Step 2 The diagram shows that 'No Methodists are Jews'. That serves as a premise for the next syllogism.

Step 3

No Methodists are Jews.
All Hassidim are Jews.

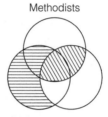

Methodists

Hassidim   Jews

Thus, no Methodists are Hassidim.

Repeat step 2 The diagram shows that 'No Methodists are Hassidim'. Continue.

Repeat step 3

No Methodists are Hassidim.
All Catholics are Hassidim.

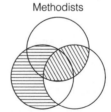

Methodists

Catholics   Hassidim

Thus, no Methodists are Catholics.

Repeat step 2 The diagram shows that the conclusion to the sorites, 'No Methodists are Catholics', can be deduced. Thus, the original argument is valid.

Let us now consider a more complicated argument:

Example 69

Something is an art form only if it involves creativity and imagination. Photography is a mechanical process of ex-

posing film to light. Mechanical processes involve no cre-
ativity and imagination. Therefore, photography is not an
art form.

First, the argument must be rewritten using categorical statements:

All art forms are things involving C and I.

All things identical to photography are mechanical
processes.

No mechanical processes are things involving C and I.

Thus, no things identical to photography are art forms.

This argument does not conform to the four rules for the sorites because, as the premises are arranged, it is not the case that each premise (except the first) has a term in common with its predecessor. However, proper form can be achieved by switching the second and third premises. Now follow the procedure for evaluating the sorites.

Step 1

All art forms are things involving C and I.

No mechanical processes are things involving C and I.

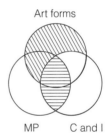

Thus, no mechanical processes are art forms.

Step 2 The diagram shows that 'No mechanical processes are art forms'.

Step 3

No mechanical processes are art forms.

All things identical to photography are mechanical
processes.

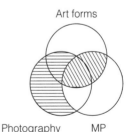

Thus, no things identical to photography are art forms.

Repeat step 2 The diagram shows that the conclusion 'No things identical to photography are art forms' can be validly inferred. Thus, the argument is valid.

Constructing sorites is a very useful method for evaluating arguments. Your own inventiveness becomes important as you explore ways to put arguments into syllogistic form. Ultimately, the basic task is to express the argument in such a way that you can check it easily with the three-circle diagramming technique.

Exercise 4.5A   Valid or Invalid?   Determine whether the following arguments are valid by using Venn diagrams. Translate sentences into categorical form if necessary and rewrite arguments in proper syllogism form where possible.

1. Few bankers voted for the new tax structure. All voters for the new tax structure were capitalists. Therefore, some bankers are not capitalists.

2. All except the candidates for officer training school were requested to submit records of their medical history. Cadet Murdoch must be a candidate because he was not requested to submit his medical record.

3. If a forecaster can predict the heat wave, then he or she is a good weather reporter. Someone is a good weather reporter only if he or she is trained in meteorology. Every forecaster who can predict the heat wave must therefore be trained in meteorology.

4. All cats except Manx cats have long tails. Iris is not a Manx cat; therefore, she has a long tail.

5. Only things capable of meaningful speech are capable of thought. Humans are capable of meaningful speech, so they must be capable of thought.

6. If you are strong you'll make it to the top. And Max is strong. So he'll make it to the top.

7. All poisonous snakes are things to avoid. But some snakes are nonpoisonous. Therefore, some snakes are not things to avoid.

8. No Californians are Easterners. Some Easterners are not unfriendly. Therefore, friendly people are non-Californians.

9. All and only Iranians are Persians. No Iraqis are Persians. Therefore, no Iranians are Iraqis.

10. Most experts on ecology are of the opinion that the use of pesticides in farming is ecologically dangerous. Since those who are of that opinion are disliked by the major chemical manufacturers, it follows that some experts on ecology are disliked by the major chemical manufacturers.

Exercise 4.5B   Sorites   Are the following arguments valid or invalid? Some of the arguments will have to be constructed as sorites before they can be evaluated. Be sure that all statements are in categorical form and that all arguments are in proper form as sorites before attempting to check them using Venn diagrams. Show your work.

1. *All X are Y.*
   All Y are Z.
   All Z are T.

   ———————————————

   Thus, all X are T.

2. *All S are R.*
   No T are R.
   All O are T.

   ———————————————

   Thus, no S are O.

3. *No A are non-D.*
   Some A are B.
   All B are C.

   ———————————————

   Thus, some C are D.

4. *No F are G.*
   No G are H.
   No H are I.

   ———————————————

   Thus, no F are I.

5. *Some humans are mortals.*
   Some mortals are Romans.
   Some Romans are Italians.

   ———————————————

   Therefore, some Italians are mortals.

6. *All Texans are ranchers.*
   No ranchers are nonsheepherders.
   All sheepherders are woolgatherers.

   ———————————————

   So, no Texans are woolgatherers.

7. *All sailors are recruits.*
   No volunteers are recruits.
   All officers are volunteers.
   All veterans are officers.

   ———————————————

   Therefore, no sailors are veterans.

8. *All Bengal tigers are carnivores.*

   All noncarnivores are nonvicious animals.

   All vicious animals are dangerous animals.

   Thus, all Bengal tigers are dangerous animals.

9. *All computer programmers are proficient in BASIC.*

   No people proficient in BASIC are computer illiterate.

   No people who are computer illiterate are mathematicians.

   Thus, no computer programmers are nonmathematicians.

10. *No letter carriers are civil servants.*

    Some letter carriers are unemployed.

    All unemployed people are job seekers.

    Therefore, some job seekers are not civil servants.

11. *All carpenters are artisans.*

    All artisans are woodworkers.

    Some carpenters are journeymen.

    So, some journeymen are woodworkers.

12. *All those looking for the elegant trogon are birdwatchers.*

    All amateur ornithologists are those who are looking for the elegant trogon.

    No people with bird books are nonamateur ornithologists.

    If a person has a large bulge in his or her back pocket, then he or she has a bird book.

    Only those with large bulges in their back pockets are holding binoculars.

    Therefore, only birdwatchers are holding binoculars.

Summary

This and the previous chapter have focused on the evaluation of both simple and complex deductive arguments according to the principles of categorical logic. We learned the four categorical forms of statements, and we saw how they can be represented in Venn diagrams, as well as how they are logically related on the traditional and the modern squares of opposition. We then learned how categorical statements can be manipulated according to the operations of conversion, obversion, and contraposition. In certain instances, these operations yield logically equivalent statements and therefore valid inferences. Using the operations we can rewrite statements within arguments to simplify the arguments and facilitate the Venn diagramming technique. By following certain guidelines we can translate most sentences in ordinary language into categorical form.

The culmination of this chapter was the logical analysis of deductive arguments called syllogisms. We applied the Venn diagramming technique to the evaluation of syllogisms, and we examined methods of analyzing arguments that are not in syllogistic form, most notably the method of constructing "chain arguments," called sorites.

You now have a good grasp of the basic concepts and techniques of categorical logic, certainly enough to apply its principles to many of the arguments you encounter in daily life. Equally important, you now understand what a deductive logical system is and how inferences may be demonstrated to be valid.

Review Questions

1. What features must a statement have in order to be in proper categorical form?
2. Which phrases in ordinary language require two categorical statements for proper translation?
3. What are proper names and singular expressions? Why do they present a special problem for categorical logic?
4. List some of the phrases that assert a conditional and illustrate how they can be translated into categorical form.
5. What is a syllogism? What features must an argument have to be in proper syllogistic form?
6. What is the bar? What does it mean, and under what conditions is it used?
7. What type of argument requires an existential assumption in order to be valid?
8. What is a sorites? Under what conditions is a sorites invalid?

True or False?

1. Syllogisms can have two, three, or four premises.
2. 'Only As are Bs' is translated as 'All As are Bs'.
3. The phrase 'if and only if' is really two conditionals.
4. It makes no logical difference whether a statement begins with the phrase 'only' or 'the only'.

5. All syllogisms can be evaluated using Venn diagrams.

6. Some uses of conversion, obversion, and contraposition do not result in logically equivalent statements.

7. Longer arguments cannot be broken down without distorting their meaning.

8. Given a three-circle Venn diagram, if an I- or an O-statement does not specify in which of two areas the X is to be placed, then you may place the X in either area.

9. The device called the bar is used whenever an existential assumption must be made.

10. Arguments with universal premises and a particular conclusion are not shown valid by the Venn diagram method unless an existential assumption is made and represented.

Discussion Questions

1. In Section 4.2, item 5, we saw that the preferred way of translating statements using nonstandard quantifiers such as 'few', 'many', and 'most' was to write them as two I- and O-form statements. Thus, 'Most officers are honest' is translated as 'Some officers are honest' and 'Some officers are not honest'. However, the same translations are recommended for 'Few officers are honest' and 'Many officers are honest'. The translations ignore the differences between the quantifiers 'few', 'many', and 'most'. Write a brief discussion in which you consider one or all of the following questions.

   a. What are the pros and cons of the rule that tells us to translate the nonstandard quantifiers, 'few', 'many', 'most', (etc.) as two particular statements, I and O?

   b. If for some reason it were important to retain a special word such as 'few', there is a way to do so. The nonstandard quantifying word can be embedded in the predicate category. For example, 'Many students are volunteers' can be rendered as 'All students who are volunteers are students many in number'. Is that form of translation better, or is it simply that circumstances might favor one translation over the other? What do you think, and why?

   c. Are there other practices of translation that seem to result in loss of meaning? Explain.

2. Venn diagramming seems to be a very useful way of representing reasoning, but is that *your* experience? Do you find it easy or difficult to "see" the structure of an inference by drawing a Venn diagram of it? Second, we have practiced diagramming three categories using three circles. Could you imagine using four circles? Five or six? What are the limits of the diagramming technique, and why?

CHAPTER FIVE
Truth-Functional Logic
Part I

Truth-functional logic analyzes statements and arguments in terms of the truth or falsity of their
component parts. In this chapter we learn the fundamentals of truth-functional logic: the symbols
and their use in symbolizing statements, the truth-
functions of the logical operators, and the truth
table as a method for displaying the truth-values of
compound statements. These fundamentals prepare
us for the use of truth-functional techniques in
evaluating arguments.

5.1 Introduction

The origins of truth-functional logic can be traced to certain ancient Greek
philosophers, in particular the Megarians (approximately 400–300 BC) and the Stoics
(approximately 330–200 BC). The most thorough formulation of truth-functional
logic—and the modern symbolization theory we use here—is primarily the work of a
group of major philosophers that includes Bertrand Russell (1872–1970), Alfred North
Whitehead (1861–1947), and Charles Sanders Peirce (1839–1914). *Truth-functional*

logic, also called *propositional logic,* takes its name from the notion of truth-functionality, the idea that the truth of a statement is a function of the truth-values of its component parts. This central notion will become clear soon.

Truth-functional logic differs from categorical logic in several important respects. First, it is not a logical system based on categories or classes. As we learned, an argument written according to the principles of categorical logic expresses a logical relationship among classes and is analyzed and evaluated in terms of class relationships. In truth-functional logic, statements, not categories, are considered basic; arguments are analyzed and evaluated in terms of the logical relationships between the truth-values of statements. Second, Venn diagrams are not used in truth-functional logic. Instead, symbolization and mechanical techniques such as truth tables are used to reveal the form of a statement or argument. Third, truth-functional logic is completely formal; that is, statements and arguments are translated from ordinary language into a symbolic form that reveals their logical structure. To some extent you will find this more mechanical system easier to use than categorical logic. For our purposes, however, neither system is more reliable than the other. Applied correctly, both categorical logic and truth-functional logic accurately evaluate many common deductive arguments for validity.

5.2 Statements and Operators

The elements of truth-functional logic are statements and *logical operators.* A statement, as we have seen, is any sentence that may be true or false. A logical operator, according to this theory, is a logical device for expressing defined logical relations among statements. So, we have statements and the operators for negating and combining statements. We employ five logical operators in our theory. They are expressed by the words 'not', 'and', 'or', 'if . . . then', and 'if and only if'. With those operators we form compound statements such as these first five examples.

Example 1	*Ted is* not *available to work on Sundays.*
Example 2	*Ted works on weekends* and *Gayle works only on Tuesdays.*
Example 3	*Ted works on weekends* or *Ted travels to visit Gayle.*
Example 4	If *Ted travels to visit Gayle,* then *he will work this weekend.*
Example 5	*Gayle takes the day off* if and only if *Ted travels to visit her.*
Example 6	*Gayle takes the day off.*

Notice that each example, except the last, uses one of the operators. Example 6 has no operator. Statements that contain no operator we call *simple statements;* all others we call *compound statements.*

> simple statement   *Any statement that contains no logical operator.*

> compound statement   *Any statement that has one or more logical operators.*

What is the significance of that decision? According to our theory, compound statements are analyzable into simpler statements, whereas simple statements cannot be further broken down. They are the "building blocks" of compounds. To attempt to further analyze a simple statement results in loss of meaning or loss of truth-value. 'The camera dropped' is an example of a simple statement. If we break this statement down further into its component parts, 'the camera' and 'dropped', we no longer have a statement, something that may be true or false. On the other hand, the statement 'The camera dropped, and Francis paid for it' can be broken down into components that are themselves statements, namely, 'The camera dropped' and 'Francis paid for it'. On this theory, the statement 'It is not snowing', because it contains an operator, is also capable of being broken: 'It is snowing'. It is therefore not a simple statement. Given this distinction, which of the following are simple? Which are compound?

Example 7	*George wins.*
Example 8	*Most people are usually hesitant to buy a car from a dealer who uses flashy gimmicks.*
Example 9	*The onions and the carrots are ready for picking.*
Example 10	*It is good to be alive and better to be healthy.*
Example 11	*The Asante of Ghana are noted for their skillfully carved statues.*
Example 12	*Men, women, and children over the age of twelve must pay full admission price.*
Example 13	*If the pain increases, then you may take two aspirins.*

The simple statements are Examples 7, 8, and 11. All others are compounds. Notice that simple statements can be as short as Example 7 or as long as Example 8. Notice also that the statements in Examples 9, 10, and 12 are compounds because logically they consist of several statements joined together. For example, statement 12 is a compound of the statements 'Men must pay full admission price', 'Women must pay full admission price', and 'Children over the age of twelve must pay full admission price'.

5.3 The Logical Operators Defined

Five important logical operators are typically used in truth-functional logic. (It is possible to present truth-functional logic with fewer than five.) Again, the five operators we will use in this account of truth-functional logic are 'not', 'and', 'or', 'if . . . then', and 'if and only if'. The five operators represent five logically different ways of forming compound statements. What follows is a survey of the operators and the functions they establish.

'Not' and Negation   The operator 'not' serves to *negate* a statement. For example, the statement 'George wins' is negated in the compound statement 'George *does not* win'. Furthermore, a negation may itself be negated, as in 'It is *not* true that George does not win'. Our language has a variety of expressions that serve the function of negation—that is, of expressing the operator 'not'—including 'it is not true that . . .', 'it is not the case that . . .', '. . . is not so', and so on. Because every statement is either true or false, if a statement is true, then its negation is false; and if a statement is false, then its negation is true.

'And' and Conjunction   The operator 'and' forms compounds called *conjunctions* (from the word 'conjoin'). In the following examples of conjunction, notice the different expressions that have the same function as 'and'.

Example 14

It is past noon, and *the men are still working.*

It is past noon, but *the men are still working.*

It is past noon, yet *the men are still working.*

It is past noon; the men are still working.

It is past noon; nevertheless, *the men are still working.*

Suppose we let P stand for 'It is past noon' and M for 'the men are still working'. Each example above then asserts that both P and M are true. The assertion of both simple statements is in effect the logical meaning of the operator 'and' serving to conjoin two statements. However, not every occurrence of the word 'and' establishes a conjunction. For example, Gandhi's remark 'Nonviolence and truth are inseparable' is not a compound even though it contains the word 'and'. It cannot be broken down into two simple statements; it is itself a simple statement. In this example, 'and' serves to connect the subjects, not two statements. (The same is true of the statement 'Water is nothing but hydrogen and oxygen'.)

'Or' and Disjunction   The operator 'or' forms compounds called *disjunctions*. A disjunction asserts of the statements it connects, called *disjuncts,* that *at least one disjunct is true.* It is consistent with this assertion that all disjuncts are true; however, a person who asserts a disjunction is making the minimal claim that *at least one* of the statements of the disjunction is true. The operator 'or' in truth-functional logic is called the *inclusive* 'or' because it includes the possibility that all disjuncts are true. For example, 'You may have mustard or relish on your hot dog' allows that you may have one or the other *or both*. On the other hand, the word 'or' in our language is sometimes used *exclusively,* that is, such that it excludes the possibility that more than one of the disjuncts may be true at the same time. For example, 'The baby may be a girl or a boy' would normally be taken to imply that the baby cannot be both. The exclusive sense of 'or' is 'one or the other but not both'. There is a special way of translating the exclusive 'or' (discussed in detail in Section 5.6), but when the context does not clearly indicate this meaning, we will use the inclusive 'or'. Thus, the disjunctive form '*p* or *q*' (where *p* and *q* stand for statements) is understood to mean that '*p* is true or *q* is true or both'.

'If . . . Then' and the Conditional   As we saw earlier, a conditional asserts that something is the case, given a certain condition. For example, 'If it rains, then the streets will be wet' asserts that the streets will be wet, given the condition that it rains. The word or phrase following the 'if' is the condition and is called the *antecedent.* The word or phrase following the 'then' is called the *consequent.* There are different ways of expressing a conditional, as these examples illustrate:

Example 15

If *it rains,* then *the streets will be wet.*

If *it rains, the streets will be wet.*

The streets will be wet on the condition that *it rains.*

The streets will be wet if *it rains.*

It rains only if *the streets are wet.*

Each example above is equivalent to 'If it rains, then the streets will be wet'. (When we examine some special cases of translating ordinary language into symbols, we will review other expressions with the same function as 'if . . . then'.)

'If and Only If' and the Biconditional   We met the phrase 'if and only if' in categorical logic. Here it is called the *biconditional,* for, as the name implies, it comprises two conditionals. Thus, 'It is a valid argument if and only if the conclusion necessarily follows from the premises' asserts that 'if it is a valid argument, then the conclusion necessarily follows from the premises, *and* if the conclusion necessarily follows from the premises, then it is a valid argument'. The biconditional can be expressed in the formula 'if *p* is true, then *q* is true, and if *q* is true, then *p* is true', where *p* and *q* stand for statements.

Using *p* and *q* to represent statements, we can summarize the five common logical operators and their functions as follows:

not *p*   Negation—asserts that *p* is not true

p and *q*   Conjunction—asserts that both *p* and *q* are true

p or *q*	Disjunction—asserts that one or the other or both are true
if *p* then *q*	Conditional—asserts that if *p* is true then *q* is also true
p if and only if *q*	Biconditional—asserts that if *p* is true then *q* is true, and if *q* is true then *p* is true

The aim of truth-functional logic is to translate statements and the deductive arguments they compose using one or more of these five logical operators. Many instances of deductive reasoning can be analyzed in terms of these five functions. Let's turn now to the symbolization of statements and operators.

5.4 The Symbols and Their Uses

In truth-functional logic there are symbols for each of the five logical operators, symbols for statements, and the symbols known as parentheses and brackets. They are shown in Table 5.1.

Symbolic Translation

We can symbolize nearly any statement with the symbols listed in Table 5.1. We symbolize a statement to reveal its form and to prepare it for further analysis, a process

Table 5.1 **Symbols Used in Truth-Functional Logic**

SYMBOL	INTERPRETATION	NAME OF THE SYMBOL
−	not	bar or "not sign"
+	and	"and sign"
∨	or	wedge
⊃	if . . . then	horseshoe
≡	if and only if	triple bar
p, q, r, s, . . .	Small letters are used to refer to types of statements or statements generally.	
A, B, C, D, . . .	Capital letters stand for actual simple statements—for example, 'G' for 'George wins'.	
(. . .)	Parentheses separate or group compounds within compounds or indicate the scope of the bar.	
[. . .]	Brackets group statements that are already within parentheses.	

that is particularly important for statements occurring in arguments. The procedure for symbolizing a statement consists of three steps:

1. *Identify the simple statement or statements.* You do this by determining that a statement cannot be further broken down into one or more simple statements.

2. *Choose capital letters to symbolize the simple statements.* The choice of capital letters is arbitrary, but it is helpful to choose a letter that reminds you of the statement. A good practice is to choose the first letter of the most significant word of the statement. *Note: Once a capital letter has been chosen for a simple statement, it must be used for every occurrence of that statement, and it cannot be used for a different statement in the same context.*

3. *For compound statements, supply the appropriate symbol for the logical operator.* (In Section 5.6 we see how to translate various phrases other than the standard five logical operators.)

Let's examine some easy examples of symbolizing.

Example 16

It is not true that evil spirits exist.

In this example we have the compound statement 'Not evil spirits exist'. The simple statement is 'evil spirits exist'. It is natural to let the letter E stand for that simple statement, giving us

It is not true that evil spirits exist. $= -E$

Example 17

It is good to be alive and better to be healthy.

The simple statements are 'It is good to be alive' and 'it is better to be healthy'. Letting G stand for the first and B for the second, we have

It is good to be alive and better to be healthy. $= G + B$

Example 18

Eliot bowls with Barb or June.

The simple statements are 'Eliot bowls with Barb' and 'Eliot bowls with June', which can be represented by B and J, respectively:

Eliot bowls with Barb or June. $= B \lor J$

Example 19

If more water goes over the dam, then the valley will be flooded.

The antecedent is 'more water goes over the dam', and the consequent is 'the valley will be flooded'. The two statements may be symbolized by W and V, respectively. The horseshoe symbol '⊃' goes between the antecedent and the consequent as follows:

If more water goes over the dam, then $= W \supset V$
the valley will be flooded.

Example 20

Statement P is a compound if and only if statement P
contains at least one logical operator.

The simple statements are 'Statement P is a compound', which can be symbolized by C, and 'statement P contains at least one logical operator', which can be symbolized by O.

Statement P is a compound if and only $= C \equiv O$
if statement P contains at least one
logical operator

Here are some other examples of symbolized statements.

Example 21	*If Rome falls, then the empire is lost.*	$= R \supset E$
Example 22	*The Civil War was not lost by lack of courage.*	$= -C$
Example 23	*Coffee, sugar, and oil are the chief exports of Venezuela.*	$= C + S + O$
Example 24	*If it does not crystallize, then it is not a salt.*	$= -C \supset -S$
Example 25	*Myles is a medical doctor if and only if he has earned an M.D. degree.*	$= M \equiv E$
Example 26	*You must take chemistry or physics.*	$= C \vee P$

Exercise 5.4   Symbolic Translation   Translate the following statements using the capital letters provided as translation cues. Name the type of compound statement—negation, conjunction, and so on—for those that are compounds.

1. If it is raining, then the forecast is correct. (R, C)

2. Congress enacts laws, and the judicial branch enforces them. (C, J)

3. If Japanese industrialists borrow heavily from American banks, then the interest rates will climb even higher. (J, I)

4. Melba left the car, and Roy cleaned the fish. (M, R)

5. Artists are not crazy about logic. (A)

6. Either breakfast is ready or I'm not staying. (B, I)

7. Pizza and beer are not recommended for people with ulcers. (P, B)

8. If the soul is not immortal, then we do not live forever. (S, W)

9. There were three people involved in the accident, and no one was injured. (T, O)

10. Smoking is harmful if and only if the Surgeon General is correct in his warning. (S, C)

11. The Pawnee and Arapahoe once occupied what is now Nebraska. (P, A)

12. There are 640 species of birds in North America. (B)

13. A person is morally responsible for his or her actions if and only if the person performed them voluntarily. (M, V)

14. If the signatures are the same, the will is genuine. (S, W)

15. The library is not closed, or the study hall is open. (L, S)

16. It's easier to make an omelet than to unmake it, easier to scratch the side of your car than to paint it, easier to mess up your room than to clean it, and so on. (Robert M. Hazen and James Trefil) (O, S, M)

17. We say that if America has entered the war to make the world safe for democracy, she must first make democracy safe in America. (Emma Goldman, 1917) (A, S)

18. I had either to submit to a system which I considered has done irreparable harm to my country or incur the risk of the mad fury of my people bursting forth when they understood the truth from my lips. (Mahatma Gandhi, 1922) (S, I)

19. Society is produced by our wants and government by our wickedness. (Thomas Paine) (S, G)

20. If, as seems likely, every bit of information in the brain corresponds to one of these connections [dendrites], the total number of things knowable by the brain is no more than 10^{14}, one hundred trillion. (Carl Sagan) (B, T)

5.5 Grouping and the Scope of Operators

Parentheses and brackets are symbols that *group statements together and indicate the scope of operators*. In more complex statements they enable us to show which parts of a compound are governed by a logical operator. For example, suppose a menu reads, 'eggs and hashbrowns or pancakes'. The words 'and' and 'or' connect the other words to indicate a choice you may make, but what exactly is the choice? Is it a choice between eggs and hashbrowns, on the one hand, or pancakes, on the other? Or is it that you may choose eggs and either hashbrowns or pancakes? Parentheses can make the phrase unambiguous, meaning either '(eggs and hashbrowns) *or* pancakes' or 'eggs *and* (hashbrowns or pancakes)'. Notice that the first version is a *disjunction*, an 'or' compound. By placing the words 'eggs and hashbrowns' together within parentheses, we indicate that it is one of the disjuncts of the larger statement. The second version is a *conjunction*, an 'and' compound; the parentheses group together the words 'hashbrowns or pancakes', indicating that that group is one of the conjuncts. Without parentheses the logical form of the example is ambiguous. Thus, parentheses serve to clarify logical form and indicate which operator "holds together" the entire compound.

Symbolizations that are ambiguous as illustrated above are unacceptable on this theory. For example, any statement of the form 'P or Q and S' must be clarified. We cannot tell whether it is a disjunction or a conjunction. We resolve the ambiguity by adding parentheses, making it either 'P or (Q and S)', which is a disjunction, or '(P or Q) and S', which is a conjunction. As you can see, a statement is classified as a conjunction, a disjunction, a conditional, a negation, and so on according to the logical operator that *governs the entire statement*. Here are some other examples illustrating the scope of operators:

Example 27	Max does not run, or Smith resigns.	$= -M \vee S$
Example 28	It's not the case that Max runs or Smith resigns.	$= -(M \vee S)$

In Example 27 the '$-$' governs only M, whereas in Example 28 it governs the compound '(M $\vee$ S)'. The first example is a disjunction; the second is a negation. Consider these examples:

Example 29	If Max does not run, then Smith resigns.	$= -M \supset S$
Example 30	It's not the case that if Max runs then Smith resigns.	$= -(M \supset S)$

Example 29 is a conditional; the antecedent alone is negated. Example 30 is a negation—a negation *of* a conditional.

Symbolizing with Parentheses and Brackets

Parentheses are used to group simple statements within a compound. Brackets are used to group compound statements within a larger compound. Let's compare the use of parentheses and brackets by carefully symbolizing a complex sentence.

Example 31

*If the president vetoes the bill or if Congress balks and the
people protest, then the chances of passing this year's new
tax amendment are not good.*

The first step in translation is to identify the simple statements and assign capital letters
to them. It may help to read through the example first and mark the words or phrases
that express logical operators. Notice the circled operator words:

V
(If) the president vetoes the bill, (or) (if) Congress balks (and)
P   G
the people protest, (then) the chances of passing this year's new tax amendment are (not)

good.

You recognize an 'if . . . then', an 'or', an 'and', and a 'not'. You also see that we have
several simple statements, which we can symbolize as follows:

the president vetoes the bill $=$ V

Congress balks $=$ C

the people protest $=$ P

*the chances of passing this year's new tax amendment are
good* $=$ G

Now we write out the compound in skeleton form using those symbols and the
operators:

If V or if C and P, then not G.

Before we supply symbols for the operators, it may help to supply parentheses and brackets. It is immediately clear that the compound 'C and P' should be grouped together:

If V or if (C and P), then not G.

The consequent of this statement is 'not G', and the antecedent is the disjunction 'If
V or if (C and P)'. (The second 'if' within the statement clarifies for us that the antecedent, the condition that must be met, is that either the president vetoes the bill or both
Congress balks and the people protest.) Thus, the compound 'If V or if (C and P)' must
be grouped together, and since it already contains a grouped compound, brackets are
used as follows:

[If V or if (C and P)], then not G.

Now the symbols for the operators can be supplied, producing the following symbolic
translation:

$$[V \vee (C + P)] \supset -G$$

What type of statement is this? That is, what operator governs the entire compound? It is the horseshoe; therefore, this compound is a conditional statement. Its antecedent is a disjunction, and its consequent is a negation.

Here are two more examples. Try to symbolize them and identify what type of compound each is. Check your results with the answers that follow.

Example 32

It's not true that if Max runs then Bill swims and Cheryl bowls.

Example 33

It's not true that if Max runs and Bill swims then Cheryl bowls, and it's not true that Max runs or Bill swims.

Example 32 is a negation and can be symbolized as $-[M \supset (B + C)]$. Example 33 is a conjunction and can be symbolized as $-[(M + B) \supset C] + -(M \vee B)$.

Exercise 5.5   Translating and Grouping   Translate the following statements into symbolic form and identify the type of compound. Not all the statements require parentheses or brackets.

1. It's not true that if you have money then you are happy. (M, H)
2. Not a soul made a sound, and not an eye was dry. (S, E)
3. The test was not very hard, or I studied well. (T, I)
4. If you live in the Southwest and don't water your lawn, it will die. (Y, W, D)
5. If John plays quarterback, then Todd gets fullback position and Randy is on the bench. (J, T, R)
6. If Sven plays quarterback, then either Marsh or Steve is replaced. (Q, M, S)
7. The baritones and the altos are in the choir, but not the sopranos. (B, A, S)
8. If the lines go down, then the transformer will blow. (L, T)
9. If the lines go down, then the transformer blows and the power goes out. (L, T, P)
10. If the lines go down and the transformer blows, then the power goes out. (L, T, P)
11. If the lines go down or the transformer blows, then the power goes out. (L, T, P)
12. Either the lines go down or if the transformer blows, then the power goes out. (L, T, P)
13. The power goes out if the lines go down or the transformer blows. (L, T, P)
14. It's not true that either the lines go down or if the transformer blows, then the power goes out. (L, T, P)

15. Either all the tickets are sold or if the council retained their share, then there are no seats available. (T, C, S)

16. If all the tickets are sold and the council retained their share, then either there are no seats available or we miscounted. (T, C, S, M)

17. If it's not true that if you are a Parisian, you're a Frenchman, then it's not true that if you are a Berliner, you're a German. (P, F, B, G)

18. It's false that the construction will continue and the men will go back to work if and only if the banker releases the funds or the purchaser closes escrow. (C, M, B, P)

19. The birds will migrate if either the temperature drops and the days get shorter or the insects move south. (B, T, D, I)

20. Each taxpayer or an authorized tax preparer must file an income tax report and complete a statement of earnings. (T, C, A, S)

21. It's not true that the average number of new millionaires created in Silicon Valley last year is more than a hundred.

22. If anyone desired knowledge beyond such as could be obtained by his own observation, or by common conversation, his first necessity was to learn the Latin language, inasmuch as all the higher knowledge of the western world was contained in works written in that language. (T. H. Huxley, 1880) (A, H)

23. If I wanted to contemplate what is to me the deepest of all mysteries, I should choose as my object lesson a snowflake under a lens and an amoeba under the microscope. (Joseph Wood Krutch, 1929) (I, C, A)

24. If we succeed in creating truly aligned incentives among all the players in the health care marketplace, we will restore public trust in health care in America — and we will benefit those who need care the most. (Advertisement for Blue Cross/Blue Shield Association) (W, R, B)

5.6 Special Cases for Translation

Truth-functional logic analyzes deductive reasoning in terms of the five logical operators 'not', 'and', 'or', 'if . . . then', and 'if and only if'. Ordinary language contains a variety of other phrases that can express the same ideas. We have already noted some different expressions of negation and conjunction. Consider now the sentences below, each of which expresses the same statement and is symbolized in the same way:

Example 34

Wilson will not run for office.	$= -W$
It's not true that Wilson will run for office.	$= -W$
It's not the case that Wilson will run for office.	$= -W$
It's false that Wilson will run for office.	$= -W$

In this section we consider how some of the more troublesome phrases in ordinary language can be symbolized using the five operators. We look first at variations on constructions of conjunction and disjunction and then at variations on the conditional. Using the symbols *p*, *q*, and *r* to stand for any statements, we will give a formula for translating constructions from ordinary language into symbolic form.

Variations on the Conjunction and Disjunction

1. *'Neither p nor q'; 'both p and q are not'; and variants*   The sentence 'Neither Wilson nor Smith runs' is an example of the construction 'neither *p* nor *q*'. It asserts that Wilson does not run and Smith does not run. The construction 'neither *p* nor *q*' therefore asserts 'not *p* and not *q*'. The same is true for the constructions 'not either *p* or *q*' and 'both *p* and *q* are not'. Consider these examples and ask yourself whether they do not all say the same thing:

Example 35

Neither Wilson nor Smith runs.

It's not the case that either Wilson or Smith runs.

Both Wilson and Smith do not run.

It's not the case that Wilson runs, and it's not the case that Smith runs.

Each of these statements can be translated as $-(W \lor S)$ or as $-W + -S$, for, as we see later, those two translations are equivalent. Thus, the formulas for these constructions are as follows:

neither p *nor* q		$-(p \lor q)$
not either p *or* q	=	*or*
both p *and* q *are not*		$-p + -q$
not p *and not* q		

2. *'Not both p and q'; 'not p or not q'*   Consider these examples:

Example 36

It's not the case that both Wilson and Smith run.

It's not the case that Wilson runs, or it's not the case that Smith runs.

Wilson does not run, or Smith does not run.

Each sentence makes the same assertion: it's not the case that both Wilson and Smith run. That assertion permits that one or the other runs or that neither runs; it rules out the possibility that both run. The constructions illustrated by the examples above are translated as follows:

not both p *and* q	$-(p + q)$
it's not the case that p, *or it's not the case that* q =	*or*
not p *or not* q	$-p \lor -q$

Notice that the two constructions 'not both *p* and *q*', discussed in this section, and 'both *p* and *q* are not', discussed in item 1, are not logically equivalent. The first denies that both *p* and *q* are true together. The second denies *p* and denies *q*. Consider the difference between these two statements and their different translations:

Example 37

It's not the case that both Wilson and = $\quad -(W + S)$
Smith run.

Both Wilson and Smith do not run. = $\quad -W + -S$

As you can see from their translations, the first is a negation, with the '$-$' sign governing the compound (W + S). The second is a conjunction, with the '+' sign governing the entire compound. (As the formulas above indicate, each translation has an equivalent, and you may use either one. But be careful not to confuse the two equivalent translations for 'not both', and so on, with the equivalent translations for 'both . . . are not', and so on.)

3. *'Either* p *or* q *but not both'; the exclusive 'or'* A commonly misunderstood construction is 'either *p* or *q* but not both'. For example, the statement 'Either Wilson runs or Smith runs but not both' appears to be a disjunction—'Wilson runs or Smith runs'—symbolized as W ∨ S. However, it is not a disjunction, and translating it as one misrepresents the logical content of the statement. A disjunction—that is, a statement using 'or' in the inclusive sense—says, in effect, 'one or the other *or both*'. But the sentence above clearly states, 'one or the other *but not both*'. This is the *exclusive sense of 'or'*, which is translated according to this formula:

$$\text{p } or \text{ q } but \text{ } not \text{ } both \quad = \quad (p \lor q) + -(p + q)$$

Written schematically, the example above asserts

(Wilson runs or Smith runs) and not both (Wilson runs
and Smith runs).

It is translated as $(W \lor S) + -(W + S)$.

Consider another example: 'The baby will be a boy or a girl'. On the surface it appears to be a simple disjunction, and by the rules of truth-functional logic, it would not be incorrect to translate it that way. However, anyone who hears that statement takes it to mean that 'The baby will be a boy or a girl and not both'. We interpret it as the exclusive 'or', not the inclusive 'or'. Thus, the statement would be translated as follows:

Example 38

The baby will be a boy or a girl.   = $(B \lor G) + -(B + G)$

Variations on the Conditional

We have already seen several different equivalent phrases that express conditionals, including the following:

if p, *then* q
if p, q
p *only if* q   = $p \supset q$
q *on the condition that* p
q *if* p

Notice that the last two constructions—'on the condition that' and '. . . if . . .'—place the antecedent and consequent in reverse order as compared with 'if . . . then' and the others.

There are other common expressions that also express conditionals. We will look at three groups: (1) necessary and sufficient conditions; (2) the pair consisting of the constructions '*p* unless *q*' and '*p* or else *q*'; and (3) the pair consisting of 'implies' and 'is implied by'.

1. *Necessary and sufficient conditions*   A *sufficient* condition is the *antecedent* of a conditional; a *necessary* condition is the *consequent*. Thus, in the statement 'If Marsha is a mother, then Marsha is a female', Marsha's being a mother is a sufficient condition for her being a female, whereas Marsha's being a female is a necessary condition for her being a mother.

The concepts of necessary and sufficient conditions permit us to describe the logical relationship between the two characteristics of being a mother and being a female:

Example 39

Being a mother is a sufficient condition but not a
necessary condition for *being a female.*

This means that if something is a mother then it is a female, but it is not true that if something is a female then it is a mother. We can describe the relationship in the converse as well:

Example 40

Being a female is a necessary condition but not a
sufficient condition for *being a mother.*

(How would the relationship between being red and having color be described in terms of necessary and sufficient conditions?)

There are also cases in which two characteristics are both necessary and sufficient for one another, as in this example:

Example 41

Being a bachelor is a necessary and a sufficient condition for *being an unmarried man.*

Finally, there are relationships in which several things are jointly necessary or jointly sufficient for another, as in these examples:

Example 42

Being a mother of a mother or a father and being a female is jointly necessary and sufficient for *being a grandmother.*

Example 43

Being two-legged and featherless is jointly necessary but not sufficient for *being a human.*

Sentences using the words 'necessary condition' or 'sufficient condition' are easily translated symbolically. Whatever is described as the sufficient condition is represented by the antecedent, and whatever is described as the necessary condition is represented by the consequent:

p *is a sufficient condition for* q	=	$p \supset q$
p *is a necessary condition for* q	=	$q \supset p$
p *is a necessary and sufficient condition for* q	=	$p \equiv q$

2. '*p or else* q'; '*p unless* q'   These two constructions may both be translated using the disjunction symbol '$\vee$'. That is, the truth-functional interpretation of these constructions is to treat them as disjunctions. Such an interpretation may not be immediately obvious. Let's consider the construction '*p or else q*' more closely, as in this example:

Example 44

The Iraqis leave Kuwait, or else the United States attacks.

Assuming a speaker asserts that statement, what circumstances would affirm the statement? What circumstances would falsify the statement?

	IRAQIS LEAVE	OR ELSE	U.S. ATTACKS
Case 1	true	TRUE	false
Case 2	false	TRUE	true
Case 3	true	TRUE	true
Case 4	false	FALSE	false

Case 1 describes that situation in which it is true that the Iraqis leave and that the U.S. does not attack. Were this the case, then the assertion of the compound "The Iraqis leave, or else the United States attacks" would be true.

Case 2 describes that situation in which the Iraqis do not leave and the U.S. attacks. Were this the case, the compound would be true.

Case 3 describes that situation in which the Iraqis leave and the U.S. attacks. Why is the compound statement true in that case? The simple answer is that it is true because the situation does not falsify it. To assert that the Iraqis leave or else the U.S. attacks is *not* to assert that if the Iraqis leave, then the U.S. does not attack. On the contrary, it is to assert no more than that if the Iraqis do not leave, then the U.S. attacks. It asserts, in other words, *at least one condition* in which the U.S. attacks, namely, the Iraqis do not leave. It is consistent with that assertion—that is, it does not falsify it—that the U.S. attacks even though the Iraqis leave.

Case 4 describes precisely that situation that does falsify the assertion. Having asserted that the Iraqis leave or else the U.S. attacks, then if the Iraqis do not leave and the United States does not attack, the assertion is false. Notice that this is the case in which neither simple statement is true.

By considering those circumstances that would affirm or falsify the assertion that 'The Iraqis leave Kuwait, or else the United States attacks them', we see that the compound is true just in case *either one or both* of the simple statements is true. It is false just in case *both* simple statements are false. This conforms to the truth-functional definition of the disjunction: true in case at least one part is true, otherwise false. Thus, the symbolic interpretation of 'or else' is as a disjunction.

$$\text{p } or\ else \text{ q } = \text{ p} \lor \text{q}$$

The construction '*p* unless *q*' expresses the same relationship between *p* and *q* as does '*p* or else *q*', but the statements are in reverse order. Consider this example:

Example 45

The United States attacks unless the Iraqis leave Kuwait.

	U.S. ATTACKS	OR ELSE	IRAQIS LEAVE
Case 1	true	TRUE	false
Case 2	false	TRUE	true
Case 3	true	TRUE	true
Case 4	false	FALSE	false

Again, it seems clear that the compound is true in cases 1 and 2 and false in case 4. Case 3 describes the situation in which the U.S. attacks and the Iraqis leave Kuwait. Recognizing that the assertion 'The U.S. attacks unless the Iraqis leave Kuwait' means no more than that the U.S. attacks *if* the Iraqis do *not* leave Kuwait, we see that the assertion is true even in that case in which the U.S. attacks and the Iraqis leave.

Thus, both constructions 'p or else q' and 'p unless q' may be translated as '$p \lor q$'.

$$\left.\begin{array}{l} \text{p } \textit{or else} \text{ q} \\ \text{p } \textit{unless} \text{ q} \end{array}\right\} = p \lor q$$

3. *'Implies'; 'is implied by'* The construction 'p implies q' is normally taken to assert that the statement represented by q follows from that represented by p. On the other hand, 'p is implied by q' is understood to assert that the statement represented by p follows from that represented by q. Thus, these expressions are translated as follows:

$$\begin{array}{lcl} \text{p } \textit{implies} \text{ q} & = & p \supset q \\ \text{p } \textit{is implied by} \text{ q} & = & q \supset p \end{array}$$

Table 5.2 summarizes the formulas for translating the various special constructions we have examined. You should have no difficulty symbolizing a statement if you look at the formula carefully and follow the changes exactly.

Let's examine a few examples.

Example 46   *You are not my friend, or else you would help me.*

Table 5.2   Special Cases for Translation

CONSTRUCTION	TRANSLATION
neither p nor q not either p or q both p and q are not not p and not q	$-(p \lor q)$ *or* $-p + -q$
not both p and q not p or not q	$-(p + q)$ *or* $-p \lor -q$
p or q but not both	$(p \lor q) + -(p + q)$
if p then q if p, q p only if q p is a sufficient condition for q p implies q	$p \supset q$
p if q p is a necessary condition for q p is implied by q	$q \supset p$
p or else q p unless q	$p \lor q$

Schematically, this statement may be represented as 'not friend or else help me'—it often helps to "strip away" some of the nonlogical words of the statement to see its structure. Write the schema underneath the formula for 'or else' and follow the changes exactly.

$$\begin{array}{c} \text{p } \textit{or else} \text{ q} \\ \textit{not friend or else help me} \end{array} \quad = \quad \text{p} \lor \text{q}$$

The formula requires that simple statements remain the same and 'or else' is changed to '$\lor$'. Thus, the symbolic translation is as follows:

$$\begin{array}{l} \textit{You are not my friend,} \\ \textit{or else you would help me.} \end{array} \quad = \quad -\text{F} \lor \text{H}$$

Example 47   *He cannot be a lawyer and a doctor both.*

Schematically, this statement asserts 'not both lawyer and doctor'. The construction is 'not both p and q', for which the formula is

$$\begin{array}{ll} \textit{not both} \text{ p } \textit{and} \text{ q} & = \quad -(\text{p} + \text{q}) \\ \textit{not both lawyer and doctor} & = \quad -(\text{L} + \text{D}) \end{array}$$

The formula indicates that the two statements following 'not both' are conjoined inside parentheses and then the whole conjunction is negated.

Exercise 5.6   More Symbolic Translations   Translate the following statements into symbolic form. Use the translation cues provided.

1. You cannot be a sailor and a marine both. (S, M)
2. If you are a sailor, then you are not a marine, and if you are a marine, then you are not a sailor. (S, M)
3. There is a decline in crime only if there is a decrease in poverty. (C, D)
4. Macbeth can be killed only if Burnam Wood comes to Dunsinane and he is attacked by someone who is not born of a woman. (M, B, A)
5. If you send your child to a private school, you can deduct half the cost of tuition from your income tax. (S, D)
6. Each taxpayer must file an income tax report, or else the taxpayer will be penalized. (T, P)
7. You will help me, or else you are not my friend. (H, F)
8. Unless the heat wave ends, the corn crops will be ruined. (H, C)

9. The heat wave must end, or else the crops will be ruined. (H, C)

10. It is false that having money is a sufficient condition for being happy and living contentedly. (M, H, L)

11. Congress will ignore the president's request for increased military spending if the president refuses to approve more aid to education. (C, P)

12. Military pressure should be used in Central America if and only if it is coupled with serious efforts to negotiate a peace settlement. (M, S)

13. Neither the chemists nor the physicists were expecting the awards. (C, P)

14. That 91 percent of all adult Americans have married implies that marriage is still an important institution in our culture. (A, M)

15. (a) Either you are male or female but not both. (b) You cannot be both male and female. (M, F)

16. The pullout of the Israelis is a necessary condition for the withdrawal of the Syrians from the Bekaa Valley. (P, W)

17. 'If you look closely at our quality and judge for yourself, you'll understand that at Ford Motor Company quality is not just an abstract idea, it's very, very real.' (Ford advertisement) (L, J, U)

18. Honduras is the poorest country in Central America but not the ripest for revolution. (H, R)

19. Neither the Chinese nor the Russians have been willing to engage in a cultural exchange. (C, R)

20. Either you're with us or you're against us. (W, A)

21. Both *Desire in the Dust* and *The Redrock Canyon* are not worth reading. (D, R)

22. If the airline pilots settle their dispute with the managers, then we'll see a resumption of service unless some other obstacle arises. (A, R, O)

23. The whole biomedical scientific community is in trouble if the secretary does not resist pressure from demonstrators and insist upon the protection of scientific research. (B, S, I)

24. Even if there are no new sources of funding, the problem of poor-quality elementary education must be addressed, or else we face a national disaster. (S, P, F)

25. In profession of his love for her, he carved her name on the tree trunk, and neither she nor her young sister ever suspected it was he. (H, S, Y)

26. (a) Smoking is harmful. (b) Smoking is not harmful. (c) It's not the case that smoking is not harmful. (S)

27. That the congressional subcommittee leaders gathered in Los Angeles over the weekend is a necessary condition of the facts that the speaker selects the site of the yearly meeting and this speaker chose L.A. (C, S, T)

28. It's not the case that both the blue jay and the scrub jay reside in Iowa. (B, S)

29. That the number of English majors is increasing implies that the new courses in literature and creative writing form an attractive program. (N, C)

30. More educators, more administrators, and more students are turning to philosophy to provide them with the skills of reasoning. (E, A, S)

31. If we are finally allowed to become full people, not only will children be born and brought up with more love and responsibility than today, but we will break out of the confines of that sterile little suburban family to relate to each other in terms of all of the possible dimensions of our personalities—male and female, as comrades, as colleagues, as friends, as lovers. (Betty Friedan, "A Woman's Civil Right," 1969) (F, C, B, W)

32. If I own a business that is making money, it makes sense to keep it open; but if the business is losing money, I would be imprudent to wait until there was no money left at all before closing. (Gregory Pence, *Classic Cases in Medical Ethics*) (O, S, L, I)

5.7 The Truth-Functions

In this section we examine closely the logical operations expressed by the five logical operators. Consider the following examples:

Example 48	*Dallas is not the capital of Texas.*
Example 49	*Dallas is the capital of Texas,* and *Texas is a state.*
Example 50	*Dallas is the capital of Texas,* or *Texas is a state.*
Example 51	If *Dallas is the capital of Texas,* then *Texas is a state.*
Example 52	*Dallas is the capital of Texas* if and only if *Texas is a state.*

In these sentences the different operators produce logically different types of statements, making the truth-value of each compound distinctly different. A conjunction, for instance, asserts that 'this *and* this' are true; therefore, the conjunction itself is true only if both of its parts are true. A disjunction asserts that 'this *or* this' is true, which means that the disjunction itself is true if at least one of its parts is true. Each logical operator forms a compound with distinct conditions for its truth-value. Those conditions define the *truth-function* represented by the operator. The *truth* of the compound is a *function of* the truth or falsity of its component parts. Now let's examine each of the operations.

1. Negation   To negate a statement is to form a new statement whose truth-value is the opposite of that of the original. A negation is true if what it negates is false and false if what it negates is true. For example, 'Dallas is not the capital of Texas' is true if 'Dallas is the capital of Texas' is false. A statement and its negation have opposite truth-values. If a statement p is true, then its negation is false, and if p is false, then its negation is true.

We can conveniently see the truth-function represented by an operator by constructing a *truth table*. A truth table shows the possible truth-values of a statement, that is, the conditions under which the statement is true or false. Given a statement p and its negation, we ask first how many possible truth-values there are for p. Obviously, there are only two: true (T) and false (F). Given what we know about the truth-function of negation, we can represent the truth-values of the negation of p in a truth table that looks like this:

p	$-p$
T	F
F	T

negation   *The truth-value of the negation is the opposite of the truth-value of the statement.*

When p is true, $-p$ is false, and vice versa. The table shows the truth-function represented by negation.

2. Conjunction   The statement 'Dallas is the capital of Texas, and Texas is a state' is true if and only if it is true that both Dallas is the capital of Texas *and* Texas is a state. In other words, the conjunction is true if and only if *all* of its parts are true, as indicated by the word 'and'. The truth table displaying the truth-function of conjunction represents two statements, p and q, so it must show each of four possible combinations of truth-values for those two statements, as below:

p	q
T	T
F	T
T	F
F	F

This table shows each possible combination of truth-values for *any* two statements: both are true, both are false, or one is true and the other false. Now we can show the truth-value of the compound formed with the symbol '+'.

p	+	q
T	T	T
F	F	T
T	F	F
F	F	F

conjunction   *True only if all parts are true; otherwise false.*

The column of Ts and Fs under the '+' sign indicates the truth-value of the compound when p is true, q is true, and so on. The table makes it easy to see that the conjunction is true in only one case: when *all* parts are true. It is false in every case in which one or more of its parts are false.

3. Disjunction   The truth-function given by disjunction—that is, by 'or'—is obviously different. 'Or' means one or the other element of the compound is true or both of them are true. The disjunction is true if at least one element is true.

p	v	q		
T	T	T	disjunction	*True if at least one part is true; false if both are false.*
F	T	T		
T	T	F		
F	F	F		

4. The Conditional   The conditional asserts that if *p* is true then *q* is true. Consider the conditional statement 'If Dallas is the capital of Texas, then Texas is a state'. Under what conditions is that conditional true? Obviously, if the antecedent 'Dallas is the capital of Texas' is true and 'Texas is a state' is true, then the conditional itself is true, for that is precisely what the conditional asserts. It is also obvious that if the antecedent is true and the consequent is false, then the conditional is false, for that is exactly the opposite of what the conditional asserts. Thus far, the conditional is true when both antecedent and consequent are true and false when the antecedent is true and the consequent false.

What is the value of the conditional when the antecedent is false? If Dallas is *not* the capital of Texas, is the conditional false? No, it is not. Remember that the conditional asserts a hypothetical situation: It says *if* the antecedent is true, then the consequent follows. The conditional is not shown false because as a matter of fact the antecedent is not true. The conditional is therefore regarded as true whenever the antecedent is false. The complete truth-function of the conditional is displayed in the following table:

p	⊃	q		
			conditional	*True in all cases except those in which* p *is true and* q
				is false.
T	T	T		
F	T	T		
T	F	F		
F	T	F		

5. The Biconditional   The truth-function represented by the biconditional is similar in a certain respect to that of the conditional. As explained above, the conditional is false whenever the antecedent is true and the consequent is false. The biconditional is really two conditionals joined together ('if *p* then *q*' and 'if *q* then *p*'). Whenever one statement of a biconditional is true and the other false, one of the conditionals composing it will be false, and therefore the biconditional will be false. The biconditional is true when the truth-values of its components are the same and false when they are not the same.

p	$\equiv$	q		biconditional	*True only when truth-values are the same.*
T	T	T			
F	F	T			
T	F	F			
F	T	F			

The truth-functions given by the five logical operators can be summarized as follows:

OPERATION	SYMBOLIZATION	TRUTH–FUNCTION
Negation	$-p$	True when p is false; false when p is true
Conjunction	$p + q$	True only when all parts are true; false if one or more are false
Disjunction	$p \vee q$	True when at least one part is true; false only if all parts are false
Conditional	$p \supset q$	True in all cases except those in which p is true and q is false
Biconditional	$p \equiv q$	True whenever all parts have same truth-value; false if there are different truth-values

5.8 Constructing Truth Tables

The purpose of the truth table is to display in a completely systematic and mechanical way the truth-values of statements (and, as we will see later, the validity of arguments). We have already seen how the tables can display the truth-functions given by the logical operators. But we can also apply the truth table method to any statement to reveal the conditions under which it is true or false. There are five steps for constructing truth tables in the easiest and most foolproof way.

Step 1 Determine the number of rows needed. The horizontal lines of Ts and Fs are called *rows,* and the vertical lines of Ts and Fs are called *columns.* The table must be constructed so that every possible combination of Ts and Fs is displayed in an organized way. If only one simple statement is involved then there are of course only two possible truth values, T and F, and the number of rows in the table is two, as shown below:

	p	One simple statement; two rows
1	T	
2	F	

If there are two different simple statements, then there are four possible combinations: Both are true, both are false, the first is true and the second false, and the first is false and the second true. Thus, there must be four rows of Ts and Fs, as follows:

	p	q	Two different simple statements: four rows
1	T	T	
2	F	T	
3	T	F	
4	F	F	

For three different simple statements, eight rows are needed:

	p	q	r	Three different simple statements: eight rows
1	T	T	T	
2	F	T	T	
3	T	F	T	
4	F	F	T	
5	T	T	F	
6	F	T	F	
7	T	F	F	
8	F	F	F	

We can put this pattern into a formula:

$$\text{Number of rows} = 2^{\text{number of different simple statements}}$$

The number of rows equals 2 taken to the power of the number of different simple statements. Or you can simply remember that each additional different simple statement doubles the number of rows needed.

1 simple statement	=	2 rows
2 simple statements	=	4 rows
3 simple statements	=	8 rows
4 simple statements	=	16 rows

Step 2 Fill in Ts and Fs for each simple statement. To make sure you capture every possible combination of Ts and Fs, follow this simple procedure:

1. Begin with the leftmost simple statement and alternate the Ts and Fs.

2. Double the Ts and Fs for the next *different* simple statement.

3. For the next different statement double the number of Ts from the previous column, then double the Fs. Do this until each column is completed for each new simple statement.

If a simple statement occurs more than once in a compound, it receives exactly the same values for each occurrence. No matter how many simple statements you are dealing with, you always follow the same procedure: alternate Ts and Fs for the first column, then double the number of Ts in the previous column and then the number of Fs. Here is a sample table for four simple statements:

	p	q	r	s
1	T	T	T	T
2	F	T	T	T
3	T	F	T	T
4	F	F	T	T
5	T	T	F	T
6	F	T	F	T
7	T	F	F	T
8	F	F	F	T
9	T	T	T	F
10	F	T	T	F
11	T	F	T	F
12	F	F	T	F
13	T	T	F	F
14	F	T	F	F
15	T	F	F	F
16	F	F	F	F
	a	b	c	d

Column a alternates Ts and Fs. Column b doubles Ts and Fs. Column c doubles the number of Ts of the previous column, then doubles the Fs. The procedure continues for any number of simple statements.

Step 3 Supply the truth-values of all negations of simple statements. Go through the compound you are displaying and check for any negations of simple statements. Fill in the column of Ts and Fs for such negations, as illustrated below:

p	v	−r
T		F T
F		F T
T		T F
F		T F

The column immediately underneath the '−' represents the truth values for −r based on the original values of r. The negation of any compounds is always done afterward.

Before continuing be sure that the truth-values for all negations of simple statements have been filled in.

Step 4 Supply the truth-values for compounds inside parentheses. If there are any compounds inside parentheses, you must fill in their truth-values before continuing. The guiding rule is *always work from the inside outward*. Notice in the following example how the compounds inside parentheses are completed before the operators outside parentheses can be done.

	(p	⊃	s)	+	−	(r	v	−	s)
1	T	T	T			T	T	F	T
2	F	T	T			T	T	F	T
3	T	F	F			T	T	T	F
4	F	T	F			T	T	T	F
5	T	T	T			F	F	F	T
6	F	T	T			F	F	F	T
7	T	F	F			F	T	T	F
8	F	T	F			F	T	T	F
	a	b	c	d	e	f	g	h	i

Column b represents the truth-values for the compound p ⊃ s. Column h shows the truth-values for the negation of s. And column g shows the truth-values for the compound r ∨ −s.

Step 5 Supply the truth-values for the outer operators. Once you have filled in the truth-values for all negated simple statements and for compounds within parentheses, you are ready to write the truth-values for the operators outside the parentheses. A negation of a compound must be treated before operators between compounds. Thus, fill in the truth-values for any negated compounds next. Then compute the truth-values for the remaining operators outside parentheses. The truth-values for the final operator will be the truth-values of the entire statement as a whole. Here is our sample completed:

	(p	⊃	s)	+	−	(r	v	−	s)
1	T	T	T	**F**	F	T	T	F	T
2	F	T	T	**F**	F	T	T	F	T
3	T	F	F	**F**	F	T	T	T	F
4	F	T	F	**F**	F	T	T	T	F
5	T	T	T	**T**	T	F	F	F	T
6	F	T	T	**T**	T	F	F	F	T
7	T	F	F	**F**	F	F	T	T	F
8	F	T	F	**F**	F	F	T	T	F
	a	b	c	d	e	f	g	h	i

Notice that column e, the negation of r ∨ −s, is determined from the values of r ∨ −s in column g. Notice also that the truth-values of the final operator, the '+' sign, are determined by the values of column b and column e. We can box in the column under the final operator to show that it represents the truth-values for the entire compound. Thus, we can see clearly for what values of the simple statements the entire compound

$(p \supset s) + -(r \vee -s)$ is true or false. Its truth-value is a function of the truth-values of its component parts.

SUMMARY OF STEPS

Step 1 Determine the number of rows required.

Step 2 Fill in Ts and Fs for each simple statement by first alternating Ts and Fs, then doubling the number of Ts from the previous column and then doubling the Fs. Give the same values to each occurrence of the same sign for a simple statement.

Step 3 Fill in the truth-values for all negations of *simple* statements.

Step 4 Fill in the truth-values for all compounds *inside* parentheses.

Step 5 Fill in the truth-values for all operators outside parentheses, completing negations of compounds first.

Exercise 5.8A   Truth Tables for the Operators   Construct truth tables for the five logical operators.

1. Negation	$-p$	2. Conjunction	$p + q$
3. Disjunction	$p \vee q$	4. Conditional	$p \supset q$
5. Biconditional	$p \equiv q$		

Exercise 5.8B   The Truth-Values of Compounds   Construct truth tables for the following compounds. Box in the column that displays the truth-values for the whole compound.

1. $R + -S$	2. $P \vee (Q + R)$	3. $P \vee (Q \supset R)$
4. $-P \supset Q$	5. $Q \supset (P + Q)$	6. $P \supset Q$
7. $-(P + R)$	8. $-P + -Q$	9. $-(P \vee Q)$
10. $P \vee (Q \vee R)$	11. $R \equiv (S \supset T)$	12. $-[S \equiv (P + -Q)]$

Exercise 5.8C   Translating and Truth Tables   Translate the following statements into symbolic form and then construct truth tables to show their truth-values. Put a box around the column that displays the truth-values for the compound.

1. If it snows, then it does not rain. (S, R)
2. Either it rains or it snows but not both. (R, S)

3. If the temperature is not above freezing and it snows, then either the maintenance crews will salt the roads or classes will be canceled. (T, S, M, C)

4. If classes are canceled, then the temperature is not above freezing and it is snowing. (C, T, S)

5. If the Israelis leave Lebanon, then the Lebanese government must keep the Syrians out unaided. (I, L)

6. Max and Mildred live in the South, and Max practices medicine. (X, M, P)

7. Abraham Lincoln was born after George Washington, and if Thomas Jefferson was president before Lincoln, then Lincoln was born after Jefferson, too. (L, J, B)

8. Citizens of the United States have the right to vote if and only if the Bill of Rights is not abandoned. (R, B)

9. It is not the case that England is governed by Spain or Germany. (S, G)

10. Ben Franklin invented the television, George Washington was born in Turkey, and the president of the United States is a former heavyweight prizefighter. (F, W, P)

11. An object is a material object if and only if it occupies space and has mass. (O, S, M)

12. The lines are down, the electricity is out, and there is no heat, if reports from the police department are true. (L, E, H, R)

13. All things are either solid or not solid but not both. (S)

14. It is not the case that believers in God and believers in Krishna are both right about their beliefs. (G, K)

15. Most scientists are supporters of nuclear research only if it is not used for warfare and weaponry. (S, N, W)

16. If the human fetus is a person, then it has a right to life, and killing it is morally wrong. (P, R, K)

17. If I do get home before dark, then either I will have to leave early or I must drive over seventy miles per hour. (I, L, D)

18. If you are not a student at the college, then you are either an administrator, a staff member, or a faculty member. (S, A, M, F)

19. Hawks eat rabbits and mice, or if there is no live food, they will eat carrion. (R, M, L, C)

20. If this paper is made of wood pulp, then it is either oak or maple. (P, O, M)

21. Capital punishment neither deters crime nor protects citizens. (C, P)

22. If Max is a Marxist and Smith is a socialist, then Wilson is a Democrat. (M, S, W)

23. Unless the mandatory industrial smokestack regulations are enforced and the exhaust emission control devices are legally required on all automobiles, the decrease of dangerous hydrocarbons in the atmosphere will not be evident within the next five to seven years. (M, E, D)

24. For the first time in four years the *Contras* will be strong enough to pose a serious threat to the Sandinista government of Nicaragua only if their numbers continue to swell, they receive support from the campesinos, and the $27 million allocated by the U.S. Congress is used for equipment. (C, N, R, E)

25. If a partner in a limited partnership invests $10,000, or 10 percent of the partnership's total investment, and the venture loses $700,000, the partner will be able to write off $70,000 but will be liable for only $10,000. (P, T, V, W, L)

Exercise 5.8D   Interpreting Symbolic Statements   Using the interpretations of the symbols given below, translate the following symbolic statements into ordinary language.

S = It snows.
R = It rains.
P = There is precipitation.
T = The temperature is above freezing.
C = Classes must be canceled.
M = Maintenance crews are salting the roads.

1. $S \lor R$
2. $P \supset (S \lor R)$
3. $(T + P) \supset R$
4. $(-T + P) \supset (-R + S)$
5. $(R + -T) \supset M$
6. $-T \supset [S \supset (-M \supset C)]$
7. $M \lor (T \supset C)$
8. $S \equiv (P + -T)$

Review Questions

1. Define 'truth-function'.
2. Define 'simple statement' and 'compound statement'.
3. What are the logical operators?
4. Under what conditions is the conjunction true?
5. Under what conditions is the disjunction true?

6. Under what conditions is the conditional true?

7. Under what conditions is the biconditional true?

8. What is the difference in meaning between $-(p + q)$ and $-p + -q$?

9. What is the difference in meaning between $-p \supset q$ and $-(p \supset q)$?

10. What are the different ways of expressing the 'if . . . then' in our language?

11. When you are determining the truth-values of a compound statement using a truth table, in what order do you determine the following: (a) Ts and Fs for compounds inside parentheses; (b) Ts and Fs for negated simple statements; (c) Ts and Fs for negated compounds; (d) Ts and Fs for operators outside the parentheses?

12. What is the purpose of constructing a truth table with a precise number of rows and a systematic procedure for filling in Ts and Fs?

True or False?

1. The statement 'If the president dies in office, then the first lady becomes president' is false if the president does not die in office.

2. Simple statements are symbolized by capital letters.

3. The scope of an operator may be bound by parentheses and brackets.

4. Supposing a compound to be false, by using a truth table you can determine the truth-values of the component parts responsible for its falsity.

5. If some statement p is a necessary condition for a statement q, then it follows that q implies p.

6. The statement 'It shines unless it's cloudy' is logically different from the statement 'It shines or else it's cloudy'.

7. The logical operator 'or' is interpreted in truth-functional logic as the inclusive 'or'.

8. If p is a necessary and sufficient condition of q, then p is true if and only if q is true.

9. A conjunction is false only on the condition that all its parts are false.

10. The exclusive 'or' is symbolized as $(p \vee q) + -(p + q)$.

Discussion Questions

1. As presented, truth-functional logic employs 5 operators. Do you suppose it would be possible to do with fewer, say, 4 or even 3 operators? Could you, in other words, express certain operations by means of others? What do you think?

2. The conditional is true even if the antecedent is false. Why is that? Make up some examples to illustrate your explanation for this element of the truth-function of the conditional.

3. Make up or find some examples of ambiguous statements that can be clarified by the use of truth-functional symbolization.

CHAPTER SIX
Truth-Functional Logic
Part II

In this chapter we learn the truth table method for
determining validity, the method of the indirect
truth table for determining validity, and the
use of truth tables to identify tautologies, self-
contradictions, and equivalences.

As we saw in the previous chapter, the truth table gives us a completely mechanical and systematic way of displaying the truth-values of statements. There are, however,
far more important uses of the truth table. In this chapter we use truth tables to evaluate deductive arguments for validity, to identify the logical types of statements, and to
ascertain logical relations between two statements. By using truth tables, in other words,
we can demonstrate that an argument is or is not valid, that a statement is a contingent
statement, tautology, or self-contradiction, and that two or more statements are contradictories, equivalences, or in neither relation. We also learn how to use a shortcut version of the truth table called the indirect truth table.

6.1 Truth Tables for Evaluating Arguments

The truth table method for evaluating arguments consists of three steps:

Step 1 Translate the statements of the argument into symbolic form.

Step 2 Construct a truth table for the whole argument.

Step 3 Look for a row in which the truth-values of the premises are T and the truth-value of the conclusion is F. If there is such a row, the argument is invalid. If there is not such a row, the argument is valid.

The theory behind this method is easy to understand. First, as you recall, a deductive argument is valid if and only if, on the assumption that the premises are true, it must also be the case that the conclusion is true. Second, as we have seen, the truth table displays all possible truth-values of a statement. Applied to an argument, a truth table can show us when the premises are true or false and when the conclusion is true or false. Each row of the truth table shows a possible assignment of truth-values for the premises and conclusion. If in any one row the premises are all true and the conclusion is false, then we know the possibility exists that the premises are true and the conclusion false; hence, we know that the argument is *not* valid. Let's use the following invalid argument to examine the truth table method:

Example 1

If it rains, then my car is wet. But it does not rain.
Therefore, my car is not wet.

Step 1 Translate the argument into symbolic form:

If it rains, then my car is wet.	R ⊃ W
It does not rain.	−R
Therefore, my car is not wet.	∴ −W

The three dots '∴' introducing the conclusion is a symbol for '*therefore*'. From now on we will use this symbol to signal the conclusion of an argument.

Step 2 Construct a truth table for the whole argument. Writing a truth table for an argument is virtually the same as writing a truth table for a compound statement. Arrange the premises and conclusion on one line, as though it were one compound statement, and then follow the steps outlined in the previous chapter for assigning truth-values. Remember always to assign the same values to each occurrence of a simple statement even though it appears in different compounds.

In the example below, the symbolized argument is written on one line with the three dots separating the premises from the conclusion. The initial Ts and Fs are written following the rule of alternating and then doubling for each different simple statement. Again, each occurrence of the same simple statement receives the same values. Next, the truth-values for the operators are entered, and the truth-values for each compound are entered. When you are finished, you should have for each statement in the argument a column representing its truth-values.

R ⊃ W				- R		∴ - W	
T	**T**	T		**F**	T	**F**	T
F	**(T)**	T		**(T)**	F	**(F)**	T	← Premises T, conclusion F
T	**F**	F		**F**	T	**T**	F
F	**T**	F		**T**	F	**T**	F

Boxed columns show the truth-values of the premises and the conclusion, and the circled Ts and F show that the argument is invalid.

Step 3 Look for a row in which the premises are all T and the conclusion is F. If there is such a row, the argument is invalid. If not, it is valid. The second row of the table has a T for each premise and an F for the conclusion. It is helpful to circle the values of such a row, for it shows that there is a case in which the premises are true yet the conclusion is false. When the truth table shows us the possibility of true premises and a false conclusion, as in our example, the argument is *invalid*. The presence of even one row with true premises and a false conclusion is enough to show that the whole argument is invalid.

Here is another example:

Example 2

If it rains, then my car is wet.	R ⊃ W
My car is not wet.	-W
Therefore, it does not rain.	∴ -R

The truth table is as follows:

R ⊃ W				- W		∴ - R	
T	**T**	T		**F**	T	**F**	T
F	**T**	T		**F**	T	**T**	F
T	**F**	F		**T**	F	**F**	T
F	**T**	F		**T**	F	**T**	F

Look across each row and you will see that there is *no* row in which the premises are T and the conclusion F. The fact that in no case are the premises true and the conclusion false means that it is not possible for the premises to be true yet the conclusion false. Therefore, the argument is proven to be valid.

Consider another example:

Example 3

You have to return the money unless it was not a loan.
If it was a gift, then it was not a loan. Therefore, if you
don't have to return the money, it was a gift.

You have to return the money or it was not a loan.	R ∨ −L
If it was a gift, then it was not a loan.	G ⊃ −L
Therefore, if you don't have to return the money, it was a gift.	∴ −R ⊃ G

```
R  v  −  L      G  ⊃  −  L    ∴ −  R  ⊃  G

T [T] F  T      T [F] F        F  [T] T
F [F] F  T      T [F] F        T  [T] T
T [T] T  F      T [T] T        F  [T] T
F [T] T  F      T [T] T        T  [T] T
T [T] F  T      F [T] F        F  [T] F
F [F] F  T      F [T] F        T  [F] F
T [T] T  F      F [T] T        F  [T] F
F (T) T  F      F (T) T        T  (F) F   ←
```

The table shows that in the very last row the premises are T but the conclusion is F. Therefore, the argument is invalid.

Exercise 6.1 The Truth Table Method Use truth tables to evaluate the following arguments for validity. Circle the truth-values of the row that shows an argument invalid.

1. If people know what is right, they will do it. But people do not know what is right; therefore, they do not do it. (K, D)

2. God cannot be both loving and jealous. He is loving; therefore, he is not jealous. (L, J)

3. God cannot be both good and evil. He is not evil; therefore, he is good. (G, E)

4. Citizens of the United States have the right to vote if and only if the United States is not a monarchy. It is not a monarchy; therefore, citizens of the United States do have the right to vote. (R, M)

5. If the acid crystallizes, then either the solution was too weak or we made a mistake. We did not make a mistake. Therefore, if it crystallizes, then the solution was too weak. (C, S, M)

6. Ted cannot be both a tenor and an alto. He must be an alto, since he is not a tenor. (T, A)

7. If Sweden is in North Africa, then either Egyptians are blue-eyed or Swedes are dark and handsome. Sweden is not in North Africa; therefore, Egyptians are not blue-eyed. (S, E, D, H)

8. Neither the French nor the Belgians want to leave the Sudan. If the French do not want to leave the Sudan, then the Namibians will elect a new president. Therefore, the Namibians will elect a new president. (F, B, N)

9. The programmers will strike if management reduces their benefits. If the programmers strike, then services will suffer. But the programmers will not strike; thus, management will not reduce benefits, and services will not suffer. (P, M, S)

10. If there were no ownership or private property, then there would be no such thing as theft. Therefore, there is ownership and private property, or there is no theft. (O, P, T)

11. "No thing can be moved if there is a void." (Aristotle) It is not the case that no thing can be moved. Therefore, there is no void. (M, V)

12. The whole numbers are either odd or even. If they are even, then they are not odd. Therefore, if they are odd, then they are not even. (O, E)

13. If he loves her, he will marry her. So, if he does not love her, he will not marry her. (L, M)

14. George is tired or Fred is happy. George is not tired. Therefore, Fred is happy. (G, F)

15. If the moon can be settled, then Mars can be settled. If Mars can be settled, then Jupiter can too. Therefore, if the moon can be settled, then Jupiter can be settled. (S, M, J)

16. The facts that Wynton Marsalis plays classical and jazz trumpet imply that he is a better musician than Miles Davis. But Davis writes his own music, and if that is so, then Marsalis is not a better musician. Therefore, Marsalis is not a better musician. (C, J, B, D)

17. If Peewee Herman starred in *The Breakfast Club,* then I'm a cross-eyed polecat. Well, I'm not a cross-eyed polecat, so . . . you figure it out. (P, C)

18. "God is in me or is not at all." (Wallace Stevens) Since it is false that he is not, it follows that he is in me. (G, H)

19. "If a man has a talent and cannot use it, he has failed. If he has a talent and learns somehow to use the whole of it, he has gloriously succeeded and won a satisfaction and a triumph few men ever know." (Thomas Wolfe) He has not won a triumph few men ever know. Therefore, either he does not have a talent or he has not learned to use the whole of it. (T, U, F, L, G, W, K)

20. Unless we are to be the last generation of humans on the face of this earth, we must put an end to war. Thus, "mankind must put an end to war, or war will put an end to mankind." (John F. Kennedy) (L, M, W)

21. $-(A \lor B) \supset D$ $C + -D$ $\therefore A \lor B$

22. $L \supset (N + M)$ $-M \lor -L$ $\therefore -N$

23. $-(P + Q)$ P $\therefore -Q$

24. $S \equiv (S + R)$ $\therefore -S \lor R$

25. $T \supset W$ $-W$ $\therefore -T$

6.2 Indirect Truth Tables

Although the truth table method for determining validity is foolproof if followed correctly, it can be tedious and cumbersome, particularly for arguments with several simple statements. There is, however, a shortcut version, called the *indirect truth table method*. Rather than listing all possible assignments of truth-values, the indirect method shows quickly whether that crucial row in fact exists in which the premises are true and the conclusion false. We begin by hypothesizing (that is, assuming for the sake of argument) that there *is* such a crucial row in which the premises are T and the conclusion is F. *We assume, in effect, that the argument is invalid. We then attempt to apply that assumption consistently by completing truth-values for the simple statements.* If truth-values can be consistently assigned to all simple statements, then our hypothesis was correct: There is at least one case in which the premises are true and the conclusion false. The argument is therefore *invalid*. If, on the other hand, a consistent assignment of truth-values cannot be made, then the argument cannot have true premises and a false conclusion. Therefore, it is valid. Let us see how this works with an example.

Example 4

If it rains, then my car is wet.	$R \supset W$
It does not rain.	$-R$
Therefore, my car is not wet.	$\therefore -W$

Step 1 Assign the value F to the conclusion and T to each premise. That represents our assumption that the argument is invalid, which we will try to prove.

$$
\begin{array}{ccc}
\text{T} & \text{T} & \text{F} \\
R \supset W & -R & \therefore -W
\end{array}
$$

Step 2 Try to complete the assignment of values to simple statements. Notice what values you have to begin with: the compound $R \supset W$ is T, the compound $-R$ is T, and the compound $-W$ is F. Can you infer from those truth-values what the values of any simple statements are? Since $-W$ is F, it follows that W must be T. And since $-R$ is T, it follows that R must be F. So we can make the following assignments:

$$
\begin{array}{ccc}
\text{T} & \text{T} & \text{F} \\
R \supset W & -R & \therefore -W \\
| \quad | & | & | \\
\text{F} \quad \text{T} & \text{F} & \text{T}
\end{array}
$$

As you can see, there is no problem in assigning values to the statements. The method shows that there *is* a row in which the premises are all Ts yet the conclusion is F. Thus, this argument is shown to be *invalid*.

Consider this example:

Example 5

Hot air rises and cold air falls.	H + C
If hot air rises, then the ground will be cooler than the ceiling.	H ⊃ G
Thus, the ground is cooler than the ceiling.	∴ G

First, assign F to the conclusion and Ts to the premises.

$$
\begin{array}{ccc}
\text{T} & \text{T} & \text{F} \\
\text{H + C} & \text{H} \supset \text{G} & \therefore \text{G}
\end{array}
$$

Try to complete the assignment of truth-values. G is false, so we can place an F under the G in H ⊃ G. The conjunction H + C is true, so each of its simple statements must be true, allowing us to place Ts under H and C. The H in H ⊃ G must therefore also be T. But now a problem arises:

$$
\begin{array}{ccc}
\text{T} & \text{(T)} & \text{F} \\
\text{H + C} & \text{H} \supset \text{G} & \therefore \text{G} \\
| \quad | & | \quad | & | \\
\text{T} \quad \text{T} & \text{T} \quad \text{F} & \text{F} \\
& \text{(F)} &
\end{array}
$$

Notice that we have an inconsistency. According to our hypothesis, H ⊃ G is supposed to be T. But if H is T and G is F, then H ⊃ G must be F, which is *inconsistent with the hypothesis.* If we change H to F, then the conjunction H + C becomes F. We find that we cannot make a consistent assignment of values to this argument on the assumption that it is *not* valid. Since the hypothesis that the argument is invalid fails, it must be that the argument is *valid.*

Not all arguments are as easily evaluated as these examples. In some cases the indirect truth table requires several attempts at assigning values. The first assignment of Ts to premises and F to the conclusion may not give you much to go on. You have to try different possible assignments. Here is an example:

Example 6

$$
\begin{array}{ccc}
\text{T} & \text{T} & \text{F} \\
\text{P} \lor \text{Q} & \text{P} \supset \text{Q} & \therefore \text{P + Q}
\end{array}
$$

How should you begin? There is no initial assignment of truth-values to simple statements that must be made on the hypothesis that the argument is invalid. That P ∨ Q is T does not indicate what truth-values P and Q have; neither does P ⊃ Q. And that P + Q is F does not indicate what values P and Q have. Looking at the conclusion, we can see three possibilities that would account for a false conclusion: both P and Q are F, one is F and the other T, and vice versa. We may have to consider several possible sets of assignments to determine whether this argument can have true premises and a false conclusion, as we are assuming. Therefore, where we begin is arbitrary. Let's start with the conclusion and suppose that both P and Q are F for our first trial. We will then make the following assignments:

Trial 1

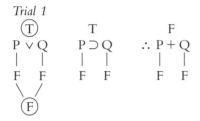

On the first trial—assigning F to P and Q in the conclusion—we see that an inconsistency results in the first premise. However, we cannot conclude that the argument is valid because we were not forced to that assignment. That is, we cannot say yet that *no consistent assignment of values is possible* for this argument on the assumption that it is invalid. We must, therefore, make other attempts. Let's try assigning T to P and F to Q in the conclusion:

Trial 2

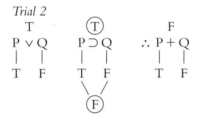

In trial 2 we encounter an inconsistency in the second premise. Again, we cannot yet conclude that no consistent assignment is possible. We must consider the last possibility, assigning F to P and T to Q in the conclusion:

Trial 3
```
    T           T            F
  P ∨ Q       P ⊃ Q      ∴ P + Q
  |   |       |   |         |   |
  F   T       F   T         F   T
```

In this assignment no inconsistency is encountered. Therefore, this third trial shows that a consistent assignment of truth-values is possible on the hypothesis that the argument is invalid. After three attempts we have shown that the argument is *invalid*.

Example 6 illustrates the important point that the purpose of the indirect truth table method is to determine whether a consistent set of truth-values can be assigned to the simple statements on the assumption that the argument has true premises and a false conclusion. The fact that a trial assignment results in an inconsistency does not show that the argument is valid. Our aim is to show whether a consistent set is possible. The key question to ask in using the indirect truth table method is expressed in the following definition:

> **indirect truth table method**   *Is there a consistent assignment of truth-values on the assumption that the premises are all true and the conclusion false?*

As the preceding examples illustrate, a consistent assignment may occur on the initial assigning of values. However, the method may require two or more trial assignments before either a consistent assignment has been reached or all possible assignments have been exhausted.

Exercise 6.2   Indirect Truth Table Method   Use the indirect truth table method to determine whether the following arguments are valid. Circle the inconsistency you find for those arguments that are shown to be valid.

1. Winters are cold and summers are hot. Therefore, summers are hot or the moon is made of green cheese. (W, S, M)

2. Russell was either a realist or an empiricist. If he was a realist, then he was not an idealist. Therefore, Russell was not an empiricist. (R, E, I)

3. If there is a God, then he is good. If we disappear into nothingness at death, then death is not good. If God is good and God creates death, then death is good. Therefore, if we disappear into nothingness at death, there is no God. (G, H, N, D, C)

4. If he loves her, he will marry her. Therefore, if he does not love her, he will not marry her. (L, M)

5. If the moon can be settled, then Mars can be settled. If Mars can be settled, then Jupiter can be settled too. Thus, if the moon can be settled, then Jupiter can be settled. (S, M, J)

6. If the acid crystallizes, then either the solution was too weak or we made a mistake. We did not make a mistake; therefore, if the acid crystallizes, the solution was too weak. (A, W, M)

7. "If a man has a talent and cannot use it, he has failed. If he has a talent and learns somehow to use the whole of it, he has gloriously succeeded and won a satisfaction and a triumph few men ever know." (Thomas Wolfe) He has not won a triumph few men ever know; therefore, either he does not have a talent or he has not learned to use the whole of it. (T, U, F, L, G, W, K)

8. The fact that animals are less intelligent than we does not imply that we may disregard their welfare. If we disregard their welfare, then we are inhumane and

no better than animals ourselves. Therefore, if we disregard their welfare, then it is not the case that animals are less intelligent than we. (A, D, I, B)

9. This argument is invalid if and only if it can have true premises and a false conclusion. This argument has a false conclusion; therefore, it is invalid. (I, T, F)

10. If people earn different amounts and everyone pays the same amount in taxes, then those who earn more keep more and those who earn less keep less. If those who earn more keep more and those who earn less keep less, then the tax laws are unfair. Therefore, either people do not earn different amounts or if everyone pays the same amount in taxes, then the tax laws are unfair. (P, E, M, L, T)

11. T ∨ O   T ⊃ O   ∴ O ⊃ −T

12. A ∨ B   B ⊃ C   ∴ −(A + C)

13. M + N   −M ∨ L   −P ⊃ −L   ∴ P + N

14. −(K + L)   R ⊃ (S + L)   R   ∴ −K

15. P ⊃ Q   Q ⊃ (S ∨ F)   −S + −F   ∴ −P

16. A ≡ T   −A ∨ −M   M   ∴ T

17. (E + F) + L   (F ∨ G) + −(F + G)   ∴ −G

18. J ⊃ V   H ⊃ J   M ⊃ H   ∴ M ⊃ V

19. −(I + O) ∨ T   ∴ I ⊃ T

20. D + [T ≡ (M ∨ R)]   −T   ∴ −M + −R

6.3 Statements and Relations

Besides evaluating arguments, truth tables can be used to identify types of statements and types of relations between statements. The types of statements are tautologies, self-contradictions, and contingent statements, and the types of relations are equivalences and contradictions.

Types of Statements: Tautologies, Self-Contradictions, and Contingencies

A tautology is a statement whose truth-value must be true, a self-contradiction is a statement whose truth-value must be false, and a contingent statement is one whose truth-value may be either true or false. In truth-functional logic these concepts of logical types of statements are given truth-functional definitions as follows:

tautology   *A compound statement whose truth-values all are Ts.*

self-contradiction   *A compound statement whose truth-values all are Fs.*

contingent statement   *A statement whose truth-values include at least one T and at least one F.*

A tautology is a statement whose truth-values are always T and cannot be F; it is a *necessary truth*. By using a truth table, we can easily demonstrate that a statement is a tautology, for the table will show that its truth-values are Ts only. Consider this example:

Example 7

The snake is cold-blooded, or the snake is not cold-blooded.

```
S   v  -S
---------
T  |T|  F
F  |T|  T
```

Here is another example:

Example 8

It is not the case that something is solid and not solid.

```
-  (S  +  -S)
-------------
|T|  T   F  F
|T|  F   F  T
```

You may recognize these types of statements as examples of the laws of excluded middle and contradiction, respectively. Any statement of either of those forms is a tautology.

A self-contradiction is a statement whose truth-values are always F and cannot be T; it is a *necessary falsehood*. The truth table shows that these statements have only F for their values:

Example 9

It is not the case that everything is heavy or not heavy.

```
-  (H  v  -H)
-------------
|F|  T   T  F
|F|  F   T  T
```

Here is another example:

Example 10

```
P  +  -  (Q  ⊃  P)
------------------
T |F|  F   T  T  T
F |F|  T   T  F  F
T |F|  F   F  T  T
F |F|  F   F  T  F
```

Contingent statements are those whose truth-values may be T or F; a truth table shows whether a statement is contingent, as in this example:

Example 11

If the paintings arrive, then we will not leave.

P	⊃	–	W
T	F	F	T
F	T	F	T
T	T	T	F
F	T	F	F

Since there is at least one T and at least one F in the column for this statement, it is shown to be contingent.

Types of Relations: Equivalences and Contradictories

There are two important relationships among statements: Statements may be equivalent or contradictory.

equivalences   *Two or more statements are logically equivalent if and only if for every assignment of truth-values to their components their truth-values are exactly the same.*

contradictories   *Two statements are contradictories if and only if for every assignment of truth-values to their components their truth-values are exactly the opposite.*

Equivalence occurs when two or more statements have exactly the same truth-values for every assignment of truth-values to their components. Their values may be true or false, but they are true or false under exactly the same conditions. The truth table shows this clearly:

Example 12

P	⊃	Q		–	P	v	Q
T	T	T		F	T	T	T
F	T	T		T	F	T	T
T	F	F		F	T	F	F
F	T	F		T	F	T	F

Notice that each occurrence of the same simple statement is given the same initial assignment of values, just as was done earlier when we displayed the truth-values of compounds. The table reveals that the two statements above are logically equivalent and are therefore interchangeable. As we see in the next chapter, Example 12 is a very useful equivalence. It is called *material implication,* and it allows us to change a conditional statement into a disjunction, and vice versa. To do so, we simply follow the pattern exhibited in the equivalence above: The antecedent is negated, the '⊃' changes to the 'v', and the consequent stays the same. Below are examples of this equivalence:

$$(P \supset Q) \lor S \quad \equiv \quad (-P \lor Q) \lor S$$
$$-P \supset Q \quad \equiv \quad --P \lor Q$$
$$(P + Q) \supset R \quad \equiv \quad -(P + Q) \lor R$$

The following two equivalences are also very useful. They are called *DeMorgan's rule:*

$$-(P + Q) \quad \equiv \quad -P \lor -Q$$
$$-(P \lor Q) \quad \equiv \quad -P + -Q$$

Among other things, these two equivalences allow us to eliminate parentheses and change disjunctions to conjunctions, and vice versa. Another important equivalence that we have already used is the *rule of double negation:*

$$--P \quad \equiv \quad P$$

This rule tells us that any statement is logically equivalent to the negation of its negation.

Contradictories are statements whose truth-values are exactly opposite for every assignment of truth-values. When one is T, the other is F. Here are some examples:

Example 13

P	⊃	Q		P	+	−Q
T	T	T		T	F	F
F	T	T		F	F	F
T	F	F		T	T	T
F	T	F		F	F	T

Example 14

P	+	Q		−	P	v	−Q
T	T	T		F		F	F
F	F	T		T		T	F
T	F	F		F		T	T
F	F	F		T		T	T

Exercise 6.3A Tautologies, Self-Contradictions, and Contingencies
Use truth tables to determine what type of statement each compound listed below is.

1. P ⊃ (P v Q)   2. (P ⊃ Q) + (−P v Q)
3. −P + (P + Q)   4. P ⊃ (P v −P)

5. $(P \supset -Q) \equiv (P + Q)$ 6. $P + -(-Q \vee P)$

7. $(P \vee Q) \vee -Q$ 8. $-(Q + -P) \equiv (Q \supset P)$

Exercise 6.3B   Equivalences and Contradictories   Use truth tables to determine whether the following pairs of statements are equivalences, contradictories, or neither.

1. $P \supset Q$ $-(P + -Q)$

2. $-P \vee -Q$ $P \supset -Q$

3. $-(P + -Q) \vee S$ $(-P \vee Q) \vee S$

4. $P + Q$ $Q + P$

5. $P \equiv Q$ $(P \supset Q) + (Q \supset P)$

6. $P + -Q$ $-Q \supset -P$

7. $-(P + Q)$ $-P \vee -Q$

8. $-(P \vee Q)$ $-P + -Q$

9. $-P \supset Q$ $P \vee Q$

10. $(P \supset Q) \vee -(-R \supset S)$ $(-P \vee Q) \vee (R \vee S)$

11. $P \supset Q$ $Q \supset P$

12. $P \supset Q$ $-Q \supset -P$

Summary

In this and the previous chapter, we have studied the fundamentals of truth-functional logic. First, we distinguished between simple and compound statements, and then we examined five common logical operators by which compound statements are formed from simple statements. We learned how sentences from ordinary language may be translated or symbolized using the standard truth-functional symbols. We used the truth table method for displaying the truth-values of compound statements and, by extension, for determining the validity of arguments. We also learned how to use the shortcut version of the truth table called the indirect truth table method. Finally, the logical types of statements and the logical relations between statements were demonstrated using the truth table method.

You now have a basic understanding of another important logical system besides categorical logic. It would be valuable at this point if you chose some arguments from previous chapters and evaluated them using the techniques of both categorical and truth-functional logic.

Review Questions

1. When you use the truth table method to determine validity, what exactly do you look for?

2. Describe the theory behind the indirect truth table method for evaluating arguments.

3. If you are using the indirect truth table method and you have an argument that, according to a trial assignment, cannot be given a consistent set of truth-values, is that argument shown valid or invalid?

4. Suppose you are using the truth table method and in one row there are all Ts. Is that argument valid or invalid?

5. Define the following terms:

   a. tautology   b. contradictory
   c. contingent statement   d. self-contradiction
   e. equivalence

6. How do you identify the concepts in question 5 with the aid of truth tables? What do you look for in the table?

7. Do all tautologies have the same truth-value?

8. Describe what the following equivalences enable you to do:

   a. material implication   b. DeMorgan's rule
   c. the rule of double negation

True or False?

1. An argument is shown to be invalid if there is a row in its truth table in which the values for the premises are F.

2. A statement and the negation of its contradictory are logically equivalent.

3. If two statements are logically equivalent, then either may be used in the place of the other.

4. One must choose carefully whether to use the truth table method or the indirect truth table because they do not give the same results.

5. If a statement is not a tautology, then it is a self-contradiction.

Discussion Questions

1. Do you believe a computer could be programmed to evaluate arguments using the full truth table method? Could a computer be programmed to use the indirect truth table method? What difficulties, if any, can you imagine computer programmers might have with such tasks? For instance, if you would agree that the indirect truth table method is less mechanical than the full-blown truth table method and requires more thinking, then would that present special difficulties for a computer?

2. Truth-functional logic provides a rule-governed and objective method for evaluating arguments. Consider some controversial issue, such as whether capital punishment is morally permissible. Find two arguments for each side of that debate. Symbolize the arguments and evaluate them for deductive validity according to the rules of truth-functional logic. Having done so, where is the issue left? What does truth-functional logic show you?

3. For those of you who have studied categorical logic as well, how does truth-functional logic compare? Which theory do you prefer and why? Which is easier for you and why?

CHAPTER SEVEN
Formal Deduction

This chapter introduces the principles of formal deduction and explains how validly to deduce the conclusion of an argument from its premises. Several valid argument forms, the rules of inference, and the equivalences are also presented.

7.1 Introduction

The advantage of truth tables is that they are almost completely mechanical and require very little creative thinking. The disadvantage of truth tables is that they are impractical and cumbersome for arguments involving several simple statements. The indirect truth table is more efficient for longer arguments, but several trials may be required before an argument can be shown to be valid. Furthermore, neither method explicitly shows the steps in reasoning. The method of formal deduction has distinct advantages over the truth table methods, particularly for longer arguments or those involving several premises. Furthermore, each step of reasoning leading from premises to conclusion is explicitly written out in deduction and can be examined.

Formal deduction is a procedure for validly deriving a conclusion from given premises according to certain valid argument forms called the *rules of inference* and the *equivalences*. A deduction consists of a sequence of statements, each written on a separate line.

Each line contains a statement that is either a premise of the argument or a valid deduction from the lines above it, deduced by the rules of inference and the equivalences. The deduction of the argument is complete when its conclusion is shown to be validly deducible from the premises by a sequence of steps, each one of which is an intermediate, validly deducible conclusion.

The key to constructing formal deductions lies in learning how to use the rules by which deductions are made. In this account of formal deduction, we learn eighteen rules of deduction: eight rules of inference and ten equivalences (sometimes called *rules of replacement*). These represent two families of rules whose differences will become clear later. Each rule represents a valid argument form whose validity can be demonstrated by the truth table method. In our discussion the symbols *p, q, r,* and *s* are used to stand for *any* statement, either simple or compound. Thus, in studying the formulas for each rule, keep in mind that *the symbols p, q, and so on, may be instantiated by simple or compound statements*. The abbreviation for each rule is shown in parentheses.

7.2 The Rules of Inference: Group I

Let us begin by examining a group of some of the simpler rules of inference, namely, simplification (Simp), *modus ponens* (MP), *modus tollens* (MT), and disjunctive syllogism (DS).

1. Simplification (Simp)

$$p + q \qquad\qquad or \qquad p + q$$
$$\overline{\therefore p} \qquad\qquad\qquad\qquad \overline{\therefore q}$$

According to simplification, if you are given a conjunction as a premise, then either one of the conjuncts is validly deducible. That is, if you have $p + q$ as a premise, then p follows as a valid deduction. Similarly, from $p + q$ you can deduce q. Consider how this rule of inference is used to deduce the conclusion of the following simple argument:

Example 1

Hydrogen is a gas, and ammonia is a liquid.
Therefore, hydrogen is a gas.

First, the argument is represented in truth-functional symbols as follows:

$$H + A$$
$$\overline{\therefore H}$$

Next, the argument is written out with each premise on its own numbered line. Each premise is identified as such by the word 'premise' at the end of the line. The conclusion to be deduced is written on the same line as the last premise and is identified as the conclusion by a slash '/' separating it from the last premise and the three-dot symbol '∴' for 'therefore'. Thus, the argument as first written out shows each premise and the conclusion that is to be deduced.

1. H + A   premise   /   ∴ H

This format shows that we want to deduce H from the premise H + A. In this example the conclusion is deducible from the premise by the use of one rule, simplification. Since we have H + A as a premise and simplification provides that either conjunct follows, we can deduce H. The deduction is written as follows, listing the rule of inference and the number of the line used from above.

1. H + A   premise   /   ∴ H
2. H   1, Simp

Each line must include a justification: Either it is given as a premise or it is derivable from lines above according to a specified rule of inference or an equivalence.

The formulas for the rule of simplification state that any compound statement that is a conjunction may be simplified. Thus, Examples 2 and 3 are legitimate uses of simplification:

Example 2

1. (T ∨ B) + −S   premise
2. T ∨ B   1, Simp

Example 3

1. (M + Y) + H   premise
2. M + Y   1, Simp
3. M   2, Simp

Example 4 is not a legitimate use of simplification, because the statement deduced, T, is not a conjunct:

Example 4

1. (T ∨ B) + −S   premise
2. T

2. *Modus Ponens* (MP)

$p \supset q$

p

$\therefore q$

Modus ponens is a rule of inference that operates with a conditional as one of the premises: $p \supset q$ states that if you have p then you may conclude q. The second premise states that you do have p; therefore, q follows. Any argument with a conditional as one premise and the antecedent of the conditional as another premise is a candidate for the rule of *modus ponens*. All the arguments below conform to this valid argument form:

Example 5	*Example 6*	*Example 7*
A ⊃ B	−S ⊃ R	−T ⊃ −V
A	−S	−T
∴ B	∴ R	∴ −V

Example 8	*Example 9*
−(P + Q) ⊃ R	(P + Q) ⊃ (S + T)
−(P + Q)	(P + Q)
∴ R	∴ S + T

In each argument above you are given the antecedent of the conditional; therefore, the consequent follows. Consider the following example:

Example 10

If it rains, then my car is wet.	R ⊃ W
It rains.	R
Therefore, my car is wet.	∴ W

From the conditional R ⊃ W and the antecedent R as premises, according to *modus ponens,* W must follow. Consider the truth-functional meaning of the '⊃'. If, for example, R ⊃ W has the truth-value T and R has the truth-value T, then W must also have the truth-value T. Thus, the conclusion W is deducible from the premises by *modus ponens,* written as follows:

1. R ⊃ W   premise
2. R   premise   /   ∴ W
3. W   1, 2, MP

Notice that the last line of the deduction indicates the rule employed and the line numbers of the statements used in that step of the deduction.

3. Modus Tollens (MT)

$$p \supset q$$
$$\dfrac{\overline{}q}{}$$

$$\therefore {}^{-}p$$

Like *modus ponens, modus tollens* is a rule of inference that operates with a conditional as a premise. In this case, however, the second premise is a negation of the consequent. Given a premise of the form $p \supset q$, if you have the negation of the consequent, then the negation of the antecedent must follow. Again, consider the truth-functional meaning of the ' $\supset$ '. If the ' $\supset$ ' has the truth-value T and the consequent has the truth-value F, then the antecedent must have the truth-value F. Thus, the argument form *modus tollens* permits us to deduce the negation of the antecedent from a conditional and the negation of the consequent. Each of the following examples exhibits the *modus tollens* argument form:

Example 11	*Example 12*	*Example 13*
$-A \supset B$	$(P + Q) \supset S$	$-S \supset -R$
$-B$	$-S$	$--R$
$\therefore --A$	$\therefore -(P + Q)$	$\therefore --S$

In each example the premises are a conditional and the negation of the consequent, from which the negation of the antecedent can be validly deduced. Consider this example:

Example 14

If it rains, then my car is wet.	$R \supset W$
My car is not wet.	$-W$
Therefore, it does not rain.	$\therefore -R$

Here is how the deduction is written:

1. $R \supset W$ premise
2. $-W$ premise   / $\therefore -R$
3. $-R$ 1, 2, MT

Line 3 shows that $-R$ is deducible from lines 1 and 2 by *modus tollens*.

4. Disjunctive Syllogism (DS)

$p \lor q$		$p \lor q$
$-p$	or	$-q$
$\therefore q$		$\therefore p$

The disjunctive syllogism is a valid argument form in which the premises are a disjunction and the negation of one of the disjuncts. Since a disjunction is true if and only if at least one of its disjuncts is true, if one part is false, then the other part must be true. The following are examples of this argument form:

Example 15

$-p \lor -q$

$--p$

$\therefore -q$

Example 16

$(R + S) \lor T$

$-T$

$\therefore R + S$

Example 17

$(-N \supset L) \lor (A + B)$

$-(-N \supset L)$

$\therefore A + B$

Consider the following example:

Example 18

The Steelers win the championship, or the Cardinals go to the Super Bowl.	$S \lor C$
The Steelers do not win the championship.	$-S$
Therefore, the Cardinals go to the Super Bowl.	$\therefore C$

If you are given as premises $S \lor C$ and $-S$, it follows that C. Consider that the statement $S \lor C$ has the truth-value T and that the premise $-S$ also has the truth-value T. For a disjunction to have the truth-value T, at least one of its component parts must be T. Since we can deduce from the premise $-S$ that S has the truth-value F, then for $S \lor C$ to have the truth-value T, C must have the truth-value T. In short, C follows from the premises given.

Let us examine a deduction using more than one rule of inference. Here is a more complex argument:

Example 19

The Australians and the Belgians have made it to the finals of the World Soccer Cup. If the Australians have made it to the finals, then the Canadians did not win their game. Either the Canadians won their game or the Danes did not win theirs. Therefore, the Danes did not win their game.

First, we symbolize the argument by writing out each premise on a line with the conclusion indicated last.

1. A + B   premise
2. A ⊃ −C   premise
3. C ∨ −D   premise   /   ∴ −D
4. ?

How can −D be deduced from the premises? It helps to locate the symbol representing the conclusion (or the simple statements of the conclusion) in the lines given as premises. (The symbols for the conclusion do not all have to be located somewhere in the premises. As we will see, one rule of inference—the rule of addition—allows us to add a statement to a disjunction.) In the example we see that −D occurs in premise 3. How can we separate −D from that disjunction?

Notice that premise 3 gives us C ∨ −D. If we could deduce −C, then we could deduce that −D must be the true disjunct in premise 3. Notice that premise 2 tells us that if A is true, then −C is true. And we are given A in the conjunction of premise 1. Thus, it appears that we can deduce −C. Our first valid step is to deduce A from premise 1. Premise 1 gives us A + B. Since a conjunction is true if and only if both its parts are true, by the rule of simplification, A must be true.

4. A   1, Simp

Now, from A in line 4 and premise 2 A ⊃ −C, we can deduce −C. The conditional A ⊃ −C means that, if we have A, then we have −C; and we do have A from line 4. Therefore, we can write line 5 using the rule *modus ponens:*

5. −C   4, 2, MP

Thus far, we have deduced −C. Now we can deduce that C is false because we have deduced −C. Thus, given that C is false and that C ∨ −D is a premise, it follows that −D must be true. Thus, the conclusion −D can be deduced. The rule for the final step is disjunctive syllogism. The whole formal deduction can be written as follows:

1. A + B   premise
2. A ⊃ −C   premise
3. C ∨ −D   premise   /   ∴ −D
4. A   1, Simp
5. −C   4, 2, MP
6. −D   5, 3, DS

Each line of the deduction is either a premise or a valid deduction from the lines above it. On the right of each line is the justification for that line. The justification either indicates that the line is a premise or shows the numbers of the previous lines appealed to and the rule used to deduce the line. Since each intermediate step validly follows from the steps before it, the conclusion is validly deduced from the premises of the argument.

For practice using the rules of inference in group I, try working through the following examples. See if you can identify the rules used in the deductions by examining the lines listed before the blanks.

Example 20

1. M ∨ P   premise
2. −M   premise   /   ∴ P
3. P   1, 2, _____

Example 21

1. H + −T   premise
2. T ∨ (A + J)   premise   /   ∴ J
3. −T   1, _____
4. A + J   2, 3, _____
5. J   4, _____

In Example 20, line 3 is deduced from 1 and 2 by *disjunctive syllogism*. The premise M ∨ P is true if at least one disjunct is true. From premise 2 −M, we can deduce that M is false. Since M is false and M ∨ P is true, then P must be the true disjunct. Thus, P.

In Example 21, since H + −T is given as a premise, it follows that −T is deducible. Thus, line 3 is deduced from 1 by *simplification*. The premises T ∨ (A + J) and −T allow us to infer A + J by *disjunctive syllogism*. Finally, the conclusion J is deducible from A + J, again by the rule of *simplification*.

Now try the exercises.

Exercise 7.2A   The Validity of Rules of Inference, Group I   Use truth tables to demonstrate the validity of the following rules of inference.

1. Simplification: $p + q$ $p + q$
                          _____   _____
                          ∴ p ∴ q

2. *Modus ponens:* $p ⊃ q$
                          p
                          _____
                          ∴ q

3. *Modus tollens:* $p ⊃ q$
                          ^-q
                          _____
                          ∴ ^-p

4. Disjunctive syllogism:

$$p \lor q$$
$$\underline{\;\;\;\sim p\;\;\;}$$
$$\therefore q$$

$$p \lor q$$
$$\underline{\;\;\;\sim q\;\;\;}$$
$$\therefore p$$

Exercise 7.2B   Deductions with the Rules of Inference, Group I   Use the rules of inference from group I to deduce the conclusions of the following arguments. Use the translation cues provided.

1. France is a member of NATO, and Great Britain is a member of NATO. Therefore, Great Britain is a member of NATO. (F, G)

2. If France is a member of NATO, then Great Britain is a member of NATO. France is a member of NATO. Therefore, Great Britain is a member of NATO. (F, G)

3. Zaire is in central Africa, or Tanzania is in central Africa. Tanzania is not in central Africa. Therefore, Zaire is in central Africa. (Z, T)

4. Minnesota is north of Arkansas. If Minnesota is north of Arkansas, then Iowa is north of Arkansas. Therefore, Iowa is north of Arkansas. (M, I)

5. If the major industry of Alaska is salmon fishing, then most of the salmon sold in U.S. markets is from Alaska. But it is not true that most of the salmon sold in U.S. markets is from Alaska. Therefore, the major industry of Alaska is not salmon fishing. (A, S)

6. 1. A + T   premise
   2. T ⊃ P   premise   /   ∴ P

7. 1. G ⊃ P   premise
   2. S + −P   premise   /   ∴ −G

8. 1. T ∨ E   premise
   2. −T   premise   /   ∴ E

9. 1. K ∨ N   premise
   2. −K + O   premise   /   ∴ N

10. 1. D ⊃ I   premise
    2. D   premise   /   ∴ I

7.3 The Rules of Inference: Group II

The remaining four rules of inference we will study are hypothetical syllogism (HS), addition (Add), conjunction (Con), and constructive dilemma (CD).

5. Hypothetical Syllogism (HS)   The hypothetical syllogism is an argument consisting of two conditionals. The statement that is the consequent of one conditional occurs as the antecedent of the other conditional.

$$p \supset q$$
$$q \supset r$$
_____
$$\therefore\ p \supset r$$

Thus, if p implies q and q implies r, then p implies r. Any argument with that form is a valid argument. Consider the following example:

Example 22

| If Max passes physics, then Max majors in science. | $P \supset S$ |
| If Max majors in science, then Max gives up French. | $S \supset F$ |

Therefore, if Max passes physics, then Max gives up $\therefore\ P \supset F$
French.

1. $P \supset S$ premise
2. $S \supset F$ premise   / $\therefore\ P \supset F$
3. $P \supset F$ 1, 2, HS

Given $P \supset S$ and $S \supset F$, it follows that $P \supset F$ by the rule of hypothetical syllogism. A truth table shows that whenever the premises $P \supset S$ and $S \supset F$ have the truth-values T, the conclusion $P \supset F$ also has the truth-value T. Thus, the argument is a valid one.

6. Addition (Add)

$$p$$
_____
$$\therefore\ p \vee r$$

Given any statement (simple or compound), a disjunction can be validly deduced with that statement as one of the disjuncts. Thus, if p is assumed true, then $p \vee r$ is deducible, because a disjunction is true if and only if at least one of its parts is true. The following arguments are valid according to the rule of disjunctive syllogism:

Example 23

$-S + T$
_____
$\therefore\ (-S + T) \vee Q$

Example 24

$A \supset B$
_____
$\therefore\ (A \supset B) \vee (X \supset Y)$

In these examples the initial disjuncts are compounds, $-S + T$ and $A \supset B$, respectively; the rule of disjunctive syllogism permits forming disjunctions from simple or compound statements. However, a compound statement may not be broken apart in order to form a disjunction. Thus, it is not valid by the rule of addition to deduce a disjunction of this form:

Example 25	*Example 26*
$-S + T$	$A \supset B$
∴ $-S \vee Q$	∴ $B \vee (X \supset Y)$

The rule requires that the entire statement be used as the initial disjunct.

7. Conjunction (Con)

p

q
_____

∴ $p + q$

A conjunction, you recall, is true if and only if all its conjuncts are true. Thus, a conjunction may be validly formed from two or more true statements. According to the rule of inference called conjunction, if a statement p occurs by itself on a line (as a premise or as a deduction from lines above it) and a statement q occurs by itself on a line (as a premise or as a deduction from lines above it), then a conjunction may be deduced consisting of p and q. For example, consider how conjunction is employed in this deduction:

Example 27

1. $H \supset P$ premise
2. H premise   /   ∴ $H + P$
3. P 1, 2, MP
4. $H + P$ 2, 3, Con

Notice that line 3 P is derived from lines 1 and 2 by *modus ponens*. Thus, statements H and P both occur alone either as premises or as deductions from lines above, so the conjunction of $H + P$ can be obtained following the rule of conjunction.

8. Constructive Dilemma (CD)

$(p \supset q) + (r \supset s)$

$p \vee r$
_____

∴ $q \vee s$

Constructive dilemma is, in effect, a variation on the *modus ponens* argument. Notice that it involves a conjunction of two conditionals as one premise and a disjunction of the antecedents of each conditional as the other premise. From two such premises it is valid to infer the disjunction of the consequents of each conditional. Consider the following deduction:

Example 28

1. (S ⊃ G) + (C ⊃ D)	premise
2. S ∨ C	premise
3. −D	premise / ∴ G
4. G ∨ D	1, 2, CD
5. G	3, 4, DS

Line 4 G ∨ D is derived from 1 and 2 by *constructive dilemma*. Notice the characteristic pattern: 1 is a conjunction of two conditionals, and 2 is a disjunction consisting of the antecedents of the conditionals. Thus, the disjunction of the consequents is deducible. G is deduced from 3 and 4 by *disjunctive syllogism*.

In this section we have examined eight rules of inference: simplification (Simp), *modus ponens* (MP), *modus tollens* (MT), disjunctive syllogism (DS), hypothetical syllogism (HS), addition (Add), conjunction (Con), and constructive dilemma (CD).

Exercise 7.3A   The Validity of Rules of Inference, Group II   Construct truth tables to demonstrate that the following rules are valid argument forms.

1. Hypothetical syllogism:
$$p \supset q$$
$$q \supset r$$

$$\therefore p \supset r$$

2. Addition:
$$p$$

$$\therefore p \lor q$$

3. Conjunction:
$$p$$
$$q$$

$$\therefore p + q$$

4. Constructive dilemma:
$$(p \supset q) + (r \supset s)$$
$$p \lor r$$

$$\therefore q \lor s$$

Exercise 7.3B   Complete the Deductions   In the blank space write the rule of inference from either group I or group II by which the line has been deduced. The line numbers are provided as hints.

1. 1. A ∨ B   premise
   2. −B   premise   /   ∴ A
   3. A   1, 2, _____

2. 1. B ⊃ (C + P)   premise
   2. B   premise   /   ∴ C + P
   3. C + P   1, 2, _____

3. 1. − −S   premise
   2. R ⊃ −S   premise   /   ∴ −R
   3. −R   1, 2, _____

4. 1. (X + Y) ∨ (Z + X)   premise
   2. −(Z + X)   premise   /   ∴ X + Y
   3. X + Y   1, 2, _____

5. 1. A ⊃ S   premise
   2. A   premise   /   ∴ S
   3. S   1, 2, _____

6. 1. R + T   premise   /   ∴ R
   2. R   1, _____

7. 1. R + T   premise
   2. R ⊃ S   premise   /   ∴ S
   3. R   1, Simp
   4. S   2, 3, _____

8. 1. B ⊃ P   premise
   2. P ⊃ X   premise   /   ∴ B ⊃ X
   3. B ⊃ X   1, 2, _____

9. 1. −(A ⊃ P) ⊃ S   premise
   2. −S   premise   /   ∴ − −(A ⊃ P)
   3. − −(A ⊃ P)   1, 2, _____

10. 1. (D ∨ S) ⊃ (P + Q)   premise
    2. D ∨ S   premise   /   ∴ P + Q
    3. P + Q   1, 2, _____

11. 1. (P + Q) + R   premise   /   ∴ P
    2. P + Q   1, _____
    3. P   2, _____

12. 1. S   premise
    2. S ⊃ (R + P)   premise   /   ∴ R
    3. R + P   1, 2, _____
    4. R   3, _____
13. 1. C ∨ −D   premise
    2. −C   premise
    3. E ⊃ D   premise   /   ∴ −E
    4. −D   1, 2, _____
    5. −E   3, 4, _____
14. 1. S ∨ (P ⊃ T)   premise
    2. P   premise
    3. −S   premise   /   ∴ T
    4. P ⊃ T   1, 3, _____
    5. T   2, 4, _____
15. 1. L + (M ∨ A)   premise
    2. −A   premise   /   ∴ M
    3. M ∨ A   1, _____
    4. M   2, 3, _____
16. 1. T ⊃ Q   premise
    2. S ⊃ Y   premise
    3. T ∨ S   premise   /   ∴ Q ∨ Y
    4. (T ⊃ Q) + (S ⊃ Y)   1, 2, _____
    5. Q ∨ Y   4, 3, _____
17. 1. (N + A) ⊃ D   premise
    2. N   premise
    3. A   premise   /   ∴ D
    4. N + A   2, 3, _____
    5. D   4, 1, _____
18. 1. (H ⊃ S) + (F ⊃ W)   premise
    2. H   premise   /   ∴ S ∨ W
    3. H ∨ F   2, _____
    4. S ∨ W   3, 1, _____
19. 1. R ∨ D   premise
    2. R ⊃ S   premise
    3. −D   premise   /   ∴ S
    4. R   1, 3, _____
    5. S   2, 4, _____

20. 1. H + (G ⊃ T)   premise
    2. G   premise   / ∴ T
    3. G ⊃ T   1, _____
    4. T   2, 3, _____

Exercise 7.3C   Rules of Inference   Use the rules of inference from groups I and II to deduce the conclusions of the following arguments. Write the line numbers and the rules used.

1. 1. K ⊃ P   premise
   2. −P ∨ D   premise
   3. −D   premise   / ∴ −K
2. 1. S + (R ⊃ J)   premise
   2. J ⊃ T   premise   / ∴ R ⊃ T
3. 1. S ⊃ P   premise
   2. −P + −A   premise   / ∴ −S
4. 1. A ⊃ B   premise
   2. A + (T ∨ J)   premise   / ∴ B
5. 1. H + −T   premise
   2. T ∨ (A + J)   premise   / ∴ J
6. 1. −L ⊃ B   premise
   2. L ⊃ S   premise
   3. −S   premise   / ∴ B
7. 1. [(A ∨ B) + C] ⊃ (T ∨ A)   premise
   2. −(T ∨ A)   premise   / ∴ −[(A ∨ B) + C]
8. 1. − −R ⊃ (R + S)   premise
   2. S ⊃ (−R ∨ J)   premise
   3. − −R   premise   / ∴ J
9. 1. −L   premise
   2. −L ⊃ (T + A)   premise   / ∴ T
10. 1. C ⊃ [(P + J) ∨ R]   premise
    2. C + −R   premise   / ∴ J
11. 1. (R ∨ T) ⊃ (T ⊃ L)   premise
    2. (T ⊃ L) ⊃ S   premise   / ∴ (R ∨ T) ⊃ S
12. 1. P + − −Q   premise
    2. −Q ∨ (P ⊃ J)   premise   / ∴ J

13. 1. $(S + A) \vee (P + M)$ premise
    2. $(S + A) \supset R$ premise
    3. $-R$ premise   / $\therefore P + M$

14. 1. $Q \supset -R$ premise
    2. $T \supset Q$ premise
    3. T premise   / $\therefore -R$

15. 1. $(T \supset Q) + (S \supset P)$ premise
    2. T premise   / $\therefore Q \vee P$

16. 1. $L + (M \supset N)$ premise   / $\therefore L \vee R$

17. 1. T premise
    2. $(T + R) \supset S$ premise
    3. R premise   / $\therefore S$

18. 1. $A \vee --B$ premise
    2. $-A$ premise
    3. $S \supset -B$ premise   / $\therefore -S$

7.4 Equivalences

Besides the rules of inference, we also use ten equivalences in formal deductions. We know that if two statements are logically equivalent, we may validly infer one from the other. In effect, these equivalences allow us to replace a statement with its logical equivalent. They differ from the rules of inference in that, given any two equivalent statements, either one may be substituted for the other, and vice versa. They are "two-way" rules, whereas the rules of inference are "one-way" rules. So, for example, it is not legitimate to employ the rule of addition in "reverse" as follows:

$A \vee B$

$\therefore B$

Some of the ten equivalences are used frequently, others less so. We will examine the most commonly used equivalences and describe how they are employed in deductions. If you are ever in doubt about the correct use of an equivalence, simply construct a truth table to determine if the statements are indeed logically equivalent. Remember that two statements are equivalent if their truth-values are identical for every assignment of values. Abbreviations for the rules of equivalence are shown in parentheses.

9. Double Negation (DN)   We have encountered this rule before. According to double negation, a statement $- -p$ is logically equivalent to p, and vice versa. Thus, whenever double negatives occur, we may cancel them out or form a double negative from a statement. However, we must be careful to use this rule only in cases in which the double negatives apply to one and the same statement. The following statements, for example, are *not* candidates for the rule of double negation precisely because they do not exemplify the negation of a negation:

$$-(-A + B) \qquad -(P \supset -Q) \qquad -X + -Y \qquad -A \lor -(C + -D)$$

The following statements *are* candidates for double negation:

$$--A + B \qquad -(P \supset --Q) \qquad --X + --Y \qquad --A \lor --(C + -D)$$

Applying the rule of double negation, the statements above are logically equivalent to these:

$$A + B \qquad -(P \supset Q) \qquad X + Y \qquad A \lor (C + -D)$$

Here are two examples showing how double negation may be used in deductions. Example 29 illustrates the use of double negation together with the valid argument form *modus tollens*.

Example 29   Double negation with modus tollens

1. $P \supset -Q$	premise	
2. Q	premise	/ ∴ $-P$
3. $--Q$	2, DN	
4. $-P$	1, 3, MT	

Example 30 uses double negation together with disjunctive syllogism:

Example 30   Double negation with disjunctive syllogism

1. $-P \lor R$	premise	
2. P	premise	/ ∴ R
3. $--P$	2, DN	
4. R	1, 3, DS	

10. DeMorgan's Rule (DeM)   DeMorgan's rule allows us to switch a conjunction to a disjunction, or vice versa. The rule follows these forms:

first form $\qquad -(p + q) \equiv (-p \lor -q)$

second form $\qquad -(p \lor q) \equiv (-p + -q)$

The first form captures our intuition that the construction 'not both p and q' is equivalent to 'not p or not q'. The second form captures the notion that 'neither p nor q' is equivalent to 'not p and not q'.

To understand the use of DeMorgan's rule, notice the changes that are made in the first form:

$$-(p + q) \equiv (-p \vee -q)$$

First p is negated; then q is negated; then the '+' is changed to '∨'. The original negation in $-(p + q)$ is "driven inside" the compound and distributed among the disjuncts. Thus, a negation of a conjunction is changed to a disjunction.

> DeMorgan's rule (DeM)   p *is negated;* q *is negated;*
> + *changes to* ∨; *or* ∨ *changes to* +.

By using DeMorgan's rule together with double negation we can formulate other useful equivalences, such as these:

STATEMENT		DeMORGAN'S		DOUBLE NEGATION
$-(-p + -q)$	$\equiv$	$(--p \vee --q)$	$\equiv$	$(p \vee q)$
$-(-p + q)$	$\equiv$	$(--p \vee -q)$	$\equiv$	$(p \vee -q)$

Finally, notice in the example below how DeMorgan's rule may be used by first applying double negation.

STATEMENT		DOUBLE NEGATION		DeMORGAN'S
$(p + q)$	$\equiv$	$--(p + q)$	$\equiv$	$-(-p \vee -q)$

Now let's see how DeMorgan's rule can be used in deductions. First, consider an example using DeMorgan's together with double negation and disjunctive syllogism:

Example 31   DeMorgan's with double negation and disjunctive syllogism

1. $-(P + Q)$ premise
2. Q premise   / $\therefore -P$
3. $-P \vee -Q$ 1, DeM
4. $--Q$ 2, DN
5. $-P$ 4, DS

Now consider DeMorgan's used together with addition:

Example 32   DeMorgan's with addition

1. −P   premise   /   ∴ −(P + Q)
2. −P ∨ −Q   1, Add
3. −(P + Q)   2, DeM

11. Material Implication (Impl)   The rule of equivalence called material implication allows us to replace a conditional with a logically equivalent disjunction, and vice versa.

$$(p \supset q) \equiv (-p \vee q)$$

Notice the changes: the antecedent is negated, the '⊃' is changed to '∨', and the consequent remains the same.

> material implication (Impl)   *Antecedent is negated;*
> ⊃ *changes to* ∨; *consequent stays the same.*

This example illustrates the use of material implication with addition:

Example 33   Material implication with addition

1. P   premise   /   ∴ −P ⊃ Q
2. − −P   1, DN
3. − −P ∨ Q   2, Add
4. −P ⊃ Q   3, Impl

12. Material Equivalence (Equiv)   This equivalence changes the biconditional to a conjunction of two conditionals, or, used in reverse, it changes a conjunction of two conditionals to a biconditional.

$$(p \equiv q) \equiv [(p \supset q) + (q \supset p)]$$

Recall that the biconditional is an 'if . . . then' statement going in "both directions." Thus, changing a biconditional to a conjunction of two conditionals is simply forming an equivalent statement. Doing so allows us to simplify to that part of the biconditional that may be of some use to us in a deduction. Notice the use of material equivalence together with simplification in this example:

Example 34   Material equivalence with simplification

1. P ≡ Q   premise   /   ∴ Q ⊃ P
2. (P ⊃ Q) + (Q ⊃ P)   1, Equiv
3. Q ⊃ P   2, Simp

Consider now the use of material equivalence with implication and conjunction to form a biconditional:

Example 35   Material equivalence with implication and conjunction

1. $P \supset Q$ premise
2. $-Q \vee P$ premise   / $\therefore P \equiv Q$
3. $Q \supset P$ 2, Impl
4. $(P \supset Q) + (Q \supset P)$ 1, 3, Con
5. $P \equiv Q$ 4, Equiv

13. Distribution (Dist)   One final equivalence worth close examination is distribution. In its first form, distribution allows us to "distribute" a conjunct between two disjuncts. In its second form, it allows us to distribute a disjunct between two conjuncts.

first form $[p + (q \vee r)] \equiv [(p + q) \vee (p + r)]$
second form $[p \vee (q + r)] \equiv [(p \vee q) + (p \vee r)]$

Notice in the following example how distribution can be used with the disjunctive syllogism:

Example 36   Distribution with disjunctive syllogism

1. $P + (Q \vee R)$ premise
2. $-(P + R)$ premise   / $\therefore P + Q$
3. $(P + Q) \vee (P + R)$ 1, Dist
4. $P + Q$ 2, 3, DS

The remaining equivalences are listed below, and all the rules of inference and equivalences are shown in Tables 7.1 and 7.2.

14. Commutation (Com) $(p \vee q) \equiv (q \vee p)$
                               $(p + q) \equiv (q + p)$

15. Association (Assoc) $[p \vee (q \vee r)] \equiv [(p \vee q) \vee r]$
                               $[p + (q + r)] \equiv [(p + q) + r]$

16. Transposition (Trans) $(p \supset q) \equiv (-q \supset -p)$

17. Exportation (Exp) $[(p + q) \supset r] \equiv [p \supset (q \supset r)]$

Table 7.1   Rules of Inference

1. Simplification (Simp)	$p + q$	or	$p + q$
	$\therefore p$		$\therefore q$
2. *Modus ponens* (MP)	$p \supset q$		
	p		
	$\therefore q$		
3. *Modus tollens* (MT)	$p \supset q$		
	$-q$		
	$\therefore -p$		
4. Disjunctive syllogism (DS)	$p \vee q$		$p \vee q$
	$-p$	or	$-q$
	$\therefore q$		$\therefore p$
5. Hypothetical syllogism (HS)	$p \supset q$		
	$q \supset r$		
	$\therefore p \supset r$		
6. Addition (Add)	p		
	$\therefore p \vee q$		
7. Conjunction (Con)	p		
	q		
	$\therefore p + q$		
8. Constructive dilemma (CD)	$(p \supset q) + (r \supset s)$		
	$p \vee r$		
	$\therefore q \vee s$		

Table 7.2   Equivalences

9. Double negation (DN)	$--p \equiv p$
10. DeMorgan's rule (DeM)	$-(p + q) \equiv (-p \vee -q)$
	$-(p \vee q) \equiv (-p + -q)$
11. Material implication (Impl)	$(p \supset q) \equiv (-p \vee q)$
12. Material equivalence (Equiv)	$(p \equiv q) \equiv [(p \supset q) + (q \supset p)]$
13. Distribution (Dist)	$[p + (q \vee r)] \equiv [(p + q) \vee (p + r)]$
	$[p \vee (q + r)] \equiv [(p \vee q) + (p \vee r)]$
14. Commutation (Com)	$(p \vee q) \equiv (q \vee p)$
	$(p + q) \equiv (q + p)$
15. Association (Assoc)	$[p \vee (q \vee r)] \equiv [(p \vee q) \vee r]$
	$[p + (q + r)] \equiv [(p + q) + r]$
16. Transposition (Trans)	$(p \supset q) \equiv (-q \supset -p)$
17. Exportation (Exp)	$[(p + q) \supset r] \equiv [p \supset (q \supset r)]$
18. Tautology (Taut)	$p \equiv (p \vee p)$
	$p \equiv (p + p)$

Exercise 7.4A   Equivalences and Rules of Inference   Use the equivalences and the rules of inference to make the following deductions. Write the line numbers and the equivalence or rule used for each step.

1. 1. A ⊃ B   premise   /   ∴ −A ∨ B
2. 1. −C + −D   premise   /   ∴ −(C ∨ D)
3. 1. −E   premise   /   ∴ −(E + D)
4. 1. Q   premise
   2. −S   premise   /   ∴ −(−Q ∨ S)
5. 1. −A   premise   /   ∴ A ⊃ B
6. 1. −A   premise
   2. C ⊃ S   premise   /   ∴ A ⊃ S
7. 1. −(A ∨ B)   premise   /   ∴ −B
8. 1. −(−S ∨ −R)   premise   /   ∴ S
9. 1. P ∨ −Q   premise   /   ∴ − P ⊃ −Q
10. 1. −F ⊃ −G   premise   /   ∴ F ∨ −G
11. 1. −P ∨ (−R ∨ S) premise   /   ∴ P ⊃ (R ⊃ S)
12. 1. −P ∨ (R + S) premise   /   ∴ P ⊃ (R + S)
13. 1. A ∨ C   premise   /   ∴ −A ⊃ C
14. 1. −S ∨ −(R + P) premise   /   ∴ −S ∨ (−R ∨ −P)
15. 1. −S ∨ −(R + P) premise   /   ∴ S ⊃ −(R + P)
16. 1. −(R + S)   premise   /   ∴ R ⊃ −S
17. 1. −(R + S) ∨ T premise   /   ∴ (R ⊃ −S) ∨ T
18. 1. A ⊃ (−B + −C) premise   /   ∴ −A ∨ −(B ∨ C)
19. 1. −(S + R)   premise   /   ∴ S ⊃ −R
20. 1. D   premise   /   ∴ A ⊃ D
21. 1. A   premise
    2. B   premise   /   ∴ A + (B ∨ C)
22. 1. L + M   premise
    2. S + A   premise   /   ∴ L + S
23. 1. A ⊃ B   premise
    2. S + A   premise   /   ∴ B + S
24. 1. S   premise
    2. R   premise   /   ∴ (S ∨ T) + R

Exercise 7.4B   More Deductions   The following deductions are more difficult. Use both equivalences and rules of inference to complete the deductions.

1. 1. $-P \lor Q$ premise
   2. $(P \supset Q) \supset R$ premise   / $\therefore R$

2. 1. $A \supset C$ premise
   2. $T \lor -(-A \lor C)$ premise   / $\therefore T$

3. 1. $-P$ premise
   2. $(P + R) \lor S$ premise   / $\therefore S$

4. 1. $D + -A$ premise   / $\therefore A \supset C$

5. 1. $(L + P) \supset Q$ premise
   2. $-Q$ premise   / $\therefore -L \lor -P$

6. 1. $(S + L) \lor -A$ premise   / $\therefore A \supset L$

7. 1. $-(P + Q)$ premise
   2. Q premise   / $\therefore -P$

8. 1. $T \equiv Q$ premise
   2. $-Q$ premise   / $\therefore -T$

9. 1. $R \lor (P + S)$ premise   / $\therefore R \lor S$

10. 1. $-Q \supset -P$ premise
   2. $-(R \lor -T)$ premise   / $\therefore T + (P \supset Q)$

11. 1. $-(P \lor T)$ premise   / $\therefore -T$

12. 1. $-S + -R$ premise
   2. $-(S \lor R) \supset L$ premise   / $\therefore L$

13. 1. $A \equiv -C$ premise
   2. $-A$ premise   / $\therefore C$

14. 1. $K \equiv N$ premise
   2. $N \supset L$ premise   / $\therefore K \supset L$

15. 1. $-(A + B)$ premise
   2. B premise
   3. $D \supset A$ premise   / $\therefore -D$

16. 1. $L + N$ premise
   2. $(L \lor E) \supset F$ premise   / $\therefore L + F$

17. 1. $C \supset D$ premise
   2. $D \supset G$ premise
   3. $F \supset N$ premise
   4. $C \lor F$ premise   / $\therefore G \lor N$

18. 1. $-A \supset (B \supset C)$ premise
    2. $F \supset T$ premise
    3. $A \lor (F \lor B)$ premise
    4. $-A$ premise   / $\therefore T \lor C$

19. 1. $(A \supset B) + (C \supset D)$ premise
    2. $A \lor C$ premise
    3. $D \supset -S$ premise
    4. $A + S$ premise   / $\therefore F \supset B$

20. 1. $-H$ premise
    2. $-G \lor H$ premise
    3. $(R + G) \lor (S + A)$ premise   / $\therefore S$

21. 1. $P \supset (A \supset B)$ premise
    2. $D \lor -B$ premise
    3. $-D + A$ premise   / $\therefore -P$

22. 1. $A \lor B$ premise
    2. $-P \supset -A$ premise
    3. $-P$ premise   / $\therefore B$

Exercise 7.4C   Symbolize and Deduce   Translate the following arguments into symbolic form and then deduce the conclusion using the rules of inference and the equivalences. Use the translation cues provided.

1. If John keeps the house, then either Carol leaves or Mrs. Nussbaum will rent the room. If John is promoted, he will keep the house. John is promoted and Carol does not leave. Therefore, Mrs. Nussbaum rents her room. (J, C, N, P)

2. Either oxidation or reduction is the cause of the explosion. If the substance contains no potassium, then oxidation is not the cause of the explosion. The substance contains no potassium. Therefore, reduction is the cause. (O, R, S)

3. If the coalition collapses, then the Labor party will assume the leadership in the cabinet. If the Labor party assumes leadership, then the Senate will not reorganize and no coalition members will be seated. If no coalition members are seated, then there will have to be an election of a new prime minister. There will be no election of a new prime minister; therefore, the coalition does not collapse. (C, L, S, M, E)

4. Eating meat is essential neither for survival nor for good health, nor is it a cost-efficient way of producing nutritious food. All of that implies that eating meat is not a necessity. Eating meat requires raising animals for slaughter. If this is so and eating meat is not a necessity, then it is morally wrong to kill animals for food in these circumstances. Therefore, it is morally wrong to kill animals for food in these circumstances. (E, G, C, N, R, M)

5. If Fischer does not win the tournament, then Spassky wins. Spassky does not win. If Fischer wins, then neither Geller nor Krogius will play. Therefore, Geller will not play. (F, S, G, K)

6. Hydrogen and oxygen are gases. Silicon is not a gas. If hydrogen is a gas and silicon is not a gas, then either potassium is a liquid or it is a solid. If potassium is unlike silicon, then it is not a liquid. It is unlike silicon; thus, potassium is a solid. (H, O, S, P, I, U)

7. If people earn different amounts and everyone pays the same amount in taxes, then those who earn more keep more and those who earn less keep less. If those who earn more keep more and those who earn less keep less, then the tax laws are unjust. Therefore, either people do not earn different amounts, or if everyone pays the same amount in taxes, then the tax laws are unjust. (P, E, M, L, T)

8. "If a man has a talent and cannot use it, he has failed. If he has a talent and learns somehow to use the whole of it, he has gloriously succeeded and won a triumph few men ever know." (Thomas Wolfe) He has not won a triumph few men ever know. So it follows that he has no talent or he's not learned to use the whole of it. (T, U, F, L, G, W)

9. It is false that film making is not an art form, because if film making involves the possibility for creativity, then it is an art form, and it does involve that possibility. (F, P)

10. Deregulation of the energy industry is now a fact. Neither the airlines nor the Bell System have benefited from deregulation. That may be concluded from the facts that deregulation of the energy industry implies higher expenses for the airlines and increased costs for the Bell System. In turn, if there are higher expenses for the airlines and increased costs for the Bell System, then it's not true that either the airlines or the Bell System benefit from deregulation. (A, B, D, H, I)

11. Argument 10 above is either deductive or inductive and not both. Argument 10 is deductive. Therefore, it is not inductive. (D, I)

12. If the Steelers win, then the Oilers lose; and if the Cowboys win, then the Broncos lose. Either the Steelers or the Cowboys win. The Broncos do not lose. Therefore, the Oilers lose. (S, O, C, B)

13. That peace is achieved in the Mideast is a necessary condition of the Mideast nations' engaging in successful negotiations. But neither is peace achieved nor are alliances formed. Therefore, the Mideast nations do not have successful negotiations. (P, M, A)

14. The choir will tour if and only if the administration funds the trip. If the administration funds the trip, then the expenses incurred by the new construction are not excessive. Those expenses are excessive if and only if the board decreases the year's budget. The board does decrease the year's budget, and so the choir will not tour. (C, A, E, B)

15. Most Indians are Hindus. Most North Africans are Muslims. Therefore, most Indians are Hindus and either most North Africans are Muslims or most Chinese are Buddhists. (I, N, C)

Review Questions

1. What are the advantages and disadvantages of the truth table method and the indirect truth table method?

2. What is a formal deduction?

3. What are the advantages of the method of formal deduction? Can you see any disadvantages to this method?

4. Which rules of inference involve the conditional? Which equivalences?

5. Which rules of inference involve the disjunction? Which equivalences?

6. Why is it valid to form a disjunction from a statement known to be true? That is, why is addition a valid argument form?

7. What rule would you use to change a disjunction to a conjunction?

8. What rule would you use to change a disjunction to a conditional?

9. According to material implication, $p \supset q$ is equivalent to $-p \vee q$. Explain how a conditional can be equivalently expressed as a disjunction.

10. According to DeMorgan's rule, we can change a disjunction to a conjunction. Thus, we should be able to change a conditional to a conjunction. Demonstrate how this can be done and check your answer with a truth table.

True or False?

1. If a conjunction is a premise or deducible from the premises, you may validly deduce either conjunct.

2. If a disjunction is a premise or deducible from the premises, you may validly deduce either disjunct.

3. DeMorgan's rule tells us, in effect, that 'neither p nor q' is equivalent to 'not both p and q'.

4. Whenever there are two "not" signs within a compound, you may eliminate them according to the rule of double negation.

5. Given the statement p you may deduce $q \supset p$ by addition, commutation, and material implication.

6. Every step in a deduction represents a conclusion drawn validly from premises.

CHAPTER EIGHT
Inductive Logic

This chapter examines inductive strength, the kind
of inferential support possible in those arguments
that are not deductively valid. We examine three
types of inductively strong arguments: the inductive
generalization, the causal argument, and the argument from analogy.

The title "Inductive Logic" implies that there is a logic of inductive reasoning that
is distinguishable from the logic of deductive reasoning. That needs some explanation.

First, it is safe to say that all logicians agree that deductive reasoning is not the
whole of logic. But if deductive reasoning is not the whole, what is the rest? Here logicians do not all agree. Some call the rest "nondeductive reasoning." Some may have
other distinctions to make. We will call all reasoning that fails to be deductively valid
"inductive." Therefore, according to some logicians, we use the term 'inductive'
broadly, perhaps too broadly for them. What matters, however, is that we recognize and
appreciate central forms of reasoning that are good yet not deductively valid.

Second, that logicians do not agree on what to call reasoning that is not deductive
is not a mere disagreement over words. There is good reason why nondeductive—what
we will call inductive—reasoning is a subject of controversy. The field of inductive reasoning is not homogeneous. Unlike deductive reasoning, much of which is fairly uniform and can be formalized symbolically, inductive reasoning consists of importantly
different types of arguments. Facing inductive reasoning, one is like an early ornitholo-

gist (scientist who studies birds) wanting to develop a science of birds but overwhelmed by the variations in species. All have wings and lay eggs, but beyond that the differences resist any easy generalizations.

Why is inductive logic so complex? There are several reasons. First, as we have defined it, it includes all reasoning that is not deductively valid reasoning. Thus, whenever we provide evidence or reasons from which the conclusion does not follow necessarily, we are reasoning inductively. For example, to consult a different physician for a second opinion is to obtain evidence that favors or disfavors the first physician's opinion. How is that new evidence to be weighed? To cancel a trip because of the weather is to make an inductive inference. To move one's bank account hoping to get higher interest rates and better service is to make an inductive inference. To vote for a Republican this time rather than a Democrat, to switch from butter to margarine, to change academic majors, to bet on the 49ers, to research the causes of disease—all these are usually examples of nondeductive reasoning.

Second, inductive reasoning is usually about things that are not now observable, things that we believe are or are not the case but that we cannot now check. Consider the examples above.

Third, inductive reasoning is always *a matter of degree*. Whereas an argument either is or is not deductively valid, an argument is *more or less* inductively strong. Whereas no new evidence, no new experience, further strengthens deductive validity, new evidence or experience does strengthen or weaken an inductive argument. Since inductive reasoning is a matter of degree, it is more complex.

As a final note, if it is not already apparent, most everyday reasoning is inductive reasoning. Some of the most important areas of our lives and the beliefs and decisions we make about them involve inductive reasoning: our beliefs about how the world works, about human behavior, about the social policies we should adopt, and about the ways we should spend our time, to mention just a few. Thus, we are studying an area of immense importance when we study inductive reasoning.

8.1 Inductive Strength

In Chapter 2 we defined a good argument as one in which the premises are true and the conclusion follows from them. We also defined two senses in which a conclusion may be said to follow from the premises, deductive validity and inductive strength. In Chapters 2 through 7 we studied various techniques for determining deductive validity. In this chapter we concentrate on those arguments that are not deductively valid yet may be inductively strong.

Recall from Chapter 1 that inferential support—the support passed by premises to a conclusion—may range in strength from the strongest to the weakest. Deductive validity exemplifies the strongest support possible. Short of that, arguments descend in degrees of strength. Think of the analogy of boiling water and degrees of heat. The water either boils or it doesn't. Analogously, an argument is either deductively valid or not. If the water isn't boiling, it still has some temperature ranging from very hot to cold. We have studied how to identify "boiling water." Now we will study how to identify "degrees of heat."

Let us define inductive strength as follows:

> **inductive strength**   *An argument is inductively strong just in case, given its premises, (1) it is deductively invalid and (2) it is more probable than not that the conclusion follows.*

Let us say further that an argument lacks inductive strength—that is, it is *inductively weak,* given 1 above and failure to meet condition 2.

> **inductive weakness**   *An argument is inductively weak just in case, given its premises, (1) it is deductively invalid and (2) it is more probable than not that the conclusion does not follow.*

In contrast to the concept of deductive validity, inductive strength cannot help but appear vague. An inductively strong argument is one in which the conclusion is "more probable than not." In further describing inductive arguments we say such things as "it is very probable that," "it is highly unlikely that," "there is slight probability that," and so on. Compare the following examples of deductively invalid arguments.

Example 1	*Example 2*
Most MDs are conservatives.	*Few MDs are conservatives.*
Max is an MD.	*Max is an MD.*
Max is a conservative.	*Max is a conservative.*

It is clear that the conclusion is more strongly supported in Example 1 than in 2. But it is not clear why that is so; neither is it clear just how much more probable the conclusion of 1 is in comparison with 2. How do we assess inductive strength? Is it possible to be more precise in the assessment of inductive strength? Let us consider the second question first.

One way to think about the probability of an inductive conclusion's following from its premises is to think about the way probability is described mathematically. The mathematical theory of probability assigns values ranging from 0 to 1 to statements and events. For example, statements that are always true and cannot be false are assigned a probability value of 1. On the other hand, statements that are always false and cannot be true have a probability of 0. Most statements fall somewhere between 0 and 1. A statement that is just as likely to be true as false is given a value of .5.

We can apply the mathematical description of probability to talk about arguments. An argument is a claim that, given the premises, the conclusion follows. Thus, an argument can be viewed as a claim about the likelihood of the conclusion, given the premises. A deductively valid argument is one in which, given the premises, the conclusion has to be true and cannot be false. Thus, the highest probability value, 1, is assigned to the conclusions of deductively valid arguments. An inductively strong argument, then, is one in which, given the premises, the conclusion has a probability value greater than .5 and less than 1. A weak argument has a probability value of less than .5. This helps us see that we are interested in identifying those arguments that have a degree of inductive support falling within the range less than 1 and greater than .5:

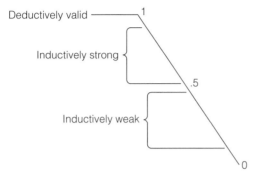

It is possible, then, to be more precise in describing the degree of probability of a conclusion, given its premises. However, applying the mathematical theory of probability to inductive arguments requires two things: (1) We can assign numerical values to a premise or premises, and (2) we have a theory about how to assess the strength of different types of inductive arguments.

For example, we could assign a precise probability value to the argument in Example 1 if we had statistical data describing the percentage of MDs who are conservative.

Example 3

Seventy-five percent of all MDs are conservatives.

Max is an MD.

Max is a conservative.

In this example the conclusion has a probability of .75, so we ought to regard it as inductively well supported.

The calculation of mathematical probability goes beyond the scope of our study. For our purposes, we need to understand that it is possible to provide precision in the assessment of inductive probability and that doing so requires attention to the differences in kinds of inductive arguments. Consider the following examples.

Example 4

Seventy-five percent of 500 MDs interviewed are
conservatives.

Therefore, probably 75 percent of all MDs are
conservatives.

Example 5

When a mild electrical current is applied to a muscle, the muscle contracts.

When the current stops, the muscle relaxes.

Therefore, the application of a mild electrical current to a muscle is the cause of contraction.

Example 6

This mushroom looks and smells like a morel.

Morels are edible.

Probably, this mushroom is edible.

Each example above represents a distinctly different way in which premises bear on a conclusion. In Example 4, a generalization is formed from premises describing some of the group. What determines whether it is a strong or weak generalization? In Example 5, a cause-and-effect relationship is concluded from premises describing a correlation of events. In Example 6, a property is attributed to something because it is similar to something else. These kinds of arguments are called *inductive generalization, causal argument,* and *argument from analogy,* respectively. Our purpose is to examine these three types and provide criteria for recognizing and assessing their inductive strength.

8.2 Inductive Generalization

Inductive generalizations are arguments with the conclusion that something is the case about all or many things on the basis of what is observed about some of them. They may be as commonplace as a neighbor's complaint that a recent scandal shows that all politicians are corrupt or as esoteric as elaborately designed statistical studies of public opinion. And they may vary in reliability from the irresponsible generalizations of prejudice to statistical calculations of probabilities and margins of error. Our concern is with what can be said in general about inductive generalizations: their typical forms, how they can be recognized, and how they can be assessed for inductive strength.

Let's focus on common features of inductive generalizations and develop a vocabulary for talking about them. Suppose we reason that all teachers in Boston are underpaid because all *those we have interviewed* are underpaid.

Example 7

All the teachers in Boston we interviewed are underpaid.
Thus, all teachers in Boston are underpaid.

This example illustrates the basic features of an inductive generalization: (1) a conclusion describing what is inferred about all or many members of a larger group, called the *population,* based on (2) a premise or premises describing a subset, called a *sample,* of that population. A third element in an inductive generalization is (3) that characteristic observed in the sample and concluded to be true of the population. We will call this the *target characteristic.* If this is a research project, it is the characteristic that we are seeking in our sample. In Example 7, the target characteristic is "being underpaid."

The reasoning in an inductive generalization is that, although we have not observed all members of the population, we can *infer* their characteristics from information we have gathered from the sample. We reason *from what we have observed to a generalization about what we have not observed.* We can represent the form of an inductive generalization as follows:

FORM

All observed *As are f. Thus, probably all As are f.*

If we have more complex information about the sample, we may be able to make what is called a *statistical generalization.* For example, if our sampling showed that 40 percent of all those interviewed were underpaid, we can then argue statistically:

Example 8

Forty percent of all Boston teachers interviewed are underpaid. Thus, it is likely that 40 percent of all Boston teachers are underpaid.

A statistical generalization has the form:

STATISTICAL GENERALIZATION

X percent of observed As are f. Therefore, probably X percent of all As are f.

In such an argument, the premise or premises contain numerical data that characterize an observed sample of the population. The conclusion is an assertion of the probability that the same characterization will be true of the population.

How do we assess the reliability of an inductive generalization? How do we tell whether it is strong? Considering that an inductive generalization is an inference from some to all, common sense would suggest that the larger the sample, the stronger the generalization. After all, the more As found to be *f,* the more likely all As are *f.* There is truth to common sense here, but the truth is below the surface. Consider this example:

Example 9

Of a sample of 60 percent of all Boston teachers, all of whom are primary grade teachers, all are underpaid. Therefore, it is likely that all Boston teachers are underpaid.

The sample, 60 percent of all Boston teachers, is remarkably large for a survey. If size were the definitive factor, then we should consider this a strong inductive generalization. But notice that the sample consists of primary grade teachers only. Despite the fact that the sample is well over half of all teachers, can we be confident that what we learned about the salaries of primary grade teachers will be reflected in the salaries of all teachers? Our suspicion is that the salaries of primary grade teachers may not be representative of all teachers' salaries. This suggests that the size of the sample is less important than how representative it is. As a matter of fact, public opinion polls, such as Gallup polls and Nielsen TV ratings, are typically based on surveys of a very small number of people carefully selected to accurately represent the larger group. So the truth behind the commonsensical idea that size determines reliability is really a function of the fact that size *may* increase representativeness. In the assessment of an inductive generalization, the degree to which a sample is representative is what matters most.

The more representative the sample, the stronger the inductive generalization. We have seen that it is much more important that a sample be representative than that it be large relative to the population. But what makes a sample *representative*?

> representative   *A sample is representative of a population to the degree that the target characteristics found in the sample occur with the same frequency or in the same proportion as they occur in the population.*

That defines representativeness, but how do we know when we have it? As you can see from the definition, one way to tell that a sample is representative is to examine the entire population! But if we could do that, we wouldn't bother with inductive generalization. So, in light of the fact that we want to infer rather than examine what may be the case about all members, how can we tell whether we have a sample whose characteristics are typical?

To tell whether a sample is representative, we must already know something about the population and about how the target characteristic is related to other characteristics of members. In Example 9, for instance, we assess the representativeness of that sample by using certain background information we already have. For instance, we know that there are different levels of teaching and that salaries vary accordingly. We also know that salaries are influenced by such factors as seniority and school district. Thus, to be representative in this case, a sample should be composed with those differences taken into account. The fault with Example 9 is that the sample lacks the variety that we know to be present in the larger population.

To consider how a representative sample is selected, let's design our own study. Suppose we want to determine what percentage of students at the university own automobiles. Suppose further that we believe that a sample consisting of 100 members will be sufficient. The method by which we compose that sample will bear on the reliability of our generalization. For instance, if we interview 100 students at the entrance to the parking lot, we are almost certain to have skewed results. On the other hand, if we interview 100 students near the campus bus stop, again our sample is not likely to be representative. What we need to consider is whether other characteristics of the members might bear on the occurrence of the target characteristic. In those two instances, they do. Clearly, students found near a parking lot are more likely to be car owners. Students near a bus stop are not. Neither group gives us a representative sample. Thus, since where we select members bears on the results, it is best to avoid selecting members who have the characteristic of location in common. Our interviewers should take their data from various locations.

Simple Random Sampling   The science of statistics provides carefully devised procedures for designing samples. One of these, *simple random sampling*, is a commonly used way to achieve variety in our sample. If we can reasonably assume that car ownership is randomly distributed throughout the student population, then we may use a simple random sample. One way to do this would be to assign a number to each university student—something the registrar's office is likely to have done already—and to randomly select students with the use of a random number generator. Even simpler, we could pick 100 names out of a hat.

What makes either of these methods a *random* sample? The selection is random in the mathematical sense that each name has an even chance of being selected. The theory of simple random sampling as a method for designing a representative sample assumes that (1) each possible member has an equal chance of appearing in the sample and (2) the characteristic sought is evenly distributed throughout the population. In our example, we can use simple random sampling because we have assumed that the characteristic in question, car ownership, is likely to be distributed evenly throughout the population. If that is an acceptable assumption, then the generalization we infer about all the students has a high likelihood of being accurate.

Stratified Random Sampling   A more sophisticated method of sampling is appropriate when we know that the population consists of different groups and the groupings bear differently on the presence of the characteristic we are interested in. The generalization in Example 7 is more appropriately handled using this method, *stratified random sampling*. We know that teachers in Boston are not a homogeneous group but comprise instead several overlapping subgroups, or *strata*. Therefore, a more representative sample will draw from those groups in proportion as they occur in the population. Suppose that 38 percent are primary grade teachers, 27 percent are secondary grade teachers, 19 percent are two-year college teachers, and so on. Suppose further that we factored in representative proportions of teachers at different levels of seniority for each strata. The final sample will consist of randomly selected members from each substrata and, thus, each strata. This sample, now quite complex, is more likely to reflect the characteristics we can expect to find throughout the population.

> random sample   *The random sample is a sample selected by a method that gives each element in the population an equal chance of being selected. The idea is that if each element has an equal chance to appear in the sample, then whatever characteristics are typically distributed throughout the group have the same probability of occurring in the sample.*

As the two sampling methods above show, assessing representativeness involves bringing background information to the argument. The more we already know about the population, the better we can assess the sample. If we know the population is diverse and we know that those differences bear on the presence of the target characteristic, then we know the sample must reflect that relevant diversity to be representative. Suppose, for example, we are interested in estimating the percentage of good eggs produced at an egg ranch. Suppose also that egg size is related to quality. Then the sample should contain a variety of sizes. On the other hand, those characteristics that make no difference can be ignored. For example, if the size of a marble makes no difference in its color and we are estimating the percentage of red marbles, a representative sample need not include variety of sizes.

To summarize: To assess the representativeness of a sample, we need to know (1) what different characteristics occur in the population and (2) whether those characteristics are relevant to the occurrence of the target characteristic. In general, we can say that the more relevant the diversity in the sample, the more representative it is. Interestingly enough, it also follows that the more relevant the diversity in the population, the larger the sample will need to be to reflect that diversity. Thus, size is a function of the requirement for representativeness.

If strong inductive generalizations are ones that are based on representative samples, then weak ones are those that are not. A sample that is unrepresentative is called a *biased sample.* In statistics the concept of sample bias is mathematically defined. For our purposes a biased sample occurs when the sample fails to reflect relevant differences in the population either because it is too small or because it is not proportionately composed. One of the virtues of random sampling is that it avoids the likelihood of a biased sample. Nevertheless, sometimes an argument purportedly based on a random sample has members too much alike to have been randomly selected. When a sample is biased, the resulting generalization is unreliable, and the argument is said to commit the *fallacy of hasty generalization* (see Section 9.11).

Other telling flaws in an inductive generalization have to do with the reliability of the premises themselves. Consider asking of the premises: How is the target characteristic defined? How is the information obtained? In Example 7, the premise reports that so many teachers are underpaid. What does "being underpaid" mean here? Is it the subject's perception of his or her salary? Is it a measurement of subjects' salaries relative to the cost of living, to salaries of other comparable jobs, or to salaries of teachers elsewhere?

If teachers are interviewed, as the example suggests, what questions are they asked? Consider the difference between being asked "How does your salary compare with that of other comparable jobs?" and "Are you underpaid?" The way in which a question is framed can affect the responses; thus, the way the information is obtained can introduce what is called *interviewer bias* into the results.

Three reasons why size is not what matters most!

1. If sample size is the measure of strength of an inductive generalization, then equally sized surveys would have the same degree of strength. However, this is not true as the following arguments show.

Example A

Mr. Smith, a mathematician, is cold and unemotional.

Therefore, all mathematicians are cold and unemotional.

Example B

This raccoon is rabid.

Therefore, all raccoons are rabid.

Example C

Mr. Spock, a Vulcan, has a two-chambered heart.

Therefore, all Vulcans have two-chambered hearts.

All three arguments are based on samples with only one member. Are they equal in strength? No. Argument C is stronger than A and B. Why? The answer has to do with the nature of the target characteristics and what we know about how they occur. For example, emotional qualities are highly variable within a population. Some people are unemotional; some are not. Similarly, rabies is highly variable. It is not a defining feature of mammals but tends to occur in special circumstances. If we know that a feature is variable within a population, then a sample size of one case is not good enough evidence. On the other hand, if a feature is invariable, such as anatomical structure, then a sample of one may be good evidence. One Vulcan with a two-chambered heart is a good indicator of what other Vulcans are like because heart structures do not vary in species. Therefore, *equally sized surveys are not necessarily equal in strength*. Size is not what matters.

2. A large sample, constructed in a biased manner, is not good evidence. Imagine a study to determine what percentage of students out of a student body of 2500 are married. In sample S1, 1200 students were interviewed in the college dormitories. In sample S2, 400 students, randomly selected by ID number, were surveyed by phone. Sample S2 is smaller but more reliable because Sample S1 is biased. S1 is not representative of the student body, since not every student has an equal chance of appearing in the sample. Therefore, it is not true that of two generalizations, the one with the larger sample is the stronger. Again, *size is less important than how the sample is constructed*.

3. Providing survey information is big business. Large samples are not only expensive to conduct but unnecessary. Very small surveys may provide very good evidence if they are carefully constructed.

Summary: Inductive Generalization

1. Inductive generalizations are arguments concluding that something is the case about all or many things on the basis of what is observed about some of them. Presupposed in every inductive generalization is the idea that what we observe in the sample is likely to be true of all members of the group.

2. An inductive generalization consists of (1) premises describing a *sample* (2) as having a *target characteristic* as reason for (3) a conclusion that all or some percentage of the *population* has that target characteristic.

3. The strength of an inductive generalization is a function of the representativeness of the sample. The more representative the sample, the stronger the argument.

4. A sample is *representative* of a population to the degree that the target characteristics found in the sample occur with the same frequency or in the same proportion as they occur in the population.

5. To assess the representativeness of a sample, we need to know (1) what different characteristics occur in the population and (2) whether those characteristics are relevant to the occurrence of the target characteristic. In general, we can say that the more relevant the diversity in the sample, the more representative it is.

6. In general, a random sample is a sample selected by a method that gives each member in the population an equal chance of being selected.

   A simple random sample is a sample selected by a method that gives each member in the population an equal chance of being selected without regard to differences. The assumption is that if each member has an equal chance to appear in the sample, then whatever characteristics are typically distributed throughout the population have the same probability of occurring in the sample.

   A stratified random sample is a sample consisting of subgroups, or strata, in proportion as they occur in the population, with each member randomly selected. The assumption is that the occurrence of the target characteristic in the population is related to the occurrence of other characteristics. Strata are differentiated by relevant differences within the population.

7. A sample that is unrepresentative is called a biased sample. An inductive generalization based on a biased sample commits the fallacy of hasty generalization.

8. The premises describing what is learned about a sample may be unreliable if the target characteristic is not clearly defined or if the method of obtaining information adversely influences the results. Either is a case of interviewer bias.

Exercise 8.2A   Inductive Generalization   Write out the argument in argument form. Then identify these elements: (a) the *sample,* (b) the *population,* and (c) the *target characteristic.*

Sample Exercise   *Based on a 1999 survey of 20 major corporations throughout the U.S. with a total of 3,822 employees, the Employee Benefit Research Institute concluded that nationally approximately 70 percent of working people are saving for retirement.*

1. A 1999 survey of 3,822 employees at 20 major corporations in the U.S conducted by the Employee Benefit Research Institute showed that 70 percent of the employees were actively saving for retirement.

---

2. Therefore, nationally approximately 70 percent of working people are saving for retirement.

   a. *Sample:* 3,822 employees at 20 major corporations in the U.S.

   b. *Population:* working people in the U.S.

   c. *Target characteristic:* actively saving for retirement

1. From a one-gallon jar filled with 1,000 variously colored gumballs, Teddy grabbed five handfuls for a total of 157. Sixty-three out of the 157 gumballs were red. Therefore, she concluded, almost fifty percent of all the gumballs in the jar are red.

2. In a study comparing the brain size of opossums and raccoons, a researcher could fit only 21 beans into the brainpan of an opossum skull but needed 150 to fill the brainpan of a raccoon. Therefore, opossums have smaller brains than raccoons. (Reported in *Audubon*)

3. Pat has been counseling families for ten years and has never yet seen a family that does not exhibit some form of dysfunction. "There are no functional families," she says.

4. Lauren says that she gets at least thirty minutes of happiness a day from her Barbie doll. When asked what she wanted for Christmas, she said she wants every six-year-old to have a Barbie doll so that each would have at least thirty minutes of happiness every day!

5. Debbie concluded that the nursing department can expect an attrition rate of about one-third of all freshmen nursing students each year, since about that many have failed or dropped out for the past three years.

6. Based on a survey of 1,500 businesses nationwide, which found that 16.4 percent of businesses used the Internet for selling, with Web-based sales accounting for an average of 14.3 percent of total store sales, economists concluded that the Internet is drawing customers away from shopping at the malls.

7. Researchers studied approximately 200 Canada geese migrating through New England last year. They found that 6% had a virus that causes brain damage. They concluded that probably 6% of the 300 thousand geese who migrate through New England suffer from that viral disease.

8. After watching her real estate business slow to a standstill in winter and pick up in spring for the past six years, Mary Jane has concluded that from now on she'll close shop and spend winters in the Bahamas.

9. The U.S. Air Force Space Command uses radar to track roughly 8,000 pieces of garbage in space, debris left by hundreds of satellites and rockets. Based on those observations, scientists estimate that the actual amount of debris floating in our atmosphere is easily three times as much. (Reported in *Audubon*)

10. In 1999 more than 16.5 million tons of rock salt was used to de-ice roads in the United States. Since the amount increased in 2000 to approximately 19 million, it is reasonable to conclude that greater quantities will be used each year for the next several years. (Reported in *Audubon*)

Exercise 8.2B   More Inductive Generalizations   Write out the argument in argument form. Identify: (a) the *sample*, (b) the *population,* and (c) the *target characteristic.* State whether (d) the sample is *representative.* Last, (e) given the premises, discuss whether the argument is *inductively strong or weak.* If no judgment can be made, describe what information you need.

Sample Exercise   *According to a* New York Times *article on pelvic inflammatory disease (P.I.D.), a sexually transmitted disease affecting about one in seven women of reproductive age, Dr. Harold Kaminsky of the American College of Obstetrics and Gynecology (ACOG) reports that "The men who passed the disease to the women often do not get treated. One study that looked at 60,000 cases of P.I.D. found that relatively few of the women's partners were treated. Because some of the women had more than one sexual partner at risk, the number of men treated should have been more than 60,000. In fact, only 29,000 were treated."*

1. A study of 60,000 cases of P.I.D. in women showed that only 29,000 men were treated.
2. P.I.D. is a sexually transmitted disease.

---

3. Therefore, men who pass the disease to women often do not get treatment.

   a. *Sample:* 60,000 cases of P.I.D.

   b. *Population:* all cases of men and women with P.I.D.

   c. *Target characteristic:* evidence of treatment for P.I.D.

   d. It is not clear whether the sample is representative. Although the sample is large, the report does not tell us how the sample was constructed. Presumably the data reflect reports of the disease made to the ACOG.

   e. If we assume that most reports of the disease are reported to the ACOG, then we may conclude that the sample is representative. Therefore, the argument is a strong inductive generalization.

1. In 1991 a study of a nursery ward for newborns in Chicago showed that nurses followed appropriate hand-washing guidelines about half the time; doctors in the ward followed the guidelines half as frequently as that. Apparently the effectiveness of antibiotics in U.S. hospitals has caused generations of hospital staff to rely on antibiotics rather than on hygiene. (Paul E. Ewald, *Plague Time,* 2000, p. 19)

2. In trying to decide how to spend an additional $8000 in entertainment funds, the UConn Student Council took a poll of students entering the campus center one Thursday morning when, by coincidence, the UConn Birders Society meets. Sixty-eight percent of those polled favored donating the money to the American Birding Association Wildlife Refuge. The rest were evenly divided among "more movies," "hiring a magician," and "the Bread and Puppet Theatre." On the basis of the sample the council concluded that the majority of UConn students would want to donate the money to the American Birding Association.

3. Don has skied the same terrain weekly for the past five ski seasons. He always sees at least one person skiing with reckless abandon. "These slopes are crawling with people who have no regard for safety. You take risks when you ski up here," he says.

4. A survey by the American Academy of Actuaries reports that 72 percent of pension fund actuaries polled predict that half the baby boomers won't have the wherewithal to retire at age 65. The number of actuaries polled was 326; the number of registered actuaries in the nation is 7,854. The reasonable conclusion to draw is that well over half of all actuaries would agree that half of the nation's baby boomers will not be able to retire at age 65.

5. A recent study at a large teaching hospital involving 82 physicians and 75 patients found that there were 154 cases of resuscitation. Although 86 percent of the patients who received resuscitation were considered competent to make medical decisions, only 19 percent were asked for their consent prior to resuscitation being administered. From this study it is reasonable to conclude that the practice at most hospitals is to administer resuscitation without first discussing it with patients.

6. According to an essay by Mary McGrory, the American Bar Association aims to have its 129,000 law students throughout the country contribute 50 hours of public service before graduation. The ABA bases this recommendation on a report that 54 percent of law students at 100 out of 175 law schools voted in favor of mandatory public service.

7. Tim has done a nonscientific survey of a two-square-mile tract of woodlands near his home in order to estimate this coming spring's population of gypsy moth caterpillars. Following the same path through the woods at approximately the same time of year, Tim counted the number of egg cases on tree trunks visible from the path. The first count totaled 1,090 egg cases; the second year's count totaled 650. Tim concluded that there will be 40 percent fewer gypsy moth caterpillars feeding on the trees this coming spring because he observed 40 percent fewer egg cases.

8. The National Medical Care Expenditure Survey of 1977 conducted a survey, consisting of six household interviews, of over 40,000 individuals over an eighteen-month period during 1977 and 1978. Among their findings were that approximately 18 million Americans are without health insurance the entire year, and as many as 34 million may be uninsured for some period of time during the year.

9. Macro Market Research of Burlington, Vermont, conducted a phone survey of 508 Vermonters representing .1 percent of the total state population of approximately 500,000 people. Callers were selected through random digit dialing. The number of calls within each of the state's fourteen counties was proportional to the counties' population and distributed geographically according to population. Callers were given the names of candidates for election and asked which they would be inclined to vote for if the election were held today. For governor the survey showed that 49 percent were likely to vote for Richard Snelling, 29 percent for Peter Welch, and 21 percent were undecided. The margin of error is plus or minus 4.5 percent with a confidence level of 95 percent. That means that 95 times out of 100 this survey would produce results within 4.5 percent of these findings. Based on these statistics it is nearly certain that Snelling will be the state's next governor. (*Rutland Herald*)

10. To determine the percentage of Alameda County drivers wearing seat belts, tollbooth operators were instructed to make observations of all drivers going through the toll at the Hill Bridge. A survey of approximately 8,000 drivers over a twenty-four-hour period showed that 37 percent were wearing seat belts. County officials concluded that approximately 37 percent of all local drivers wear seat belts.

11. By randomly selecting names from the phone book, surveyors for Ace Phone Company asked people whether they owned an Ace phone. Out of 450 calls, 14 percent owned an Ace phone, 36 percent did not know, 2 percent hung up, and 48 percent owned another brand. Marketing researcher Victor Kay concluded that 14 percent of all area phone owners have an Ace and that Ace should print its name boldly across the front of each phone it produces. He is convinced, he argued, that a large percentage of those who "did not know" were Ace owners who couldn't find the label.

12. A survey of the buying habits of residents in Franklin County showed that the most commonly purchased commodities were coffee, long underwear, and ammunition. Researchers interviewed 500 rural residents during the month of January. Franklin County consists of approximately three thousand rural residents and 67,000 urban dwellers. On the basis of the survey, researchers recommended that area retailers are looking at an exciting untapped market, particularly in long underwear and ammunition.

8.3 Causal Arguments

Probably few interests in life occupy us as much as wanting to know how things work. We want to know why things happen, how to make things happen, how to avoid things happening, and how to predict what will happen. Our lives consist of events, and our success in life consists in part in our ability to explain, predict, and alter events. This is surely why newspapers, magazines, books, and everyday conversations are filled with discussions about what causes what. However, an interest in causes and effects is not the same as an interest in good reasoning about causes and effects. The latter is the subject of this section.

How do we identify strong causal arguments? In this section we first clarify what a causal argument is. Then we look at the kinds of arguments in which causal statements occur. From there we see that our main concern is with causal statements as conclusions of arguments. Thus, we focus on the strength or reliability of reasons supporting a causal conclusion, and we study John Stuart Mill's methods for identifying causal relations.

Causal Statements

Causal arguments, as we illustrate shortly, consist of at least one causal statement as either a premise or the conclusion. Let's begin with an account of causal statements.

A causal statement is a statement that asserts or denies that one thing or type of thing causes another or that one thing or type of thing is caused by another.

> causal statement   *Any statement that asserts or denies that "A causes B," in which A and B refer to things, people, events, states of affairs, or their types.*

Whatever is an instance of A in the schema "A causes B" is said to be the cause; whatever is an instance of B is said to be the effect. For example:

Example 10

Increased stress causes increased risk of heart attack.

Example 11

Increased stress does not cause increased risk of premature delivery in pregnant women.

Example 10 asserts a causal relationship. Example 11 denies one. Besides being assertions or denials, there is a distinction to be made between specific causal statements and causal generalizations. A *specific causal statement* asserts, for example, that some specific thing caused or is caused by some other specific thing.

> *Specific causal statement: A causes B.*

where A and B refer to particular things or events. For example:

> *The power failure caused the loss of my document in the computer's memory.*
> *The paint is drying slowly because of the high humidity.*
> *The pesticide I used killed my neighbor's roses.*

On the other hand, a *causal generalization* asserts or denies a causal relationship between *types* of things or events.

> *Causal generalization: As cause Bs.*

where A and B refer to types of things or events. For example:

> *Power failures are common causes of loss of data in a computer's memory.*
> *Lightning bursts can disrupt the navigational devices on airplanes.*
> *Some kinds of pesticides harm flowering roses.*

The Senses of the Word 'Cause'

In the most general terms, to assert that A causes B is to assert that A brings about, produces, or makes B happen. But if we look at various examples, we see that there are different senses of the word 'cause' in different causal statements.

Example 12

Power failures cause loss of data in a computer's memory.

Example 13

The presence of oxygen caused the combustion.

Example 14

Smoking causes cancer.

When we say that one thing causes another, sometimes we mean that one brings about the other, sometimes that one is required for the other to occur, and sometimes that one contributes to the occurrence of the other. A precise way to characterize these different senses is to use the concepts of necessary and sufficient conditions encountered in Section 5.6. Recall that, given a statement of the form 'if p, then q', p is a sufficient condition for q and q is a necessary condition for p.

Consider first the causal relationship asserted in Example 12. How is the event of a power failure related to the effect, loss of data in a computer's memory? We know that if a power failure occurs during the operation of a computer, loss of data in memory will occur. We can say that a power failure is a *sufficient condition* for loss of data. However, if there is loss of data in a computer's memory, it does not follow that a power failure occurred. (Other causes are possible: You accidentally pressed "delete," for example.) Thus, power failure is not a *necessary condition* for loss of data. Example 12 illustrates a causal relationship in which the cause is a sufficient but not a necessary condition for the effect.

In Example 13, the presence of oxygen is not sufficient for combustion; fuel is also required. But the presence of oxygen is a necessary condition, for without it there would be no combustion. The statement asserts a cause in the sense of a causally necessary condition for the effect.

Considering Example 14, from what we know about the relationship between smoking and lung cancer, we know that the statement does not assert that smoking is a sufficient condition for lung cancer, since some people smoke but never get cancer. Neither does it assert that smoking is a necessary condition since not all causes of lung cancer are cases in which the person smoked. Rather, the causal relationship observed between smoking and lung cancer is that the incidence of lung cancer is higher in those cases in which a person smokes. Thus, smoking is a *contributing factor* or *partial cause* of lung cancer.

These examples illustrate three basic senses in which one thing may be said to cause another. They are summarized below.

In the case that A causes B, then

    i. A is a *sufficient condition* for B if and only if, given that A occurs, B occurs. If B does not occur, then A has not occurred.

        For example, a dead battery causes failure of the engine to start. That is, if the battery is dead, the car won't start.

    ii. A is a *necessary condition* for B if and only if, given that B occurs, A occurs. If A does not occur, then B does not occur.

        For example, cessation of functioning in the human cerebellum causes the death of the person. That is, if a person is dead, then the cerebellum has ceased functioning.

    iii. A is a *partial cause* of B if and only if, given factors $f, g, h,$ the occurrence of A increases the likelihood of B, and A is neither sufficient nor necessary for B.

        For example, rapidly falling atmospheric pressure indicates the likelihood of precipitation. That is, if rapidly falling atmospheric pressure occurs along with other factors, then precipitation occurs.

As an example, consider how the concepts defined above are used in describing fog. Fog, the phenomenon in which visibility is reduced below 1 km by water droplets in the air, is the product of a number of factors occurring simultaneously. As the evening progresses, Earth radiates its heat into the atmosphere. If atmospheric pressure is high—permitting the warm air to ascend, the temperature to fall, and cooler air to be trapped near the ground—and if relative humidity increases in the absence of wind, fog is formed. No single factor is sufficient to produce fog. Rather, the factors listed are *jointly sufficient* and some but not all are *individually necessary*. The occurrence of evening and the absence of wind, to be specific, are not necessary, since fog may occur as long as the surface temperature is cooler and the wind is bringing in moist air. Evening and the absence of wind, in our example, may be called *partial causes*.

Fog is a complex phenomenon because it occurs only if a number of factors are present. Some of the phenomena we would most like to understand—for example, disease, crime, educational success, economic shifts, and environmental pollution—are significantly more complex. Crime, for instance, is not a single phenomenon but a family of more or less closely related phenomena. Furthermore, each kind of crime involves a network of factors. Even if we were to focus exclusively on a specific type of crime—arson, for example—we would find a number of contributing factors and few necessary conditions for cases of arson.

The Structure of Causal Relationships

Events take place against a background of circumstances. A woman falls in a store and breaks her hip because the floor is wet. But also at play are any number of other circumstances: the texture of the flooring; the high-heeled shoes she happened to be wearing, but might not have, had her others been repaired on time; the fact that she lingered at the meat counter; the custodian's being distracted by a spill in the next aisle and thus forgetting to get the caution sign; her age and increased vulnerability to fractures; the physical laws of falling bodies; the law of gravity, and so on. How do we begin to ferret out relevant causes?

In looking at the complexity of events, it is useful to apply some distinctions. First, we can distinguish between events that occur in sequence and events or circumstances that converge. In our example, there are *causal chains* or sequences of events: Something caused the woman to be at the store at that time; something caused her to linger at the meat counter, bringing her to the place where she stepped, slipped, fell, and was injured. But other factors converging at different places in that sequence also have bearing on the complex event: her other shoes being unavailable, the wet floor, the spill in the next aisle, and the absence of a caution sign. Independently occurring events converge to form a network of circumstances that make the accident possible. A diagram of the accident shows both causal chains and the convergence of circumstances.

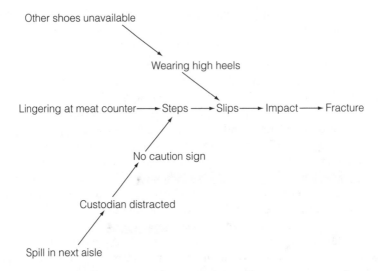

Second, we can distinguish causal factors in terms of their proximity, or nearness, to the effect in question. A *proximate cause* is a causal factor that occurs immediately prior to or simultaneous with the effect. In our example, it seems that the proximate cause of the fractured hip is the impact of the woman's body on the hard floor, which in turn was caused by slipping on water. Elaborating on the explanation, we may specify other events as *intermediate causes*—say, the absence of a caution sign—or *remote causes* even further removed from the accident—say, the spill in the next aisle. Usually in explaining an event, we single out an event or events immediately prior as bearing the weight of *the* cause. Although it may be true that the accident would not have occurred had some other events not taken place, we would probably not say that she fell and broke her hip because she lingered at the meat counter or because her other shoes were not repaired on time. And we would not say that the fall was due to the law of gravity.

> proximate cause   *A causal factor that occurs immediately prior to or simultaneous with the effect.*

intermediate cause *A causal factor whose occurrence links a more distant or remote cause to a proximate cause.*

remote cause *A factor causally relevant to an effect but not immediately responsible for the effect. Typically, a remote cause is a cause occurring at some distance temporally or spatially from the effect.*

Adapting an illustration from Robert Blank's *Rationing Medicine,* we can see how the structure of very complex causal relationships might be displayed. Blank is illustrating the factors causally responsible for the crisis in health care.

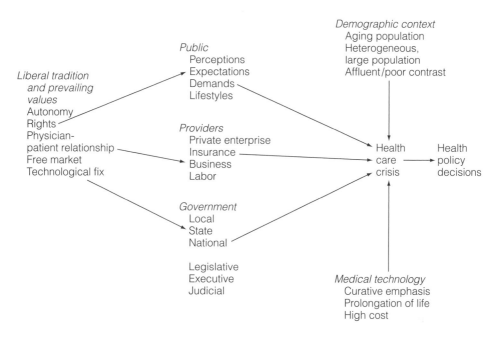

Exercise 8.3A   Causal Structure   Using the concepts of causal chain, convergent events, proximate cause, intermediate cause, and remote cause, draw diagrams representing the following descriptions of events or circumstances.

Sample Exercise   *Freezing followed by thawing followed by freezing causes the water to get under your shingles, freeze again, and then melt between the roofing boards. Pretty soon you have a leak in the roof.*

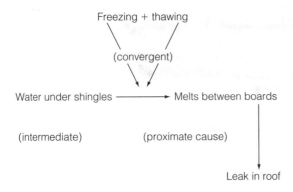

Freezing + thawing

(convergent)

Water under shingles ⟶ Melts between boards

(intermediate)   (proximate cause)

Leak in roof

1. Max hit the baseball so hard it flew over the fence and broke Mr. Porter's picture window.

2. Maxine passed the history final because she stayed up all night studying.

3. The brilliant reds, yellows, and oranges of the leaves in autumn result from the shortening of daylight hours, which decreases the production of chlorophyll in the leaves.

4. The conflict over slavery caused the Civil War.

5. Sitting at a computer keyboard for prolonged periods can produce inflammation of the tendons in the wrist, arm, and elbow, a syndrome known as repetitive strain injury (RSI).

6. The car backfired, startling Mr. Potts, who dropped the can of paint on Fido, causing him to leap at Mrs. Potts, who was carrying the turkey dinner, which hit the floor with a splat.

7. The increase in consumer spending is directly affected by the availability of low-interest-rate borrowing. The interest rates local banks charge are in turn determined by their access to secondary mortgage holders. Secondary holders will buy groups of mortgages from local banks, depending on the interest rates set by the Federal Reserve Board for loans to preferred customers.

8. The passenger in Ted's car was wearing a seat belt and therefore received only slight injury when Ted lost control of the car, due to poor visibility and icy roads, and hit a retaining fence that spun the car around and into a telephone pole.

9. Evelyn ran eight miles, causing repeated strain of her Achilles tendon. She packed her ankle in ice and prevented swelling, thus reducing the pain she otherwise would have experienced.

10. A recent study shows that, on the whole, women who work outside the home tend to have fewer chronic ailments than women who are homemakers. Specifically, the incidence of chronic ailment is lower for women employed in nonindustrial jobs with a high degree of social interaction. Those in industrial occupations have a higher incidence of chronic ailment due to physical exertion and occupational hazards. The study suggests that the absence of daily social interaction is a significant factor in producing chronic ailments in women who are homemakers.

Exercise 8.3B   Describing Causes   Using the concepts of necessary condition, sufficient condition, jointly sufficient condition, individually necessary condition, and partial cause, discuss the examples listed in Exercise 8.3A.

Sample Exercises

1. Max's hitting the baseball as he did is a sufficient condition for the breaking of the window, but it is not a necessary condition since the window's breaking can occur without Max's hitting the baseball.

3. If decreased production of chlorophyll occurs, the leaves change color. Thus, decreased production of chlorophyll is a sufficient condition for color change. Conversely, if there is color change, it must be that the leaves are producing less chlorophyll. Thus, decreased production is a necessary condition as well. Decreasing daylight seems to figure the following way: Decreased daylight is a sufficient condition for decreased chlorophyll, but not a necessary condition. Other factors might cause a tree to produce less chlorophyll. Thus, daylight is sufficient but not necessary for color change in leaves.

Types of Causal Arguments

A causal argument is any argument in which a causal statement occurs either as a premise or as a conclusion. Consider first causal statements as premises.

Example 15	FORM
Reduction in swelling causes relief of pain.	Cs cause Es.
The swelling in my arm is diminishing.	A C occurs.
Therefore, relief of pain will occur.	An E will occur.

Example 16	
Reduction in swelling causes relief of pain.	Cs cause Es.
There is relief of pain.	E occurs.
Therefore, the swelling in my arm is diminishing.	C occurs.

Example 17	
Reduction in swelling causes relief of pain.	Cs cause Es.
Therefore, if relief of pain is desired, reduce the swelling.	If E is desired, do C.

Each example employs a causal generalization as a premise, yet each illustrates a different kind of causal inference. In Example 15, an inference is made to the occurrence of the effect, here symbolized by E. It is a *causal prediction*. In Example 16, an inference is made to the occurrence of a cause. It is a *causal explanation*. Thus, given a causal generalization and a specific instance of a circumstance, we can make an inference about what will happen or what has happened. Example 17 illustrates a *causal prescription*. Given a causal generalization, we can conclude that if an effect is desired (or not desired), we should (or should not) produce the cause. These three types are summarized below.

Causal predictions: Given C, E will occur.
(What will happen if C occurs?)

Cs cause Es.

A C occurs.

E will probably occur.

Causal explanations: E occurred because C occurred.
(Why did E occur?)

Cs cause Es.

E occurs.

C probably occurred.

Causal prescriptions: If E is (is not) desired, do (not do) C.
(How do we make E occur or prevent E from occurring?)

Cs cause Es.

If E is desired, do C.
(Or, if E is not desired, do not do C.)

Each type of causal argument employs a causal generalization, but none establishes or concludes with a causal generalization. Rather, the strength of the argument forms depends upon the reliability of the causal premise 'Cs cause Es.' In our examples, the prediction, explanation, and prescription all presuppose that reduction in swelling causes relief of pain. Such arguments are only as good as the evidence in support of the causal premise. This means that, in assessing causal arguments of the kind illustrated above, we are ultimately drawn back to those arguments that attempt to establish the relevant causal statement. Consider, as an example, how the causal generalization in the preceding arguments might be supported.

Example 18

Whenever swelling is reduced, pain is relieved.

Therefore, reduction in swelling causes relief of pain.

The example has the form:

Whenever event C occurs, event E occurs.

Therefore, events of type C cause events of type E
(that is, Cs cause Es).

Example 18 illustrates a type of causal argument we call a *causal conclusion:* an argument that employs premises to establish a causal statement. Since the arguments we have called predictions, explanations, and prescriptions employ causal statements as premises, we focus on the assessment of those arguments in support of a causal statement. In the following section we examine what have been called Mill's methods for making and assessing causal conclusions.

Below is a summary of this section.

causal statement   *A statement asserting or denying that one thing (or event) or type of thing (or event) causes or is caused by another thing (or event) or type of thing (or event).*

causal argument   *An argument in which at least one causal statement occurs either as a premise or as a conclusion.*

causal prediction   *An argument consisting of a causal generalization and an instance of a causal circumstance, and concluding that a specific effect occurs.*

causal explanation   *An argument consisting of a causal generalization and an instance of an effect, and concluding that an instance of a specific cause explains the occurrence of the effect.*

causal prescription   *An argument consisting of a causal generalization and concluding with a prescription or recommendation for producing or preventing some effect.*

causal conclusion   *An argument consisting of premises in support of a causal statement.*

Exercise 8.3C   Types of Causal Arguments   In the following exercises, (1) write the argument in *argument form,* (2) identify the causal statement, and (3) state whether the argument is a causal prediction, causal explanation, causal prescription, or causal conclusion. You may need to supply missing premises or conclusions. If so, mark them with an asterisk (*).

Sample Exercises

A. Some insects have the ability to survive freezing in winter by producing nucleating proteins in their body fluids. These proteins prevent ice crystals from spreading and causing cell destruction. Since mature green beetles reappear immediately with the first thaw, they have survived the winter by producing proteins that protect their body cells from freezing.

Answer

1. *Some insects have the ability to survive freezing by producing nucleating proteins in their body fluids.*

2. *These nucleating proteins prevent ice crystals from spreading and causing cell destruction. (causal statement)*

3. *Mature green beetles reappear immediately with the first thaw.*

4. *Therefore, they produce nucleating proteins that protect their body cells from freezing.*

Statement 2 is a causal statement. The argument offers a *causal explanation* for the effect that mature green beetles reappear when temperatures thaw them out.

B. Since underwater weevils have been consistently found in those ponds that have an unusually diminished amount of milfoil weed present, it seems reasonable to conclude that the weevils are causing the disappearance of the milfoil weed.

Answer

1. *Underwater weevils have been consistently found in ponds that have an unusually diminished amount of milfoil weed present.*

2. *Probably, weevils are causing the disappearance of the milfoil weed. (causal statement)*

Statement 2 is a causal statement. The argument is a *causal conclusion* providing evidence—the occurrence of weevils and diminishing weeds—in support of the causal statement.

1. Improper cabin pressure in an airplane causes earache. Several passengers have complained of earache; there is probably a problem with the cabin pressure.

2. Passing an electrical current through wire wrapped around a piece of metal produces an electromagnet. Thus, if you want to make an electromagnet, attach a battery to wire wrapped tightly around a piece of iron, for example.

3. Whenever an orange female cat is mated with a black male, the resulting male kittens will be orange and the resulting female kittens will be tortoiseshell. Thus, your black male and my orange female will probably produce no black kittens.

4. Fumbles in football cause more losses of games than any other player error. Because Mudd dropped the football, he will probably do it again, and the Tigers will lose this one.

5. According to Robert J. Samuelson in "Diapers: The Sequel," studies comparing cloth and disposable diapers show that the absorbent in disposable diapers draws moisture from the skin and reduces diaper rash. If you are interested in protecting your infant from diaper rash, you'd be wise to use disposable diapers.

6. Children who are born unable to hear often are also mute and require special attention to learn speech. This is because there seems to be corrective feedback between the part of the brain that hears sound and the part that controls speech. With the absence of sound, the child does not learn speech, at least not easily.

7. The mammalian eye may exhibit two types of nerve receptors, cone-shaped receptors for color vision and rod-shaped receptors for low-intensity light. Owls can hardly see in daylight because they have only rods; hens can hardly see at night because they have only cones.

8. High tide consistently occurs with the rising of the moon and subsides with its setting. Therefore, the tides are caused by the position of the moon.

9. Shaking a bottle filled with carbonated liquid releases the gas and increases the pressure inside the bottle. That is why the soda bubbled out and all over when you opened it.

10. If at night you see something out of the corner of your eye and then turn to look directly at it, it will seem to disappear. This is because the nerve receptors that are most sensitive to low light are displayed on the perimeter of the retina, not in the center.

11. It has recently been concluded that measurable levels of stress do not increase the likelihood of complications in pregnancy, based on a study correlating stress levels and the incidence of complications.

12. Fred's car went out of control and off the road because the roads were icy and, as we all know, ice on the road significantly reduces traction.

13. The fate that befell the Amerinds when they first came into contact with the European invaders is among the best-documented illustrations of the effects that epidemics in general and smallpox in particular have exerted on the course of wars. Shortly after the arrival of Cortez and his Conquistadores, smallpox spread like wildfire through the Indian population. As smallpox was then prevalent in Europe, the Spaniards had probably developed immunity to it through early exposure, whereas the Indians, who had no racial experience with it, proved very susceptible. By killing at least half the Indians and demoralizing them at a critical time, the epidemic certainly played a part as important as Spanish arms and valor in bringing about the conquest of the South American continent. (Rene Dubos, *The Mirage of Health*)

14. In light of the fact that Congress included significant increases in income tax in the new budget and that higher income tax results in decreased consumer spending and deepening recession, the likely result of the new budget will be to deepen the current recession.

15. According to *Newsweek*, "a new study headed by doctors from the University of Minnesota provided the strongest evidence yet that cholesterol does indeed contribute to heart disease. The 838 subjects of the study had survived a previous heart attack and had cholesterol levels above 220. Half were told to modify their diets; some of them were given drugs. The other half underwent a surgical procedure to reduce absorption of cholesterol into the bloodstream. In the

surgery group, cholesterol levels dropped to an average of 196, compared with 241 in the control group. Over a 10-year period the combined rate of second heart attacks or death from heart disease was 35 percent lower in the treated patients—and they required less than half as many cardiac operations as the controls. The study also showed convincingly, for the first time, that the progression of heart disease could be accurately forecast by X-rays taken to monitor plaque buildup inside the arteries." (*Newsweek*, 10/15/90)

Mill's Methods

John Stuart Mill (1806–1873), in his *System of Logic*, describes five methods for identifying causes and effects. They are the methods of agreement, difference, concomitant variation, residue, and the joint method of agreement and difference. We examine the first four and comment on the last. Philosophers do not agree about the adequacy of Mill's methods. Some think Mill claims too much for them. But our purpose is not to enter the debate; it is to adapt the methods as seems reasonable to the assessment of arguments that conclude with a causal statement.

1. The Method of Agreement   According to the method of agreement, the cause of an event E is that circumstance common to all cases in which E occurs. Thus, to paraphrase Mill:

> method of agreement   *If two or more instances of a phenomenon E have only one antecedent circumstance in common, then probably that antecedent circumstance is the cause or a partial cause of E.*

Reasoning that whenever a phenomenon occurs, the cause will be present, Mill's first method for identifying a cause tells us to look for an antecedent circumstance present in all those cases in which the phenomenon occurs.

Suppose, for example, five friends have lunch at a restaurant, and an hour later three get sick from food poisoning. The method of agreement suggests that we can identify the spoiled food causing the sickness by looking for the antecedent circumstance common to the three cases of illness.

Example 19

	ATE	GOT SICK
Denise	salad, roast beef, apple pie, tea	No
Amy	clam chowder, salad, apple pie, coffee	Yes
Beth	clam chowder, apple pie, cola	Yes
Ellen	hamburger, fries, cola	No
Clara	clam chowder, chicken, coffee	Yes

Following the method of agreement, we focus on those cases in which the illness occurred and look for a common element.

Case A   Amy's illness has antecedents: *clam chowder,* salad, apple pie, coffee.

Case B   Beth's illness has antecedents: *clam chowder,* apple pie, cola.

Case C   Clara's illness has antecedents: *clam chowder,* chicken, coffee.

The three cases of illness have only one circumstance in common: clam chowder. On the principle that the cause is probably that circumstance common to otherwise different instances of a phenomenon, it is reasonable to conclude that the clam chowder is at least a causal factor in producing the illness.

The form of an argument using the method of agreement is:

1. *Case A of phenomenon E has antecedent circumstances* f, g, h, *and* i.

2. *Case B of phenomenon E has antecedent circumstances* f, h, *and* j.

3. *Case C of phenomenon E has antecedent circumstances* f, k, *and* i.

---

4. *Therefore, circumstance* f *is probably the cause or a partial cause of E.*

Although the case of the food poisoning illustrates Mill's first method, it seems contrived. Isn't it fortunate that *only one* dish was common to the cases of illness? What if there had been two or three common items eaten by those who got sick? Furthermore, isn't it possible that there are other circumstances common to the three? In fact, looking at our example, there are others: All three are women and, let us suppose, all three are wearing red. On what grounds, then, do we single out food items as antecedent circumstances and not, say, color of clothing? These questions require some discussion of the adequacy of Mill's first method. (Indeed, Mill's other three methods raise similar problems, which, however, we will not stop to address. Let the present discussion suffice.)

Let's take the second problem above first. On what grounds do we single out food items as antecedent circumstances and not such things as wearing red? What is to count as an antecedent circumstance? In practice we distinguish between circumstances thought to be relevant to a phenomenon and those that are not. Wearing red, we say, is not relevant to getting sick after lunch. In other words, we form a *hypothesis,* a reasonable guess based on past experience, as to what circumstances are relevant candidates for the cause of a phenomenon. Using a hypothesis, we significantly narrow the field of antecedent circumstances and thus may apply a method like Mill's first method to isolate the cause. This qualification is required for the application of Mill's first method (and, with the appropriate changes, the others as well):

Given the hypothesis that antecedent circumstances f, g, h, i, *etc. are* causally relevant *to E, then, according to the method of agreement, if two or more instances of a phenomenon E have only one antecedent circumstance in common, probably that antecedent circumstance is the cause or a partial cause of E.*

Second, given two or more occurrences of a phenomenon E, how likely are they to have *only one relevant* antecedent circumstance in common? What do we do when *two or more relevant* antecedent circumstances are common to the otherwise different cases of E? In our example, we may imagine that, besides each woman having clam chowder, each also ate apple pie. The first thing to notice is that the antecedent of Mill's method of agreement does not obtain: We do not have two or more instances of E with only one circumstance in common. Thus, in such a case Mill's first method does not identify the cause of E. We must turn to Mill's second method. Nevertheless, the first method does allow us to eliminate from further consideration all those circumstances not present in instances of E. It provides, in other words, positive evidence that the cause of E is, at least, among those antecedent circumstances common to E. We may state this as a modified version of Mill's first method:

> modified method of agreement   *If two or more in-*
> *stances of a phenomenon E have antecedent circumstances*
> f *and* g *in common, then probably (*f *causes E) or (*g
> *causes E) or (*f *and* g *cause E).*

Naturally, this modified version can be rewritten to apply to cases in which there are more than two common antecedent circumstances. The essential point is that, while Mill's method of agreement may not be sufficient to identify *the* cause of a phenomenon, it does allow us to identify potential causes.

2. The Method of Difference   Using Mill's second method, the method of difference, we can continue the investigation. According to this method, we compare cases in which the phenomenon occurs with those cases in which it does not occur to discover in what way they differ. If there is a single antecedent circumstance present when the phenomenon occurs but absent when it does not occur, that circumstance is causally involved in the phenomenon. For example, you may conclude that touching the TV antenna is the cause of the clear picture on your TV screen when you observe that it is clear when you touch it but not clear when you take your hand away. Or, to take another example, you may conclude that it is the ham that causes the salty taste in your stew when you notice that the salty-tasting batch has ham in it while the other batch does not.

> method of difference   *If an instance of phenomenon*
> *E and an instance in which E does not occur differ only in*
> *the presence of one antecedent circumstance with the in-*
> *stance of E, then that antecedent circumstance is probably*
> *the cause or a partial cause of E.*

The form of an argument employing the method of difference is

> 1. *Case A of phenomenon E has antecedent circumstances*
>   f, g, h, *and* i.

2. Case B without phenomenon E has antecedent circumstances g, h, *and* i.

---

3. Therefore, circumstance f *is probably the cause or a partial cause of E.*

By using the method of difference in conjunction with the method of agreement—actually what Mill calls the joint method of agreement and difference—we can handle the problem raised above: those cases in which two or more instances have *more than one* antecedent circumstance in common. Let's suppose that Amy, Beth, and Clara also have apple pie in common. By the method of agreement, we can say that the three cases of illness are caused by apple pie, clam chowder, or the combination of apple pie and clam chowder. Now we compare their cases with those in which one of the two antecedents is present yet the illness is not.

Example 20

Case A   Amy's illness has antecedents *clam chowder,* salad, *apple pie,* coffee.

Case B   Beth's illness has antecedents *clam chowder, apple pie,* cola.

Case C   Clara's illness has antecedents *clam chowder,* chicken, *apple pie,* coffee.

Case D   Denise, no illness, has antecedents salad, roast beef, *apple pie,* tea.

By using the method of difference, we see that the apple pie cannot be the cause of the illness because Denise had apple pie but did not get sick. Thus, of the two common antecedents, the apple pie may be eliminated as a cause.

When we use the method of agreement, we look for what is common to instances of a phenomenon we are investigating. Thus, we eliminate those antecedent factors not present in all cases in which the phenomenon occurs. When we use the method of difference, we look for some difference between instances of a phenomenon and instances without the phenomenon. Thus, we eliminate those antecedent factors present whenever the phenomenon fails to occur.

Below is the form of an argument employing both the method of agreement and the method of difference.

METHOD OF AGREEMENT AND METHOD OF DIFFERENCE

1. If f *and* g *are common to E, then probably (*f *causes E) or (*g *causes E).*	*(modified method of agreement)*
2. f *and* g *are common to E.*	*(by observation)*
*3. Therefore, probably (*f *causes E) or (*g *causes E).*	*(by 1 and 2, MP)*
4. If circumstance g *but not E, then probably not (*g *causes E).*	*(method of difference)*
5. g *and not E.*	*(by observation)*

6. Therefore, probably not (g causes E).   (by 4 and 5, MP)

_____

7. Therefore, probably f causes E.   (by 3 and 6, DS)

3. The Method of Concomitant Variation   Any number of things in our experience exhibit variations. Hot plates get hotter; people get physically stronger or weaker. Frequently, we observe that such variations coincide with (are concomitant with) variations in other circumstances.

Example 21

The more Smith exercises, the stronger he seems to get.

Example 22

The higher the humidity, the longer it takes the paint to dry.

The fact that instances of two different kinds of phenomena consistently vary together provides some evidence that they are causally related. To paraphrase Mill:

> **method of concomitant variation**   *If variations in phenomenon E coincide with variations in phenomenon P, then it is probable that E and P are causally related.*

A virtue of the method of concomitant variation, Mill claims, is that it is particularly useful for those cases in which the method of difference cannot be applied. Mill's example is the phenomenon of the tides. Suppose we suspect that the moon's gravitational pull on Earth is the cause of the tides. In this case, there is no possibility of applying the method of difference because we cannot get rid of the moon (which is what we'd have to do to see what effect, if any, that had on the tides). But what is possible, Mill says, is to observe the variations in the position of the moon and look for concomitant variations in the tides. Hence, we see that the tide rises with the rising moon and ebbs with the latter's setting.

Now the fact that two phenomena vary consistently is evidence that they are causally related but not evidence about which is the cause and which the effect. Thus, for example, we should not conclude that the moon is causing the tides just because we observe a concomitant variation between the two. Odd as it may sound, perhaps the tides cause the moon to rotate! By itself the method of concomitant variation gives us only correlations of phenomena and, hence, evidence of a causal connection. To conclude which phenomenon is causing which, we need evidence beyond what the method of concomitant variation provides, evidence that is perhaps provided by the other methods.

In thinking about two phenomena that vary in relation to each other, it is useful to make a distinction. In some cases a phenomenon varies *simultaneously* with some other circumstance. For example, variations in humidity and paint-drying time occur simultaneously. The moon's rotation occurs simultaneously with the changing of the tides. On the other hand, some phenomena vary *subsequent to* variations in some other circumstance. For example, one's muscles get bigger subsequent to increased exercise. Next year's crop of insects varies with the severity of this year's winter.

About the second kind of case above, we can conclude that the antecedent phenomenon is the cause of the subsequent because we know that what comes after cannot be the cause of what comes before. If we know, in other words, that some phenomenon E has circumstance *f as an antecedent,* then we could reason that variations in E are caused by variations in *f*. Letting the symbols '+' and '−' represent increases or decreases, we can express the form of the argument by the method of concomitant variation as follows:

Case A   *Phenomenon E has antecedent* f.

Case B   *Phenomenon E+ has antecedent* f+.

Case C   *Phenomenon E− has antecedent* f−.

Therefore, probably variations in antecedent f *cause variations in E.*

Of course, for those cases in which phenomena vary inversely, the form of argument would differ accordingly. For example, 'phenomenon E+ has antecedent *f−*.'

About those kinds of cases in which phenomena vary simultaneously, Mill suggests that, if possible, we try to produce variations in one phenomenon by controlling variations in the other. For example, in a tightly sealed room we vary the humidity and see whether that produces variations in drying time. Then we try the reverse. We speed drying time by thinning the paint, say, to see if that alters the room's humidity. Or, as another example, we observe that increasing the temperature of a gas increases its volume but increasing volume does not increase temperature. Such experiments enable us to say which of two simultaneously occurring events is varying because of which.

Example 23

Given a balloon filled with air to a volume of fifteen cubic inches at room temperature, say, 70°F, I then step outside into the cold, 20°F, and observe that the balloon nearly collapses. When I return to the warm house, the balloon resumes its previous volume.

Experiments in which we produce variations in some phenomenon by controlling others borrow from what we have learned with the method of difference. In effect, we try to produce a difference in one by making a difference in the other. In short:

Case A   *Phenomenon P increases (or decreases);*
          E increases (or decreases).

Case B   *Phenomenon E increases (or decreases);*
          P neither increases nor decreases.

Therefore, variations in P probably cause variations in E.

What finally entitles us to say that the moon causes the tides and not the reverse? We cannot experiment on the moon and the tides. However, in this kind of case, the method of difference provides a way of testing the hypothesis that the tides cause the moon's variations. Comparing our moon with planets having a moon but no oceans, we conclude that the tides cannot be the phenomenon causing variations in the moon; it must be the reverse.

4. The Method of Residue   Suppose we are investigating some complex phenomenon such as the increased incidence of AIDS in our community. Let us say that we already know certain facts: (1) The AIDS virus is transmitted through exchange of body fluids, typically blood or semen; (2) in all the cases of AIDS we have observed, the antecedent circumstances have been either contaminated needles in IV drug use, unsafe sex, or blood transfusions; (3) we have established that IV drug use is a causal factor in 65 percent of the cases and unsafe sex is a causal factor in 25 percent of the cases. Thus, we can conclude that the remaining cases are caused by blood transfusion. Our argument is

Example 24

1. *All observed instances of AIDS have as their antecedent circumstances IV drug use, unsafe sex, or blood transfusion.*

2. *IV drug use is a causal factor in 65 percent of cases of AIDS.*

3. *Unsafe sex is a causal factor in 25 percent of cases of AIDS.*

_____

4. *Therefore, blood transfusion is a causal factor in the remaining cases of AIDS.*

That argument illustrates Mill's method of residue, which he describes as follows:

method of residue   *Subtract from any phenomenon such part as is known by previous inductions to be the effect of certain antecedents, and the residue of the phenomenon is the effect of the remaining antecedents.*

An example of the form of an argument using the method of residue is this:

1. *Phenomenon E consists of parts E1, E2, and E3.*

2. *E has antecedent circumstances f, g, and h.*

3. f *causes E1.*

4. g *causes E2.*

_____

5. *Therefore,* h *(the residue) causes E3.*

In short, if we know what part one antecedent plays in a complex phenomenon, we can infer the part played by the other. Suppose we want to clarify for ourselves what effect the strings are having in an orchestra, given that we can hear the horns well. Following the method of residue, we ask the horn section to sit out while the strings play.

The method of residue may be used to identify interfering causal factors as well. Suppose a patient is being given an antihypertensive drug that we know should have the effect of a reduction in blood pressure. Yet we observe that the patient is not responding as predicted. In searching for other antecedent circumstances, we discover that the patient has been taking epinephrine to control a cold. Assuming that we can rule out other factors and given that the antihypertensive drug normally dilates blood vessels, we can reasonably conclude that the epinephrine is interfering. Letting f refer to the antihypertensive drug, g the epinephrine drug, and E reduced blood pressure, we are reasoning as follows:

> 1. *Antecedent circumstance f is known to cause E—that is, all other things being equal, in cases where f is present, E occurs.*
>
> 2. *Case A Antecedent circumstances f and g, E does not occur.*
>
> ---
>
> 3. *Therefore, in Case A, probably g causally interferes with f.*

As the examples illustrate, the method of residue presupposes some causal knowledge of a phenomenon. Perhaps by means of the other methods, we have a partial understanding of the phenomenon. This method allows us to identify at least one, perhaps other causal factors contributing to the phenomenon.

Summary: Mill's Methods   Mill's methods provide four criteria for assessing the strength of arguments having a causal conclusion. In applying Mill's methods, the following points should be observed.

First, Mill's methods assume that relevant circumstances or factors have been identified. That is, the use of Mill's methods requires a hypothesis about which kinds of circumstances are to be considered. Thus, in assessing an argument in support of a causal statement, we should consider whether a premise asserting that, for example, "in all instances of E, only antecedent circumstance f is present" is true. Are there relevant circumstances that have not been considered?

Second, consider the methods as *providing evidence* in support of or contrary to a causal claim. That is, if a causal claim—X causes Y—is supported by premises based on one of the methods, we will say that that causal claim is strengthened. Let us say, further, that a causal claim is given additional strength by premises based on more than one method.

Below is a shorthand summary with simple explanations, not rigorously expressed, of the four methods we have studied. In examining a particular argument, use this general summary to direct you to the previous, more detailed discussions.

AGREEMENT

If a circumstance *f* is the only circumstance always present whenever E occurs, then we have supporting evidence for the conclusion that *f* is the cause of E.

Why? Because whatever is the cause of E will be present whenever E is present.

DIFFERENCE

If E occurs when *f* is present but not when *f* is absent, then we have supporting evidence for the conclusion that *f* causes E.

Why? Because the nonoccurrence of E is attributable to some difference in antecedent circumstances.

CONCOMITANT VARIATION

If one phenomenon varies consistently with another phenomenon, then we have supporting evidence that the two are causally related.

Why? Because if two variable phenomena are causally related, then they will exhibit concomitant variation.

1. Given two phenomena that vary consistently, if one precedes the other, then we have supporting evidence that the former causes the latter.

2. Given two phenomena that vary consistently, if by altering one we can produce concomitant variations in the other, then we have supporting evidence that the former causes the latter.

RESIDUE

If one or more parts of a phenomenon can be causally explained by one or more parts of the antecedent circumstances, then we have supporting evidence that the remaining part of the phenomenon can be causally explained by the remaining antecedent circumstance.

Why? Given a complex phenomenon represented as E1, E2, and E3 and antecedents *f, g,* and *h* and given that E1 is causally explained by *f,* and E2 is causally explained by *g,* then the only remaining factor to explain E3 is *h.*

Since these four methods provide evidence in support of a causal statement, we can say in summary that

A causal conclusion is strong to the degree that it is supported by premises with evidence of one or more of Mill's methods.

Exercise 8.3D   Mill's Methods   In the following exercises, (a) identify the causal statement that is asserted; then (b) explain which method or methods are employed or should be employed to support the causal statement.

Sample Exercise *Researchers reported in* Scientific American *recently that some species of frogs are able to survive the winter by existing in a frozen state. Ice on the skin of the frog causes the liver to excrete large amounts of glucose into the blood system. The glucose in the blood acts to control the formation of ice crystals in the body and to prevent cellular collapse.*

Answer (a) The causal connection asserted in the passage is that between the presence of glucose in the frog's blood system and effects of freezing. (b) Mill's methods of agreement and difference are appropriate in this example. First, researchers have identified the glucose in the blood as the causal factor inhibiting the effects of freezing. Second, it would strengthen the causal claim to observe those cases in which the frog is frozen but the liver is prevented from excreting glucose into the blood.

1. Smith needs some more lavender paint. Previously he mixed red, blue, and white to make the shade he wanted. He knows that red and blue make purple, so he reasons that adding white must produce lavender.

2. Ralph reasons that his grades are improving over last semester's because this semester he is sleeping an extra hour each night.

3. Alice suspects that she is allergic to Bud's cat because every time she visits his house the cat is there and she starts sneezing. But when he visits her house, the cat isn't and she doesn't. Does she have good evidence for her suspicion? If so, by what method? If not, by what method can she confirm or disconfirm her suspicion?

4. Max plugged in the vacuum cleaner and flipped the 'on' switch but nothing happened. Then he plugged in a lamp; it worked. Max concluded that the cause of the problem lies in the vacuum cleaner, not in the electric outlet.

5. Kay-kay, a precocious three-year-old, reasoned that turning the knob on the stereo caused the music to get louder or softer because no matter how far or how fast she turned the knob, the sound changed along with it.

6. At the first weighing, the mother stepped onto the scale alone. Her weight caused the scale to show 150 lb. At the second weighing, the mother stepped onto the scale holding her baby. Their combined weight registered 165 lb. Thus, the weight of the baby, being the cause of the difference, is 15 lb.

7. Comparing the cases in which women are employed in jobs involving a high degree of social interaction with cases in which women are not, we can conclude that, all other things being equal, social interaction reduces the incidence of chronic ailment.

8. Seventeen customers reported being shortchanged during one week. All seventeen had receipts showing that Max was their cashier. It appears that Max is responsible.

9. Caffeine does not increase the risk of heart disease, for as a recent study shows—comparing caffeine users, users of decaffeinated products, and those who use neither—heart disease is as low for caffeine users as it is for those who use neither. The incidence of heart disease is slightly higher for those who use decaffeinated products.

10. Airplane crashes have a number of causes: equipment malfunction, weather conditions, pilot error, ground control error. Studies show that equipment malfunction, weather conditions, and pilot error account for 87 percent of airplane accidents examined in the past nineteen years. We conclude that 13 percent are due to ground control error.

11. If the cycle goes over a bump and the engine misfires, and then goes over another bump and the engine misfires, and then goes over another bump and the engine misfires, and then goes over a long smooth stretch of road and there is no misfiring, and then goes over a fourth bump and the engine misfires again, one can logically conclude that the misfiring is caused by the bumps. (Robert M. Pirsig, *Zen and the Art of Motorcycle Maintenance*)

12. Cigarette smoking and exposure to secondhand smoke both significantly hasten hardening of the arteries . . . [according to a study in the January 1998 *Journal of the American Medical Association*]. An estimated 30,000 to 60,000 deaths a year in the United States can be attributed to secondhand smoking, wrote the authors, led by epidemiologist George Howard. . . . Howard and colleagues used ultrasound to measure how much carotid-artery walls thickened over a three-year period in 10,914 adults age 45 to 65. Subjects who had smoked on average one pack a day for 33 years had 50 percent increase in the progression of hardening of their arteries when compared to nonsmokers. Among past smokers—who had previously smoked a pack daily for 25 years—a 25 percent increase in progression was found. Among nonsmokers who reported exposure to secondhand smoke for an average of 18 to 20 hours weekly, there was a 20 percent increase . . . when compared with people without such exposure. (*New York Times,* Jan. 14, 1998)

13. The following is an excerpt from a *New York Times* report on studies showing that "birds can calibrate their innate sense of magnetic north with the movement of celestial objects across the sky."

In a study performed by Kenneth P. and Mary A. Able of the State University of New York at Albany, 20 Savannah sparrows were divided into four groups and exposed to a rotating disk with dim lights resembling stars.

In the wild, young birds learn the location of true north by noting the axis of the rotation of the night sky.

But in the Ables' test, only one group of birds observed the rotation of the artificial stars at true north. For the other three groups, that point was located to the magnetic east, south, or west.

When the birds were ready to migrate, they were placed in darkened boxes without the star patterns. Only the birds exposed to the "normal" pattern migrated south.

The others calibrated their compass to a point they believed to be north and veered off in the wrong direction.

In comparison, another group of sparrows raised seeing neither the actual sky nor the artificial patterns migrated according to magnetic north only.

14. According to a report in *Newsweek:*

People with two X chromosomes are usually female; an X and a Y make a male. But sometimes an XX is male and an XY is female. By studying these exceptions, researchers narrowed the search for the maleness gene to a smidgen of the Y—a piece that was absent from an XY female's Y, but present on an XX male's X. Researchers at the Imperial Cancer Research Fund in London used biochemical scissors to chop this smidgen of human DNA into 50 bits; they then mixed those bits with DNA segments from other mammals, male and female. Because a trait as basic as maleness is expected to have deep evolutionary roots and thus can be shared across species, the bit that found a match in every male was the best candidate for the masculinity gene.

15. A *New York Times* essay by William K. Stevens reports on a study showing that if a new analysis of the link between weather patterns in West Africa and the tropical Atlantic is correct, communities along the United States East Coast that experienced relatively few dangerous hurricanes in the 1970s and 1980s may face more frequent killer storms in the next two decades or so.

　　The analysis by William M. Gray of Colorado State University, an expert on tropical cyclones, found that when rain in the Western Sahel region of Africa is plentiful, more strong hurricanes develop in the Atlantic and strike the United States. The years from 1947 through 1969 were just such a time. In that period, the study found, 13 hurricanes with winds of more than 110 miles an hour slammed into the East Coast and Florida.

　　But when there is drought in the Western Sahel, fewer strong Atlantic hurricanes develop. According to this study, that was the case in the Sahel from 1970 through 1987, when only one storm with peak winds of more than 110 miles an hour struck the East Coast and Florida.

　　The study suggests that this relatively calm period is ending and that a more violent period is about to begin or may already have begun. And the potential for damage is greater now, Dr. Gray said. "There are more people and more development along the Atlantic Coast. . . . There is more property to damage."

8.4 Argument from Analogy

　　An argument from analogy draws a conclusion about something on the basis of an analogy to some other thing. For example, you may reason that since your last car was a Ford and it held up well, then your present car, also a Ford, will hold up well, too. What is true of your previous car is likely to be true of your present car because they are both Fords. The reasoning is that if two or more things are alike in some respects, they are alike in some other respect. Letting A and B represent two different things, events, or practices and letting f, g, h, and j represent features or properties, we can represent the form of analogical reasoning as follows:

FORM OF ARGUMENT FROM ANALOGY

(A and B are analogous in that . . .)

A and B are both f, g, *and* h.

A is also j.

Therefore, probably B is j.

Let us call the thing, event, or practice at issue in the argument the *subject*. In the formal expression above, B is the subject. Let us call that to which the analogy is drawn the *analogue*. Further, let us call the feature *j* possessed by A and concluded to be possessed by B the *inferred feature*. Last, we call the similarities that form the basis of the analogy the *common features*. Thus, the reasoning is that subject B has inferred feature *j* because B has common features *f, g, h* with A, the analogue. Although this is cumbersome, it will help in talking about this type of argument.

Consider now some examples of arguments from analogy and notice the assertion of an analogy between the subject of the argument and the analogue.

Example 25

The economic depression of the thirties was turned around by extensive federal job programs. We are currently in a similar economic situation, so it is probable that federal job programs are needed to solve the current economic problem.

Example 26

Machines are the products of intelligence. They are ordered systems consisting of parts deliberately designed to perform certain functions. The universe, too, is an ordered system, albeit on a much greater magnitude, consisting of parts perfectly adapted to certain ends. Thus, it is reasonable to conclude that the universe is also a product of intelligence.

Example 27

Just as no one is under an obligation to donate his or her kidney to a person who needs one to live, so no pregnant woman is under an obligation to donate the use of her womb to the person, the fetus, who requires it to live.

In each of Examples 25 to 27, a conclusion is drawn about the subject under discussion—the current economic situation, the universe, and the obligation of a pregnant woman to the fetus, respectively—on the basis of what is asserted to be true of an analogue: the previous economic depression, machines, and the obligation of persons with healthy kidneys to persons in need of a kidney. How do we assess such arguments? What do we look for in evaluating the strength of analogical reasoning?

The inductive strength of an analogical argument essentially depends on two considerations: (1) How does the possession of the common features bear on the possession of the inferred feature? Is being like A in features *f, g,* and *h* good reason for concluding that B also possesses *j*? (2) Is there any relevant dissimilarity between A and B? Is there a difference between the two that might bear negatively on B's possessing the inferred feature? A summary description of the inductive strength of the argument from analogy can be put as follows:

An argument from analogy is inductively strong to the degree that
1. *the common features are relevant to the inferred feature and*
2. *there are no relevant dissimilarities.*

We will call these two considerations the criteria of inductive strength in arguments from analogy. There is a third consideration we must look at, the *extent of the similarity* between the subject and the analogue. However, we will see that the extent of similarity between subject and analogue is less important than whether the similarities are relevant and there are no relevant dissimilarities, that is, criteria 1 and 2 above.

Assessing an argument from analogy frequently requires that we attempt to make explicit information that is not provided in the premises. What are we told in the argument and, more important, what do we already know about the subject, the analogue, or the relevance of the purported analogy? Both Examples 25 and 27 are typical arguments; they leave much unstated. In assessing Example 25, for instance, we need to ask, what are the features common to the depression of the thirties and today's economic situation? Is it because of those features that federal job programs succeeded in changing the economy? Or are there relevant differences today that would make federal job programs ineffective? Given that background information is presupposed in the typical argument from analogy, if we were to make explicit and express formally those claims, then the form of an inductively strong argument from analogy is this:

1. *A and B are* f, g, *and* h.

2. *A is also* j.

3. *Features* f, g, *and* h *are relevant to the possession of feature* j.

4. *There is no feature* k *possessed by B but not A that bears negatively on the presence of* j.

---

5. *Therefore, B is probably* j.

Premises 3 and 4 express what is presupposed in a strong analogical argument. Thus, to the extent that an argument meets the criteria of relevant features and no relevant dissimilarities, it is strong. In what follows, we examine and illustrate statements 3 and 4 to see how they bear on the strength of analogical arguments.

1. The Similarities Are Extensive   The first premise in our construction of the form of an inductively strong analogical argument asserts that the subject and the analogue have some number of features in common. (The form of the premise lists three common features. This is only for illustration, of course.)

Now it would seem that the greater the similarity between two things, the stronger the argument, but in fact this consideration turns out to be less reliable than the other two. The situation with the extent of similarity is reminiscent of what we saw about sample size in inductive generalizations. But let's see why sheer number of similarities is generally no real virtue in an analogical argument. Consider an example in which two things are said to be alike in a number of ways:

Example 28

In respect of color, shape, and size, an orange is more like a peach than a pineapple. Furthermore, oranges and peaches come from trees that are very similar in appearance, whereas the pineapple comes from a short, tough, lance-leaved shrub. The orange contains citric acid. Probably, a peach contains citric acid, whereas a pineapple does not.

In this example, the extensive similarities mislead us; just the opposite is true of peaches and pineapples. Why does that argument fail in spite of the numerous similarities? It is because the stated similarities do not bear on whether a fruit has citric acid. The example suggests two points: (1) If the features two things have in common are *not* relevant to the inferred feature, then the number of common features does not matter; and (2) two things, like the orange and pineapple, may have few, if any, observable similarities, yet still be alike in possessing the inferred feature.

How, then, does extent of similarity bear on the strength of an analogical argument? It is important in three ways. First, just as a matter of probability, the greater the points of similarity between two things, the more likely a relevant similarity, if present, will appear in the set of common features. Thus, *extent of similarities* may be indirectly related to the criteria of (1) relevance and (2) no relevant dissimilarity.

Second, if we have no grounds for judging the relevance of common features to the inferred feature, then knowing only that two or more things are similar in a number of ways is positive evidence of further similarities.

Example 29

A and B are spherical, yellow, waxy, small, and light. A is sweet-tasting. Probably B is sweet-tasting.

If all we know is that A and B are alike as described, then the conclusion drawn seems reasonable. Indeed, given the premises in Example 29, expecting that A and B are of the same kind is reasonable.

Third, having a number of similarities in common is usually what we expect of things that are members of the same kind. (Think of two or more Fords, gumballs, No. 2 pencils, Shetland ponies, etc.) Some arguments from analogy are based on a premise stating that the subject is a member of a kind. For example, the following argument illustrates this type of reasoning by analogy:

Example 30	FORM
Most sociologists are liberals.	Most Xs are *j*.
Max is a sociologist.	B is an X.
Therefore, Max is probably a liberal.	B is *j*.

Implicit in the argument is that Max shares common features with sociologists in virtue of being a sociologist. (If it sounds odd to you to say that Max is analogous to or similar to sociologists when, after all, he *is* one, consider that Max could be a sociologist only if he did in fact share some common features with them, such as, for example, the same kind of training.)

Although B's being a member of kind X provides some reason for thinking that B has some feature common to Xs, nevertheless the argument assumes that B is typical of Xs. The strength of an argument such as Example 30 depends on whether Max is a *typical* sociologist. Max might have those features that make him a sociologist, yet be a rather atypical one. Thus, while being a member of a kind is some positive evidence for an inference, again we see that the *number* of similarities between two things or types of things is less important than the *kinds* of similarities, the criterion expressed in 2 above. We need to consider that criterion next.

2. The Similarities Are Relevant to the Inferred Feature   If the conclusion of an analogical argument is strongly supported by its premises, then implicit at least in the premises is that the common features are relevant to the inferred feature. Let's focus on statement 3 in the formal expression of a strong argument.

1. A and B are f, g, and h.

2. A is also j.

3. Features f, g, and h are relevant to the possession of feature j.

4. There is no feature k possessed by B but not A that bears negatively on the presence of j.

Therefore, probably B is j.

What makes common features relevant to the possession of the inferred feature? Features the subject and analogue have in common may be relevant to the inference in different ways. Let's consider four kinds of relevance, giving us four different kinds of analogical arguments. This classification is not exhaustive, but it does illustrate some of the variations found in analogical reasoning. The four we consider are causal, statistical, moral, and aesthetic analogies.

2a. Causal Analogies   One way in which common features may be relevant is that they are *causally connected* to the inferred feature. Perhaps it is the case that features *f, g,* and *h* are causally sufficient or necessary for *j*. Consider this example.

Example 31

Although jalapeño and Serrano chiles are different in size and color, both contain the acid capsaicin. Jalapeños leave a strong burning sensation in the mouth. Probably Serranos do as well.

The acid capsaicin causes the burning sensation; thus, having that acid in common with jalapeños provides good evidence that Serranos are hot too.

A common method of reasoning in science is to explore one phenomenon by means of what is purported to be an analogue called a model. For example, one very important and deservedly controversial area in which analogical reasoning is assumed to be valuable is in scientific research using animals to gain information about humans. Regarding the animal as a model of human physiology, researchers draw conclusions about, for example, human susceptibility to disease on the basis of the animal's susceptibility to disease. The inferences made are causal analogies.

In the following example, a physical model is used as evidence of the activity of atoms.

Example 32

In support of the theory of molecular motion, Einstein at-
tempted to produce an observable mechanical consequence
of the action of atoms. Searching for phenomena large
enough to be viewed through a microscope yet small
enough to respond to the mechanical actions of atoms, he
found it in the phenomenon known to biologists as Brown-
ian motion. If one suspends a fine powder . . . in a liquid
and studies the grains through a microscope, he notes that
they are in continual trembling, random motion.
(Adapted from *Contemporary Physics* by David Park)

2b. Statistical Analogies   Another way in which common features may be relevant to the inferred feature is that they are frequently found together. A frequently occurring correlation of features gives some evidence for inferring the one whenever the other or others are present. Since such correlations can be studied and described statistically, we can call analogical arguments based on correlations statistical analogies. Our observations suggest that the probability is high that whenever features f, g, and h are present, the inferred feature j is also present.

Example 33

In district 4 the majority of residents have incomes above
$80,000. They almost always elect the Republican can-
didate in their district elections. District 6 is also popu-
lated with high-income residents; therefore, they will
probably vote Republican.

Example 34

A study of physicians' attitudes toward patient autonomy
showed that physicians at Boston University Medical
Center, a teaching hospital, rated patient autonomy an
important value. Physicians at an equally large but non-
teaching metropolitan hospital rated patient autonomy as

having less value in their practice. Since the Dartmouth hospital is a large teaching hospital, we should expect physicians' attitudes like those of the BU hospital.

2c. Moral Analogies   To draw a moral conclusion on the basis of an analogy is to reason that what is morally true about one case is true about another because they are similar cases. It is presupposed that features *f, g,* and *h* support the same moral judgment about the subject as is made about the analogue. For example, since case A is a case of lying and therefore morally wrong, case B, also a case of lying, is also morally wrong. Consider these examples.

Example 35

A pet of any sort is certainly as dependent on its owner as a child is on its parents. Neither pet nor child can live and develop well without basic attention to its needs, consistency in treatment, and affection. Thus, since what's good for a child should always be considered, so also what's good for a pet should be considered.

Example 36

Because Smith was punished with a fine and two months in jail for driving while intoxicated, Jones, who committed the same offense, should receive the same punishment.

Example 37

Recently, the parents of a child dying from kidney failure made their plea for a kidney donor on national television. Some weeks later the host of that show proudly announced that a donor had been located and the child was doing well after a successful transplantation of a new kidney. There is a serious injustice in a case like this, an injustice to those children and parents who happen not to have access to national television but who wait patiently and bravely, following the nationally agreed-upon rules for allocation of organs. There is a child just like the child of those TV parents, whose turn was taken by someone else.

In Example 37, the argument is that an injustice is done when two similar cases are not given the same treatment.

2d. Aesthetic Analogies   To draw an aesthetic conclusion about something is to conclude that it has or lacks aesthetic merit or some particular aesthetic quality. You might support your conclusion on the basis of an analogy to a case you think is uncontroversial. For example, since performance A was dynamic, sensitive, and intelligently executed and you judged it aesthetically good, then performance B, also dynamic, sensitive, and intelligently executed, should also be judged aesthetically good. Consider these examples.

Example 38

The movie Lethal Weapon II *is worth seeing because it has the same actors as* Lethal Weapon *and it maintains the same fast-paced excitement and comic irony that we saw in the first one. Much of the success of the first version is due to the improbable pairing of actors Mel Gibson and Danny Glover, playing two opposite-personality types.*

Example 39

These two shades of turquoise and orange will really liven up your kitchen and make it cheerful and inviting. Just look at how exciting these colors look together when you hold up these samples in the light.

Example 40

On the Metropolitan Museum exhibit "Mexico: Splendors of Thirty Centuries," a Newsweek *reporter writes: "The whole idea of . . . squeezing the art history of an entire nation of nearly 90,000,000 people and three distinct civilizations into part of a floor of the Met seems a little sad, if not absurd. Would the Italians have sat still for a few galleries each of imperial Rome, the Renaissance, and the industrial age?"*

Example 40 argues that the exhibit is aesthetically flawed because the cultures it represents are as complex as the Italian cultures and a similar presentation of the Italians would be aesthetically flawed.

3. There Are No Relevant Dissimilarities   Let us focus on the second criterion of a strong inductive analogy by considering statement 4 in the formal account:

> 4. *There is no feature* k *possessed by B but not A that bears negatively on the presence of* j.

If there is a dissimilarity between the subject and the analogue, then there is some feature possessed by one and not the other. Differences per se do not create a disanalogy; differences are to be expected. For instance, in Example 28, it matters little that oranges and pineapples come from plants that are so different in appearance. However, when a difference bears negatively on the possession of the inferred feature, a disanalogy exists. For example, in thinking about Example 27—where it is argued that mothers have no more obligation to bring a fetus to term than healthy people do to those who need a kidney transplant—it is arguably a relevant difference that a fetus may have a right to use the mother's womb, whereas a donor hardly ever has a right to another's kidney. If that difference can be supported, then criterion 2 has not been met, and the argument is weakened. Consider this example.

Example 41

Maxine has demonstrated that she knows how to apply CPR (cardiopulmonary resuscitation) and how to remain calm and controlled in simulated cases of cardiac arrest using a dummy. Therefore, she can be expected to treat actual cardiac patients effectively and calmly.

The argument concludes that Maxine can be expected to handle actual cardiac patients effectively because she has done so in demonstrations with dummies. Yet there is certainly a significant psychological difference between treating a dummy and treating a person who might die because of one's actions. An awareness of that risk is liable to produce anxiety and affect Maxine's behavior; she may freeze or fail to remember the proper procedure. Suppose, however, the analogy had been constructed on the basis of Maxine's performance in some previous case of actual cardiac arrest. No disanalogy could be raised and the argument would be stronger. As it is, Example 41 fails to meet criterion 2.

We show that an argument from analogy is weak or at least weakened by showing that a relevant difference exists between the cases. Conversely, we add strength to an argument by showing that no such relevant difference exists. For example, in defense of Example 41, two kinds of replies are appropriate. One is to show that the purported dissimilarity, the anxiety, is not adversely relevant to proper behavior in actual cases. Repeated practice does not reduce anxiety, but it does ensure proper behavior. She will be frightened, but her actions will be almost automatic. Another reply is to argue that the adversely relevant factor, anxiety, does not usually occur in people who have been so thoroughly tested as has Maxine. She is unlikely to be frightened. In short, the debate about the strength of an analogy is likely to turn on whether the relevant negative feature is present or whether, being present, it does indeed make the inferred feature less probable.

Summary: Argument from Analogy

1. An argument from analogy draws a conclusion about one thing on the basis of an analogy to some other thing.

2. The form of an argument from analogy is

A and B are both f, g, and h.

A is also j.

_____

Therefore, probably B is j.

3. The terms we employ to talk about the argument are the following:

Subject   That person, thing, or event, represented by B, about which a conclusion is drawn

Analogue   That person, thing, or event, represented by A, to which B is claimed to be analogous

Common features   Those features—here *f, g,* and *h*—possessed by both A and B that are the basis for the analogy

Inferred feature   That feature, *j,* present with A and concluded as belonging as well to B

4. There are two criteria of the inductive strength of an argument from analogy. They are

    a. the common features are relevant to the inferred feature; and

    b. there are no relevant dissimilarities.

5. A common feature is relevant to the presence of the inferred feature if it increases the likelihood of the presence of the inferred feature. Specifically, common features may be relevant to an inferred feature in ways such as the following.

Causal analogy   Common features are causally connected to the presence of the inferred feature.

Statistical analogy   Common features are statistically correlated with the presence of the inferred feature.

Moral analogy   Common features justifying a moral judgment about the analogue justify the same moral judgment about the subject.

Aesthetic analogy   Common features justifying an aesthetic judgment about the analogue justify the same aesthetic judgment about the subject.

Exercise 8.4   Arguments from Analogy   Identify the subject and analogue. Discuss whether the analogy is relevant or irrelevant by supplying, where necessary, background information about common features. Given the information provided, would you judge it to be inductively strong? If not, why?

Sample Exercise   *A* Newsweek *article reports concerns over the use of mercury in dental fillings. At a meeting of the American Physiological Society scientists presented evidence that mercury "seriously compromises" organ systems in test animals. Researchers at the University of Calgary placed twelve amalgam fillings in the mouths of six ewes. Within two months, the test animals experienced a loss of kidney function of between 16 percent and 80 percent; control animals suffered no loss. And in the first study in primates, the Calgary team reports that in monkeys the mercury winds up in the kidneys, intestinal tract, and jaws. Canadian and American researchers concluded that mercury in fillings should be banned immediately.*

Answer

Subject: Humans

Analogue: Ewes and primates

Argument: Mercury amalgam fillings cause organ problems in ewes and primates. Ewes and primates are like humans. Therefore, mercury amalgam fillings probably cause organ problems in humans. Therefore, they should be banned.

Relevant analogy? We might wonder how alike ewes and humans are, but primates are the closest, physiologically, of all animal groups to humans. The study reports no relevant dissimilarities. It is reasonable to conclude that this is a strong analogical argument.

1. Police officers routinely practice the use of their service revolvers at a firing range. An officer who does well in target practice ought to do well in actual situations requiring the use of a revolver.

2. Like a religion, dianetics has a comprehensive body of beliefs about what we are, where we came from, our purpose, a diagnosis of our ills, and a prescription for how to live well. Furthermore, like a religion it postulates supernatural forces at work in human nature. Dianetics purports to be a science, but it should be classified as a religion.

3. Organisms—plants and animals of all varieties—are highly organized systems composed of parts that cannot exist independently, that work together harmoniously, and whose activities are irreversible. Every organism we know of is the product of the natural processes of chemical interaction and biological reproduction. The universe is like an organism, for what we see in it is exactly what we see in them. Thus, it is probable that the universe is a product of natural processes.

4. I wouldn't buy a Zephyr. Marie bought a new one, and within a year she had to have the transmission completely replaced.

5. The other day Dad and I happened to see Madonna on TV, and Dad said she was pretty. So when I saw this tie with a picture of Madonna on it, I knew it would be a perfect present for him to wear at Bab's wedding on Saturday!

6. The problem with Bart Simpson is that he looks like a pencil eraser with eyeballs. Anybody with those looks has got to be a lot of trouble.

7. When I observe myself, I see that if fire touches me I jump and feel pain. What I see in others is that when fire touches them, they also jump. Since they behave as I do, and since they are so much like me, I reason that they too feel pain.

8. Konrad Lorenz, a pioneer in the study of animal behavior, has observed that many species of animals are innately aggressive. Given that humans are animals too, the same conclusion about us seems to follow.

9. Cats lack the special nerve cell that in humans is believed to be responsible for color vision. Since they lack that nerve cell, and since they are like us in so many other ways, it is likely that on this score they differ. They don't see color as we do.

10. Consider a child who reacts to a first stimulus of thirst by drinking from his glass of milk. One day the glass is filled with buttermilk, and the child receives an unexpected second stimulus. The next time he is thirsty he may refuse his milk until convinced that it is not buttermilk.

When a household appliance is plugged in, the outlet provides the necessary electric current. This is normal behavior; it corresponds to the child habitually drinking his milk. Then one day a defective lamp is plugged in and the fuse burns out. The burnt fuse corresponds to the child's memory of the buttermilk. The outlet will no longer provide current to appliances until the memory has been removed by inserting a new fuse. Both the child and the electric circuit have "learned by experience." (Marshall Walker, *The Nature of Scientific Thought*, p. 14)

11. The tackling dummy constitutes a material model of a football player because its inertia corresponds to the inertia of the player. The coach can use it to make predictions. "If our 140-pound center tends to bounce off the tackling dummy, he will probably bounce off an opposing player also." The dummy may look somewhat like a football player, but such a resemblance is irrelevant. (Marshall Walker, *The Nature of Scientific Thought*, p. 3)

12. Just as we see that fallow land, if rich and fertile, teems with a hundred thousand kinds of wild and useless weeds, and that to see it work we must subject it and sow it with certain seeds for our service; and as we see that women, all alone, produce mere shapeless masses and lumps of flesh, but that to create a good and natural offspring they must be made fertile with a different kind of seed; so it is with minds. Unless you keep them busy with some definite subject that will bridle and control them, they throw themselves in disorder hither and yon in the vague field of imagination. (Montaigne, "Of Idleness")

13. We can point to the fact that the nervous systems of all vertebrates, and especially of birds and mammals, are fundamentally similar. Those parts of the human nervous system that are concerned with feeling pain are relatively old, in evolutionary terms. Unlike the cerebral cortex, which developed only after our ancestors diverged from other mammals, the basic nervous system evolved in more distant ancestors common to ourselves and the other "higher" animals. This anatomical parallel makes it likely that the capacity of animals to feel is similar to our own. (Peter Singer, *Practical Ethics*)

14. Regarding the use of scientific experimentation on animals, Peter Singer argues in *Animal Liberation:* If experimentation on retarded, orphaned humans would be wrong, why isn't experimenting on nonhuman animals wrong? What difference is there between the two, except for the mere fact that, biologically, one is a member of our species and the other is not? But *that,* surely, is not a morally relevant difference. . . .

15. Since the probability of winning $1 million in the national clearinghouse sweepstakes is 1 in 70,000 and the MacDonald's sweepstakes is also a national lottery for $1 million, it is likely that it, too, has a winning ratio of 1 in 70,000.

16. Suburban residents interviewed outside Albany said, eight times out of ten, that education should have priority in local funding. Troy is a suburb of Albany, so probably residents of Troy support giving priority to education.

Summary

1. An argument is inductively strong just in case, given its premises, (1) it is deductively invalid and (2) it is more probable than not that the conclusion follows. An inductively weak argument is one that is deductively invalid and it is more probable than not that the conclusion does *not* follow.

2. Inductive generalization: an argument with the conclusion that something is the case about all or many things on the basis of what is observed about some of them.

   An inductive generalization is inductively strong to the degree that the sample on which the generalization is based is representative of the population. Otherwise it is inductively weak.

   criterion of inductive strength   *Representativeness of the sample.*

3. Causal argument: an argument in which at least one causal statement (a statement of the form 'X causes Y') occurs as a premise or as the conclusion.

   causal conclusion   *An argument consisting of premises in support of a causal statement.*

   A causal conclusion is inductively strong to the degree that its premises describe evidence from one or more of Mill's methods. Otherwise, it is inductively weak.

   Agreement: If f is present whenever E occurs, then probably f causes E.

   Difference: If f is present whenever E occurs, but absent whenever E fails to occur, then probably f causes E.

   Concomitant variation: If f varies consistently with E, then f and E are probably causally related.

   Residue: If f causes E1 and g causes E2, then the remaining factor h probably causes the remaining effect E3.

   criterion of inductive strength   *Premises with evidence from one or more of Mill's methods.*

4. Arguments from analogy: an argument in which a conclusion is drawn about one thing on the basis of an analogy to some other thing.
      An argument from analogy is inductively strong to the degree that the common features are relevant to the inferred feature and there are no relevant dissimilarities.
      Criteria of inductive strength:

   a. *Common features are relevant to the inferred feature.*

   b. *There are no relevant dissimilarities.*

Exercise 8.5A   Identifying Types of Arguments   Each passage below contains an argument. First write it in argument form. Then classify the argument according to the types we have studied: *deductively valid argument, inductive generalization, causal arguments (causal conclusion, causal prescription, causal prediction, causal explanation),* and *argument from analogy.*

1. According to business consultant Mary Smith, who specializes in downtown business trends, downtowns are winning the war against suburban malls. She supported her contention by citing a Price Waterhouse survey of randomly selected families that found that the average number of monthly trips to the mall has dropped from 3.7 in 1980 to 3.1 in 1998.

2. Tornadoes have been predicted for tomorrow in northwestern Missouri's Atchison County. Since tornadoes always follow strong winds and usually hailstones as well, it is likely that there will be hail tomorrow in that area.

3. In 1900, the three top killers of Americans were all infectious diseases: pneumonia, tuberculosis, and "diarrhea, enteritis, and ulceration of the intestines." By wiping out infectious diseases, medical science made an astounding contribution to human longevity. American Demographics reports that a baby girl born in 1900 could be expected to live to age forty-nine; but a girl born in the year 2000 will probably live almost eighty years. My children can expect, on average, to live half as long again as their grandparents. (John F. Ross, *The Polar Bear Strategy,* 1999)

4. If mind and brain are identical, then to say "I am confused" also means "My brain is confused." But, whereas it is not absurd to say that my mind is confused, it is absurd to say that "My brain is confused." Therefore, it cannot be the case that my mind and brain are one and the same thing.

5. A six-year decline in murders by teenagers brought the 1999 homicide arrest rate for juveniles down 68 percent from its 1993 peak to the lowest level since 1966, the Justice Department reported. Experts say the decline of crack cocaine and the violent gangs that peddled it, combined with big city police crackdowns on illegal guns and expanded after-school crime prevention programs, have turned around the juvenile crime wave that pushed murder arrest rates for youths, age 10 to 17, up from 1987 to a peak in 1993. (Associated Press, 2000)

6. Mutation of a gene . . . can double the life span of fruit flies. . . . Researchers at the University of Connecticut Health Center have found that the life span of a fruit fly was extended from an average of 37 days to 70 days when a gene was modified on a single chromosome. The same life gene exists in humans. In human terms, a doubled life span would be about 150 years. (Associated Press, 2000)

7. The lifetime risk of depression (defined as the probability that a subject will suffer at least one episode lasting a year or more) ranged from 1.5 percent in Taiwan to 19 percent in Lebanon. (John Horgan, *Scientific American*) Those data indicate that the risk of depression is much lower in Asia than in the Middle East.

8. Viagra, a godsend to impotent men, set off protests among women who argued that health insurance companies that cover a male sex drug also should cover birth control for women. Now a federal agency agrees, saying it's against the law for many health plans to exclude contraception. (Associated Press, 2000)

9. If children are to develop into mature, healthy adults, then they should have consistent parental guidance. But that is something that children do not have. Therefore, they do not develop into mature, healthy adults.

10. Crash tests of side impact air bags show they can help prevent serious head injuries, even in collisions between passenger cars and high-riding light trucks, insurance industry researchers report. In its first such tests, the Insurance Institute for Highway Safety rammed a pickup truck traveling at 32 mph into the side of a Volvo S80 going 16 mph and found the car's side air bags protected the crash dummy's head against what could have been a fatal head injury. In a crash test without the air bag, the heads of the driver and rear passenger dummies were hit by the hood of the pickup truck. The force was high enough to kill the passenger, while the driver dummy's head barely escaped severe impact . . . . In a test with the head protection air bag, . . . instruments on the dummy heads recorded a low impact. The test demonstrates that lives could be saved. . . . (Associated Press, 2000)

Exercise 8.5B   Identifying More Difficult Arguments   Each passage contains an argument. Write the argument in argument form. Then classify the argument according to the types we have studied: *deductively valid argument, inductive generalization, causal arguments (causal conclusion, causal prescription, causal prediction, causal explanation),* and argument from analogy.

1. I believe that ignorance, or lack of familiarity, is the parent of fear. We are generally afraid of what we don't understand. And fear is the parent of hatred. Though some hatred is learned, we otherwise often hate what we are afraid of. Homophobia [". . . the fear and hatred of homosexuality in ourselves and others"] is most often caused by a lack of accurate information about and familiarity with gay people. I believe that the problem of homophobia in the workplace is most effectively addressed through education. (Brian McNaught, *Gay Issues in the Workplace*)

2. Since its beginnings, sea kayaking has been a relatively safe sport, with few injuries or fatalities. However, the large influx each year of paddlers new to the sport is worrisome. Sea kayaking is so easy to learn that anyone with a few minutes' practice can unknowingly paddle into a hazardous predicament. In fact, in the roughly 50 degree Fahrenheit (10 degree C) water of the Pacific Northwest, capsizing less than one-half mile from shore could easily be fatal to a lone kayaker unable to get back in the kayak, get his or her body out of the water, or attract the attention of rescuers. (Matt Broze and George Gronseth, *Sea Kayaker's Deep Trouble*)

3. A 1990 *Fortune* magazine survey of 799 of the largest U.S. industrial and service companies showed that only nineteen women—less than one-half of 1 percent—were listed among the more than 4,000 highest-paid officers and directors. In business as in academe, women earn less than men . . . , are promoted more slowly and work in less prestigious institutions. (Virginia Valian, "Running in Place," *The Sciences*)

4. Some people find it helpful to think of the distinctions among [sexual] orientation, behavior, and identity in terms of "handedness." We know that there is a predictable percentage of people in the world who are left-handed. Parents don't create left-handed children. It happens prenatally (in the womb). Being left-handed is the person's orientation.

The culture can and does influence the behavior of left-handed people. Left-handedness can be so stigmatized that left-handed people learn to write with their right hand and identify themselves as right-handed.

There was a time when left-handedness was seen as a sign of the devil. Left-handed women were thought to be witches. People quoted Scripture to support their bias and essentially forced left-handedness into the closet. Recent studies have shown that left-handed children who are forced to function with their right hand experience major trauma that takes a terrible toll on their development. The same is being said about homosexual people who are forced to behave heterosexually. When our behavior and/or our identity are different than our orientation, it can take a terrible toll.

In working with gay, lesbian, and bisexual people over the last twenty years, I have found that the people who are most open about their sexual orientation experience the least conflict in their lives. They are generally happier in all aspects of their lives than are people who are secretive or in denial. This, obviously, has major ramifications for the business world. (Brian McNaught, *Gay Issues in the Workplace*)

5. *Headline:* "Kentucky Doctors' Warning: Don't Eat Squirrel Brains" Doctors in Kentucky have issued a warning that people should not eat squirrel brains, a regional delicacy, because squirrels may carry a variant of mad cow disease that can be transmitted to humans and is fatal.

In the last four years, 11 cases of a human form of transmissible spongiform encephalopathy, called Creutzfeld–Jakob disease, have been diagnosed in rural western Kentucky, said Dr. Erick Weisman. . . . "All of them were squirrel-brain eaters." Within the small population of western Kentucky, the natural incidence of this disease should be one person getting it every 10 years or so, Weisman said. While the patients could have contracted the disease from eating beef and not squirrels, there has not been a single confirmed case of mad cow disease in the United States, Weisman said. Since every one of the 11 people with the disease ate squirrel brains, it seems prudent for people to avoid this practice until more is known, he said. (*Rutland Herald*)

6. I'll have a hotdog with mustard and . . . mosquito legs? According to a recent study, the sizzling flash of a bug zapper may do more than kill bugs. James Urban, a microbiologist at Kansas State University, has found that zappers placed near food may spread bacteria from the insects to the tasty treats nearby. Urban and Alberto Broce, a Kansas State entomologist, sprayed flies with bacteria, then released them in a room with a bug zapper. They determined that when bugs are zapped, parts of their bodies can land at least six feet from the zapper. Says Urban, "I think our study shows that a reasonable and prudent person should not feel comfortable with a bug zapper hanging over a condiment table, a take-out window, a barbecue grill, or even where baby toys are stored." (Amy Erikson, *Audubon, 2000*)

7. *Does sex need a justification?* Most people, and this includes most U.S. Roman Catholics, no longer believe that sex must be limited to procreation. But most

people, and this includes many who are cosmopolitan and educated, still believe that sex needs justification. You're allowed to eat spaghetti because you enjoy it, listen to Sinatra because you enjoy it, ride a bicycle because you enjoy it, but not have sex because you enjoy it. Sex for the sake of sex is not permissible. Sexual encounters, goes the argument, have consequences that make them different from these other pursuits. Pleasure, by itself, is not a sufficient justification for sex. (Joshua Halberstam, *Everyday Ethics*)

8. One way to put the argument for patients' autonomy with regard to assisted dying is to compare a person's life to a business: If I own a business that is making money, it makes sense to keep it open; but if the business is losing money, I would be imprudent to wait until there was no money left at all before closing. Similarly, a terminally ill patient owns his or her body and need not "stay in business" till the very end. (Gregory Pence, *Classic Cases in Medical Ethics*)

9. As every boat owner knows, equipping a boat with an engine that is twice as powerful as the original one will not make the boat go twice as fast. In fact, if the engine tries to force the boat to go faster than its "hull speed," the craft may lower its nose and drive itself underwater. Similarly, it is fallacious to think that if the efficiency of computers doubles (or rises a thousandfold), the whole set of industrial inputs should therefore become twice as efficient. (Alan S. Binder and Richard E. Quandt, "The Computer and the Economy," *Atlantic Monthly*)

10. *The Sunday New York Times* has a full-page article headlined, "It's pretty, it's trendy, but skiing is also much too dangerous." Yet exaggeration is easy. Carl Ettlinger, an expert on skiing injuries, has studied the subject for two decades. A resort used by 10,000 skiers a day, he believes, is liable to have one bad injury every 75 days, a death only every four months. True, that adds up to 32 deaths a year in the whole country, the National Safety Council reckons. But swimming and boating kill over 4,500 Americans a year, hunting about 90, and twice as many golfers get hurt as skiers. Indeed, skiers are seven times likelier to suffer death or serious injury while driving to the slopes, says Mr. Ettinger. (*The Economist*)

11. Most people assume that the jobs of the future will be related to the technologies of the future. They imagine that we will become a society of telecommuting nerds. Historically, however, the opposite has happened: job growth tends to be greatest in the occupations that new technology affects the least. We have become supremely efficient at growing food; that is why there are so few farmers.

    In the Labor Department's list of "occupations with the largest job growth," the top five categories are cashiers, janitors and cleaners, salespeople, waiters and waitresses, and nurses. All of these jobs involve "being there"—having face-to-face contact with the consumer, or dealing in a hands-on way with the unpredictable messiness of the physical world. To put it a bit differently: The typical worker of the 21st century will be doing precisely the kinds of thing that you can't do over the Internet. [* *The economic trends of the future will be like those of the past.* Therefore, it is not true that *the jobs of the future will be related to the technologies of the future . . . that we will become a society of telecommuting nerds.*] (Paul Krugman, "What's Ahead for Working Men and Women," *New York Times*)

12. Ask people what they think about the prospect of retail competition for electric power and many say, "*Why? My telephone bill didn't go down* when they deregulated the telephone industry." [This argument is] based on faulty assumptions.

First, telephone rates. The belief that telephone bills increased after the breakup of AT&T is a widely held misconception. In fact, long-distance rates have declined by more than 50 percent in real dollars (adjusted for inflation) since 1984—the year that long-distance competition began in earnest. In 1982, prior to its divestiture, AT&T charged an average of $5.40 in real dollars for a 10-minute residential call from New York to Los Angeles. In 1996 that same call could be placed for about $2.30 with AT&T, MCI, Sprint, or dozens of other carriers.

Contrary to another common misconception, the savings in long-distance bills did not come at the expense of in-state residential ratepayers. In Vermont, average annual in-state bills between 1986 and 1994 fell by more than 20 percent, or about $130 per line, after adjusting for inflation.

Competition has brought enormous financial savings to consumers in a variety of other industries as well. In the airline industry, for example, the price of an economy-class airline ticket has dropped by roughly one-third in real dollars since deregulation occurred in 1978. Similarly, railroad freight costs have dropped steadily since the Staggers Act of 1981 created competition for railroad shipping. In 1970 it cost 3.2 cents to move one ton of product one mile by train. By 1993 that figure had dropped to 1.85 cents.

Those are real savings that show up in consumers' pockets in the form of lower prices for retail products. [*Therefore, deregulation saves consumers money.*] (John H. Hollar, "Deregulation Saves Money")

13. To put it simply, our current economic relationship with China is fundamentally against the national interests of the United States. To remedy this, we must start by taking steps that will reduce the trade deficit with China. It is important to note here that it is not necessary to reduce imports from China. Many imports from China, as we stated above, are beneficial to Americans, and they are beneficial to the cause of economic development in China as well. The goal should not be reducing sales of Chinese goods in the United States but increasing American exports to China, something that will happen once China drops its various barriers to imported goods. (Richard Bernstein and Ross H. Munro, *The Coming Conflict with China*)

14. In a 1996 survey of the twenty highest-paid women in U.S. corporations, the lowest total compensation was $833,350. But 615 men earned more than the twentieth woman on the list. And again, as in academe, to the extent that performance can be accurately measured, men and women appear to perform equally well. Independent of all other factors, gender appears to play a key role in people's ability to get ahead. (Virginia Valian, "Running in Place," *The Sciences*)

15. I must express my teeth-grinding impatience with the New Age nonsense about science being a "belief system," or even a religion. Science is not a belief system, for this reason: Scientific knowledge is subject to revision pending new real-world evidence. Every week the *New York Times* comes out with news of some discovery that makes scientists rethink their theories. A recent *Newsweek* had a cover story about how the observations made with the Hubble telescope have forced astronomers to change their view of the universe. Science is the opposite of faith: it is a perpetual "Show me!"

Religious belief, on the other hand, is not subject to such revision; it is not falsifiable by any real-world evidence. The existence of God cannot be disproved. Religious beliefs are "leakproof"—there's no evidence that will contradict them. (Letter to the editor, *Mother Jones*)

Review Questions

1. According to your text, what are the features of an inductive generalization and the terms used to refer to them?
2. What is the difference between a simple random sample and a stratified random sample?
3. What is a random sample? Explain how random sampling improves the likelihood of obtaining a representative sample.
4. Briefly explain these terms as they are used in your text:
   - a. Causal statement
   - b. Causal prediction
   - c. Causal explanation
   - d. Causal argument
   - e. Proximate cause
5. In your own words, explain Mill's method of
   - a. Agreement
   - b. Difference
   - c. Concomitant variation
   - d. Residue
6. What, according to your text, are the terms used to talk about the elements of an argument from analogy?
7. What are the criteria for inductive strength in arguments from analogy?
8. Briefly define the four kinds of analogical argument in your text.

True or False?

1. Given that the car starts whenever the temperature, with wind chill, is above freezing, but fails to start when the temperature is below freezing, you could infer by the method of agreement that the freezing temperature is causing the car failure.
2. If a person reasoned that her chemistry class will be difficult because it is a lab class like biology and biology was difficult, then she would be making an inductive generalization.
3. Two criteria of a strong causal conclusion are that a phenomenon has been found present in all cases in which circumstance C is present and absent in all cases in which C is absent.
4. Causal arguments are arguments that include a causal statement as a premise or conclusion.

5. In the statement "Bovine growth hormone (BGH) causes increased milk production," a sufficient condition of increased production is the introduction of BGH.

6. Strong inductive generalizations require large samples.

7. A moral analogy is a kind of argument in which a moral conclusion is supported by some moral authority.

8. A sample is randomly constructed if every member of the sample is of the same generic type.

9. According to your text, every inductively strong argument is inductively invalid.

10. If an argument fails to be deductively valid, it fails to be a good argument.

Discussion Questions

1. What makes an inductive generalization strong? It is common to think that the size of the sample is what determines the degree of inductive strength. For instance, most people think a small sample is not a good one, but in fact sample size is not what matters. Size is less important than the representativeness of the sample. Professional pollsters, for example, routinely use very small samples from which to make their generalizations. Discuss this point by using examples to explain why it is not size that counts in inductive generalizations.

2. How do the three types of inductive argument compare? Do they seem to you equally capable of providing reliable conclusions? Do they seem to you easily distinguishable? Are all three necessary, or would it be possible to reduce inductive reasoning to one or two rather than the three?

3. Write an essay describing the differences between inductive and deductive reasoning. What is your perception of the role of each in daily life?

 ## INFOTRAC Assignments

Using INFOTRAC look up any of the subject words below for articles containing inductive arguments. Write the arguments in argument form.

LOGIC, INDUCTIVE REASONING
ADVERTISING; ADVERTISING AND CHILDREN
ANALOGY
CAPITAL PUNISHMENT
LAUGHTER; And HEALTH; And MEDICINE; And SUCCESS
HUNTING
STATISTICAL SAMPLING

CHAPTER NINE
Informal Fallacies

This chapter presents a survey of several common informal fallacies—errors in reasoning that we can detect only by examining the content or meanings of the words in the argument. The study of informal fallacies is one of the major enterprises of informal logic.

A *fallacy* is an error in reasoning. Both deductive and inductive arguments may be fallacious. Some fallacies are detectable by an examination of the *form* of the argument; they are called *formal fallacies*. (The techniques for evaluating deductive validity that we learn in categorical and truth-functional logic enable us to recognize many sorts of formal fallacies.) All other fallacies are called *informal fallacies,* and they must be detected by an examination of the *content* of the argument.

Logicians have distinguished many types of informal fallacies, although they have by no means agreed on uniform classifications. Nevertheless, certain common types are recognized fairly universally, and these are the ones surveyed in this chapter. Many informal fallacies are traditionally referred to by their Latin names, so those Latin names appear in parentheses in the headings.

9.1 Appeal to Authority
(*Argumentum ad Verecundiam*)

An *appeal to authority* is an argument in which the testimony of someone believed to be an authority is cited in support of a conclusion. The fallacy occurs when the person cited is not in fact an authority on the matter or for some reason should not be relied upon. Here are three examples:

Example 1

Well, I wouldn't listen to Bishop Desmond Tutu's version of the situation in South Africa, because Jerry Falwell says that Tutu is a phony.

Example 2

According to my physics professor, Emily Dickinson's poetry is for the birds. That's good enough for me.

Example 3

Marvis Frazier is America's greatest boxer. I have that on the authority of Marvis's father, Joe Frazier.

The underlying idea of such arguments is that some statement S is true because some authority A has said it is true. The argument's basic structure is this:

Authority A asserts that S.

Therefore, S.

You see immediately that such an argument is neither valid nor inductively strong, since the mere fact that someone asserts S neither makes it so nor makes it probable. Typically, however, the arguer believes more than the mere fact that A asserts that S. The arguer very likely is assuming such things as that A is someone who knows what he or she is talking about regarding S, and that A is speaking without bias, and that A is telling the truth. If those or similar assumptions are well founded, then the appeal to authority A *may* constitute good—that is, nonfallacious—reasoning. Not all appeals to authority are fallacious; some may be inductively strong. After all, we should accept the testimony of qualified and unbiased experts, for we cannot be experts in every field ourselves.

The fallacy of appeal to authority occurs when the authority cited is not qualified in the relevant matters or, less typically, is not free from adverse influences. Thus, the arguer is relying upon the assertions of someone who is not truly in a position to know.

To identify the fallacy of appeal to authority, we ask two questions: (1) Is the authority in fact a *qualified* authority about matters related to S? (2) Is there any good reason to believe that the authority may be biased in matters related to S? Regarding Example 1, we should ask, Is Jerry Falwell qualified to claim that Bishop Tutu is a phony? Is Falwell an expert on South Africa and the political representation of the pro-testers? Regarding Example 2, we should ask, Is a physics professor likely to be an authority on American poets? And regarding Example 3, although we know that Joe Frazier *is* a boxing expert, we may ask if he is impartial when it comes to his own son.

A common variation on the appeal to authority is an appeal to a magazine or newspaper article or a radio or TV program. Consider this example: 'They've found a cure for cancer. I read about it in *Popular Mechanics*'. In such cases we ought to ask the same question: Is the source cited a reliable one in this matter? Ordinarily, we should be very suspicious of medical breakthroughs reported in *Popular Mechanics,* though not of such breakthroughs reported in, say, the *Journal of the American Medical Association.* On the other hand, we would not expect to get reliable advice on automobiles in a medi-cal journal. The fallacy occurs when an argument is supported by reference to a publi-cation or program not known for specialization on the subject.

In summary, not all appeals to authority are fallacious. The fallacy occurs when an arguer appeals to someone who is not an expert in the field for which he or she is cited as support or who is not unbiased.

To recognize the appeal to authority, look for an argument based primarily on the premise that some person (or some publication) reports that S is true. The fallacy occurs when the person (or publication) is not relevantly qualified or is not speaking without bias.

9.2 Appeal to the People
(*Argumentum ad Populum*)

The *appeal to the people* fallacy is a variation on the appeal to authority. It consists in arguing that some statement S is true because most people believe S. It is in effect an appeal to commonly or traditionally held beliefs. Many advertisements recommend a product by asserting that "everyone uses it," as for example, in this ad for Ford trucks:

Example 4

America's best-selling pickups: Ford.

The unstated premise is that the best-selling pickup truck is the *best* pickup truck, and the conclusion is that since you ought to buy the best, you ought to buy a Ford. But of course the fact that Ford sells the most pickups entails neither that Fords are the best nor that you ought to buy one.

Here are some other examples of the appeal to the people.

Example 5

Well, for centuries people have believed in God, and I just don't see how so many people could be mistaken. So that's why I choose to believe.

Example 6

Working one's way through college is a cherished American concept. (Dr. Newman, former president of the University of Rhode Island)

In Example 5, the arguer bases a decision to believe in God on the fact that, as he or she claims, people throughout the centuries have so believed. The implicit inference of Newman's statement is that working one's way through college is good because it is "a cherished American concept." Both arguments commit the fallacy of appeal to the people.

To recognize the fallacy of appeal to the people, look for an argument in which the conclusion is based on assertions about commonly or traditionally held beliefs.

9.3 Appeal to Force (*Argumentum ad Baculum*)

An *appeal to force* is an argument based upon a threat. Arguers use this type of appeal to try to persuade you by pointing out their power over you or by warning you of the bad consequences of refusing to accept their argument. Consider these examples:

Example 7

Ladies and gentlemen of the jury, if you do not bring in a verdict of guilty, you may be this killer's next victim!

Example 8

Look, I give out the grades in this course, so I guess I should know that your answer is wrong!

Example 9

Smith, we can't have this statement on expenditures coming to the attention of the president. You've been the accountant here for nearly twenty years. It would be a shame to ruin all that now. I think it would be wise of you to take another look at the books, don't you?

Rather than offering a relevant reason for the conclusion, the arguer poses a threat to the listener, saying, in effect, "Accept my conclusion or you'll be sorry." Obviously, the fact that the arguer poses a threat does not make the arguer's conclusion true or even probably true.

To recognize the fallacy of appeal to force, look for the presence of a threat that is either explicit or, as in Example 9, subtly disguised.

9.4 Appeal to Pity
(Argumentum ad Misericordiam)

Someone offering an *appeal to pity* is reasoning, in effect, "You should accept my conclusion out of pity." Such arguers urge you to believe something by arousing your sympathy for them or their cause. For example, imagine an attorney defending his client to the jury:

Example 10

There is no question that what this young man did is intolerable and repugnant. He admits it himself. But you're not here to evaluate this man's conduct morally; you're here to try him and determine his guilt or innocence. And as you think this over, I want you to think hard about this young man, his home life and his future, which you now hold in your hands. Think about his broken home, never knowing his father, being left by his mother. Think about the poverty he's known, the foster homes, the birthdays going unnoticed, and the Christmas he's never had. And think hard about what life in prison will do to him. Think about these things, and I know you will acquit him of this crime.

This clever lawyer makes quite a case for his client's miserable and unfortunate life. Although all of it may be true, it would be fallacious to conclude that the defendant is *not* guilty because his life has been hard or because finding him guilty would add to his misery.

To recognize the fallacy of appeal to pity, look for premises that appeal to your sympathy.

9.5 Appeal to Ignorance
(Argumentum ad Ignorantiam)

When arguers claim that some statement S is true because, they say, we have failed to show that S is false, they are guilty of the fallacy of *appeal to ignorance*. If they argue that S is false because we have failed to show that S is true, they are also guilty of this fallacy. In each case the lack of proof or good evidence for the truth (or falsity) of S is used as a reason for concluding that S is false (or true). The two forms of the appeal to ignorance look like this:

We do not know that S is false.
_____

Therefore, S is true.

We do not know that S is true.
_____

Therefore, S is false.

Consider this example:

Example 11

Well, I've examined all the arguments for the existence of God, and I've seen that none of them proves that God exists. That's reason enough for me: there is no God!

The speaker concludes that there is no God because there are no successful proofs of God's existence. But the absence of a successful proof of God's existence does not justify concluding that there is no God. What the speaker *is* justified in concluding is that we do not know.

Similarly, some people have been behaving irrationally about the disease AIDS. For example, several Hollywood actors have refused to play scenes opposite potential AIDS carriers. Scientists say that although their research has not proven that AIDS *cannot* be transmitted by casual contact, neither has it produced evidence that it *can* be transmitted by such contact. Yet some people interpret this as follows:

Example 12

Scientists have not proven that AIDS cannot be transmitted through casual contact. Therefore, we should avoid casual contact with suspected AIDS carriers.

Here the fact that the possibility of contracting the disease through casual contact has not been disproven is taken as a reason for acting on that possibility.

Lack of evidence that S is true is not normally evidence against it, and vice versa. However, there are at least two kinds of cases that resemble the appeal to ignorance in which a lack of evidence may justify the conclusion that S is true (or not true). In a court of law, the failure to establish that a person has committed a crime is considered sufficient to allow us to conclude that the person is not guilty. Thus, lawyers may argue that their clients are innocent because there is no evidence of their guilt. Notice, however, that finding a person innocent or not guilty in a court of law is not a determination that the person did not commit the crime; it is a determination that the evidence does not justify a judgment of guilt. So if we concluded that a defendant did not commit the crime because he or she was found not guilty, we would be committing the fallacy of appeal to ignorance. Similarly, in scientific reasoning a failure to disconfirm or disprove a hypothesis lends support to the hypothesis, although it does not usually justify concluding that the hypothesis is true. Rather, each failure to disconfirm the hypothesis indicates that it is more probable.

The second kind of case in which a lack of evidence may justify a conclusion about a statement is one in which investigation can be expected to tell us what is or is not so. For example, the fact that X-rays reveal no evidence of a fracture is a good reason for concluding that there is no fracture, since we can expect a fracture to show up on X-rays. Or consider the case of the Loch Ness monster. The fact that repeated searches have produced no evidence of this monster makes it probable, though not certain, that it does not exist. If there were a Loch Ness monster, we would expect some indication of its presence. As you can see, these are cases in which the results of an investigation are relevant to the truth-value of a statement. The fallacy of appeal to ignorance occurs when the lack of evidence or proof is not relevant to the conclusion but the arguer believes that it is.

To recognize the fallacy of appeal to ignorance, look for a conclusion based upon an absence of proof or evidence. Be aware of the two types of cases in which lack of evidence for S is relevant to the truth or falsity of S.

9.6 *Ad Hominem*

An *ad hominem* argument is an attack upon the person rather than the person's ideas. The name of this fallacy comes from the Latin and means literally "against the person." There are three common types of *ad hominem* arguments: abusive, circumstantial, and *tu quoque* ("you, too!").

The *ad hominem* abusive argument is an attack on the opponent's character, implying that what he or she says should not be believed because of this character flaw. Consider these examples:

Example 13

Well now, you've all heard Professor Clark tell us about the theory of evolution. But I'm not surprised that he neglected to tell you that he is a godless atheist! How can this man speak the truth, I ask you?

Example 14

Franklin Putnam says he'd make a good president. But he's no man for the White House; not only has he been divorced, but he's a Catholic and divorced!

The abusive *ad hominem* argument, in effect, involves two claims: first, that the opponent possesses a certain undesirable or negative characteristic and, second, that the opponent's words or abilities are not to be trusted because of that characteristic. Thus, an abusive *ad hominem* argument may be fallacious either because the person does not possess the characteristic ascribed to him or her or because possessing that characteristic is not relevant to the truth of his or her statements. For example, the fact—if it is one—that Professor Clark is an atheist does not make it even probable that what he has said is false. Similarly, the fact that Franklin Putnam is a divorced Catholic does not make it probable that his claim that he would be a good president is false. The underlying idea of this type of argument can be exposed as follows:

> *Whatever anyone with undesirable characteristic X says is probably not true.*
>
> *Person A has undesirable characteristic X.*
> _____
>
> *Therefore, whatever A says is probably not true.*

To identify the ad hominem *abusive fallacy, look for an attack on the person's character rather than the person's statements.*

The *ad hominem* circumstantial argument implies that the opponent has special, usually self-interested, reasons for his or her claims. Thus, the argument attempts to refute the person's statement, not by offering reasons against it but by suggesting that the person himself does not have good reasons or honest motives for the position. Here are some examples:

Example 15

> *The auto industry lobbyists have been arguing that tax reform is unnecessary. But just remember this: It is the auto industry that stands to benefit the most if there is no change in the current tax laws.*

Example 16

> *I'm not surprised that your mechanic recommends a complete engine overhaul. Do you know how much money he stands to make from that?*

Rather than offering reasons against the others' claims, these speakers suggest that the persons are not to be believed because they have self-interested motives. In Example 15, for instance, the speaker implies that the auto industry lobbyists would not be arguing against tax reform if they did not stand to gain from it. Thus, the speaker argues that we should not accept the lobbyists' position because they do not have logically relevant reasons for it.

The structure of the *ad hominem* circumstantial argument may be represented as follows:

> *Person A has self-interested reasons for asserting S.*
> _____
>
> *Therefore, S is probably not true.*

The fallacy is apparent if you consider that even if the charge of self-interested motives is true, it still does not follow that what the person says is not true or even probably not true.

To identify the ad hominem *circumstantial fallacy, look for an argument that claims that the opponent advances his or her argument not because it is true but because the opponent has some other, usually ulterior, motive for wanting his or her argument accepted.*

The *ad hominem tu quoque* (or "you, too!") argument is an argument in which one defends oneself by accusing one's attacker, usually of a similar wrongdoing. For example, suppose you have been accused of cheating on a test. If you respond to your critic by saying "Well, I saw you cheating, too!" you are committing an *ad hominem* fallacy. Your defense is in effect to accuse your attacker. But even if you are correct in your accusation, you have not defended yourself against the charge. The fact that someone else has done wrong does not excuse you from doing wrong. Appropriately, this fallacy is sometimes called the fallacy of "two wrongs make a right." Here are some other examples:

Example 17

Yes, I admit, I did lie to you about last night. But you've lied to me.

Example 18

Congressman Pyle accuses me of wasting taxpayers' money on political junkets. Well, you'll be interested to know that he has the track record in Congress for so-called working vacations. Working in the Bahamas! Come now, Mr. Pyle.

To identify the fallacy of ad hominem tu quoque, *look for an argument that attempts to offer a defense by accusing the accuser of a similar wrongdoing.*

To identify an ad hominem *fallacy in general, look for an argument that attempts to offer a defense or a response by attacking the opponent rather than the opponent's argument.*

9.7 False Cause

The fallacy of *false cause* is committed when an arguer concludes that one event or thing A causes another event or thing B when in fact there is no good evidence of a causal relation. In Section 8.3 we saw that evidence supporting a causal statement is strong to the degree that it conforms to one or more of Mill's methods. Absent that, the fallacy occurs. One common type of false cause, called *post hoc, ergo propter hoc* (Latin for "after this, therefore because of this"), consists of concluding that A causes B because A *preceded* B. The fallacious reasoning is obvious: Because one event A occurs before another event B, it does not follow that A causes B. Here is an example:

Example 19

Statistics show that nearly every heroin user started out by using marijuana. It's reasonable to conclude, then, that marijuana smoking naturally leads to the harder drug.

The arguer asserts that the majority of heroin users tried marijuana before using heroin, which may be true. However, the arguer concludes that smoking marijuana leads to using heroin, which has in fact been shown to be false. The arguer is mistaking the concurrence of two things for a causal connection.

Another example illustrates an unwarranted feeling of responsibility a person might have about wishing misfortune on others:

Example 20

Last night I was so angry at my brother I wished he was dead. And now he's in the hospital. God, if only I hadn't thought that. It's all my fault. I'll never feel hatred again, not of anyone!

Although the speaker in the example may simply regret having had ill feelings toward his brother, if, on the other hand, he literally believes that his wishing misfortune on his brother contributed to the misfortune, then he is guilty of the fallacy of false cause. There is no good reason to believe in this case that wishing it so has caused it to be so.

Another type of fallacy of false cause may be called *oversimplification*. This fallacy occurs when an arguer explains the occurrence of some event or phenomenon in terms of one (or more) of its least important causes. Suppose, for example, that some event E is caused by a combination of several factors, A, B, C, and D. The arguer asserts that E is caused by A and then proceeds to show how A can be eliminated. The arguer appears to have a solution to the problem regarding E when, in fact, the other, more important causal factors are being neglected. Thus, the arguer oversimplifies what is really a complex matter. Consider this example:

Example 21

I blame the television media for the epidemic of hijackings, kidnappings, and other acts of terrorism. If we would stop televising terrorist acts, they'd stop.

The arguer implies that televising terrorist acts causes more terrorist acts. It may be true that television coverage partially contributes to terrorism by giving the terrorists the attention they seek for their causes, but the speaker neglects other, more important causes.

Is it really likely that terrorism would cease if the media refused to provide television coverage? Thus, although the element of truth in this argument may draw us in, the arguer's solution to the problem is on examination naive.

To identify the fallacy of false cause, look for a claim that one thing B is caused by or explained as the result of some other thing A. Then consider whether there is any good evidence that A causes B. The variation called oversimplification can usually be spotted when an arguer proposes a solution to a problem while at the same time overlooking more plausible causal factors.

9.8 Slippery Slope

The fallacy of *slippery slope* is actually a variation of the fallacy of false cause; it involves a claim that a chain of causal events will occur. This fallacy is committed when a person argues that some event or practice he or she disapproves of will trigger a sequence of events ultimately leading to some undesirable consequence. The reasoning is that since we do not want the undesirable consequence, we ought therefore to oppose the initial event or practice. The fallacy in the reasoning consists in the false assumption that the chain of events will in fact occur.

Recently, the slippery slope argument has been made against physician-assisted suicide. The argument has been that physician-assisted suicide will lead to nonvoluntary euthanasia. That is, if we permit physicians to assist people who want to end their lives, then there will be a natural and logical progression to legalizing assistance in dying for those who are not terminally ill, for those who are not conscious, and eventually for those who have not asked for assistance. As bioethicist Daniel Callahan writes

If we believe in relief of suffering, then it seems cruel and capricious to deny it to the incompetent. There is, in short, no reasonable or logical point once the turn has been made down the road to euthanasia, which could soon turn into a convenient and commodious expressway. (Hastings Center Report, "When Self-Determination Runs Amok")

We have the fallacy of slippery slope in this reasoning if one maintains that legalizing physician-assisted suicide is likely to lead to the undesirable consequences described.
Here is another example:

Example 22

You've all heard of grade inflation. Well, I want to speak to you about grade depression: the serious harm we do to students by grading them too hard rather than too easily. What does it do to students to measure them by too strict a standard? It frustrates them. It conditions them to expect failure. They recoil from responsibility, always taking the easy route rather than learning to challenge and hence improve themselves. They develop habits of dependency, and many develop the symptoms of neurosis and other psychological disorders. Can we afford a generation of weak, dependent people unsuited for the demands of contemporary society?

In this example the arguer opposes a strict grading policy by claiming that it will ultimately lead to "a generation of weak, dependent people." The first step in the causal chain—that strict grading leads to frustration—is perhaps plausible. But from that point on the series of occurrences is unlikely. There is no good reason to believe that harsh grading will lead to expectations of failure, withdrawal from responsibility, and eventually dependency or neurosis. Thus, the arguer commits the fallacy of slippery slope.

To recognize the slippery slope fallacy, look for an argument claiming that a certain practice or event will initiate a series of events ultimately leading to some undesirable consequence.

9.9 Either/Or Fallacy

The *either/or* fallacy, sometimes called *false dichotomy*, consists of mistakenly assuming that there are only two possible solutions to some problem or that solving some problem consists of choosing between only two alternatives. The argument moves by showing that one of the alternatives is false or unacceptable and concludes that the other must be true. (We can imagine variations of the either/or fallacy in which an argument rests on the mistaken assumption that only three alternatives or four alternatives are available. The fallacy in each case consists in overlooking some other, less extreme alternative.) Here is a typical example:

Example 23

As I see it, either we enforce the death penalty or we eventually find the convicted murderer out on parole. We cannot have murderers going free, so we had better start enforcing the death penalty.

Let's expose that argument and examine its form.

1. *Either we enforce the death penalty or we eventually find the convicted murderer out on parole.*

2. *We cannot have murderers going free.*

---

3. *Therefore, we must enforce the death penalty.*

The form of the argument is

Either X or Y.
Not Y.

Therefore, X.

Notice that this is a valid argument form, Disjunctive Syllogism. Therefore, the fallacy does not consist in its logical form. It consists rather in a false premise—the premise stating that only two alternatives are available, the death penalty or parole for murderers. The either/or fallacy consists in assuming a false dichotomy; the arguer overlooks other possible alternatives. In the case of Example 23, the arguer neglects the possibility of mandatory life imprisonment without the chance for parole.

Here are some other examples:

Example 24

I don't like Smith any more than you do, but voting for
him is better than voting for Brown.

The speaker assumes one has only two choices, whereas, one could choose some other candidate, write in a name, or not vote at all.

Consider this attempt to justify the government's policy of refusing to negotiate with terrorists holding Americans hostage:

Example 25

Either we give in to these terrorists' demands and jeopar-
dize the lives of thousands of Americans or we refuse and
risk the lives of the hostages. Well, I for one will not risk
the lives of Americans all over the world. So we must not
give in to these terrorists.

And consider this attempt to justify subjecting animals to head injuries for research purposes:

Example 26

The idea of deliberately causing trauma, deliberately in-
juring the head of a living baboon, is extremely distaste-
ful. But if we are not allowed to continue this research,
then we will simply not learn how to treat human beings
with head injuries. It is unfortunate, but it must be done.

In studying Examples 25 and 26, consider whether there may not be other alternatives the speaker is overlooking. If you can describe such alternatives, then you have a way of showing the fallacious either/or reasoning of the argument.

To identify the either/or fallacy, look for an argument that makes the false assumption that there are only two alternatives (or perhaps three or more) available and that one must be taken because the other is unacceptable.

9.10 Equivocation

The fallacy of *equivocation* occurs when the conclusion of an argument rests upon the equivocal use of a word or phrase, that is, its use in two different senses. Consider this example:

Example 27

1. *Philosophy is an art.*
2. *Art is studied by art historians.*

3. *Therefore, philosophy is studied by art historians.*

The premises of the argument are plausible, and the argument appears to be valid. However, the word 'art' is used in two different senses. In its first occurrence it refers to a skill requiring creativity and imagination, whereas in its second occurrence it refers to the fine arts or the cultural institution involving the fine arts. When we rewrite the argument replacing 'art' with those different meanings, it becomes obvious that the argument is not valid:

1. *Philosophy is a* skill requiring creativity and imagination.
2. The fine arts *are studied by art historians.*

3. *Therefore, philosophy is studied by art historians.*

Although it may be true that art historians study the fine arts, it is not true that art historians study all skills involving creativity and imagination; and so it is not true that philosophy is studied by art historians.

Consider this second example:

Example 28

Logic is the study of argument. Well, that's one course I could ace. I know all about arguments. I've learned from experts. You should hear the arguments my parents have.

The speaker concludes, in effect, "I would do well at the study of argument because I know all about arguments." The word 'argument' is being used here in two different senses. In the first occurrence it means 'reasoning', and in the second it means 'quarreling'. Substituting the two senses of the word clarifies what is in fact being said: I could do well at the study of *reasoning* because I know all about *quarreling*. That, of course, does not follow.

A rather farfetched but dramatic instance of the fallacy of equivocation occurs in Shakespeare's play *Macbeth*. Macbeth has been told by the three witches that "none of woman born / Shall harm Macbeth." Macbeth reasons as follows:

Example 29

". . . for none of woman born shall harm Macbeth."
Since all persons are born of woman, it follows that I shall
not be harmed by anyone.

Believing that he cannot be harmed by anyone, Macbeth confidently confronts his rival Macduff in the following exchange:

MACBETH:
  Let fall thy blade on vulnerable crests.
  I bear a charmèd life, which must not yield
  To one of woman born.
MACDUFF:
  Despair thy charm,
  And let the angel whom thou still has served
  Tell thee, Macduff was from his mother's womb
  Untimely ripped.
                              (*Macbeth*, act 5, sc. 8)

Macbeth is the victim of the fallacy of equivocation. In one sense of the phrase "of woman born," what the witches said was true: Macbeth shall not be harmed by anyone *born naturally*. Unfortunately, and quite understandably, Macbeth took them to mean Macbeth shall not be harmed by anyone *conceived and carried by a woman*.

To identify the fallacy of equivocation, look for reasoning that involves a shift between two or more senses of a key word or phrase in the argument.

9.11 Hasty Generalization

The fallacy of *hasty generalization* occurs when a generalization is formed on the basis of an unrepresentative sample. As we saw in Section 8.2, to be accurate, a generalization about a group should be based upon a sample reflecting the diversity of that group. One way to ensure a representative sample, in some cases, is to select as large a sample as possible. The more people polled, for example, the more likely it is that the results truly represent the group. However, an accurate generalization does not necessarily require a large sample. In Gallup opinion polls, generalizations are typically based on surveys of a very small number of people. However, the pollsters are careful to select a typical or representative group of people for their sample. Consider these two examples:

Example 30

I've surveyed twenty-five students—each from a different campus organization—out of a student body of two thousand, and all of them prefer to use the activity fund for a film series. So probably the majority of all students would prefer a film series.

Example 31

I've spoken to the members of the campus Audubon Club, and they prefer to use the activity fund for a film series on birds. So probably a majority of the two thousand students would prefer a film series on birds.

The arguer in the first example forms a generalization about the preferences of two thousand students on the basis of a sample drawn from various campus groups. It is reasonable to assume that this sample accurately reflects the diversity of opinion among the students. Thus, this generalization does not commit the fallacy of hasty generalization. In the second example, however, the generalization is based solely upon a survey of one, rather select group, the members of the Audubon Club. Although their preferences should be considered, it is not likely that their group is representative of the student body as a whole; neither is it a random sample of opinions. Thus, the generalization rests on an unrepresentative sample.

Here is another example to consider. Columnist Ann Landers conducted an informal survey in which she asked her women readers to reply to this question: "Would you be content to be held close and treated tenderly and forget about 'the act'?" She reports that 100,000 women responded, with 72 percent answering yes. Among the conclusions she draws is the following:

Example 32

The most surprising aspect of this survey was that 40 percent of the yes votes were from women under forty years of age. What does this say about the sexual revolution? It says, in the boudoir at least, it has been an abysmal failure.

Landers reports that 72,000 women answered yes and that of that group, 42 percent, or 28,800, were under forty years of age. She concludes that the sexual revolution "has been an abysmal failure" on the basis of the 28,800 women under age forty who answered yes. Setting aside problems with the survey question itself and, in particular, the meaning of a yes answer, can we say that her sample of 28,800 women is large enough to support a generalization about a majority of the nation's approximately 2 million women under forty years of age? Although it is a significant sample, we may wonder whether it is indeed representative of the nation's women under forty. Landers provides no further information about the makeup of the sample. We know only that it is composed of women forty years or under who read the survey and responded. Lacking such information we cannot conclude that it is an accurate generalization, and we may suspect the fallacy of hasty generalization.

To identify the fallacy of hasty generalization, look for a conclusion that generalizes over a group. Notice whether the basis for the generalization is both representative of the group and sufficiently large to justify the generalization.

9.12 Fallacy of Composition

The fallacy of composition and the fallacy of division consist of fallacious reasoning about the relationship between a whole and its parts or a group and its members. They are sometimes called the part/whole fallacies. The fallacy of *composition* occurs when an arguer *mistakenly* concludes that the whole must have some characteristic because each part or member has the characteristic. Letting W stand for the whole and *f* for some feature, we can represent the form of this type of reasoning as follows:

Each member of W is f.

Therefore, W is f.

Here is an example:

Example 33

Each member of the orchestra is excellent, so the orchestra is excellent.

The assumption of the argument is that what is true of the parts is true of the whole. However, that assumption is often false. It is false, for instance, in many of those cases in which "the whole is *more than* the sum of its parts." In Example 33, an orchestra is not excellent simply because each musician is excellent. It is excellent because, in addition, the musicians work well together. Thus, the fact that the members are individually excellent does not itself justify inferring that the orchestra is excellent. More needs to be supplied to save the argument from the fallacy of composition.

Here are some other examples:

Example 34

The pink sweater is gorgeous. The purple skirt over there is smashing. I love those red shoes in the window, and how about that terrific yellow vest on the mannequin! Let's face it, it will make a great outfit for you!

Example 35

Smoking this cigarette surely can't harm me. So how can smoking cigarettes harm me?

Example 36

The movie Cleopatra *must be great. After all, it stars Elizabeth Taylor, Richard Burton, Rex Harrison, and Hume Cronyn—each a superb actor.*

To recognize the fallacy of composition, look for an argument that moves from a claim about the parts or members of a group to a conclusion about the whole. Consider then whether it is justifiable to attribute what is true of the parts to the whole.

9.13 Fallacy of Division

The fallacy of *division* is fallacious reasoning from the whole to the parts. It is in effect the reverse of the fallacy of composition. In this case the arguer mistakenly concludes that each part or member of the whole must have some characteristic because that characteristic is possessed by the whole. Letting W stand for the whole and f for some feature, we can represent the form of this argument as follows:

W is f.

Therefore, each member of W is f.

Here are some examples:

Example 37

The union voted to strike. Therefore, every member of the union voted to strike.

Example 38

Humans are the only animals capable of philosophical thinking. Thus, every person is capable of philosophical thinking.

Example 39

Tornadoes are common in the Midwest. Therefore, since Kansas City is in the Midwest, tornadoes are common in Kansas City.

Example 40

The team won a trophy. Therefore, every player won a trophy.

In Examples 37 and 38, the characteristics of the group as a whole—having voted to strike and being capable of philosophical thinking, respectively—are erroneously attributed to the members comprising the group. As the examples illustrate, a group may have characteristics *as a group* that are not possessed by all members taken individually. Examples 39 and 40 illustrate how a characteristic possessed by the group is not necessarily possessed by *any* member. For example, although tornadoes may be common in the Midwest, it does not follow that tornadoes are common in Kansas City or in any particular city in the Midwest. Likewise, that the team won a trophy does not mean that every member or any member won a trophy. Thus, what is true of the whole is not necessarily true of the parts.

To recognize the fallacy of division, look for an argument that moves from a claim about a whole or a group to a conclusion about one or all of the members of the whole. Then consider whether it is justifiable to attribute what is true of the whole to its parts.

9.14 False Analogy

An argument from analogy draws a conclusion about something on the basis of an analogy with or resemblance to some other thing. The assumption is that if two or more things are alike in some respects, they are alike in some other respect. Letting A and B represent two different things, events, or practices and letting f, g, h, and j represent features or properties (any number of features is possible), we can represent the form of the argument from analogy as follows:

A and B are both f, g, and h.
A is also j.

Therefore, probably B is j.

As we saw in Section 8.4, the strength of an argument from analogy depends on (1) the relevance of the possession of features f, g, and h to the possession of feature j and (2) the absence of relevant dissimilarities. If either criterion is not satisfied, then the argument commits the fallacy of *false analogy*. For example, the following argument lacks a relevant resemblance:

Example 41

Professor Hart teaches philosophy, and he is no fun at parties. Professor Milton teaches philosophy too, so he is probably no fun at parties either.

Now consider a variation on this argument with the addition of further points of resemblance between the two professors:

Example 42

Professor Hart teaches philosophy, has a pet cat, reads German, drives a foreign car, likes to cook, and is no fun at parties. Professor Milton teaches philosophy, has a pet cat, reads German, drives a foreign car, and likes to cook. So he is probably no fun at parties either.

The resemblance is stronger, yet the features that the two professors have in common are not relevant to the further feature of being no fun at parties. A strong resemblance or analogy is not by itself sufficient to warrant the conclusion.

On the other hand, the same conclusion is more probable if it is based upon points of resemblance that *are* relevant to the feature in question, as in this example:

Example 43

Professors Hart and Milton both teach philosophy. Both are happy only when talking about philosophy. Both frequently get into lengthy, abstract debates on nearly any subject with anyone. Professor Hart is no fun at parties. So Professor Milton is probably no fun at parties either.

Not only is the analogy between Hart and Milton more extensive, but the characteristics they are said to have in common do provide a reasonable basis for the conclusion that Milton is no fun at parties.

Examples 41 and 42 illustrate simple cases of the fallacy of false analogy. Let's consider a more difficult and more typical example:

Example 44

Regarding Iowa House Minority Leader Delwyn Stromer's proposal to get teenagers drunk in order to teach them their drinking limitations, a letter to the editor in the September 22, 1985, Des Moines Register *contained this statement:*

Perhaps Stromer would also be an advocate of Russian roulette to teach gun safety.

The writer's argument can be exposed as follows:

1. *It is foolish to advocate Russian roulette to teach gun safety.*

2. *Getting teenagers drunk to teach them their drinking limitations is like using Russian roulette to teach gun safety.*

---

3. *Therefore, getting teenagers drunk to teach them their drinking limitations is foolish.*

The analogy between getting teenagers drunk and Russian roulette is faulty. Getting teenagers drunk in the proposed experimental setting is not potentially fatal and could be conducted without harm. Russian roulette *is* potentially fatal and could not be conducted in such a way as to ensure no harm. Thus, the argument does not succeed in raising a legitimate objection to Stromer's proposal.

Consider another example:

Example 45

A study conducted in Argentina has shown that the IQs of mentally defective children can be raised 12 to 25 points by administering large doses of vitamin E. The implications of this study are astounding. If it works for retarded children, just think what it would do for normal children! We could greatly improve the IQs of the next generation of young people and, perhaps, raise the level of intelligence of our people for generations to come.

The argument assumes that mentally defective children and normal children are enough alike that what will work for the former will work for the latter. The obvious neurological differences are discounted, as though they were no factor in the children's body chemistry. We ought to be suspicious of this. It is very likely that the neurological differences are such that large doses of vitamin E will not have the same effects on normal children. It is possible, that is, that the addition of vitamin E makes up for some chemical deficiency in abnormal children or, perhaps, inhibits some of the symptoms of their mental condition; whereas normal children have no such deficiency or no mental condition that is inhibited by the vitamin. Whatever the case, the neurological differences between the mentally defective and the normal child are important enough to make us suspect the fallacy of false analogy.

To recognize the fallacy of false analogy, look for an argument that draws a conclusion about one thing, event, or practice on the basis of its analogy or resemblance to others. The fallacy occurs when the analogy or resemblance is not sufficient to warrant the conclusion, as when, for example, the resemblance is not relevant to the possession of the inferred feature or there are relevant dissimilarities.

9.15 Begging the Question

Begging the question is the fallacy of assuming the conclusion in one's premises. Suppose the question is whether God exists, and a person argues for the affirmative on the grounds that 'God's existence is clearly stated in the Bible, and the Bible is God's revelation of the truth'. The arguer is assuming the existence of God already in the reasons she gives; she is not providing reasons that can be accepted independently of the conclusion. This is made clear by exposing the argument:

Example 46

1. *The Bible asserts that God exists.*
2. *The Bible is the truth revealed by God.*

___

3. *Therefore, God exists.*

The argument is valid. Indeed, arguments that beg the question are usually valid. However, premise 2 is true only if the conclusion 3 is true. In other words, the premise does not offer independent support for the conclusion; it assumes the conclusion. Thus, the argument assumes the very thing that it purports to prove. A person using an argument of this form is often said to be guilty of "circular reasoning," for, as you can see, the support for the conclusion is itself supported *by* the conclusion.

There are various forms of question begging. Example 46 illustrates the type of question begging in which the premise itself rests upon or assumes the conclusion it is meant to support. Usually the fallacy is not as obvious as this. In other cases question begging occurs when the arguer uses a premise that is merely a restatement of the conclusion. The premise asserts the conclusion in different words, perhaps so subtly that the arguer may not notice. Consider this example:

Example 47

It is plain to see that suicide is morally wrong because, as any thinking person will admit, no one is ever justified in taking his or her own life.

The example claims that suicide is morally wrong because it is not justified. Saying that it is not justified is merely another way of saying that it is morally wrong. Thus, the arguer has not advanced the issue, for the issue is precisely whether suicide *is* morally justified.

Question begging also occurs when a question is expressed in such a way that a certain position or a certain answer is already assumed. Consider these two examples:

Example 48

I'm sorry I missed your class today, Professor Hart. Did I miss anything important?

Example 49

Mr. President, are you going to support further unnecessary military spending?

The question in Example 48 carries the implication that nothing of importance takes place in the class and missing it is thus of little consequence. In Example 49, the question assumes, before hearing the president's answer, that the military spending is unnecessary. A related form of question begging is called the *complex question,* so called because it typically hides more than one question and assumes an answer, usually incriminating, to one of them. Consider this question you might ask of a friend as a joke: "Are you still cheating on your taxes?" It actually involves two questions:

1. *Did you cheat on taxes?*
2. *Given that you cheated on taxes, do you still do it?*

The original question—"Are you still cheating on taxes?"—leaves the respondent no simple yes or no reply, for it already assumes that the answer to 1 is yes. Notice that if the respondent says no to the question, the implication is that he *did* cheat on taxes; whereas, if he answers yes, then again he implies that he cheats. Thus, either way he incriminates himself. The only response to such a question is to refuse to answer it as stated and to take it apart, as it were, so that it can be dealt with. Thus, one might say, "You assume that I cheat on taxes, and the fact is I never have!"

To recognize the fallacy of begging the question, look for an argument, reply, or question that assumes already the very issue under debate. Be aware that a question-begging argument may appear to offer legitimate, independent support, but on closer examination a premise in fact either itself rests upon the conclusion or restates the conclusion in different words.

9.16 Straw Man

The *straw man* fallacy occurs when an arguer responds to an opponent's argument by misrepresenting it in a manner that makes it appear more vulnerable than it really is, proceeds to attack that argument, and implies that he or she has defeated the opponent. It is called the straw man fallacy because, rather than attacking the "real man," the opponent sets up and knocks over a "straw man."

One form of the straw man fallacy involves a misrepresentation of an opponent's position as much too strong and therefore unacceptable. For example, in the argument below the arguer interprets an inductive argument as a deductive argument and shows that it is invalid.

Example 50

Don't be fooled by statistics showing some sort of correlation between smoking and lung cancer. Any logic student can tell you that it does not necessarily follow that a person will get cancer from smoking cigarettes.

The arguer misrepresents a causal correlation between smoking and lung cancer as a necessary connection and then easily provides an argument against it. The arguer thus appears to have a relevant response to the opponent's position, when in fact no such necessary connection is intended by the opponent.

Another example of interpreting an opponent's position in an unacceptably strong way is this:

Example 51

Councilman Winters says that all home owners should be required to put fences around their swimming pools in order to warn children. But we all know that any child who really wants to get to a neighbor's pool will find some way to get over any fence.

The arguer is probably right, but Councilman Winters does not claim that putting up fences makes it impossible for children to gain access to pools. The arguer is unfairly interpreting Councilman Winters' argument as involving an extremely strong and rather implausible claim.

Another form of the straw man fallacy occurs when an arguer represents an opponent's position as crucially depending upon some rather minor point that he or she then proceeds to attack. In this kind of case, the arguer's response attributes too little to the opponent. Consider this example:

Example 52

Robert Ardrey and others have argued for the theory of evolution by adducing evidence that humans evolved from a rather smallish, apelike hominid, Australopithecus africanus, who, they say, was an aggressive, territorial hunter and carnivore. In their zeal to establish this theory of theirs, they overlook one crucial fact: We are not all carnivores! How does their theory of descent from the apes account for the fact that many humans, indeed, most humans in the world, live on a diet of vegetables and grains, not meat?

The arguer misconstrues the theory of evolution as dependent on a rather minor point—that the hominids from which we evolved were carnivores—which can then be refuted.

Consider one final example of the straw man fallacy:

Example 53

MR. HUNTER:
Among the reasons I have for supporting sport
hunting is that it is in point of fact beneficial to
the species. If we abolished sport hunting, then
the deer populations in many parts of the country
would multiply without check, leading to massive
starvation as the deer placed impossible demands
upon their habitat. There would simply be too
many deer and not enough food for them all.

MR. AUDUBON:
Well, that's the most foolish and cruel argument
I've ever heard. How can it be good for a deer to
be shot?

Mr. Audubon distorts the argument by interpreting it to mean that it is beneficial to the particular deer, whereas the argument claims that it is good for the species as a whole.

To recognize the straw man fallacy, look for a response that misrepresents an opponent's argument in order to defeat it more easily. The arguer appears to be attacking the opponent's position, but in fact the arguer is attacking a misrepresentation of it.

9.17 Red Herring

The fallacy of *red herring* gets its name from the practice of using a herring, a particularly smelly fish when cooked, to divert hunting dogs from the scent of a fox. To commit the fallacy of red herring in an argument is to draw attention away from an issue by raising some other, seemingly related issue. In so doing, the arguer attempts to sidetrack the opponent's argument, as in this example:

Example 54

*Friends and neighbors, I urge you to defeat the proposal
to make jail sentences mandatory for drunk drivers. My
opponent claims that it will reduce the number of accidents
caused by drunk drivers. But if we really want to reduce
traffic accidents, then we should stand behind those men
and women whose chief responsibility is our safety. I am
referring, of course, to our valiant police officers. What we
need to do is increase their salaries, beef up the police
force, and, most importantly, stop butting into their business
with troublesome proposals!*

The issue is whether mandatory jail sentences should be used to combat drunk driving. The arguer does not advance the issue but instead diverts attention to the issue of supporting the police force. The tactic is clever because it raises an issue of loyalty that is likely to capture a crowd's attention and sympathy.

Here is another example:

Example 55

I agree with my opponent that pornography is a national problem, and I am almost persuaded by his argument that women are being degraded and victimized by pornography. I say, almost *persuaded . . . until I remember the facts that my opponent obviously overlooks: namely, that the people of Tibet are not merely degraded and victimized, they are deprived of every right due a human being. And what I don't understand is how we convince ourselves that our so-called national problem takes precedence over genuine oppression and suffering.*

Although the speaker may well have a point about the relative unimportance of pornography in comparison with the situation in Tibet, and although it is interesting to ask how we determine our priorities, nevertheless, this response is not relevant to the issue at hand. The question is not, Should we devote our time and energy to the consideration of pornography? but, Does pornography pose a serious moral harm to society or segments of society? Thus, this response involves the fallacy of red herring.

To recognize the fallacy of red herring, look for an argument in which the speaker responds by directing attention away from the issue to other, seemingly related issues.

9.18 Inconsistency

The fallacy of *inconsistency* involves reasoning from inconsistent premises, that is, statements that cannot be simultaneously true. For example, the statements 'Love is the desire for what is good' and 'Love is not the desire for what is good' are clearly inconsistent. It is impossible for both to be true.

The above example illustrates what we may call *explicit* inconsistency, because the inconsistency is readily apparent: One statement is the denial of the other. Such cases of inconsistency are rare, since they are so easily recognized. More common is what can be called *implicit* inconsistency. Two statements are implicitly inconsistent if one or both imply statements, one of which is the denial of the other—that is, if what follows from one is explicitly inconsistent with the other. For example, in President Reagan's 1984 campaign for the presidency, he promised, on the one hand, to achieve a balanced budget without diminishing funds to other government programs and, on the other hand, to increase the defense budget without raising taxes. Many critics charged Reagan with inconsistency on the grounds that increasing defense spending without cutting into other programs would require more federal money at the same time that attempting to balance the budget without raising taxes would decrease the amount of federal money. Thus, Reagan appeared to be endorsing (1) an increase in federal spending and (2) no increase in federal spending. Without explaining how both goals could be achieved, Reagan was guilty, critics claimed, of an inconsistency.

Consider another example of an implicit inconsistency:

Example 56

SENATOR:

Parents are the sole authority on the education of their children. Nothing we do should restrict the rights of parents to determine the kind of education they want for their children.

INTERVIEWER:

Senator, does the state, as a major contributor to the funding of education, have an interest in the content of education?

SENATOR:

Most certainly it does. One of the primary responsibilities of the state is to ensure a quality and equal education for all children. That is why we give the state the authority to license teachers, determine educational goals, and monitor the use of funds in education.

The senator is inconsistent. It cannot be the case that parents are the sole authorities on education and that the state has the authority to regulate education. Even if by a happy accident the wishes of parents and the decisions of the state coincide, the senator's position is inconsistent. He maintains that (1) the parents have the sole right to determine the quality of education and that (2) the state has the right to determine the quality of education. If 1 is true, then it follows that (3) the state does not have the right to determine the quality of education; and 3 is the denial of 2.

The fact that speakers assert one thing at one time and its denial on another is not in itself sufficient to charge them with inconsistency. Speakers may change their minds, in which case they do not assert both the statement and its denial. Rather, they conclude that one of the statements is false. For example, when it was learned that the hijackers of the ship *Achille Lauro* were likely to be turned over to the PLO, President Reagan was asked if he would accept the PLO's claim that it would bring the hijackers to justice. Reagan said that he would. Later in the day, however, he responded to the same question by saying that he would not. He explained to the reporters that he had considered the matter further and concluded that he spoke hastily the first time. At no time did he maintain that it both was and was not acceptable to him. Thus, Reagan cannot be charged with inconsistency in his remarks.

What is wrong with inconsistency? From the practical standpoint the most obvious answer is that we cannot rely on a person who argues inconsistently or maintains inconsistent positions. If a politician asserts S on one occasion and not S on another, without explaining it as a change of mind, then we do not know what the politician thinks or will do. Such a person is unreliable, if only regarding that issue. But there are two other reasons why inconsistency is a serious error in reasoning.

First, arguments with inconsistent premises necessarily fail to be good arguments because it cannot be the case that all premises are simultaneously true. Second, an argument with inconsistent premises does not distinguish good reasoning from bad because *any* statement can be validly deduced from inconsistent premises. Suppose, for example, we have as premises the two statements 'It is raining' and 'It is not raining.' We can validly deduce any statement whatsoever. Consider the following nested argument:

Example 57

1. It is raining.

---

2. Therefore, it is raining or Mexico is north of the United States.

3. It is not raining.

---

4. Therefore, Mexico is north of the United States.

The inference from 1 to the conclusion 2 is a valid deduction. Given that it is raining, it necessarily follows that 2 'It is raining *or* Mexico is north of the United States'. Notice that 2 does not assert that 'It is raining' is true *and* 'Mexico is north of the United States' is true. It asserts only that one *or* the other is true. Thus, from a statement S assumed to be true we may always combine it with any other statement P in a statement of the form 'S or P'. Now premise 3—the denial of 1—asserts that it is not the case that it is raining. Thus, since 'It is raining' is false and 'It is raining or Mexico is north of the United States' is true, 'Mexico is north of the United States' must follow as a valid inference. From inconsistent premises we have validly deduced 4. The significance of this is that inconsistent arguments are particularly pernicious. Any argument form from which *any* statement (including S and not S) is deducible is one that necessarily fails to distinguish good reasoning from bad. It is understandable, then, that inconsistency is the logician's nightmare. Imagine working long and hard to establish some highly important thesis only to discover that one's premises are implicitly inconsistent.

To recognize the fallacy of inconsistency, look for an argument with premises that are either implicitly or explicitly inconsistent.

Summary

The following summary is no substitute for the detailed explanations given in this chapter. Use the summary as a quick reference when you are explaining the fallacious reasoning in the exercises.

1. Fallacious appeal to authority: an argument that relies upon the assertions of someone who is not relevantly qualified or is not speaking without bias.

2. Appeal to the people: an argument in which a conclusion is said to be true because it is commonly or traditionally believed.

3. Appeal to force: an argument in which a threat is used to win the listener's acceptance of the conclusion.

4. Appeal to pity: an argument in which an appeal to the listener's sympathy is used to win the listener's acceptance of the conclusion.

5. Appeal to ignorance: an argument in which it is concluded that some statement is true (or false) because there is no evidence that the statement is false (or true).

6. *Ad hominem:* an argument that attacks the person rather than the person's ideas.

   Abusive: reasoning that a person's arguments are not to be believed because the person is of poor character.

   Tu quoque: excusing or defending oneself by accusing one's critic of a similar wrongdoing.

   Circumstantial: reasoning that a person's arguments are not to be believed because the person has ulterior motives.

7. False cause: an argument that concludes without justification that one thing or event causes another.

   Post hoc, ergo propter hoc ("after this, therefore because of this"): concluding that one thing or event, A, causes another, B, because A preceded B; whereas, from the fact that A precedes B it does not follow that A causes B.

   Oversimplification: proposing a solution to a problem that oversimplifies the matter by overlooking other important causal factors.

8. Slippery slope: an argument that reasons without justification that some thing or event will cause a series of events ultimately leading to some undesirable consequence.

9. Either/or: an argument involving the mistaken assumption that there are only two alternatives available and that one must be taken because the other is unacceptable.

10. Equivocation: an argument in which the conclusion rests upon the use of a word or phrase in two different senses.

11. Hasty generalization: an argument in which a generalization is formed on the basis of an unrepresentative sample.

12. Fallacy of composition: an argument involving the mistaken assumption that what is true of the parts or members of a whole is true of the whole itself.

13. Fallacy of division: an argument involving the mistaken assumption that what is true of the whole is true of the parts or members of the whole.

14. False analogy: an argument that reasons that if two things are alike in certain respects, then they are alike in some other respect. The fallacy occurs when the analogy is not relevant to the possession of the inferred feature or there is a relevant disanalogy.

15. Begging the question: an argument that assumes as true the very point under question. Question begging occurs when a premise assumes the truth of the conclusion or the conclusion is a restatement of the premise.

    Complex question: a question framed in such a way that the answer is already assumed.

16. Straw man: a rebuttal to an argument in which the speaker misrepresents the opponent's argument as more vulnerable than it is and then proceeds to attack that misrepresentation.

17. Red herring: a rebuttal to an argument that diverts attention away from the main issue by raising other, seemingly related issues.

18. Inconsistency: an argument based on inconsistent premises, that is, premises that cannot be simultaneously true.

Exercise 9A Identifying Fallacies Almost all of the following arguments commit a fallacy. Identify the fallacy and explain your judgment.

1. Those who keep quiet about this funding won't have to look for other jobs. Do you all understand?

2. I know your doctor says you need your appendix removed, but according to *Reader's Digest,* people with your symptoms just need a change in their diet. So forget about having your appendix out.

3. Certainly Leo Tolstoy was a great novelist, and I admit his stories are excellent. But if we are supposed to take his sermonizing on the value of unselfishness and love for humanity as a prescription for the good life, then I strongly object. If the man has a philosophy, it is not worth the paper it's written on for the simple reason that he was himself a failure at living unselfishly and benevolently.

4. I don't have any mice in my house. I haven't seen a single one.

5. Aw, c'mon, go out with me. My ship's been out at sea for six months, and I haven't seen a girl in all that time.

6. Well, I don't like Hollings, but either I vote for him or I vote for Miller, and you know what I think about Miller.

7. People have no reason to be afraid of love, for love is just a four-letter word.

8. It's no wonder there's so much divorce, crime, and political corruption in our nation today. Have you seen what's on TV these days?

9. I can't understand why people talk about how beautiful California is. Last summer I spent three days at a convention in Los Angeles, and I can tell you, Cali-

fornia is not beautiful. There are too many people, too many cars, too much concrete, not enough fresh air, and not enough peace and quiet.

10. I believe that God's word is our commandment, for he is all-good and he knows what is right and wrong. After all, he created us and gave us the freedom to act as we choose; so it is up to each individual to follow his or her idea of what is right.

11. Studying philosophy is a dangerous thing to do. It makes you critical, which in turn makes you skeptical of your religious beliefs. And once you've begun to lose faith in your religion, it's a small step to atheism and immorality, and a life of immorality is damned.

12. I find the proposal to permit students to take part in the development of the college curriculum utterly ridiculous. How can students be in a position to judge which courses are worthwhile and which are not before they have had those courses? It's preposterous!

13. Simpson, it has come to my attention that some of the employees want to form a union. Their representative tells me that they are not satisfied with their working conditions. Well, some people are never satisfied and never think of anyone but themselves. You can tell them for me that it will be a cold Fourth of July before we cater to the whimperings of malcontents.

14. George: That must be a pretty heavy book you're carrying.
    Jeff: It ought to be; it's got the weight of authority in it.

15. I know my paper is late, Professor Hart, but my roommate was sick last night, and my folks'll kill me if I flunk this course.

16. Max: Maestro, tell me, what is the secret of composing a beautiful symphony?
    Maestro: Ah, that's easy. Just make sure that you select only beautiful notes.

17. Professor Scott, my American Literature professor, warned us about the dangers of nuclear power plants, so I'm voting against proposition N, the nuclear power plant initiative.

18. I don't see why you get down on me for smoking pot. You guys have a couple of martinis every night.

19. If you don't accept Christ in your heart this very night, you will lose your immortal soul.

20. Max: Are you going out with that cheerleader this weekend?
    Fred: Yep.
    Max: Wow! What did she say when you asked her out?
    Fred: She didn't say no.
    Max: Well, what *did* she say?
    Fred: She didn't say anything.

21. A: Do you see what I'm saying?
    B: No, how could I? We can see only what is visible.

22. Ginger: I believe in the theory of reincarnation.
    Diane: What is that?
    Ginger: Well, it is the idea that we never *really* die. What happens at death is that our soul leaves the body and is reborn into another human body to live another life. So we always come back and never really die.

Diane: So you mean we're sort of recycled?

Ginger: Yes, in a sense.

Diane: Well, that's got to be false. If we all just keep coming back, then what are we having funerals for?

23. No one on the weight-lifting team can lift more than 250 pounds, so the team won't be able to push that 2000-pound car.

24. The sign read, "All you can eat for a dollar," but when I went back for more the manager said, "No more! That's all you can eat for a dollar."

25. Sure I was speeding, officer, but so were you! How else would you ever have caught me?

26. My opponent argues that women do not have the right to choose abortion. That means he denies that women have the right to control their own bodies, and he thus endorses a kind of sexual discrimination. Well, we've worked too long and too hard to ensure equality between the sexes to revert back to that kind of unjust treatment of women.

27. I recommend that we not rehire Professor Buzz. We simply can't have teachers who cannot keep discipline in the classroom. Professor Buzz is cross-eyed and, as everyone knows, a cross-eyed teacher cannot control his pupils.

28. We haven't heard any sounds from the rubble of that collapsed building, so we figure that no one remains alive inside.

29. My art professor, Mr. Crowley, recommends using marble slab for the lithos. So you should use it, too.

30. Art: Well, I've decided to take the course in philosophy of art because I already have a theory worked out. It's that all art is the communication of emotion.

Phil: That's interesting. Does it matter what kinds of emotion art communicates?

Art: Yes, it does. Good art communicates only noble and fine emotions.

Phil: And bad art? What does it communicate?

Art: Aha! That's just it! Bad art doesn't communicate at all.

31. Plato said that man is the rational animal. Aristotle said that man is the featherless biped. Both of them were wrong. After all, not everybody is rational, and not everybody has two legs. Those Greeks!

32. Reports of extraterrestrials, visitors from Mars, and so on are numerous, but not one report is worth believing. All of them come from people who lack credibility, as is clear from the fact that they make these incredible claims!

33. Well, I was shocked to learn from my daughter that racial discrimination is being *taught* at her college. In her last letter she said that her art teacher is teaching them to make discriminations on the basis of color.

34. When people have typhoid fever, we quarantine them so that others will not be infected. Malaria is certainly as serious a disease as typhoid, so we should quarantine malaria patients, too.

35. Of course there are extraterrestrials. Haven't you read that article in the *National Enquirer* about those UFOs spotted in Texas last month?

36. Every year a few snowy owls are spotted in Nebraska. So every year a few snowy owls are spotted in Omaha, because Omaha is in Nebraska.

37. Son, I have to tell you that I strongly disapprove of your living with your girlfriend. People just do not do that.

38. Special Investigator Griffin Bell's committee concluded that there was no evidence of wrongdoing on the part of top executives at E. F. Button, so we may all rest assured that Button's top executives had nothing to do with those illegal practices.

39. I read in the obituary column this morning that the multimillionaire J. P. Vanderbilt died, leaving his entire estate to his brothers. Well, since we are all brothers under the skin I expect I'm entitled to my share of his millions.

40. Phil: The philosopher Spinoza said that if we know God, then we know all things, because God *is* all things.

    Max: That sounds very nice, Phil, but you're surely not going to believe a man who is an avowed pantheist.

Exercise 9B   More Informal Fallacies   The following excerpts from letters to the editor and from newspaper and magazine articles contain fallacious reasoning. Some excerpts may contain more than one fallacy. State what fallacy or fallacies you find in the passages, and give an explanation for your judgment.

1. *Gerald F. Uelmen describes an incident in which Justice Oliver Wendell Holmes, Jr., hearing a motion for a continuance of a murder trial by a lawyer named Swasey, appears to commit a fallacy. Justice Holmes speaks:*
   "Mr. Swasey, the record shows that the trial of this case has at your request been continued once. Last summer, when I was in England visiting the law courts, Mr. Justice Stephen commented to me on the importance of speedy trials in the administration of justice, particularly in capital cases while witnesses were available, evidence fresh in the mind, and before suggestions could create false psychological memories."
   As Holmes paused before ruling, Swasey inquired, "Has Your Honor read the morning papers?" An annoyed Holmes inquired what bearing the morning papers could possibly have on the motion. "None," replied Swasey, "but they do report that yesterday Mr. Justice Stephen was judicially committed to an institution for the feeble-minded." Amidst harrumphs, Holmes granted the motion. (*New York Times*)

2. *A letter to the editor of the* St. Joseph Gazette *claiming that spanking children leads those same children to become child abusers when they grow up gives this argument:* To say it is proper to whip a child mildly, is like saying it is all right to steal a few things, just don't carry it too far.

3. Despite the fact that the case against cigarette smoking has by no means been proven, the tobacco industry has in recent years suffered a notable degree of harassment: It has stopped advertising cigarettes on television. It has had to print on its packs the flat assertion that smoking "is dangerous" to one's health. We

have seen effective and often very creative anti-smoking ads. Some magazines won't accept cigarette advertising. Some periodicals won't publish articles which tend to exonerate tobacco. Aboard commercial airlines and on interstate trains and buses, it is not only permissible to segregate smokers; it is federally mandated. (Smokers usually have to sit in the back of the plane where there is more engine noise and more chance of being served a cold meal.) Recent lawsuits have sought to ban smoking in the New Orleans Superdome and to limit it in federal office buildings. And sales and excise taxes, particularly at state and local levels, have climbed to the sumptuary point in many places. (James Council, "The Case for Tobacco," in *The Language of Argument*, by Daniel McDonald)

4. A few of us just get kind of sick and tired of the Catholic Church and our U.S. government always being fair game. Every Christian owes his Christianity, and a word of appreciation, to the treasury of faith, history and tradition due to the uninterrupted Catholic lineage leading back to Christ. And every American owes his freedom, and rights and thanks to the continuity of our government. It is the greatest success story in the history of the world, and the envy of those who cannot share it. (Letter to the editor, *Des Moines Register*)

5. *Phyllis Schlafly, spokesperson for the pro-life position on abortion, accused women working for abortion rights* of wanting to protect women's rights to kill their babies. That isn't what American women really want. (*U.S. News & World Report*)

6. Unless the homosexuals end their perverted way of life, which is unlikely, we can forget a nuclear holocaust and prepare for the AIDS holocaust. Something has to be done. Should the AIDS cases be allowed to roam freely like walking time bombs, or should they be isolated, as discussed on TV, in their own colony as was done in the past with leprosy cases? (Letter to the editor, *Riverside Press-Enterprise*)

7. Religion *is* being taught in our public schools today, and the government's own brand of "brainwashing" is going on. It is called secular humanism. (Letter to the editor, *Des Moines Register*)

8. While I certainly don't feel the Japanese attack on Pearl Harbor was justified, I can't believe there is so little knowledge of what actually took place. Several books now out tell of how Roosevelt was simply a frontman for the industrialists who were hoping to reap fat profits from war. Roosevelt cut off trade with Japan, refused to negotiate with her, and when he got word she was going to attack Pearl Harbor, deliberately withheld the information. . . . Later, Truman deliberately ignored the overtures to surrender by Japan and dropped the A-bombs. All governments are usually run by those who put profits above freedoms and life, and an ill-informed, apathetic public allows it. (Letter to the editor, *Riverside Press-Enterprise*)

9. [Black Muslim leader Louis] Farrakhan calls Judaism a "dirty religion." Jewish teachers believe the Old Testament is the inspired word of God. Christian teachers believe both the Old and the New Testaments are the inspired word of God. Therefore by implication Farrakhan really says that the Judeo-Christian religion is dirty.

Farrakhan is evil, Farrakhan is satanic. I am very distressed more Christian leaders did not make an outcry against this evil man and his sinful remarks. (Letter to the editor, *Riverside Press-Enterprise*)

10. *Regarding the "Farm Aid" benefit designed to help alleviate the U.S. farm crisis, one writer made the following comment in the letters to the editor column:* Only a man of Willie Nelson's caliber can understand who really feeds the world—the American farmer.

11. Until we as a nation, take a stand against any kind of corporal punishment of our children, we will continue to abuse them in the name of discipline. (Letter to the editor, *St. Joseph Gazette*)

12. *Ann Landers commented as follows on a survey in which she asked people to answer yes or no to the question, "Would you be content to be treated tenderly and forget about the 'act'?":* If my survey had any value, it was in the revelation that a great many women choose affection over sex. Those yes votes were saying, "I want to be valued. I want to feel cared about. Tender words and loving embraces are more rewarding than an orgasm produced by a silent, mechanical, self-involved male." (*Family Circle,* June 1985)

13. *The following letter was in response to an editorial by Mary McGrory in which she argued that AIDS is not God's punishment for homosexuality because it is also being contracted by those who are not homosexuals.* Never once as a Christian have I thought that AIDS was God's punishment of homosexuals. I always have thought of AIDS as being a good example of what happens when a person puts his own interests and pleasures ahead of what God's will is on the matter. God did not bring AIDS upon homosexuals and drug addicts; they brought it upon themselves by means of an unclean, unbiblical lifestyle. That mainstream people and even children are contracting AIDS only points out the fact that many people must pay the price for the reckless behavior of a few. (Letter to the editor, *Omaha World Herald*)

14. *On a television interview regarding his new book,* Macdougal's Medicine, *Dr. Macdougal answered questions from callers. Two separate callers asked about having surgery to remove a suspicious lump.*

To the first caller: Have the lump removed. If the tumor hasn't spread, then by all means remove it. If it has spread, then don't let yourself be disfigured by surgery which won't save you.

To the next caller: If there are no symptoms from this breast tumor, then follow the advice of the doctor who told you to wait. You can always have the surgery later. The one thing about surgery is that it's a last-ditch effort in most cases. You can always have it done later.

15. We dare to challenge the seat-belt law because it is an infringement on our personal freedom, and no excuse that it saves money in any way is going to change that fact. It's not what I fought for in World War II. We have a state government in Lincoln that is doing its best to create a police state. (Letter to the editor, *Omaha World Herald*)

16. If it were really demonstrated that cigarettes are *the* cause of cancerous growths, the tobacco industry would join the rest of the world in rejoicing that the cause of cancer had at last been identified. It would celebrate the medical breakthrough which would bring protection and new hope to everyone, including tobacco people. It would be most happy to stop cigarette production and diversify into new areas. (James Council, "The Case for Tobacco," in *The Language of Argument,* by Daniel McDonald)

17. We have an obligation to stop playing games, hiding behind euphemisms, arguing over shades of meaning of the word "viability" and face a very distasteful fact: when we perform an abortion, we are destroying a life. We may choose to do that—some of us do choose to do it—but abortion is murder and there is no way we can, if we are honest, deny that revolting fact. (William A. Nolen, M.D., *The Baby in the Bottle*)

18. Apparently Secretary of State George Schultz does not believe in God for he has said that we must ensure that there is "no escape from justice" for the terrorists responsible for the recent shipjacking of the *Achille Lauro*. If he believed in God, he'd know that God brings all men to justice no matter what *we* do. If he thinks they might escape justice, then he cannot be a believer in a God of justice; it's that simple. (Letter to the editor)

19. In regard to a recent article . . . about the intolerable conditions in the county jails and the statistics on inmate population increases: One comment was that inmates were forced to eat near toilets and urinals in their cells. Oh, for shame! Who forced them into jail! It would be nice if they could be housed in Motel 6 and have catered meals plus a membership in Jack LaLanne's. But in my and other law-abiding citizens' books, they are getting their just desserts. The solution is simple: Stay out of jail. (Letter to the editor, *Riverside Press-Enterprise*)

20. A Romanian farm journal reports that extremely large amounts of vitamin E, plus vitamin A, were given to 77 sterile cows. Within one to one and a half months, their sexual cycles were restored, and 70 percent of them conceived. (Ruth Adams and Frank Murray, "Vitamin E in the Hands of Creative Physicians," in *Vitamin E, Wonder Worker of the 70's*)

21. *Jerry Falwell of the Moral Majority sent out a poll soliciting viewers' opinions on the presence of violence and sex on television. Respondents were asked to answer the following questions and then send a donation to the Moral Majority to "help clean up television once and for all!"*

   Please answer each of the questions below by checking the appropriate box:

   1. Are you in favor of America's children being subjected to the presentation of homosexuality as an acceptable lifestyle in prime-time television?

   2. Do you favor the showing of obnoxious and unedited R-rated movies on network television?

   3. Are you in favor of television programs which major in gratuitous violence such as murder, rape, beatings, etc.?

   4. Are you in favor of cable television now bringing hard-core pornography into America's living rooms?

22. Seventy-five percent of the people in California believe the death penalty is a protection which they need and are entitled to. Now, this question is not subject to any scientific analysis; not something one person knows a great deal about and another person knows nothing about. You can't come up with a right answer by using a slide rule. Everyone in this room, and most of the citizens in this state are just as well qualified to arrive at a correct conclusion in this as I am, or as is Professor Amsterdam, or as is Governor Brown. This is not something that's subject to expert testimony. I think every citizen has a stake in this and the fact that 75 percent of our citizens support the reenactment of the death

penalty is significant. (Evelle J. Younger, "Capital Punishment: The People's Mandate," address of the California Attorney General to the Commonwealth Club of California, July 1977)

23. The extraordinary courageous action of the citizens who captured the "Night Stalker" and those providing vital information leading to the arrest, are really entitled to any reward previously offered; however I believe if I had been in the position of these noteworthy captors, I would have killed him myself. . . . Of course, I realize the decision to take the law into my own hands would be wrong, but equally wrong would it be to let this criminal be released after a prison term—to kill again and again. (Letter to the editor, *Riverside Press-Enterprise*)

24. Prior to World War II, we heard nil about Alzheimer's [disease] and we hardly heard of anyone who acquired it. At this point in time, post–WWII, we tossed out iron and enamel cookware for aluminum cookware and bakeware. Then the popular new TV dinners wrapped in aluminum foil, ice cream bars, not to forget soda pop and beer in aluminum cans. We also receive a lot of aluminum into our system through buffered aspirins, and stomach anti-acids and underarm deodorants. We are taking a lot of a toxic poisonous substance aluminum which affects the ions of the brain. Was the overuse of aluminum and the upsurge of so much Alzheimer's disease surfacing coincidental? (Letter to the editor, *Riverside Press-Enterprise*)

25. Another argument, a favorite of those who oppose the death penalty, is that we can accomplish the same thing by life imprisonment without possibility of parole. There are several things wrong with that. There is no such thing in our nation or in our state as true life imprisonment, nor should there be. The governor has, and always should have, the power to commute. That's the safety valve that will work when everything else fails. So I wouldn't be in favor of, if we could, and it would be impossible, to try and take away the governor's power to commute. Given that power to commute, there's no such thing as life imprisonment. (Evelle J. Younger, "Capital Punishment: The People's Mandate," address of the California Attorney General to the Commonwealth Club of California, July 1977)

26. Frederick J. Stare, a founder and chairman of the Department of Nutrition at Harvard University's School of Public Health, remains one of the country's leading defenders of sugar in our diet. He thinks the substance has been "unduly maligned." He applauds it as "the least expensive important source of calories" and "an important nutrient and food." General Foods Corporation, the second-largest user of sugar in the country, paid for the Nutrition Research labs at Harvard's School of Public Health. Other contributors to Harvard's Department of Nutrition—Amstar, Domino Sugar, Coca-Cola, Kellogg, the International Sugar Research Association, and the Sugar Association—are no more eager for the true sugar story to emerge. (Jeanne Shinto, "Is Our Diet Driving Us Crazy?" *The Progressive*)

27. *The following exchange took place on the* Dick Cavett Show *during an interview with G. Gordon Liddy, who spent five years in prison in connection with the Watergate burglary:*
    Cavett: You spent several years in prison and we hear about the high incidence of homosexuality. Did you find it hard to adjust to the homosexuality there?

Liddy: No.
Cavett: You heard it, folks. He said he had no trouble adjusting to homosexuality in prison.

28. We can talk and plan and agonize about child abuse until the cows come home, but we shall never approach the cure until we stop planting the seeds. Every time we strike a child and tell him it is for his own good that we must whip him to make a good child of him, we have planted a seed of belief that violence to the body will control actions; will control others. That tiny seed becomes a monstrous tree that is resulting in a violent society. (Letter to the editor, *St. Joseph Gazette*)

29. In fairness, any legal effort to curtail cigarette smoking on the ground that it may be a health hazard, should also work against other possible health hazards: There should be no television advertisements for wine or beer. Every bottle of whiskey and of cough syrup should bear a health warning. T-bone steaks should carry a printed brand warning of cholesterol. It should be illegal for a restaurant to serve pecan pie to anyone who is twenty pounds overweight. To avoid danger to health, no one should be allowed to buy a gun—or a football—or a king-size bottle of aspirin. Clearly, very heavy regulations should govern the sale of something as deadly as an automobile. No one should be permitted to sunbathe on the beach or to shop in high-crime areas. (James Council, "The Case for Tobacco," in *The Language of Argument,* by Daniel McDonald)

30. *The New Republic* refers to fetuses as "not yet self-conscious." On what grounds does *The New Republic* say that fetuses are not "self-conscious"? A sixteen-week-old fetus will kick and squirm if prodded by a needle. That, it would seem to me, is very simple evidence that the fetus is self-conscious. Perhaps a sixteen-week-old fetus does not spend time, as it bobs around in the amniotic sac, thinking about the meaning of life or musing on the works of Plato, but neither does a two-year-old toddler. (William A. Nolen, M.D., *The Baby in the Bottle*)

31. I am a Christian woman, and I am also a feminist. I am writing to share with all your readers the fact that there *are* Christian sisters who, though they believe abortion is wrong, *uphold a woman's right to do with her body as she wishes.* This is a point I cannot get across to most fanatical Christians, especially men. I hope that non-Christians aren't lumping all Christians in with Jerry Falwell and Ronald Reagan, because that is not accurate. I am appalled by the Moral Majority, and it frightens me that they are trying to change the current abortion laws. Christians have a nasty habit of imposing their views and doctrine upon people, and this marriage of religion and state is not good. (Letter to the editor, *Ms.* magazine)

32. Cartoonist Walt Handelsman charges MTV with what fallacy?

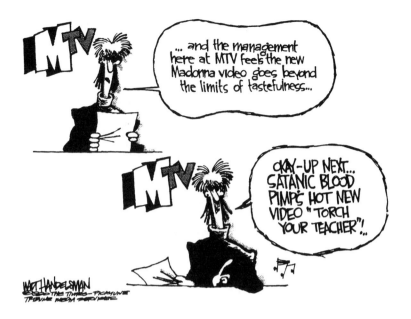

33. It [the pope's position against birth control] is insane, yet it reflects the ambition of the Catholic Church for power by sheer numbers. Each female member of every diocese becomes a baby factory, by papal decree—being urged to produce as many children as possible in her lifetime. This pressure makes the Catholic Church the greatest menace in the world today. . . .

    The Catholic churches . . . should be picketed until the pope and the church renounce their stand against birth control and do as other churches do: preach Christianity, love for their fellow man, and follow in the footsteps of Jesus Christ. (Letter to the editor, *Riverside Press-Enterprise*)

34. I was filled with awe and admiration when I read of the determination of the men searching for the killer bees. Why couldn't we conduct just such a thorough search for missing children? Why couldn't we search every single home in the United States for these children? I think very few people would object to a legal search. (Letter to the editor, *Riverside Press-Enterprise*)

35. What mergers are doing to America is a national disgrace. They are the real reason the U.S. can no longer produce goods of quality at a reasonable price. Why produce goods when mergers are the product? Keep on merging, America; the Orient loves it. (Letter to the editor, *U.S. News & World Report*)

36. Many people fear that Fundamentalists will influence the passage of laws that infringe on their personal choices. However, this claim can never be an argument against the movement since all laws quite properly limit the individual's freedom for the collective good. (Letter to the editor, *Time*)

37. *What is this writer accusing the editor of the* Economist *of doing?* Sir—You state that 1,300 cinema screens are available in the United States for a major film release. Yet later in the same issue . . . , you say that "almost all big movies now open on 2,000 or more screens." One hopes that your newspaper has greater precision in financial reporting than in counting cinema screens. (Letter to the editor)

38. *Is there a fallacy in this argument?* Big Tobacco recently settled Florida's lawsuit against it for $11.3 billion—the largest monetary concessions the industry has ever paid. But there is another huge carcinogen out there. And despite knowledge of the deadly risk, one state in particular has nevertheless encouraged innocent victims from around the world to come and be exposed to that carcinogen. I am referring, my friends, to Mr. Sun—which causes deadly skin cancer. Florida has always been aware of this. And yet Florida calls itself "The Sunshine State." Let's call Florida the Cancer State! They have built whole industries around keeping you on the beach. Has Florida ever mentioned in its ads: "Warning: Exposure to sun can cause deadly cancer"? No. Not a single tourism ad warns of the cancer risk of Florida sunshine.

How much has been spent caring for these unsuspecting tourists? What strains have been placed on the health care systems of other states, whose citizens return home to suffer and die? And what of Florida's own residents?

I suggest that citizens with skin cancer sue the state of Florida, which has knowingly contributed to this crisis. Yes, health groups have put out warnings left and right. But can we trust the people to inform themselves of the risks? I think not. After all, people are unwitting dupes. It's time for a class-action suit. Because nobody's responsible for what they do. It's not the idiots who lit the tobacco cigarettes. It's not the people who bake in the sun. It's everybody else's fault for deceiving them in advertisements. Besides . . . it's a fast track to a quick buck. (Rush Limbaugh, *The Limbaugh Letter*)

39. *The following passage is an editorial critical of Norwich University for recruiting army officers from Indonesia for its military college on the grounds that Indonesia's military "has a horrendous human rights record." What fallacy does the editor accuse President Schneider of?* In defending the college's Indonesian ties, President Richard Schneider said, "Would the Catholic Church send missionaries to Indonesia? Absolutely. Why do they do it? To convert them?"

True enough. But when the Blessed Sisters of Mercy do missionary work abroad, they don't expect money for their pains. And the sisters don't urge those to whom they are ministering to protest the government's autocracy. (Editorial, *Rutland Herald*)

40. *Does this moving argument commit a fallacy, such as appeal to pity or appeal to force, perhaps? What do you think?* Every part of this country is sacred to my people. Every hillside, every valley, every plain and grove has been hallowed by some fond memory or some sad experience of my tribe. Even the rocks, which seem to lie dumb as they swelter in the sun along the silent sea shore in solemn grandeur, thrill with memories of past events connected with the lives of my people.

The very dust under your feet responds more lovingly to our footsteps than to yours, because it is the ashes of our ancestors, and our bare feet are conscious of the sympathetic touch, for the soil is rich with the life of our kindred.

The noble braves, fond mothers, glad, happy-hearted maidens, and even the little children, who lived and rejoiced here for a brief season, and whose very names are now forgotten, still love these sombre solitudes and their deep fastnesses which, at eventide, grow shadowy with the presence of dusky spirits.

And when the last Red Man shall have perished from the earth and his memory among the white men shall have become a myth, these shores will swarm with the invisible dead of my tribe; and when your children's children shall think themselves alone in the fields, the store, the shop, upon the highway, or in the silence of the pathless woods, they will not be alone. In all the earth there is no place dedicated to solitude.

At night, when the streets of your cities and villages will be silent and you think them deserted, they will throng with the returning hosts that once filled and still love this beautiful land.

The white man will never be alone. Let him be just and deal kindly with my people, for the dead are not powerless. Dead—did I say? There is no death. Only a change of worlds! (Chief Seattle, January 1855)

41. *Commenting on a scheme to fool people into depositing their money into a fake, bank night-deposit box, Rush Limbaugh says the following:* On Labor Day Saturday, a box and sign were put up at a Warwick, R.I. bank. The sign instructed customers that the regular night-deposit box was broken, so they should put their money into the new box in the foyer. And, people did. But there was one problem. The box was not installed by the bank. Police say that whoever put the sign up returned Sunday night, grabbed the box and made off with a "substantial amount" of money.

Imagine that, friends. People willingly putting their hard-earned money somewhere they were tricked into believing was safe, legitimate, and ultimately for their benefit—but the cash went to feed someone else's greed. In this case, certain words were attached to the event: Theft. Robbery. Crime. Excuse me, ever hear of *taxes*? (Rush Limbaugh, *The Limbaugh Letter*)

42. *The following two passages are from two separate essays written by Rush Limbaugh in his* The Limbaugh Letter. *What fallacy, if any, do you find here?*

Remember, my friends, what has made America great is freedom. And that's what you should always be on guard to protect, as every new day arrives. Because, as I always say, it is freedom that has allowed ordinary people to do extraordinary things. Ordinary people becoming extraordinary people is this country's legacy and promise—it doesn't matter if it's 1956 or 2056. ("Why I Believe in You")

Joshua Smith, 25, isn't happy that after customer complaints, the owners of Noah's Bagels instituted what he calls "conservative" policies. They limited the kinds of face piercings employees can have. And he says they cut back on health benefits. So employees voted to join the United Food & Commercial Workers Local 870. "We're not out to gouge the company," says Smith. No, they're out to gouge their skin. So what if they offend customers? If kids want to wear rings in their noses, their eyelids, their cheeks, their tongues, and who knows where else . . . the unions will pin down those rights! ("News Digest")

Exercises 43–45 are letters to the editor of Harper's Magazine. *They were written in response to an essay by Joy Williams defending animal rights. What fallacies, if any, do you find present?*

43. When a grizzly bear bites the face of a woman in the Pacific Northwest, do you think it feels any sense of shame? Do you think that great white sharks have traumatic nightmares after they bite surfers? Or perhaps there is a self-help group for chickens who have pecked another chicken to death, which is a real problem in that community. If we think that such feelings in animals would be absurd, why do we expect more from ourselves?

Speaking about animals' rights is like spitting into the wind. Our own rights are abrogated on a daily basis in thousands of ways. It is difficult enough for us to uphold, defend, and protect these rights without concerning ourselves with the so-called rights of those who cannot communicate with us and whom we happen to find quite tasty. (Letter to the editor)

44. Joy Williams' article includes genuinely amazing descriptions of how some animals are regularly mistreated, but I was not moved to action. Although the world's supply of sympathy is infinite, the resources of time and energy are not. It is for this reason that truly compassionate individuals devote themselves to helping other people.

    Until humans everywhere can live in comfort, health, and safety, the huge amounts of time and money devoted to the cause of animals' rights strikes me as decidedly inhumane. (Letter to the editor)

45. Just a thought for Joy Williams: If we're not supposed to eat animals, how come they're made out of meat? (Letter to the editor)

Exercise 9C   Composing Fallacies   In the following exercises, complete the statement in such a way that the resulting reasoning commits the fallacy requested.

Sample   *Euthanasia ought to be permitted because . . .*

   a. (fallacious appeal to authority) . . . my uncle is a police officer and he is in favor of it.

   b. (either/or fallacy) . . . it's the most sensible solution when you consider that the only alternative is a protracted and painful death.

1. The death penalty should be abolished because . . . (either/or fallacy):

   _____

2. I completely reject Professor Gordon's statement that we should not give money to people panhandling on the streets because . . . (*ad hominem* abusive):

   _____

3. The personal use of marijuana should not be legally permitted because . . . (begging the question):

   _____

4. I think that extraterrestrials probably have visited the earth thousands of years ago because . . . (appeal to ignorance):

   _____

5. I know that I was caught plagiarizing my final essay, but I do not believe I should be failed in the course because . . . (appeal to pity):

   _____

6. Proponents say that the strongest argument in support of physician-assisted suicide is that it relieves suffering, but I say that . . . (straw man):

   _____

7. People argue that television violence is causing an increase in crime but I say that . . . (red herring):

_____

8. The faculty should reconsider the student council's proposal for a two-week break in the spring because . . . (appeal to force):

_____

9. I decided not to have my wisdom teeth removed because . . . (fallacious appeal to authority):

_____

10. Some people say that out of respect for animals we ought to stop eating meat, but I say that . . . (straw man):

_____

11. Why does it surprise you that the garage door repairman recommends that you buy a new garage door opener? After all . . . (*ad hominem* circumstantial):

_____

12. The student council voted to reinstate the film series. Therefore . . . (fallacy of division):

_____

13. The faculty opposes serving alcohol in the student dining hall. I support that. After all, serving alcohol in a student dining hall is like . . . (false analogy):

_____

14. There is a lot of support in this city for a new hockey rink. Almost everyone I asked was in favor of the idea. I spent the afternoon polling people at . . . (hasty generalization):

_____

Review Questions

1. What is a fallacy?
2. What is the difference between formal and informal fallacies?
3. What is fallacious about the *ad hominem tu quoque* argument?
4. What is the difference between the straw man and the red herring fallacies?
5. What fallacies do the following phrases express?
    a. If we cannot show that S is true, we may conclude that S is not true.
    b. What is true of the whole is true of its parts.
    c. Accept my conclusion if you know what is good for you.
    d. Don't believe him; he's not a good person.
    e. This must be true because so many people believe it.
    f. A and B are always observed together, so A must cause B.
    g. Believe what I say, I need your support.

h. If A and B are alike in those respects, they are probably alike in this respect.

i. This premise is true only if the conclusion is true.

j. Refuting a misrepresentation of an opponent's argument.

True or False?

1. An argument that cites an authority in support of its conclusion is always fallacious.

2. The fallacy of composition consists of reasoning that what is true of the whole is true of the parts.

3. The fallacy of hasty generalization consists of generalizing over a small sample.

4. If a person asserts S and then asserts not-S after changing his or her mind, the person is not guilty of inconsistency.

5. Informal fallacies are always deductively invalid.

6. Arguments from analogy are always fallacious.

7. An arguer who uses a word in two different senses is not necessarily guilty of the fallacy of equivocation.

8. Any statement whatsoever is validly deducible from inconsistent premises.

9. The fallacy of slippery slope may be thought of as an assertion of a series of causal connections, at least one of which commits the fallacy of false cause.

10. At the heart of the either/or fallacy is the mistake of overlooking some other possible alternative.

Discussion Questions

1. Explain the difference between the fallacy of composition and the fallacy of hasty generalization. They are similar but not the same. How *do* they differ?

2. Explain in your own words why inconsistency is a failure of good reasoning. Then consider the question, *Why, if at all, is it important for people to try to be consistent in their beliefs and avoid inconsistency?*

3. The abusive *ad hominem* fallacy involves rejecting a person's position because of some purported undesirable characteristic of the person. Can you think of any examples in which the fact that a person has a certain characteristic *would* be a good reason for rejecting what he or she says? Explain your example.

4. Are there any examples you can think of, real or imaginary, in which pity or sympathy for a person's circumstance might be a good reason for accepting the person's argument?

CHAPTER TEN
Evaluating Arguments

In this chapter we show how the various concepts
and techniques presented in this text can be applied
to the evaluation of real arguments—that is, the
arguments found in books, magazines, newspapers,
and so on. A procedure for argument evaluation
is described. Then we practice preparing long
passages for evaluation, extend our study of the
enthymeme and the skill of supplying missing parts,
and examine what logic can tell us about determining the truth-value of premises. Finally, the entire
procedure of argument evaluation is illustrated with
some examples.

10.1 A Procedure for
Argument Evaluation

The purpose of argument evaluation is to decide by examination whether an argument is good. That involves at least three major steps, which logically would proceed
in the following order. First, we expose the argument, clarifying the conclusion, the
premises, and the inference involved. Second, we can use the techniques of the deductive theories of categorical logic or truth-functional logic to check the deductive

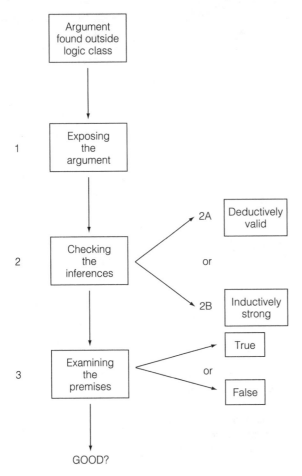

Figure 10.1   Evaluation Flowchart

validity of the inference. If deductively invalid, we can then examine the argument in terms of one of the three types of inductive standards. And last, we assess the truth-value of the premises. Depicted as a flowchart, the procedure would look like Figure 10.1.

Up to this point in the text we have concentrated on step 2: *checking the inferences* for deductive validity or inductive strength. Now we return to step 1: exposing the argument in lengthy passages. And we develop step 3: examining premises for truth-value. Let's begin by focusing on exposing real arguments.

10.2 Exposing Real Arguments

Arguments found in books, essays, newspapers, and conversations are frequently challenging for logical analysis, because they may be long, wordy, and incomplete and may contain rather complex lines of support with subsidiary arguments. Even the initial step of exposing the argument can be very difficult, and one may see different ways of doing it. What kinds of problems might you face with real arguments?

To begin with, for longer passages, essays, and the like, the sheer length of the passage can be an obstacle. It raises an important issue: *How much detail do we need to include in our exposure of the argument?* Every claim the arguer makes, or something less than that? Well, it depends, doesn't it? It depends on how important the argument is. Those arguments that address vital concerns deserve close attention; others perhaps do not. Logic tells us that we must provide at least as much detail as necessary for us to say what and how the argument is made, or, in other words, at least enough detail so that we can pass to steps 2 and 3. But beyond that, logic does not tell us—there are no rules for determining—how closely and completely, and with what degree of detail, we should treat a long passage. To put it differently, logic, the study of the principles of good reasoning, does not define our vital concerns; ethics perhaps does. So, how much detail to develop in evaluating a lengthy argument has more to do with our own interests than with the principles of logic.

Nevertheless, one of the more useful skills in treating real arguments is *paraphrasing,* or restating the argument in a shorter, more manageable version. This is a skill we can develop. It involves such challenges as the following. First, a passage may include sentences that on the surface are not *statements;* we may need to rewrite them as statements. Second, the passage may contain sentences or paragraphs that serve no purpose in the argument; those we may omit. Third, the passage may leave out statements that need to be supplied. There may be missing premises or conclusions. Thus, these are three ways that we may edit an argument to produce a restatement or paraphrase suitable for evaluation: rewriting sentences, omitting sentences or paragraphs, and supplying missing parts.

Proficiency in exposing real arguments involves these important skills. Not every argument requires these tasks, but we do not have mastery of handling arguments without them. Therefore, in the following sections we concentrate on these skills: omitting sentences, rewriting sentences as statements, and paraphrasing.

10.3 Omitting, Rewriting, and Paraphrasing

Omitting Sentences

Some sentences or passages in an argument serve no inferential purpose. They state neither premises nor conclusions. Therefore, they may be omitted when we expose the argument. The typical kinds of sentences or passages that may be omitted are those serving only to introduce the subject, identify the arguer, illustrate, or clarify with examples, and so on. They may help the arguer communicate and clarify the argument, but they do not state premises or conclusions. What follows are examples of the kinds of statements that may be omitted.

Example 1

I am a member of People for the Ethical Treatment of Animals as well as other groups dedicated to a more compassionate interpretation of our world. I see an animal, or a plant for that matter, as a living organism that is unique by the fact of its life force. Creatures have only one life to live . . . and should be allowed to do so with dignity and in their natural environments. (Letter to the editor, Scientific American)

The statement called out in underline identifies the writer but does not provide any inferential support for the conclusion expressed in the last sentence. Similarly, in Example 2, this writer opens by identifying the subject and then proceeds to his or her argument.

Example 2

I was surprised that few of your writers looked at the politics of travel from the perspective of indigenous peoples, local communities or responsible-tourism groups. The last remaining pristine areas on earth are the homelands of indigenous peoples. These areas and peoples are under serious threat from rapidly expanding tourism development. Anyone traveling . . . should be aware of the real effects of their tourism: It is likely to contribute to environmental devastation, conflict within communities, accelerated globalization and less reliance on local resources, among other problems.

As the world's largest industry, tourism is a force to be reckoned with for peoples all over the world. We encourage travelers to learn more about the implications of travel, support responsible-tourism organizations and indigenous peoples and demand responsibility of the global tourism industry. (Letter to the editor, The Nation)

In Example 3, the underlined sentence illustrates the premises, 'it is wrong to punish someone for something which he could not help' and 'no one can help being sick'. The sentence does not add a new premise to the argument, so you would not include it in your exposition.

Example 3

Everyone would agree that it is wrong to punish someone for something which he could not help; furthermore, no one can help being sick. In the words of the Supreme Court of the United States: *"Even one day in prison would be cruel and unusual punishment for the 'crime' of having a common cold." It just so happens to be the case that everyone who commits a crime is sick. Hence, it is morally wrong to punish someone who commits a crime.* (Richard Wasserstrom)

In the next example, the first statement identifies the subject. The other two underlined statements are examples of the premise that 'Scientific knowledge is subject to revision pending new real-world evidence.' All could be omitted from the argument exposition.

Example 4

I must express my teeth-grinding impatience with the New Age nonsense about science being a "belief system," or even a religion. Science is not a belief system, for this reason: Scientific knowledge is subject to revision pending new real-world evidence. Every week the New York Times comes out with news of some discovery that makes scientists rethink their theories. A recent Newsweek had a cover story about how the observations made with the Hubble telescope have forced astronomers to change their view of the universe. Science is the opposite of faith: It is a perpetual "Show me!"

Religious belief, on the other hand, is not subject to such revision; it is not falsifiable by any real-world evidence. The existence of God cannot be disproved. Religious beliefs are 'leakproof'—there's no evidence that will contradict them. (Letter to the editor, *Mother Jones*)

In Example 5, writer Joshua Halberstam illustrates his point that bad things are usually events, not continuing states of affairs, with several examples.

Example 5

Why don't we notice the good stuff in our lives? Because good things don't happen. The good things in life are continuing states of affairs, not events. In the next five minutes countless bad things could happen to you. You could fall and fracture your shoulder, your ankle, your hip. Your dear aunt Christina could break her shoulder, ankle, or hip. The light fixture above you could explode and send glass into your eye. You could get a menacing call from the IRS. With a minimum of effort you can come up with an infinite number of unhappy events that could befall you. (Everyday Ethics)

His examples help us understand his point, but they do not provide evidentiary support or reason for accepting the statement they illustrate.

Using Examples to Support Inferences Do not conclude from the preceding examples that illustrations or examples never provide inferential support. Offering an example is sometimes the writer's way of presenting a new premise. In a letter written to the editor of *Rider,* a magazine for motorcyclists, on the practice of "lane splitting"—that is, passing cars within the lane—the author writes:

Example 6

The debate rages on concerning the safety of lane splitting, but for me the question has been answered many times. As long as it is approached in an intelligent manner, it is no less safe than staying in the lane, and in many circumstances it is actually safer. <u>For example, if I am sitting in traffic between two cars, someone in the next lane can (and frequently does) change lanes into what appears to be a gap between those cars only to find an outraged motorcyclist already occupying said gap. The various responses to this situation can be imagined, and none of them is pretty.</u>

The writer asserts that lane splitting may be done safely and may in fact serve to avoid unsafe situations. He then offers an example. Should the example (called out in underlining) be omitted, or does it support the author's conclusion? A reasonable answer, it seems, is that it does not merely clarify or illustrate; it provides evidential support for this claim. In this case providing an example is tantamount to providing an assertion that the described situation is unsafe. We can interpret the author to be reasoning as follows:

It is an unsafe situation when a car driver changes into a lane that appears to be unoccupied only to find a motorcycle sitting there. Therefore, it may in fact be safer for motorcyclists to practice lane splitting.

In that case we are in fact rewriting the author's example as a statement that supports the conclusion.

Here is another case in which examples seem to function as an important part of the argument. Example 7 is one of several arguments for the conclusion that scientific literacy is essential to education. Notice the underlined sentences.

Example 7

<u>*Finally, we come to the argument of intellectual coherence.*</u> *It has become a commonplace to note that scientific findings often play a crucial role in setting the intellectual climate of an era. <u>Copernicus' discovery of the heliocentric universe played an important role in sweeping away the old thinking of the Middle Ages and ushering in the Age of Enlightenment. Darwin's discovery of the principle of natural selection made the world seem less planned, less</u>*

directed than it had been before; and in this century the
work of Freud and the development of quantum mechan-
ics have made it seem (at least superficially) less rational.
In all of these cases, the general intellectual tenor of
the times—what Germans call the Zeitgeist—was in-
fluenced by developments in science. How, the argument
goes, can anyone hope to appreciate the deep underlying
threads of the intellectual life in his or her own time without understanding the science that goes with it? [There-
fore, scientific literacy is important.] (Robert M.
Hazen and James Trefil, *Science Matters: Achieving*
Scientific Literacy)

First, the argument is named. Then, the writers state a premise and proceed to list four
examples; they summarize the examples and then assert a premise expressed as a rhetorical question. Do the examples provide inferential support? In fact, they do. They
provide reasons for accepting the first premise. This becomes clear when you consider
that one way to challenge this argument would be to criticize the examples. Suppose
you could show that neither Copernicus, Darwin, nor the rest have had much cultural
impact. That would weaken the premise. In that case, the examples should be included
in the exposition of the argument. Leaving aside the rewrite of the rhetorical question,
the last premise, here is how Example 7 is written in argument form.

1. *Copernicus's discovery of the heliocentric universe*
   played an important role in sweeping away the old
   thinking of the Middle Ages and ushering in the Age
   of Enlightenment.

2. *Darwin's discovery of the principle of natural selection*
   made the world seem less planned, less directed than it
   had been before.

3. *In this century the work of Freud and the develop-*
   ment of quantum mechanics have made it seem (at
   least superficially) less rational.

4. *In all of these cases, the general intellectual tenor of*
   the times—what Germans call the Zeitgeist—was
   influenced by developments in science.

---

5. *It has become a commonplace to note that scientific*
   findings often play a crucial role in setting the intellec-
   tual climate of an era.

6. *How . . . can anyone hope to appreciate the deep*
   underlying threads of the intellectual life in his or her
   own time without understanding the science that goes
   with it?

---

7. *Therefore, scientific literacy is important.*

The examples, listed above as premises, lend support to statement (5), so it strengthens the larger argument to include them in the exposition.

Rewriting Sentences

Recall from Chapter 1 that we defined a statement as any sentence or part of a sentence that makes an assertion that something is or is not the case. Not all sentences, we noted, make assertions; thus, not all sentences are statements. When necessary, we may rewrite sentences or sentence parts as statements.

For our purposes, rewriting a sentence is done in order to make explicit a statement that functions as a premise or conclusion. Relatedly, paraphrasing is restating a text or passage. In relation to exposing an argument, the purpose of both rewriting and paraphrasing is the same: to make clear what is said or written.

We need to approach the task of rewriting and paraphrasing with caution because restating a person's words runs the risk of misinterpreting them. How do we avoid misinterpreting what someone has written or said? (1) Ask the person to clarify. A lot of fuss and bother is saved by this simple courtesy; but, of course, how often is the person there when you need him or her? Almost always we have to fall back on our best efforts. Thus, (2) stay as close as possible to the very words the person uses. If certain phrases are crucial, try to leave them intact. Be aware of key logical terms such as the categorical quantifiers and the logical operators. And last, (3) apply the principle of charity. Carefully choose those words that provide the most plausible interpretation. (For review, see Section 1.6 on the principle of charity.) Keeping in mind the sensitive nature of interpreting people's words, let's move directly to the task of rewriting sentences and then paraphrasing passages.

Common types of nonstatements are questions, exclamations, commands, and requests. Nevertheless, we often can tell from the context of the sentence that a statement may be inferred or supplied in its place. In Examples 8–10, we have sentences that would reasonably be taken to make the assertions shown. Notice the commands and questions and how they can be rewritten as statements.

Example 8

Sentence: *Make your own decision!*

Statement: *You should decide for yourself.*

Example 9

Sentence: *Eureka!*

Statement: *I have found it.*

Example 10

Sentence: *Why fear death?*

Statement: *Death is not to be feared.*

Now consider Example 11 and its exposition in argument form. Notice how some simple rewriting clarifies the second premise.

Example 11

The computer in some ways enhances the power of the individual, but it also depletes our individuality. A degree of space and isolation is required for a healthy sense of self, which may be threatened by the constant stream of other people's opinions on computer networks. (Robert D. Kaplan, "Was Democracy Just a Moment?")

1. *A degree of space and isolation is required for a healthy sense of self.*

2. *[Space and isolation] may be threatened by the constant stream of other people's opinions on computer networks.*

---

3. *The computer in some ways enhances the power of the individual, but it also depletes our individuality.*

Rewriting Rhetorical Questions Let's develop some more difficult examples and consider two particularly common practices—using rhetorical questions and following a question with an answer—as they occur in real arguments.

First, a *rhetorical question* is really a statement that, for effect, is put in the form of a question. Here is the rhetorical question at the end of Example 7.

Example 12

How, the argument goes, can anyone hope to appreciate the deep underlying threads of the intellectual life in his or her own time without understanding the science that goes with it?

REWRITTEN AS A STATEMENT

No one can hope to appreciate the deep underlying threads of the intellectual life in his or her own time without understanding the science that goes with it.

In this next example, a writer begins an argument that we should not go to war in the Middle East, with the following rhetorical question:

Example 13

If you think we have problems now, what do you think will happen if we go to war?

In this rhetorical question, the writer is making the statement 'If we go to war, matters will be much worse'.

Now consider this letter to the editor:

Example 14

① *When will our leaders learn that "two wrongs don't make a right; that might is not right; that when our enemy hungers we should feed him, not starve him?"*

Our poor old earth is suffering from our mistreatment of her for too many years. ② *Shall we burn and bomb and kill and maim to "preserve our way of life," i.e., go on polluting the air, wasting our natural resources . . . and refusing to face up to our real problems, the obscenely rich, the hopelessly poor, the neglected children. Wake up America!*

A rewrite of sentence ① would seem to be

> *Our leaders should know that two wrongs don't make a right, that might is not right, and that when our enemy hungers we should feed him, not starve him.*

Sentence ② is complex. Here is a reasonable restatement.

> *We should not go to war (burn, bomb, kill, and maim) to preserve our way of life.*
>
> *We should not go on polluting and wasting our natural resources.*
>
> *We should face up to our real problems: the obscenely rich, the hopelessly poor, and the neglected children.*

Here is another example, an excerpt from a tongue-in-cheek newspaper editorial entitled "Who Are the Rich?"

Example 15

Suppose you know a major league baseball player who has just signed a contract that is supposed to supply him with $1 million a year for the next seven years. ① *Is he sitting back smiling contentedly? Not a bit. You see him on television with a frown creasing his face, complaining about his teammates, his team manager, his lawyer, or the umpire—and sometimes all at once.* ② *And is such a person, beset with such woes, someone you want to nail hard with a soak-the-rich tax scheme?* ③ *Who among us would be so pitiless and brutally callous as to contemplate such a thing?*

Focusing just on the numbered questions in the passage, we can restate them as follows:

① *The million-dollar-a-year baseball player is not feeling content.*

② *You shouldn't want to further burden with taxes a person who is already beset with woes.*

③ *No one among us is so pitiless and brutally callous as to contemplate raising the taxes of people such as the million-dollar-a-year baseball player.*

Following a question with an answer is a common stylistic device by which writers try to engage their readers. The question serves to introduce a subject and stimulate the reader's interaction. For example, in a *Newsweek* essay, "The Necessity of Dissent," Jonathan Alter argues that in a democracy it is essential to raise critical questions about the wisdom of going to war. During the course of his argument, he asks

Example 16

① *Why should American soldiers die in the name of cut-rate oil?*

② *It's immoral to shed so much blood just to make the world safe for rich sheiks and gas guzzlers.*

Sentence ① is rhetorical as is obvious in the context of the passage. Alter is arguing that American soldiers should not die in the name of cut-rate oil, and he offers statement ② as a reason.

Later in the essay, Alter asks this question:

Example 17

① *How scarce is mainstream dissent? Last week the father of a U.S. Marine wrote a critical piece in the* New York Times. . . . *The author, Alex Molnar, was besieged by requests for TV appearances to explain his novel views. No one had heard them before.*

There's some token antiwar sentiment showing up in newspapers in the Midwest. . . . And polls show that black Americans . . . are less supportive than the population as a whole. But that still leaves a deafening silence.

Sentence ① introduces the subject with a question: 'How scarce is mainstream dissent?' The last sentence of the passage is the answer: 'It is a deafening silence'. That is, it is almost nonexistent. In between Alter provides reasons for that answer. Here is how the passage may be written in argument form.

① *The author of a critical piece in the* New York Times *was besieged by requests to explain his novel views because no one had heard them before.*

(2) *There's some token antiwar sentiment showing up in newspapers in the Midwest. . . .*

(3) *Polls show that black Americans . . . are less supportive than the population as a whole.*

_____

(4) *Therefore, mainstream dissent to the war is almost nonexistent.*

Notice how the first sentences of the passage and the conclusion are written for the argument.

Paraphrasing

Paraphrasing is restating a text or passage usually for the purpose of simplifying it. We try to capture in a few statements the meaning of a passage consisting of many sentences. Example 17, again, presents a good example for paraphrasing. The passage in Example 17 is in fact part of a larger argument not presented here. It is one of Jonathan Alter's premises for the point that dissent is essential to a democracy. If our aim were to simplify Alter's essay as much as possible, then we would paraphrase the passage in Example 17 to be stating the premise:

Mainstream dissent is almost nonexistent.

Let's work through some other arguments.

Example 18

One overarching reason must lead us to prefer modern times to any past, whatever "golden age" mythology we may be tempted to embrace: Thanks to medical knowledge and technology, almost all of our children will grow up. Read the biography of any Victorian family, however privileged; they all knew that a high percentage of their children would die. Whatever the psychological defense mechanisms then in place (from religion to wet-nursing), I cannot imagine that the pain of loss was any less then than now. This is the best of times—only I pray that we don't misuse technology to make it the worst. (Stephen Jay Gould, quoted in the *New York Times*)

Ask yourself: What is the main point the writer is making, and what reason or reasons directly support that point? Would you agree that Example 18 contains the simple argument that "This is the best of times . . ." because, given "modern medical knowledge and technology, almost all of our children will grow up"? Therefore, a paraphrased restatement is as follows.

1. *In the present, "thanks to medical knowledge and technology, almost all of our children will grow up."*

2. *In the past, people "knew that a high percentage of their children would die."*

3. *The pain of loss was no less then than it is now.*

---

4. *The present is better than the past.*

Now consider the passage below and see if you agree that the underlined sentences constitute this argument's premises and conclusion.

Example 19

<u>Many people imagine that the sun is necessary to human happiness</u> and that the South Sea islanders must be the gayest, most leisurely and most contented folk on earth. No notion could be more falsely romantic, <u>for happiness has nothing to do with climate:</u> these Eskimos afforded me decisive proof <u>that happiness is a disposition of the spirit.</u> Here was a people living in the most rigorous climate in the world, in the most depressing surroundings imaginable, haunted by famine in a grey and sombre landscape sullen with the absence of life; shivering in their tents in the autumn, fighting the recurrent blizzard in the winter, toiling and moiling fifteen hours a day merely in order to get food and stay alive. Huddling and motionless in their igloos through this interminable night, <u>they ought to have been melancholy men, men despondent and suicidal; instead they were a cheerful people, always laughing, never weary of laughter.</u>

    <u>A man is happy, in sum, when he is leading the life that suits him; and neither warmth nor comfort has anything to do with it.</u> (Gontran de Poncins, *Kabloona*)

The writer's main point seems to be expressed in the sentence "happiness is a disposition of the spirit," not a matter of the comfort associated with a sunny climate. He reiterates this compound conclusion in the final sentence. As reason for his conclusion, the writer describes his observations of the Eskimo people, people who one would expect to be miserable if happiness were a matter of climate and not disposition. Here is a restatement of the argument.

1. *If happiness is a matter of climate, then the Eskimos would be unhappy.*

2. *The Eskimos are not unhappy.*

---

3. *Happiness is not a matter of climate. (Modus tollens)*

4. *Happiness is either a matter of climate or disposition of the spirit.*

---

5. *Therefore, happiness is a matter of the disposition of the spirit.* (Disjunctive syllogism)

Notice that we can paraphrase the argument as consisting of a *modus tollens* and a disjunctive syllogism.

Here is another example. Read it through and identify the writers' overall point and premises.

Example 20

The People's Republic of China, the world's most populous country, and the United States, its most powerful, have become global rivals, countries whose relations are tense, whose interests are in conflict, and who face tougher, more dangerous times ahead.

    If China remains aggressive and the United States naive, the looming conflict between the two countries could even lead to military hostilities. The United States, after all, has been in major wars in Asia three times in the past half century, always to prevent a single power from gaining ascendancy there, and there seems little question that China over the next decade or two will be ascendant on its side of the Pacific. But even without actual war, the rivalry between China and the United States will be the major global rivalry in the first decades of the twenty-first century, the rivalry that will force other countries to take sides and that will involve all of the major items of competition: military strength, economic well-being, influence among other nations and over the values and practices that are accepted as international norms.

    We base these conclusions on two propositions: One is that China, after floundering for more than a century, is now taking up the great power role that it believes, with good reason, to be its historic legacy.

    The second proposition is that the United States for at least one hundred years has pursued a consistent goal in Asia, which is to prevent any single country from dominating that region. Since this is precisely what China seeks to do, its goals and American interests are bound to collide, and they are colliding in an area that is rapidly eclipsing Europe in economic and strategic importance. (Richard Bernstein and Ross H. Munro, *The Coming Conflict with China*)

Authors Bernstein and Munro state their conclusion in the first paragraph. In the next paragraph, they expand upon that conclusion. Then they boldly announce their reasons, making it easy to see the structure of their argument. Once we paraphrase the conclusion, we can restate the argument in a much shortened form as follows:

1. *China . . . is now taking up the great power role [in Asia] that it believes . . . to be its historic legacy.*

2. *The United States . . . has pursued a consistent goal in Asia, which is to prevent any single country from dominating that region.*

3. *[Dominating Asia] . . . is precisely what China seeks to do.*

---

4. *China's . . . goals and American interests are bound to collide.*

5. *[The emerging rivalry between] the People's Republic of China and the United States will be the major global rivalry in the first decades of the twenty-first century.*

This gives us a very manageable version of the larger passage, which, if we want to, we could easily expand by adding the statements that support premises 1, 2, and 3.

To summarize, we have been studying how to handle those frequently long and difficult arguments we find in newspapers, magazines, speeches, and so on. It greatly improves our grasp of such arguments to be able to read selectively, noticing what sentences may be omitted, what can be rewritten, and how we may summarize the thrust of an argument.

Exercise 10.3   Omitting, Rewriting, and Paraphrasing   All the following passages contain arguments. Write a paraphrase—that is, a shortened version—of each in argument form, being careful to stay close to the writer's words, omitting and rewriting where necessary.

1. Those who oppose the notion of the all-powerful coach argue that no one man can oversee everything. How, they ask, can a coach run the draft, make personnel decisions, draw up the game plan, dissect the salary cap, manage free agency, baby-sit the players and choose between lasagna or turkey sandwiches for the team lunch all by himself? (Mike Freeman, *New York Times*)

2. *There Are Two Sides to Every Moral Issue* This cliché is based on misplaced tolerance and a sense of fairness gone awry. Not every view deserves equal respect. Nancy is getting divorced. She has a horror story to tell about her husband, Paul. Not so fast, you warn yourself. There are two sides to every tale. Fairness dictates that you hear Paul's version before you condemn him. Here's where the confusion sets in. You need to hear both sides, but having done so, you no longer have to accord the same moral standing to both parties. That both claim the truth doesn't imply that both possess the truth—or even part of it. (Joshua Halberstam, *Everyday Ethics*)

3. I must express my teeth-grinding impatience with the New Age nonsense about science being a "belief system," or even a religion. Science is not a belief system, for this reason: Scientific knowledge is subject to revision pending new real-world evidence. Every week the *New York Times* comes out with news of some discovery that makes scientists rethink their theories. A recent *Newsweek* had a cover story about how the observations made with the Hubble telescope have forced astronomers to change their view of the universe. Science is the opposite of faith: It is a perpetual "Show me!"

   Religious belief, on the other hand, is not subject to such revision; it is not falsifiable by any real-world evidence. The existence of God cannot be disproved. Religious beliefs are "leakproof"—there's no evidence that will contradict them. (Letter to the editor, *Mother Jones*)

4. From Robert Thurman's interview with the Dalai Lama, which appeared in *Mother Jones*.

   THURMAN:
   How do you feel about the state of the world as
   we approach the 21st century?

   DALAI LAMA:
   I am basically optimistic. And I see four reasons
   for this optimism. First, at the beginning of this
   century, people never questioned the effectiveness
   of war, never thought there could be real peace.
   Now, people are tired of war and see it as ineffective in solving anything. Second, not so long ago
   people believed in ideologies, systems, and institutions to save all societies. Today, they have given
   up such hopes and have returned to relying on the
   individual, on individual freedom, individual initiative, individual creativity. Third, people once
   considered that religions were obsolete and that
   material science would solve all human problems.
   Now, they have become disillusioned with materialism and machinery and have realized that spiritual sciences are also indispensable for human welfare. Finally, in the early part of this century
   people used up resources and dumped waste as if
   there were no end to anything, whereas today
   even the smallest children have genuine concern
   for the quality of the air and the water and the
   forests and animals. In these four respects there is
   a new consciousness in the world, a new sensitivity to reality. Based on that, I am confident that
   the next century will be better than this one.

5. It is a complicated question, the answer to which rests on a jumble of determi-
   nations. Do you favor collective action or individual initiative? Do you trust the
   union's leaders? Do you want somebody else speaking for you in dealings with
   your employer?

   But in one regard, the choice is simple. . . . From a pocketbook perspective, workers are absolutely better off joining a union. Economists across the po-

litical spectrum agree: Turning a nonunion job into a union job very likely will have a bigger effect on lifetime finances than all the advice employees will ever read about investing their 401(k) plans, buying a home, or otherwise making more of what they earn. Over all, union workers are paid about 20 percent more than nonunion workers, and their fringe benefits are typically worth two to four times as much . . . (*New York Times*)

6. It is indeed an opinion strangely prevailing amongst men, that houses, mountains, rivers, and in a word all sensible objects, have an existence, natural or real, distinct from their being perceived by the understanding. But with how great an assurance and acquiescence soever this principle may be entertained in the world, yet whoever shall find in his heart to call it in question may, if I mistake not, perceive it to involve a manifest contradiction. For what are the aforementioned objects but the things we perceive by sense? and what do we perceive besides our own ideas or sensations? and is it not plainly repugnant that any one of *these,* or any combination of them, should exist unperceived? (George Berkeley, *Of the Principles of Human Knowledge*)

7. One occasionally sees the notion expressed that dogs and cats are perfectly natural predators, operating like any bobcat or broad-winged hawk. They are not, any more than man's cattle and sheep are natural operatives in a grazing ecology. Natural predators have, perforce, to live with their resource; they cannot afford to exterminate it. They tend to range widely, exploiting one or more ecological niches, cropping individuals of abundant prey species. The domestic dog and cat (especially former) have become *politicized* by long association with man. The instinct to kill and the territorial imperative, though largely irrelevant, have been retained and confused. Consequently, predatory pets tend to hunt the limited territory described on their owners' deeds; and the results, if the pet is a skilled killer, can be disastrous for the area's wildlife. (Alan Pistorius, *The Country Journal Book of Birding and Bird Attraction*)

8. Consider that Bill Gates, whose personal net worth has recently soared to over $40 billion, made this money in the twenty-two years or so since he founded Microsoft. If we presume that he has worked fourteen hours a day on every business day since then, that means that he's been making money at a staggering $500,000 per hour, or about $150 per second. This, in turn, means that if Bill Gates saw or dropped a $500 bill on the ground, it wouldn't be worth his time to take the four seconds required to bend over and pick it up. ("Bill Gates' Wealth Index," quoted in *Harper's Magazine*)

9. The confusion over whether women are the "same" as men, and whether they can be "different but equal," is at the heart of the current debates between (and about) the sexes. In contrast, I take as my basic premise that there is nothing *essential*—that is, universal and unvarying—in the natures of women and men. Personality traits, abilities, values, motivations, roles, dreams, and desires: all vary across culture and history, and depend on time and place, context and situation. Of course, if you photograph the behavior of women and men at a particular time in history, in a particular situation, you will capture differences. But the error lies in inferring that a snapshot is a lasting picture. What women and men *do* at a moment in time tells us nothing about what women and men *are* in some unvarying sense—or about what they can be. (Carol Tavris, *The Mismeasure of Woman*)

10. *Mathematician Christopher Zeeman argues that mathematics is "probably one of the oldest and noblest of man's activities. . . .":* My real justification is that mathematics is a natural and a fundamental language. It may well be that it's a property of human beings, that only human beings can think maths. But I think it's probably true that any intelligence in the universe would have this language as well. So maybe it's even greater than . . . no, not greater than, but more universal than, the human race. (From *A Passion for Science,* edited by Lewis Wolpert and Alison Richards)

11. What's more, creationism is an attack upon all science, not just my narrow little field. These guys believe in the literal word of Genesis, and if that's true, everything goes. If the Earth really is 10,000 years old then all astronomy is wrong, and all of cosmology is wrong, because the astronomers tell us that most of the stars are so far away that their light takes longer than 10,000 years to reach us, therefore, there's something wrong if the universe is only 10,000 years old. All of physics and atomic theory goes, because if radioactive dating consistently gives these ancient ages for old rocks then, as it's based on the fundamental behavior of atoms, there's something wrong with that knowledge of atomic structure, if it's all a delusion and the Earth is only 10,000 years old. So it's an attack on all of science; it's an attack on all of knowledge. . . . (Stephen Jay Gould in *A Passion for Science,* edited by Lewis Wolpert and Alison Richards)

12. It's nonsense to think that Americans are individualists. Deep down we are a nation of herd animals: micelike conformists who will lay at our doorstep many of our rights if someone tells us that we won't have to worry about crime and our property values are secure. We have always put up with restrictions inside a corporation which we would never put up with in the public sphere. But what many do not realize is that life within some sort of corporation is what the future will increasingly be about. (Attributed to Dennis Judd in Robert D. Kaplan, "Was Democracy Just a Moment?")

13. Most people assume that the jobs of the future will be related to the technologies of the future. They imagine that we will become a society of telecommuting nerds. Historically, however, the opposite has happened: job growth tends to be greatest in the occupations that new technology affects the least. We have become supremely efficient at growing food; that is why there are so few farmers.

In the Labor Department's list of "occupations with the largest job growth," the top five categories are cashiers, janitors and cleaners, salespeople, waiters and waitresses, and nurses. All of these jobs involve "being there"—having face-to-face contact with the consumer, or dealing in a hands-on way with the unpredictable messiness of the physical world. To put it a bit differently: the typical worker of the 21st century will be doing precisely the kinds of thing that you can't do over the Internet. (Paul Krugman in "What's Ahead for Working Men and Women," *New York Times*)

14. I have often thought it would be a blessing if each human being were stricken blind and deaf for a few days at some time during his early adult life. Darkness would make him more appreciative of sight; silence would teach him the joys of sound.

Now and then I have tested my seeing friends to discover what they see. Recently I was visited by a very good friend who had just returned from a long walk in the woods, and I asked her what she had observed. "Nothing in particular," she replied. I might have been incredulous had I not been accustomed to such responses, for long ago I became convinced that the seeing see little. (Helen Keller, quoted in *The Atlantic Monthly*)

15. A huge chunk of the universe is missing. Within the past two decades astronomers have discovered overwhelming evidence that the universe is littered with dark matter—seemingly invisible stuff that must be out there but that we can't find with our most powerful telescopes. Today no scientific question holds more mystery or significance than the puzzle over dark matter.

    Why should we care about matter no one can see? First, because the most basic task of science is to catalogue and describe the universe around us. If as much as 99 percent of the universe is unseen and hidden, as recent evidence suggests, then we have barely begun to document its contents. Second, evidence suggests that the missing mass is intrinsically different from everyday matter. Our understanding of the universe and its origin may be woefully biased and incomplete until we account for dark matter. Finally, the amount of missing mass is closely tied to the ultimate fate of the universe—whether cosmologists expect it to expand forever or eventually collapse into itself. The missing mass problem thus lies at the heart of our most fundamental attempts to understand the past, present, and future state of the cosmos. (Robert M. Hazen, *Why Aren't Black Holes Black?*)

16. Many Taiwanese claim their island has both the historical and the legal right to be independent. Taiwan has not been under the control of any government on Mainland China since 1895. During the last fifty years, moreover, while Taiwan was theoretically a part of China, it has largely taken an independent course, becoming a regional economic powerhouse with European-style standards of living and the highest degree of democratic freedom ever achieved by a large Chinese entity.

    While the other Chinese provinces, including disputed regions traditionally controlled by China, have been within the Chinese realm for thousands of years, Taiwan did not become a part of the national territory until the seventeenth century.

    Indeed, the first outsiders to settle in Taiwan were not Mainland Chinese but Portuguese, Spanish, and Dutch traders and explorers who first established forts there in the 1620's, the entire island becoming a Dutch possession around the middle of the century. (Richard Bernstein and Ross H. Munro, *The Coming Conflict with China*)

17. The single mood people generally put most effort into shaking is sadness; Diane Tice found that people are most inventive when it comes to trying to escape the blues. Of course, not all sadness should be escaped; melancholy, like every other mood, has its benefits. The sadness that a loss brings has certain invariable effects: it closes down our interest in diversions and pleasures, fixes attention on what has been lost, and saps our energy for starting new endeavors—at least for the time being. In short, it enforces a kind of reflective retreat from life's busy pursuits, and leaves us in a suspended state to mourn the loss, mull over its meaning, and finally, make the psychological adjustments and new plans that will allow our lives to continue. (Daniel Goleman, *Emotional Intelligence*)

18. *If you expect someone to know something, you have to tell him or her what it is.* This principle is so obvious that it scarcely needs defending (although you'd be

amazed at how often it is ignored within the halls of academe). It's obvious that if we want people to be able to understand issues involving genetic engineering, then we have to tell them what genetic engineering is, how DNA and RNA work, and how all living systems use the same genetic code. If we expect people to come to an intelligent decision on whether billions of dollars would be spent on a superconducting supercollider, we have to tell them what an accelerator is, what elementary particles are, and why scientists want to probe the basic structure of matter.

But this argument, as simple as it seems, runs counter to powerful institutional forces in the scientific community, particularly the academic community. To function as a citizen, you need to know a little bit about a lot of different sciences—a little biology, a little geology, a little physics, and so on. But universities (and, by extension, primary and secondary schools) are set up to teach one science at a time. Thus a fundamental mismatch exists between the kinds of knowledge educational institutions are equipped to impart and the kind of knowledge the citizen needs.

So scientists must define what parts of our craft are essential for the scientifically literate citizen and then put that knowledge together in a coherent package. For those still in school, this package can be delivered in new courses of study. For the great majority of Americans—those whom the educational system has already failed—this information has to be made available in other forms. (Robert M. Hazen and James Trefil, *Science Matters: Achieving Scientific Literacy*)

19. But why bother to quit? After all, if quitting smoking were easy, all rational smokers would do it. Why should you deny yourself the pleasure of smoking? You may die tomorrow in an automobile accident; why not enjoy smoking until then? Living is difficult and smoking is one of your few pleasures, so why bother to quit? Besides, cigarettes are relatively inexpensive. Besides, smoking is a good way to handle stress. And it goes well with other important pleasures such as eating and drinking. So why quit?

The chief reason has nothing at all to do with health or with pleasure: it has to do with being out of control. A cigarette smoker is a slave to tobacco. A smoker is not someone who is free to choose; a smoker must choose to smoke. Slavery is an evil. It is better to be free from the slavery of tobacco addiction than to be a slave to it. Isn't it better to control your own life than to let a plant control it? Who could disagree with the obvious answer?

Of course, you may pretend to yourself that you are free not to smoke. But if this freedom not to smoke is never exercised, what evidence is there for it? We human beings have a great capacity for rationalizing, for creating conceptual illusions that screen us from reality. But living life behind a veil of illusions is not living life well. If we cannot be honest with ourselves, if we cannot tell the truth to ourselves, with whom can we be honest? How can we possibly live wisely, how can we possibly make consistently good decisions, if we live in a realm of unreality? Honest smokers admit to themselves that they are slaves to tobacco, and they often have a lowered self esteem because of that assessment. They would think better of themselves if they were able to become free from the addiction of tobacco. Many want to quit but have been unable to quit. Being an honest slave is at least better than being a dishonest slave. (Dennis E. Bradford, *A Thinker's Guide to Living Well*)

20. I oppose the attribution of rights to animals not out of any religious conviction or invocation of divine authority, and not because I have no affection for animals, but because I fear animal-rights arguments diminish the special status of Homo sapiens. Respect for human beings requires that dignity be granted our species beyond any qualitative comparison with others. In insisting on that dignity, I do not shirk our responsibility toward other creatures. A position of such privilege and power imposes a special moral obligation on our species. That is why only we human beings are capable of, willing to, and even obliged to agonize about other species.

All animals are not created equal, however. Some animals have less value even than inanimate structures; some have negative value. I do not grieve for the destruction of *Treponema pallidum,* that beautiful and delicate spiral organism that is the cause of human syphilis. To destroy this entire species would be a blessing; whereas blowing up the Grand Tetons or willfully destroying Michelangelo's David would constitute a greater moral crime; these are inanimate "things."

Recently I was confronted with a difficult case of the ethical permissibility of using chimpanzee hearts in experimentation to facilitate human organ transplants. Chimpanzees have enormous charm, sensitivity, great intelligence, and a strong kinship to humanity. Should they be sacrificed for human ends? If so, what are the limits?

It seems to me that the implicit issue evolved into the following dilemmas. Assuming a promising and prudent research procedure, would you sacrifice a chimpanzee for a trivial human need? I suspect most of us would not. Would you sacrifice a chimpanzee for a child's life? I know most of us would. Would you sacrifice the entire species of chimpanzees for the entire species of Homo sapiens? I hope most of us would. Finally, the hard question: would you risk sacrificing the entire species of chimpanzees, a real and not just a theoretical possibility, to relieve the pain and suffering and premature death of many children? I emphatically would. Others would not. It is here that my bias for the specialness, for the extraordinary specialness, of the human being emerges.
. . . the magnificent potential of the human being to become something halfway between animal and God.

At this juncture, where our technology seems to be expanding our horizons for changing the nature of our species and the forms of our lives, we must be unafraid of such changes and recognize that our glory has always been not just in what we are, but in what we can become. (Willard Gaylin, M.D., *On Being and Becoming Human*)

10.4 More on Enthymemes: Plausible Interpretations

As a general rule we are justified in supplying a premise or conclusion if it is required to make the reasoning of the argument explicit. That presumes that we know what the arguer intends. Of course, we may not. Therefore, when we supply missing parts to an argument, we should be guided by the principle of charity (see Section 1.6), according to which we are to interpret the argument in its most plausible form. Let us consider some issues in completing enthymemes according to the principle of charity.

To begin with, suppose someone makes the following brief argument:

Example 21   *Abortion is wrong because it is killing.*

It would be natural to supply the missing premise (marked with an asterisk) 'All killing is wrong', yielding the following argument:

    1. *Abortion is killing.*

*   2. *All killing is wrong.*

    —————————————————————

    3. *Therefore, abortion is wrong.*

Although premise 2 completes the argument, giving it the valid logical form called Barbara, it also weakens the argument, since 2 is not a plausible statement. It is open to serious counterexamples: killing in self-defense, in time of war, and capital punishment, for example. Therefore, if we are to practice the principle of charity, we should not provide statements that weaken an argument. In this case, if we are to supply the most plausible interpretation we can think of, we might complete the argument as follows:

    1. *Abortion is the intentional killing of a human fetus.*

    2. *A human fetus is a person with a serious right to life.*

*   3. *It is wrong to intentionally violate the right to life of a person.*

    —————————————————————

    4. *Therefore, abortion is wrong.*

The speaker, if available, can tell us whether this argument is intended. Otherwise, we have done our best to provide a plausible argument from what we have been given. Now consider the following problem:

Example 22   *Mice don't lay eggs. Mice are mammals.*

What would be the most plausible way to interpret that inference? Is it an inference to the conclusion that 'Mice are mammals'? Or that 'Mice don't lay eggs'? Or could it be a generalization to the conclusion that 'Mammals don't lay eggs'? Consider each one in turn and notice what kind of argument we have. Suppose first that we construe it to be making the point that mice are mammals because mice don't lay eggs. Then we might supply the missing premise, 'Mammals don't lay eggs':

INTERPRETATION A

1. *Mice don't lay eggs.*
* 2. *Mammals don't lay eggs.*

_____

3. *Mice are mammals.*

We quickly see that interpretation A commits the fallacy of undistributed middle. That would not be a particularly happy interpretation. Next, consider that it is an inductive generalization to the conclusion that 'Mammals don't lay eggs' because mice are mammals and mice don't lay eggs. Call it interpretation B:

INTERPRETATION B

1. *Mice don't lay eggs.*
2. *Mice are mammals.*

_____

* 3. *Mammals don't lay eggs.*

Once that interpretation is exposed, we see that it is an unrepresentative sample; it commits the fallacy of hasty generalization. The third possibility is the argument that 'Mice don't lay eggs' because 'Mice are mammals' and 'Mammals don't lay eggs':

INTERPRETATION C

1. *Mice are mammals.*
* 2. *Mammals don't lay eggs.* (Barbara)

_____

3. *Mice don't lay eggs.*

Here we have a good argument: a valid logical form, Barbara, and true premises. Interpretation C is the most plausible interpretation of Example 22.

As a problem for discussion, consider Example 23. First, supply a premise to rewrite the argument as a syllogism. What possible interpretations can you devise? Which interpretation is the most plausible, and why?

Example 23   *Runners don't smoke. Runners are health conscious.*

Enthymemes are arguments that are missing a premise or conclusion. Since people tend to leave out what they consider obvious, it is often not difficult to supply the missing parts. But when an interpretation must be made, we should be guided by the principle of charity. Avoid fallacious logical forms and implausible premises.

_____

Exercise 10.4   Real Enthymemes: Missing Premises and Conclusions
Write the following arguments in argument form, supplying the necessary premise or conclusion. Indicate a supplied statement with an asterisk (*).

1. According to statistics reported in *Harper's Magazine,* the percentage of first-year medical students who believe a knowledge of nutrition is important to their career is 74. On the other hand, the percentage of third-year medical students who believe this drops to 13. Somewhere between the first and the third year of medical school, students get the idea that knowledge of their patients' diets is not important. Yet, the fact is that over 80 percent of illnesses is caused by things people put in their mouths.

2. All around us we see college-educated experts dumping garbage into our waterways, robbing people of their pensions, or just being dissatisfied and unhappy. Sadly, not every college graduate is well educated. (Douglas J. Soccio, *How to Get the Most Out of Philosophy*)

3. I am convinced that one of the best ways to make consistently good decisions is to try deliberately to make decisions that you will not later regret. What is more regrettable than wasted potential? For this reason alone, everyone should get as much formal education as possible. Furthermore, persons with more formal education are quite likely to make much more money over the course of their lives than persons with less formal education. (Dennis E. Bradford, *A Thinker's Guide to Living Well*)

4. If the proliferation of the bomb . . . is not stopped, safeguards for survival will become impossible. Before long a lunatic, a supreme egoist or an itchy finger will flip the switch. (Letter to the editor)

5. *Animals eat each other, so why shouldn't we eat them?* The decisive point . . . is that nonhuman animals are not capable of considering the alternatives open to them or of reflecting on the ethics of their diet. Hence, it is impossible to hold the animals responsible for what they do, or to judge that because of their killing they "deserve" to be treated in a similar way. (Peter Singer, *Practical Ethics*)

6. A free man is one who lives under the guidance of reason, who is not led by fear, but who directly desires that which is good, in other words, who strives to act, to live, and to preserve his being on the basis of seeking his own true advantage; wherefore such an one thinks of nothing less than of death, but his wisdom is a meditation upon life. (Spinoza, *The Ethics*)

7. For to fear death, my friends, is only to think ourselves wise without really being wise, for it is to think that we know what we do not know. For no one knows whether death may not be the greatest good that can happen to man. But men fear it as if they knew quite well that it was the greatest of all evils. (Plato, *Apology*)

8. Since marijuana is the illegal drug most popular with teenagers, who are still in school, it makes sense to consider its effect on short-term memory and motivation. A study of undergraduates at the University of Maryland found that those with the lowest grade averages were four times more likely to smoke pot than those with the highest. No such gap was observed between good and poor students who drank alcohol. (Christopher S. Wren, *New York Times*)

9. To write a successful book on the possibilities of extraterrestrial life would require good knowledge in many widely separated fields. The author would have to be a broad biologist, familiar with all the forms that have been explored by life on earth. He would have to know organic chemistry, which is concerned with carbon compounds, and also inorganic chemistry. He would have to know

the many kinds of physics that deal with conditions in the atmospheres, the oceans and on the surfaces of other planets than the earth. He would have to know enough about astronomy to read the extremely difficult literature that professional astronomers circulate in their small, charmed circle. Such a man does not exist. . . . This is a crying shame. Life is the most interesting thing in the entire universe; it deserves better treatment. (Jonathan Norton Leonard, "Other-Worldly Life," *The Sacred Beetle*)

10. No sooner have you gotten used to WordPerfect 5.0 with a manual of about 500 pages, than WordPerfect 5.1 appears—with a manual of 1,000 pages. Unlike much industrial equipment, software is easily rendered obsolete. And since software products are not perishable, the only way a software provider can grow significantly is by regularly inducing customers to buy updates. (Alan S. Binder and Richard E. Quandt, "The Computer and the Economy," *The Atlantic Monthly*)

11. In philosophy, the centrality in thought and language of the universal male affects the ability to reason about humanity. The philosopher Elizabeth Minnich reminds us of the famous syllogism:

All men are mortal.

Socrates is a man.

Therefore, Socrates is mortal.

But, Minnich suggests, try this one:

All men are mortal.

Alice is _____

Alice is—what? We can't say "Alice is a man." So we say she is a woman. Therefore—what? Alice is immortal? Alice, being female, is in a category that is neither masculine nor mortal. (Carol Tavris, *The Mismeasure of Woman*)

12. A 1990 *Fortune* magazine survey of 799 of the largest U.S. industrial and service companies showed that only nineteen women—less than one-half of 1 percent—were listed among the more than 4,000 highest-paid officers and directors. In business as in academe, women earn less than men . . . , are promoted more slowly and work in less prestigious institutions. (Virginia Valian, "Running in Place," *The Sciences*)

13. All known bodies are capable of having their dimensions reduced by pressure or percussion without diminishing their mass. This is a strong proof that all bodies are composed of atoms, the spaces between which may be diminished. (*Scientific American*)

14. Dr. John P. Morgan and Lynn Zimmer highlight what they consider fallacies of the gateway theory. [The theory "that marijuana is a gateway to the use of hard drugs."] "People using uncommon drugs have almost always used common drugs first. . . ." Calling marijuana a gateway . . . was like saying that people who ride motorcycles began by pedaling a bicycle. "If you wanted to stop motorcycle riding . . . you wouldn't start by stopping people from riding bikes." (Christopher S. Wren, *New York Times*)

15. One basic weakness in a conservation system based wholly on economic motives is that most members of the land community have no economic value. Wildflowers and songbirds are examples. Of the 22,000 higher plants and animals native to Wisconsin, it is doubtful whether more than 5 percent can be sold, fed, eaten, or otherwise put to economic use. Yet these creatures are members of the biotic community and if (as I believe) its stability depends on its integrity, they are entitled to continuance. (Aldo Leopold, *A Sand County Almanac*)

10.5 Examining Premises

Step 3 in the procedure for evaluating arguments is to examine the premises for their truth-value. How do we know whether a statement is true or false? And if we do not know, on what grounds do we accept or reject a statement?

First, notice that in an extended argument, some premises are provided with support, some are not. In Example 24, statement 3 is supported by premises 1 and 2.

Example 24

1. *We have evidence of an extremely large number of humans who have not lived beyond 500 years of age and no evidence of humans who have.*

2. *Any living thing that ceases to live is mortal.*

3. *All humans are mortal.*

4. *Joe Montana is human.*

5. *Joe Montana is mortal.*

Thus, 3 might be acceptable on the grounds that 1 and 2 are true and provide strong inferential support. Some premises, we can say then, are accepted because we believe they are supported by good argument.

On the other hand, statements 1, 2, and 4 have no support within the argument. On what grounds do we assess them? One possibility, as we saw with 3, is that they may also be supportable by further argument. Is it the case, then, that all premises, if acceptable, must be supported by further argument? If that is so, then the process of evaluating one argument involves evaluating every argument provided in support of each premise and the premises of those arguments, and so on. We step into what logicians call an infinite regress. In short, if the decision to accept or reject a premise must itself be supported by further argument, we will have no place to start.

The reasoning above suggests that if an argument is to be evaluated, at some point the search for further support must stop. Some statements must be taken as true. As a matter of practice, that is precisely what we do. Some premises are taken as starting points because (1) they accurately report what has been observed, (2) they are self-evidently true, or (3) they are accepted by the relevant authorities.

First, let's consider again the premises in Example 24. Then we explain the three common "starting points" above. Consider premise 4:

4. Joe Montana is human.

Anyone who has seen Joe Montana would accept this premise on the ground that observation is sufficient to verify it.

Premise 2, on the other hand, is not a report of observations but an assertion about the meaning of the term 'mortal'.

2. Any living thing that ceases to live is mortal.

That premise, it is arguable, is self-evidently true.

Last, consider premise 1:

1. We have evidence of an extremely large number of humans who have not lived beyond 500 years of age and no evidence of humans who have.

That premise reports observations and is verifiable certainly by those experts who have made the observations. We, however, who have not, are justified in accepting 1 on the testimony of the experts.

The three premises just discussed illustrate three different kinds of "starting points" in an argument. Premise 4 exemplifies a statement verifiable by observation. Premise 2 illustrates a statement self-evidently true; and the last example, premise 1, is a statement acceptable by appeal to authority. There is a helpful though not uncontroversial distinction to be made here. It is the distinction between what are called empirical and nonempirical statements. It needs to be explained.

Empirical and Nonempirical Statements

Let us distinguish between statements that are verifiable by experience and those that are not. The former are called *empirical statements;* the latter are called *nonempirical* or *a priori statements.*

> empirical statements   *Statements whose truth-value is determined by observation.*

Included in the first kind are all those whose truth-value we determine by making the appropriate observations or, if impossible, by providing evidence or a hypothesis about what observations might have been made or what they might reveal. For example, consider these statements:

Example 25	*It is raining outside your window now.*
Example 26	*There is no breed of dogs with blue eyes.*
Example 27	*Abraham Lincoln fractured his leg on his fourteenth birthday.*
Example 28	*Any two bodies exert forces on each other that are proportional to the product of their masses divided by the square of the distance between them.* (Newton's law of universal gravitation)
Example 29	*The temperature of the center of the sun is 1 billion degrees Fahrenheit.*

Statements 25 and 26 describe circumstances we can check by observation. Statement 27 describes an event we might have observed had we been there. (Lincoln either did or did not observe it.) Is it true? We may never know, but we do know, at least, what kind of evidence to look for: forensic evidence and reports in diaries or letters, for example. Statement 28 describes what is observable for all bodies, past, present, and future. Statement 29 could not be checked by any direct human observation but might be checked by specially designed instruments or, more likely, by estimates of the center's temperature based on knowledge of the temperatures of related bodies. All these examples illustrate statements whose truth-values are determinable by experience of the relevant sort.

> **nonempirical statements** *Statements whose truth-value is not determined by observation.*

Nonempirical statements are verifiable by means other than experience. Some nonempirical statements are said to be self-evidently true or false. That is, we see that they are true or false simply by understanding them.

Example 30	*Dermatologists are skin doctors.*
Example 31	*Dermatologists are not physicians.*

If you know what a dermatologist is, then you know that 30 is true and 31 is false.

Some nonempirical statements, although hardly self-evident, nevertheless require analysis of the meanings of the terms or concepts.

Example 32	*Love is the everlasting desire for the possession of the good.*

Example 33   *The human fetus is a person at the point of conception.*

Neither 32 nor 33 is verifiable by observation, which does not mean that observation plays no part in their verification. But each finally stands or falls on whether we think the statement correctly captures what we mean by 'love' or by 'human fetus' and 'person'.

Some nonempirical statements are verifiable by mathematical calculation, something analogous, perhaps, to the analysis of concepts.

Example 34 $12 \times 122 = 1464$

Example 35   *A rational solution of* $x^n + y^n = a^n$
is impossible when $n > 2$.
(Fermat's last theorem)

Last, some nonempirical statements are recognizable as true or false by their logical form. *Tautologies* are those statements that are always true in virtue of their form, as for example:

		LOGICAL FORM
Example 36	*It rains or it does not rain.*	p or not p
Example 37	*It can't be both raining and not raining.*	Not both (p and not p)
Example 38	*If it rains, then it rains.*	If p, then p

Self-contradictions are the counterparts of tautologies. They are statements that, in virtue of their form, are always false.

		LOGICAL FORM
Example 39	*It is raining and it is not raining.*	p and not p
Example 40	*It is not true that either it rains or not.*	Not (p or not p)

As we saw in Section 6.3, the truth-values of tautologies and self-contradictions—that the former are always T, the latter always F—can be demonstrated by the use of truth tables.

Statements accepted by appeal to authority

Some empirical statements report observations we have not personally made. Some nonempirical statements make assertions about the analyses of concepts we are not prepared to assess. In such cases, we are entitled to accept the testimony of experts, assuming we have good reasons for thinking they are experts in the appropriate matters. (See Section 9.1 on fallacious appeal to authority.)

To summarize what we have seen thus far, we can say that a premise P in an argument is acceptable if P is supported by good argument or P is (1) empirically true, (2) nonempirically true, or (3) acceptable by the relevant authorities. Obversely, premise P in an argument is not acceptable if P is denied by good argument or P is (1) empirically false, (2) nonempirically false, or (3) rejected by the relevant authorities.

The following is a brief summary of the distinction between empirical and nonempirical statements.

1. Empirical statements are those whose truth value is determined by observations.

2. Nonempirical statements are those whose truth value is not determined by observation.

   a. Some nonempirical statements are self-evidently true or false—that is, seen to be true or false by understanding the meaning of the statement.

   b. Some nonempirical statements are true or false by analysis of the terms or concepts.

   c. Some nonempirical statements are true or false by mathematical calculation.

   d. Some nonempirical statements are true or false by virtue of their logical form. Tautologies, in virtue of their logical form, are always true; self-contradictions are always false.

Exercise 10.5A   Empirical or Nonempirical?   Read each statement and decide whether it is better interpreted as an empirical statement or as a nonempirical statement.

1. The average human brain weighs about 45.5 ounces.

2. Democrats are more likely to vote for tax increases than Republicans.

3. All people are either happy or not.

4. John's kitten has webbed toes.

5. Taoism is one of the oldest religions of China.

6. One cannot truly lie to oneself.

7. Might is right.

8. The brain of a mosquito possesses roughly 40,000 neuron cells, and the brain of a human possesses about 1 trillion neuron cells.

9. Rules are made to be broken.

10. More women give up smoking than do men.

11. Pacifism is the doctrine that violence in all forms is morally wrong and must be avoided.

12. People cannot live the good life if they do not know themselves.

13. Happiness is contentment, good fortune, and virtue.

14. In the United States every citizen's right to privacy is guaranteed by the Constitution.

15. It is morally wrong to take advantage of a person in a business deal.

16. Materialism is the view that only matter exists.

17. The new wing of the library is a concrete monstrosity completely lacking in style and innovation.

18. Although body size varies considerably among the various species of living organisms, cell size does not vary much at all.

19. You should live according to your beliefs.

20. Every statement is either empirical or nonempirical.

Exercise 10.5B   More on Empirical and Nonempirical   Read each passage and explain why you consider it to be an empirical or a nonempirical assertion.

1. The function of a university is . . . first of all to help the student to discover himself: to recognize himself, and to identify who it is that chooses. (Thomas Merton)

2. Evil dwells in the heart of the criminal without being felt there. (Simone Weil)

3. At eighteen months of age, when a little toddler's head is about one-third adult size, he has the full number of neuronal connectors that we have as adults. (Joseph Chilton Pearce)

4. The place is so crowded that nobody goes there any more. (Attributed to Yogi Berra)

5. Wisdom is not just something in the head; it is a state of the whole human being. (Jacob Needleman)

6. When Mercury is at perihelion (the point in its orbit closest to the sun), it moves so swiftly that, from the vantage of someone on the surface, the sun would appear to stop in the sky and go backward—until the planet's rotation catches up and makes the sun go forward again. (Robert M. Nelson, Ph.D.)

7. Dice can be rigged in a variety of ways. Their faces may be subtly shaved so that their corners are not right angles, or they can be "loaded" with weights. Both techniques make some throws more probable than others. (Ian Stewart)

8. Far from being simply the absence of disease, health is a dynamic and harmonious equilibrium of all the elements and forces making up and surrounding a human being. (Andrew Weil, M.D.)

9. People have always looked at birds, but the hobby and sport of birding really developed in the twentieth century. (Kenn Kaufman)

10. Space is the totality of places where things can be at the same time. (Rom Harre)

11. Time does differ from space in one essential respect. While there can be places at which nothing is at some time . . . while there can be space empty of particular things or materials, there cannot be empty time. (Rom Harre)

12. People typically learn 10 words a day, 3,500 or so words a year, until about age 30. After that, people continue to build their vocabularies, but the process slows, probably because most of the easy words have been learned. Folks typically level off at about 80,000 to 100,000 words. (Lila Gleitman, psychologist)

13. It is impossible to experience one's own death objectively and still carry a tune. (Woody Allen)

14. Although international relations have changed drastically since the end of the cold war, both Russia and the U.S. continue to keep the bulk of their nuclear missiles on high-level alert. So within just a few minutes of receiving instructions to fire, a large fraction of the U.S. and Russian land-based rockets . . . could begin their 25-minute flights over the North Pole to their wartime targets. (Bruce G. Blair, Ph.D.)

15. Mythology is a validation of experience, giving it its spiritual or psychological dimension. . . . (Joseph Campbell)

16. One further element that we observe in high-performance people, in addition to goal setting, mental rehearsal, watching your self-talk, and being able to use both sides of the brain, is that they are very health conscious and very careful about the sources of stress in their lives. (Lee Pulos, Ph.D.)

17. In my exploration over the years, the most dramatic shifts in illness that I have ever encountered were in people who underwent a total change in their consciousness. (W. Brugh Joy, M.D.)

18. Every moment and every event of every man's life on earth plants something in his soul. (Thomas Merton)

19. But how does the cat actually produce its purr? Whenever the glottis narrows, air pressure increases in the larynx and on the vocal cords. The motion of the latter causes the air to vibrate and resonate throughout the entire respiratory system. (Myrna M. Milani, D.V.M.)

20. Science is distinctive in that its subject matter is the empirical world. . . . (Stephen Jay Gould)

21. Scientific knowledge is only a communal belief system with a dubious grasp on reality. (Kurt Gottfried and Kenneth G. Wilson)

22. Much of their popular presence is attributable to an obvious but deep biological analogy: computer viruses replicate by attaching themselves to a host (a program or computer instead of a biological cell) and co-opting the host's resources to make copies of themselves. (Jeffrey O. Kephart, Ph.D.)

23. Perhaps computer viruses and computer immune systems are merely precursors of an eventual rich ecosystem of artificial lifeforms that will live, die, cooperate and prey on one another in cyberspace. (Jeffrey O. Kephart, Ph.D.)

24. Of hundreds of known diseases and their predisposing characteristics, some 85 percent of our aging population will succumb to the complications of one of only seven major entities: atherosclerosis, hypertension, adult-onset of diabetes, obesity, mental depressing states such as Alzheimer's and other dementias, cancer, and decreased resistance to infection. (Sherwin Nuland, M.D.)

25. And whatever you do, every act, however small, can teach you everything—
provided you see who it is that is acting. (Thomas Merton)

10.6 Sample Evaluations

Sample Evaluation 1

Anthony Snowden, an excellent photographer himself, has argued that photography is not an art form but a craft. If this is true, then it would seem to follow that photography is not a medium for artistic creativity and should not be evaluated according to the standards of art or treated with the kind of respect and admiration appropriate to works of fine art. In short, photography should not be taken so seriously. Snowden gave the following argument during a television discussion:

> *Art requires creativity and imagination. Photography involves no such thing, for it is a mechanical process of exposing film to light. The photographer merely "opens" the camera and the resulting picture is simply what happened to be in front of it.*

Snowden's argument begins with a statement about art. It is his first premise. Then he claims that photography lacks what is required of art, he illustrates this, and he leaves the listener to draw the obvious conclusion: photography is not an art form. Here is how we may write and expose his argument.

1. *Art requires creativity and imagination.*
2. *Photography is a mechanical process of exposing film to light.*
* 3. *Mechanical processes are neither creative nor imaginative.* (missing premise)

---

4. *Therefore, photography is neither creative nor imaginative.*

---

5. *Therefore, photography is not an art.*

Notice that premise 3 needs to be supplied. Why? Clearly, if Snowden believes that something lacks creativity and imagination because it is a mechanical process, then he must be assuming that mechanical processes lack creativity and imagination. Premise 3 makes his assumption about mechanical processes explicit. Notice also that Snowden's argument consists of an argument within an argument. Is it inductive or deductive? It seems clear that the argument claims to show that photography *must* not be an art form rather than probably is not an art form. In effect, the argument defines art and then shows that photography fails to meet the definition and thus must not be art. Hence, this is a deductive argument.

First, we check validity. If we assume the premises to be true, does the conclusion have to follow? Assuming the premises, statement 4 certainly follows, and statement 5 must be true given premises 1 and 4. Thus, this argument is deductively valid.

Are all the premises true? Premise 1 claims that art must involve creativity and imagination. What type of premise is it? Is it empirical? Will observations of artworks determine whether art requires creativity and imagination? Let's think about treating this as an empirical claim. What would observations of artworks show us? Either all those artworks we observe *are* creative and imaginative or most are or most are not. We might even frame the inductive generalization from our observations that probably all artworks are creative and imaginative. But we would not have established the claim that art *must* be creative and imaginative, that, in other words, something could not be an artwork if it were neither creative nor imaginative. Thus, this premise is best understood as a nonempirical claim, a claim about the nature of art, to be exact. And it certainly seems to be true. Wouldn't our concept of art disappear or at least be radically different if we did not believe that art must involve creativity and imagination? Surely those are necessary ingredients of art. We ought then to accept this premise.

Premise 2 says that photography is a mechanical process of exposing film to light. What kind of claim is this? It seems to be a definition, however brief, designed to tell us what photography is. Is it an accurate claim about what photography is? It is certainly true that photography *involves using* a mechanical process to make pictures. But that is not the same as saying it *is* a mechanical process. If one were to provide a more accurate partial definition of photography, one should probably say that it is 'making pictures by using the mechanical process of exposing film to light'. This is a better statement of the relationship between photography and mechanical processes.

What do we say, then, about premise 2? The answer is that it is not true. Snowden overstates the connection between photography and mechanical processes, making it seem that photography is *nothing but* a mechanical process. The truth is that the camera is a tool, a machine, designed and used according to human interests. Snowden seems to overlook the elements of creativity involved in the ways cameras are designed and, more importantly, in the ways they are used by humans. Creativity and imagination are involved in the decisions to make camera lenses bend light as they do. They did not just come that way. Creativity and imagination are involved in the choices photographers make regarding subjects; composition of the image; type of film, color or black and white; degree of contrast; quality of focus; and so on. Thus, although the camera is a machine, the photographer is not.

Since premise 2 is false, Snowden's argument is not good and should not be believed. He does not establish that photography is lacking in creativity and is therefore not an art form. We do not need to go any further with his argument.

Sample Evaluation 2

In his book *Animal Liberation*, Peter Singer offers an argument for the belief that plants do not feel pain. Singer says that there are

① *three distinct grounds for believing that nonhuman animals can feel pain: behavior, the nature of their nervous systems, and the evolutionary usefulness of pain.* *②* *None of these gives us any reason to believe that plants feel pain.* *③* *In the absence of scientifically credible experimental findings, there is no observable behavior that suggests pain;* *④* *nothing resembling a central nervous system has been found in plants; and* *⑤* *it is difficult to imagine why species that are incapable of moving away from a source of pain or using the perception of pain to avoid death in any other way should have evolved the capacity to feel pain.* *⑥* *Therefore the belief that plants feel pain appears to be quite unjustified.*

If we expose Singer's argument to examine it, we have the following (notice especially the phrases I have called out with underlines):

① *There are three grounds for believing that nonhuman animals feel pain: (a) behavior, (b) the nature of their nervous system, and (c) the evolutionary usefulness of pain.*

③ *In the absence of scientifically credible experimental findings, there is no observable behavior in plants that suggests pain.*

④ *Nothing resembling a nervous system has been found in plants.*

⑤ *It is difficult to imagine why species that are incapable of moving away from a source of pain . . . should have evolved the capacity to feel pain.*

---

* ⑤a *Therefore, plants lack the three features above that in nonhuman animals are our grounds for believing pain is present.* (missing conclusion)

---

⑥ *Therefore, the belief that plants feel pain appears to be quite unjustified.*

Singer's argument is an example of the type of inductive argument we called the argument from analogy. Notice the clues. Singer's first premise is about nonhuman animals and the features they possess that justify our belief that they feel pain. His conclusion, however, is about plants. And he reaches that conclusion on the basis of a comparison of features between nonhuman animals and plants. To be exact, he finds that plants do not appear to possess the relevant features: They lack the relevant behavior; they seem to have no nervous system; and feeling pain would seem to serve no purpose for them. Thus, the analogy that would support the belief that plants feel pain is not present. The form of reasoning certainly indicates an inductive argument. In addition, notice Singer's language. The words and phrases I have underlined indicate Singer's belief that his conclusion is very probably though not necessarily true. That is another sign, though not a decisive one, that the overall argument is inductive.

Is Singer's a good inductive argument? First, assuming the premises are true, do they provide strong support for the probable truth of the conclusion? It certainly seems so. Imagine that the premises are true but the conclusion is not true. Suppose, that is, that plants do feel pain despite the fact that they lack those relevant similarities to animals. Plants feel pain although they have none of the physiological apparatus we correlate with pain perception, they exhibit no behavior that suggests pain, and pain would seem to serve no useful purpose for them. Now, none of that is a contradiction or a logical impossibility, but it would be highly unexpected and greatly surprising to our scientists. It runs completely counter to what our experience leads us to believe about living things. That little thought experiment shows us that the premises *do* provide strong support for the conclusion. Thus, we can say that this argument has a strongly supported inference.

Are the premises true? Premise 1 is not an empirical claim because observations do not show us what the grounds for a belief are. We *can* observe whether certain features are present—behavior, nervous system, and so on—but we cannot observe whether a belief is justified because of those features. Premise 1 makes a logical rather than an empirical claim. It is a claim in part about what it means to be in pain or to be a sentient creature. And it most certainly is a good claim about what justifies believing pain is present in an animal. Indeed, it describes the grounds we have for our belief that *other human beings feel pain*. If we did not accept this premise, it is hard to imagine how we would justify our belief that animals feel pain.

As for statements 3 through 5, each asserts an empirically verifiable claim, and each expresses what conforms to our own experience and what we have learned from scientists. Thus, it seems that the premises of Singer's argument are true. Therefore, his argument is a *good inductive argument*.

Exercise 10.6   Evaluating Real Arguments   Nearly every one of the following passages contains an argument. Where relevant, expose the argument using either argument form or argument diagramming. The first three exercises have statements already numbered, to get you started. As for the remaining exercises, try numbering first. Supply missing statements as you think necessary. Indicate supplied statements with an asterisk (*). Assess the inferences for deductive validity or inductive strength. Next, examine the premises for truth-value, describing what you can about the verification of each. Last, is the argument a good one? Why, or why not?

1. ① Of course human nature is fundamentally good! Why am I so sure of this? That is what I want to tell you. ② The proposition "Human nature is fundamentally good" is a logical consequence of two other propositions, both of which are as self evident to me as any axioms, but either or both of which the reader is, of course, free to reject.

   ③ The first of my two axioms is that *I* am fundamentally good. This to me is so utterly obvious! ④ By "fundamentally" good, I mean, of course, that I was born good. I say this because ⑤ I distinctly remember coming into the world in complete good faith, loving and trusting everybody, with good will to all and malice towards none. ⑥ I only developed hostilities, hatreds, pettinesses, envies, jealousies, etc. as a result of having been mistreated and distrusted. ⑦ Now, I haven't been all that badly treated, and that's why I'm not half bad as I now stand. ⑧ But whatever badness I have, 'tis nothing more nor less than a reaction to the badness I have experienced. ⑨ I did not bring this badness into the world when I arrived! Of this I am certain. Thus my first axiom is unequivocally, "I am fundamentally good."

⑩ My second axiom is that it is obvious that I am no better than anyone else! Fundamentally better, I mean. ⑪ Of course I sometimes act better than other people and sometimes worse. ⑫ But it is inconceivable to me that human natures can be so radically different that some are good and others are bad at birth! No, that is ridiculous! ⑬ So, if I am fundamentally good, then everyone is fundamentally good. ⑭ And since I *am* fundamentally good, then *everyone* is fundamentally good. (Raymond M. Smullyan, *The Tao Is Silent*)

2. Why don't we notice the good stuff in our lives? Because good things don't happen. ① The good things in life are continuing states of affairs, not events. ② In the next five minutes countless bad things could happen to you. You could fall and fracture your shoulder, your ankle, your hip. Your dear aunt Christina could break her shoulder, ankle, or hip. The light fixture above you could explode and send glass into your eye. You could get a menacing call from the IRS. With a minimum of effort you can come up with an infinite number of unhappy events that could befall you.

③ What good things could happen to you in the next five minutes? Not much comes readily to mind. You might win the lottery, but then there's no drawing today, and anyway you didn't buy a ticket. You might find a hundred-dollar bill under your seat. Peace might break out in the world. But there aren't many more obvious candidates, especially as compared to all the bad stuff that could happen.

④ This asymmetry between bad events and good events has its basis in the second law of thermodynamics (the law of entropy). ⑤ This law of physics states that there are always more ways to impair a working system than to improve it. (Thus the wise dictum: "If it ain't broke, don't fix it.") ⑥ The principle describes molecular structures, but it also applies to daily life. ⑦ A thriving relationship can come to a sudden and dramatic end—for example, one of the partners can have a fatal heart attack—but flourishing relationships don't flourish abruptly. ⑧ Good relationships, like most good things, take time and cultivation, which is why we fail to notice the healthier aspects of our lives. ⑨ Our attention is drawn to unusual occurrences, and most irregularities are negative. You aren't conscious of your breathing, but you will be if food gets stuck in your throat. A few seconds ago, you blinked and gave it no thought. You would have if a speck had entered your eye.

⑩ You need, therefore, to carve out some time to appreciate what's wholesome in your life and the lives of those you care about. ⑪ Don't take for granted that your body is in decent shape, your mental faculties are functioning, and your senses are operating. Any one of these could go wrong at any time. ⑫ Appreciate, too, your own moral decency. It's not that common. (Joshua Halberstam, *Everyday Ethics*)

3. The following essay, "Why War Is Ignoble," by Howard Morland appeared in *Newsweek* and is reprinted by permission of the author.

(Hint: Morland's conclusion is expressed in statement 44. Assuming that you agree, what reasons does he offer and how then should many of the other statements be treated?)

① Whenever young Americans depart for overseas battlefields, older men seem to envy them the adventure. ② On the eve of the Vietnam War, my college dean told me he was sorry he had not come under fire during his wartime service in the Pacific. ③ He wanted to know how he might have responded to the test of combat. ④ He assumed that I would understand, and his regrets may have led me to later join the Air Force rather than seek a draft deferment.

⑤ Today, because of the crisis in the Mideast, a new generation of young people hears of the salutary effects of the battlefield from their Vietnam-era elders. ⑥ In September, liberal essayist Roger Rosenblatt told a national television audience that he now wishes he had fought in Vietnam. ⑦ He said that even though he "disapproved of our being in Vietnam," he feels "deep regret" that he never experienced the "dependent connection to one another" of soldiers "thrown into an incomprehensible horror." ⑧ Watching him on the McNeil/Lehrer NewsHour sent me searching through my own Vietnam experiences for a clue to this curious longing for memories of combat.

⑨ My job in 1968 was to pilot C-141 transport planes of the type now hauling U.S. soldiers and gear to Saudi Arabia. ⑩ Except for one close call when a battle-damaged Phantom jet crashed and exploded near my plane at Da Nang Air Base, I never came in harm's way. ⑪ My own knowledge of combat comes from the stories soldiers told as I airlifted them from the battlefield zone. ⑫ One night, on a flight from Cam Ranh Bay to California, a young veteran the age of today's tennis champion Pete Sampras sat between the pilot seats and told the flight crew about his year in Vietnam. ⑬ He described a photograph in his duffel bag, of an American GI holding the severed heads of two Viet Cong prisoners. ⑭ The hapless prisoners were grabbed and beheaded as revenge for the death of an American, killed when another Viet Cong prisoner turned himself into a human bomb by detonating a concealed grenade in his own armpit. ⑮ In the eerie darkness seven miles above the Pacific, our narrator described the sound a bullet made as it plowed through a friend's body two feet away. ⑯ He thought it wise not to make close friends in combat. ⑰ His homecoming plan: lock himself in the bathroom, sit on the john, smoke cigarettes and shake for several hours.

⑱ Pondering this survivor's tale, I entered the cargo bay and sat with the coffins of a dozen veterans who had undergone the ultimate combat experience. ⑲ The young soldier on the flight deck may have embellished his war stories, I thought, but the boys in the boxes were testament to the truth. ⑳ I was struck by how lonely one feels in the company of the dead.

㉑ Two years later in Thailand, a Thai veteran made a point of showing me snapshots of Vietnamese bodies stretched out in a row. ㉒ He had helped kill them. ㉓ A fresh haircut on the corpse closest to the camera caught my eye; I wondered if the man with the haircut had sensed it would be his last. ㉔ My host seemed to invite me to explain the meaning of the carnage, but I was still young enough to believe people should live forever, and like the then young Mr. Rosenblatt, I saw no sufficient reason for that particular war.

"Bloody shreds": ㉕ Combat is unique in the way it celebrates untimely death at the hand of fellow human beings. ㉖ Mark Twain saw the horror in this, and, in a poem called "The War Prayer" wrote of a ghostly old man who disrupts a church service as the preacher delivers a patriotic war prayer. ㉗ The old man offers his own grim version. ㉘ "O Lord our God, Help us to tear their soldiers to bloody shreds with our shells . . . to drown the thunder of the guns with the shrieks of their wounded, writhing in pain . . . to lay waste their humble homes with a hurricane of fire." ㉙ Persuaded that it could be considered sacrilegious, Twain had his poem published posthumously. ㉚ In his bitter assessment, ". . . only dead men can tell the truth in this world." ㉛ But his warning, when it appeared, was widely ignored.

㉜ War is like other human activities in that people who enjoy it the most will do it the best, and be chosen to run it. ㉝ Obviously, not everyone enjoys it, but there is a common notion that all combatants should somehow love war, and benefit from it. ㉞ The premise of the typical Hollywood action movie is that real men love each other most when locked in a deeply fraternal exercise designed to demonstrate how short life can be. ㉟ If war is such an ennobling experience, why does it bring out the worst in people, not the best?

㊱ I have always believed that I might kill or die for a worthy enough cause. ㊲ It's the way boys were raised in my native South, as in most other places, and for good reason. ㊳ During much of history, a successful army was the most important institution a people could possess. ㊴ A bad day on the battlefield meant extinction for a number of ancient civilizations. ㊵ However, this country has never faced extinction in any of its wars. ㊶ Our recent wars have all been exercises in foreign policy, and ㊷ for such wars the worthiness of the cause must justify the slaughter. ㊸ Are we convinced that the war now brewing in the Persian Gulf is worthy of the bloodshed it would entail?

㊹ In my view, no American should ever be required to kill or die simply as a test of manhood—particularly if that test involves some politicians' perception of manhood. ㊺ And certainly no American should die simply because as a nation our imagination is too poverty-stricken to figure out how to live without cheap oil. ㊻ For lethal force to have any legitimate role, we must strictly and dispassionately confine it to legitimate questions about international law and homeland defense. ㊼ War is too brutal to be used as a rite of passage for a college dean, for an essayist, or even for a U.S. president.

㊽ I don't know why Roger Rosenblatt feels the way he feels, but I'm glad he didn't fight in Vietnam. ㊾ I wish nobody had.

4. Suppose you've got lots of colliding particles. You can think of them as molecules of oxygen, let's say, in a gas and they're in a box. You believe that they obey Newtonian mechanics.

And you measure their initial position and velocity precisely. Then one can predict their motion for all time. But wait a minute! You can only do that if the system is completely isolated and so you say, "Isolate it as best you can according to the laws of physics as we know them." Well there's one force that you can't screen out, and that's gravity. So unless you know the position of every single external particle in the universe which would have a gravitational effect on your molecules, you couldn't predict the motion. So let's estimate the uncertainty that arises from this source by considering the gravitational effect of an electron at the observable limit of the universe.

There it is at the observable limit of the universe, say ten thousand million light years away. It has its gravitational effect, but you don't know where it is *exactly,* so that's the uncertainty. Well, you ask, after how many collisions will the little uncertainty . . . be amplified to the degree where you've lost all predictability . . . ? Well, the amazing thing is that the number of collisions is only about 50 or so, which is of course over in a tiny, tiny fraction of a microsecond. That means it's really unreasonable in a large class of systems to consider Newtonian mechanics as being predictable. (Interview with Michael Berry, *A Passion for Science,* edited by Lewis Wolpert and Alison Richards)

5. Patrick Macdonald, a law student at Aberdeen University, has been granted legal aid to sue his mother for the living expenses required to complete his degree. Others are already following his example.

That a son should sue his mother . . . is more than just an offence to filial piety, it is a grotesque misuse of the legal system. Mr. Macdonald is within his rights under the Scottish Family Law Act of 1985 but that does not make his actions right. He protests that he has to go to law because he does not wish to go into debt. A proper horror of indebtedness is a decent Scots prejudice but when it leads a man to use the blunt instrument of a writ to bludgeon money from his mother it becomes not proper prudence but ugly selfishness.

Parents, if they can, may wish to support their children at university. Those who have the resources to do so, and choose not to, should certainly be thought the less of. Affection should not diminish with the end of adolescence. But enforced responsibility should. Parents should not be expected in law to indulge their adult offspring any more than grown-up children should be forced in law to turn up for Christmas lunch. (Editorial, *The Times,* London)

6. But there is no reason to believe that China will become democratic in the near future, for several reasons. The first is that it would be contrary to the Chinese political culture. China, in its entire three-thousand-year history, has developed no concept of limited government, or protections of individual rights, or independence for the judiciary and the media. It has never in its history operated on any notion of the consent of the governed or the will of the majority. China, whether under the emperors or under the party general-secretaries, has always been ruled by a self-selected and self-perpetuating clique that operates in secret and treats opposition as treason.

A second reason, related to the first, is that for there to be real democratic reform, the bureaucrats who hold power in China today would have to give up some of their power, and there is no sign whatsoever that they have ever been ready to do that. The Chinese tradition is that personal benefits stem from political power. . . .

Finally, for China's government to subject itself to the concept of popular will would mean the loss of its control in areas where it feels its national interest allows no such loss. If, for example, Tibet were to be governed by democratic principles, rather than *diktat* from Beijing, the Tibetan people would create an independence movement that would challenge sovereignty there. Democracy in China would force China's leaders to acknowledge the right of the people of Taiwan to be allowed to decide for themselves whether to keep their island's de facto independence, to move toward de jure independence, or to become part of China with its government in Beijing.

China's ruling clique is simply not prepared to suffer the losses to its prestige and the undermining of its power that a move toward real democracy would entail. (Richard Bernstein and Ross H. Munro, *The Coming Conflict with China*)

7. Gay people who have to worry about what will happen to them if they come out of the closet (acknowledge their homosexuality), generally produce at a lower level than gay people who don't worry about what will happen to them. Even when the company has a policy that forbids discrimination based upon sexual orientation, as many do today, gay employees will probably be less productive if they are afraid of coming out because of the hostility they hear and see in the workplace.

It takes a lot of energy to protect your life. On a day-to-day basis, the closeted gay person in the corporate world leaves behind who they are, what is important to them, and what motivates them to succeed. He or she puts on a mask. Keeping that mask on to avoid discrimination is hard work.

It is hard work to dodge questions about what you did for Thanksgiving and what your weekend plans are. It is difficult to refrain from participating in discussions about family and friends. It takes energy to keep from being honest about oneself.

Closeted gay employees do not put on their desk a picture of the person they care most about for fear of being asked, "Who's that?" Closeted gay, lesbian, or bisexual employees do not make or receive personal phone calls in front of their co-workers. Closeted gay employees do not attend office social functions unless they come alone and wear that suffocating mask.

Once when my partner, Ray, and I were vacationing at Disney World, he spotted a colleague. Not being "out" at the time, he did not know how to introduce me to this man, his wife, and their children. I wandered off in another direction before their chance encounter. We met up later when the co-worker was out of sight. I was angry and hurt. Ray was angry, hurt, and resentful. We had long moments of difficult silence.

That is not an uncommon scenario. Closeted gay, lesbian, or bisexual employees face work-related stress inside and outside the workplace. Not only must they keep their masks on at the office, but also, when in the company of gay friends or their significant others, at restaurants, movies, bowling alleys, supermarkets, or church. If they are afraid of coming out of the closet at work, they will probably also be afraid of writing a letter to the editor about a gay issue; of marching in a gay parade; of any behavior that might be seen by someone who knows someone who works with them. (Brian McNaught, *Gay Issues in the Workplace*)

8. Every life is different from any that has gone before it, and so is every death. The uniqueness of each of us extends even to the way we die. Though most people know that various diseases carry us to our final hours by various paths, only very few comprehend the fullness of that endless multitude of ways by which the final forces of the human spirit can separate themselves from the body. Every one of death's diverse appearances is as distinctive as that singular face we each show the world during the days of life. Every man will yield up the ghost in a manner that the heavens have never known before; every woman will go her final way in her own way. (Sherwin Nuland, M.D., *How We Die*)

9. All our theories of science are formulated on the assumption that space-time is smooth and nearly flat, so they break down at the big bang singularity, where the curvature of space-time is infinite. This means that even if there were events before the big bang, one could not use them to determine what would happen afterward, because predictability would break down at the big bang. Correspondingly, if, as is the case, we know only what has happened since the big bang, we could not determine what happened beforehand. As far as we are concerned, events before the big bang can have no consequences so they should not form part of a scientific model of the universe. We should therefore cut them out of the model and say that time had a beginning at the big bang. (Stephen Hawking, *A Brief History of Time*)

10. *Why Scientific Literacy Is Important*   Why be scientifically literate? A number of different arguments can be made to convince you it's important. We call them,

> the argument from civics
>
> the argument from aesthetics
>
> the argument from intellectual connectedness

The first of these, the argument from civics, [goes as follows]. Every citizen will be faced with public issues whose discussion requires some scientific background, and therefore every citizen should have some level of scientific literacy. The threats to our system from a scientifically illiterate electorate are many, ranging from the danger of political demagoguery to the decay of the entire democratic process as vital decisions that affect everyone have to be made by an educated (but probably unelected) elite.

The argument from aesthetics is somewhat more amorphous, and is closely allied to arguments that are usually made to support liberal education in general. It goes like this: We live in a world that operates according to a few general laws of nature. Everything you do from the moment you get up to the moment you go to bed happens because of the working of one of these laws. This exceedingly beautiful and elegant view of the world is the crowning achievement of centuries of work by scientists. There is intellectual and aesthetic satisfaction to be gained from seeing the unity between a pot of water on a stove and the slow march of the continents, between the colors of the rainbow and the behavior of the fundamental constituents of matter. The scientifically illiterate person has been cut off from an enriching part of life, just as surely as a person who cannot read.

Finally, we come to the argument of intellectual coherence. It has become a commonplace to note that scientific findings often play a crucial role in setting the intellectual climate of an era. Copernicus' discovery of the heliocentric universe played an important role in sweeping away the old thinking of the Middle Ages and ushering in the Age of Enlightenment. Darwin's discovery of the principle of natural selection made the world seem less planned, less directed than it had been before; and in this century the work of Freud and the development of quantum mechanics have made it seem (at least superficially) less rational. In all of these cases, the general intellectual tenor of the times—what Germans call the Zeitgeist—was influenced by developments in science. How, the argument goes, can anyone hope to appreciate the deep underlying threads of the intellectual life in his or her own time without understanding the science that goes with it? (Robert M. Hazen and James Trefil, *Science Matters: Achieving Scientific Literacy*)

11. These are times when the fabric of society seems to unravel at ever-greater speed, when selfishness, violence, and a meanness of spirit seem to be rotting the goodness of our communal lives. Here the argument for the importance of emotional intelligence hinges on the link between sentiment, character, and moral instincts. There is growing evidence that fundamental ethical stances in life stem from underlying emotional capacities. For one, impulse is the medium of emotion; the seed of all impulse is a feeling bursting to express itself in action. Those who are at the mercy of impulse—who lack self-control—suffer a moral deficiency: the ability to control impulse is the base of will and character. By the same token, the root of altruism lies in empathy, the ability to read emotions in others; lacking a sense of another's need or despair, there is no caring. And if there are any two moral stances that our times call for, they are precisely these, self-restraint and compassion. (Daniel Goleman, *Emotional Intelligence*)

12. Now that we are living in an era where science is the truest religion, and Darwin its reluctant prophet, the comfortable view of the animal kingdom is to visualize a continuum of creatures, all advancing in small increments up the hierarchical scale from the unicellular to the primate.

   My central argument will be an attempt to demonstrate that this conceptualization is defensible only when considering the developmental line that stretches from the virus to the chimpanzee. But the order of change between the chimpanzee and the human being is of such a magnitude as to represent a break, a discontinuity, in this great chain of life. Mankind is that noble discontinuity. We are not the next step, or even a giant leap forward. We are a parallel and independent entity; a thing unto ourselves; in a class of our own; *sui generis*. This being so, the preservation of this species, our species, is vital not only to our selfish ends but also to the preservation of something extraordinary and unique in nature.

   No one can deny that we share whole biological systems with animals much lower and more distant from us than the higher primates. But what we have done with these various systems, and, beyond that, what nature has done with these systems, is profound and immeasurable. We are not dealing with more and better. We are different. The distance between man and ape is greater than the distance between ape and ameba.

   We must come to understand how different we are from other animals. . . . Modern biologists understand this, too, and stand in awe of our uniqueness. A major geneticist like Theodosius Dobzhansky pointed out that, in developing culture, humankind has outstripped nature and found the supragenetic. In all other animals, change can occur only through mutation.

   Cultural changes, on the other hand, can be directly and universally transmitted to everyone in that culture. "By changing what he knows about the world man changes the world that he knows; and by changing the world in which he lives man changes himself. . . . Evolution need no longer be a destiny imposed from without; it may conceivably be controlled by man in accordance with his wisdom and his values."

   We and the rest of the plant and animal kingdoms, for better or worse, live in a world that is at least in part of human design. We consciously, purposely, and often foolishly and shortsightedly change the actual world in which we and our fellow travelers on this planet must abide. But we also alter our environment in a second way. Our "world" is a product of our own perception; our imagination, feelings, sensitivity, knowledge, aspirations, self-deceptions, and hopes will create a "reality" that will command our lives beyond most strictures of actual events. How we interpret and define happenings will be the primary influence on our behavior, our pleasures, our self-judgments, and our sense of purpose.

Animals live in a sensate world. We live in a world of our own imagination. (Willard Gaylin, M.D., *On Being and Becoming Human*)

13. Turning now . . . to criticisms of grades, consider first the claim that grades are inherently inaccurate. Those who defend this position argue that the same paper would be graded differently by different instructors, and therefore a student's grade is not a reliable measure of his achievement but merely indicates the particular bias of his instructor.

However, a student's work is generally not judged with significant difference by different instructors. In fact, teachers in the same discipline usually agree as to which students are doing the outstanding work, which are doing good work, which are doing fair work, which are doing poor work, and which are doing unsatisfactory work (or no work at all). Of course, two competent instructors may offer divergent evaluations of the same piece of work. But that experts sometimes disagree is not reason to assume there is no such thing as expertise. Two competent doctors may offer divergent diagnoses of the same condition, but their disagreement does not imply that doctors' diagnoses are in general biased and unreliable. Similarly, two competent art critics may offer divergent evaluations of the same work of art, but such a disagreement does not imply that a critic's evaluations are usually biased and unreliable. Inevitably, experts, like all human beings, sometimes disagree about complex judgments, but we would be foolish to allow such disagreements to obscure the obvious fact that in any established field of inquiry some individuals are knowledgeable and others are not. Clearly the opinions of those who are knowledgeable are the most reliable measure of an individual's achievement in that field. Thus, although teachers sometimes disagree, they are knowledgeable individuals whose grades represent a reliable measure of a student's level of achievement.

A second criticism of grades is that they traumatize students. Those who support this criticism argue that grades foster competition, arousing a bitterness and hostility which transform an otherwise tranquil academic atmosphere into a pressure-filled, nerve-wracking situation unsuited for genuine learning. In such a situation, it is said, students are worried more about obtaining good grades than a good education.

This criticism emphasizes only the possibly harmful effects of competition while overlooking beneficial effects. Often only by competing with others do we bring out the best in ourselves.

. . . Competition fosters excellence, and without that challenge most of us would be satisfied with accomplishing far less than we are capable of.

A third criticism of grades is that in attempting to measure people, they succeed only in dehumanizing and categorizing them, depriving them of uniqueness, and reducing them to a letter of the alphabet. Thus, it is said, grades defeat one of the essential purposes of an education: to aid each individual in developing individuality.

A grade, however, is not and is not intended to be a measure of a person. It is, rather, a measure of a person's level of achievement in a particular course of study. To give a student a C in an introductory physics course is not saying that the student is a C person with a C personality or C moral character, only that the student has a C level of achievement in introductory physics.

Grades no more reduce students to letters than batting averages reduce baseball players to numbers. That Ted Williams had a lifetime batting average of .344 and Joe Garagiola an average of .257 does not mean Williams is a better person than Garagiola, but only that Williams was a better hitter. Why does it dehumanize either man to recognize that one was a better hitter than the other?

Indeed, to recognize an individual's strengths and weaknesses, to know areas of expertise, areas of competence, and areas of ignorance is not to deny but to emphasize individuality.

Thus grades do not dehumanize an individual; on the contrary, they contribute to a recognition of uniqueness and to the possible development of individual interests and abilities. (Steven M. Cahn, "Rethinking Examinations and Grades")

14. According to some philosophers, if we were truly objective we would accord each minute of our lives—past, present, and future—equal value. In actuality, we accord far more weight to the immediate future than to the past. Interestingly, we do have this objectivity when it comes to other people's lives. The philosopher Derek Parfit explores this deeply ingrained irrationality, and the following "thought experiment" derives from his work.

Case A. You wake up in a hospital bed. The doctor informs you that you have just had a four-hour operation. The surgeons were not able to use anesthesia and you were in excruciating pain. But the operation is over and there are no postoperative side effects. You will have no recollection of the procedure because you were given a pill that expunged the memory of the operation forever.

Case B. The doctor informs you that you will have to undergo an operation one hour from now. The procedure will last only ten minutes but it will be very painful; you will not be anesthetized. Here, too, the operation will not have any enduring side effects and you will be given a pill that will eliminate your memory of it.

Most people quickly say they prefer Case A to Case B. Even though the pain in Case A is much more prolonged than the pain in Case B, it makes all the difference that the suffering in Case A is over while the suffering in Case B is still to come.

Now consider two scenarios involving the pain of someone else. Your mother, for example. You've been on a desert island for three years. Today your rescue boat arrives and you inquire about the health of your loved ones.

Case A. You are told that just yesterday your mother underwent an excruciating operation. The operation lasted for four hours and no anesthesia was administered. A pill was given to her at the end of the operation and she has no recollection of the operation. The procedure has no lasting side effects.

Case B. Your mother will undergo a painful operation in an hour, but the operation will last only ten minutes. Same deal—at the end of the procedure, she will be given a pill that will remove the memory of it, and the operation will have no side effects.

Which would you prefer? Without hesitation, most people opt for Case B. In that case your mother suffers for only ten minutes, but in the other she suffers for four hours. When we think about the pain of other people, future and past are not decisive—we opt for less pain. But when it comes to our own pain, mild or intense, it matters very much whether it's past or still to come. (Joshua Halberstam, *Everyday Ethics*)

15. That man is, in fact, only a member of a biotic community is shown by an ecological interpretation of history. Many historical events, hitherto explained solely in terms of human enterprise, were actually biotic interactions between people and land. The characteristics of the land determined the facts quite as potently as the characteristics of the men who lived on it.

Consider, for example, the settlement of the Mississippi valley. In the years following the revolution, three groups were contending for its control: the native Indian, the French and English traders, and the American settlers. Historians wonder what would have happened if the English at Detroit had thrown a little more weight into the Indian side of those tipsy scales which decided the outcome of the colonial migration into the cane-lands of Kentucky. It is time now to ponder the fact that the cane-lands, when subjected to the particular mixture of forces represented by the cow, plow, fire, and axe of the pioneer, became bluegrass. What if the plant succession inherent in this dark and bloody ground had, under the impact of these forces, given us some worthless sedge, shrub, or weed? Would Boone and Kenton have held out? Would there have been any overflow into Ohio, Indiana, Illinois, and Missouri? Any Louisiana Purchase? Any transcontinental union of new states? Any civil war?

We are commonly told what the human actors in this drama tried to do, but we are seldom told that their success, or the lack of it, hung in large degree on the reaction of particular soils to the impact of the particular forces exerted by their occupancy. In the case of Kentucky, we do not even know where the bluegrass came from—whether it is a native species, or a stowaway from Europe.

In short, the plant succession steered the course of history; the pioneer simply demonstrated, for good or ill, what successions inhered in the land. Is history taught in this spirit? It will be, once the concept of land as a community really penetrates our intellectual life. (Aldo Leopold, *A Sand County Almanac*)

Review Questions

1. According to your text, what are the steps in the procedure for evaluating an argument?

2. What two formats may be used for writing an exposition of an argument?

3. Define extended argument.

4. What kinds of problems might extended arguments present for exposition?

5. What is the purpose of exposing an argument? How explicit should the exposition be?

6. What is an enthymeme?

7. Define empirical statement and nonempirical statement.

8. Under what circumstances are we justified in accepting a premise of an argument?

9. Why are tautologies nonempirical statements?

10. Why can't a good argument have a false premise?

True or False?

1. Statements accepted by appeal to authority may be empirical or nonempirical statements.

2. Tautologies are nonempirically true, but self-contradictions are empirically false.

3. Arguments with a missing premise are always deductive arguments.

4. If we see immediately that a premise of an argument is false, then as far as the evaluation of the argument is concerned, it is not good.

5. A premise of one argument may be the conclusion of another.

6. If the premise of one argument is supported by a good argument, then that premise is true.

7. Both tautologies and self-contradictions can be formally determined using truth tables.

8. A statement that serves no inferential purpose in an argument may be omitted without affecting the argument.

9. Causal statements—statements asserting that one event causes another—are empirical statements.

10. Given that an inductive generalization employs a premise asserting what has been observed about a sample of a larger group, it follows that such a premise is an empirical statement.

Discussion Questions

1. Earlier in this chapter (p. 309) you read that "logic, the study of the principles of good reasoning, does not define our vital concerns. . . ." What does that claim mean and do you agree with it? Explain your judgment.

2. Write an essay in which you describe and illustrate with examples what you have learned about preparing long passages or essays for analysis.

3. Find a poem that argues a point. Provide a logical analysis and evaluation of it. That is, rewrite it in argument form using the techniques of argument exposition. Examine the premises and then discuss the plausibility of the argument. Now discuss the merits of evaluating a poem for its logical character.

4. In general, we can say that the sciences and the humanities provide us with many of the premises we use in reasoning. Given what you have learned about logic, how would you characterize the relationship between logic and the sciences and humanities?

INFOTRAC Assignments

Using INFOTRAC look up any of the subject words below for articles containing inductive arguments. Write the arguments in argument form or draw an argument diagram. Evaluate the argument.

ANIMAL RIGHTS

ASSISTED SUICIDE

ETHICS

CAPITAL PUNISHMENT

PROFESSIONAL ATHLETICS

Answers to Selected Exercises

Chapter 1

Exercise 1.2
1. Statement, conditional   **3.** Statement   **5.** Not a statement   **7.** Statement
9. Statement   **11.** Not a statement   **13.** for *tomorrow we shall die;* statement
15. Statement   **17.** Statement   **19.** Statement   **21.** for *loan oft loses both itself and friend . . .;*
statement   **23.** Statement   **25.** Statement

Exercise 1.3

1. *1. Every literature major must take a course in Shakespeare.*
2. John has taken the Shakespeare course.
3. Therefore, he must be a literature major.

5. *1. If the president dies in office, then the first lady becomes the new president.*
2. Laura Bush is the first lady.
3. She will take over if President Bush dies in office.

9. *1. A person can't be a marine and a sailor both.*
2. Max is a sailor.
3. Therefore, it must be that he is not a marine.

3. *Not an argument*

7. *1. If the creationists are right, then the universe was created and has a beginning.*
2. Now, whatever has a beginning must also have an end.
3. Therefore, if the creationists are right, the universe must have an end as well.

11. *1. There is freedom in the sense of being able to move as one pleases . . .*
2. There is freedom in the sense of being able to do and speak as one pleases . . .
3. There is freedom in the sense of being able to think for oneself.
4. This last type makes the others possible.
5. Therefore, it is our most important freedom.
[NOTE: *Premises 1–3 may be combined as one compound premise.*]

13. *Not an argument*

17. 1. *You cannot hold a person liable for something he or she did not know about.*
  2. *You have not shown that your client did not know about the faulty wiring in the house he sold.*
  _____
  3. *Therefore, we can conclude that your client cannot be excused for damages.*

21. 1. *The mind directly perceives only ideas.*
  2. *Material objects are not ideas.*
  _____
  3. *Therefore, the mind does not directly perceive material objects.*

25. 1. *Mice are just smallish rats.*
  _____
  2. *Therefore, housecats are just smallish tigers.*

29. 1. *The most common large woodpecker in our area is the redheaded woodpecker.*
  2. *What I saw was a large woodpecker.*
  _____
  3. *So, even though I did not see its head, it probably was a redheaded woodpecker.*

Exercise 1.4A   Diagramming Arguments
1. ① *All humans are mortal.*
  ② *Socrates is a human. Therefore,*
  ③ *Socrates is mortal.*

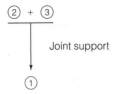

5. ① *There is no reason for fearing death because*
  ② *if there is no afterlife,*
  ① *then at the moment of death we are nothing. Or*
  ③ *if there is an afterlife, at the moment of death we are born into new life.*

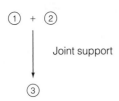

15. 1. *Only living things can have feelings.*
  2. *Computers are not living things.*
  _____
  3. *Therefore, computers do not have feelings.*
19. 1. *The workday is often more than eight hours long.*
  2. *There is heavy lifting to do.*
  3. *There is the possibility of injury.*
  4. *There are cranky supervisors.*
  5. *The weather does not always cooperate.*
  _____
  6. *Therefore, house builders work awfully hard.*
[NOTE: Premises 1–4 may be combined as one premise.]
23. 1. *Being in jail is frightening enough for kids.*
  2. *Locking them up with adults is inviting tragedy.*
  _____
  3. *Therefore, kids should not be put behind bars with adults.*
27. 1. *If there is no afterlife, then at the moment of death we are nothing.*
  2. *If there is an afterlife, then at the moment of death we are born into a new life.*
  _____
  3. *Therefore, death is not to be feared.*

3. ① *Housebuilders work awfully hard.*
  ② *The workday is often more than eight hours long;*
  ③ *there's heavy lifting to do,*
  ④ *the possibility of injury, and*
  ⑤ *cranky supervisors; and*
  ⑥ *the weather doesn't always cooperate.*

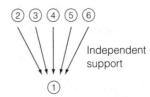

7. ① *Parents are principally responsible for the education and upbringing of their children and*
  ② *are, therefore, the most qualified persons to select the formal schooling for their children.*

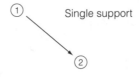

9. ① *The United States spends nearly $2000 per year per capita on health care.*
② *Yet the indicators of national health show that we are getting less for our dollars than countries that spend less per capita.*
③ *This is the reason why we need to thoroughly re-examine our health care system in the U.S.*

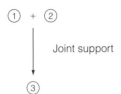

① + ②

Joint support

③

11. ① *If people want good roads, then they must pay for them.*
② *That is the reason why you should support increased highway taxes.*

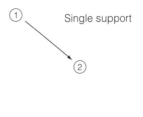

① Single support

②

13. ① *Whenever a solid is heated, its color changes from red to orange, yellow, and then bluish white.*
② *Since this change is the same for all solids,*
③ *it would seem that it could be explained without knowing much about the actual structure of any particular solid. Furthermore,*
④ *it seems reasonable to conclude that there could be a unified theory of radiant energy.*

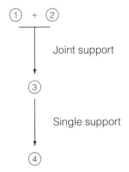

① + ②

Joint support

③

Single support

④

15. ① *In general the child from a large family makes a better team player.*
② *Such a child develops better interpersonal skills because*
③ *he or she learns to cooperate with others, to share responsibilities, and to see things from the other's viewpoint.*

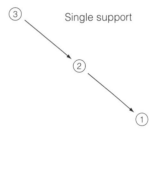

③ Single support

②

①

Exercise 1.4B
In this exercise, students compose their own arguments for or against the given propositions.

Exercise 1.5
1. Supplied premise: You can vote only if you have registered.   **3.** Supplied premise: Professor Pipes is a scientist.   **5.** Supplied premises: A fetus is an innocent human being. Killing an innocent human being is murder.   **7.** Supplied premise: Her brain is dead.   **9.** Supplied premise: We are living longer than the age of eighty.   **11.** Supplied conclusion: The theory of evolution is not correct.
13. Supplied premise: Reliance on gasoline-fueled vehicles makes us vulnerable to Persian Gulf politics.
15. Supplied premise: Having language is necessary for reasoning.   **17.** Supplied premise: The Arctic Circle provides so little light.

Exercise 1.6
NOTE: For convenience, statements are abbreviated by using '. . .' (ellipses). These answers represent reasonable analyses of the passages in the exercises. Yours might differ. Compare yours and be prepared to discuss and defend your analysis.

1. ① *If two events happen . . . minutes*
② *Different observers . . . legitimate.*

3. ① *[Under present law] federal regulations . . . study.*
② *In 1982, . . . agony . . .*
③ *As moral beings, . . . misery.*

5. The first sentence does not figure in the argument and may therefore be omitted. The second sentence contains as a premise the statement "I want to be free to practice my religion."
① *I want to be free . . . my religion.*
② *I believe that if my government . . . and my kind need.*

7. The first sentence, a rhetorical question, and the second sentence in the passage are rewritten as statements ① and ②.
① *Critics should know that if it weren't for the electoral college, then the consequences for smaller states would be unfortunate.*
② *If it weren't for the electoral college, then all a candidate . . . population.*
③ *The electoral . . . a real vote.*

9. ① *I submit that the state of our sexual life is a mess.*
② *Our culture . . . muddle.*
③ *Traditional morality . . . sex life.*
④ *For teenagers . . . they don't.*
⑤ *When it . . . moral confusion.*

11. ① *There are . . . bad idea,*
② *The main one being . . . that way. . . .*
③ *"Coaches come and go.*
④ *When a coach is fired, all of his people go, then the next guy . . . people.*
⑤ *The organization suffers.*

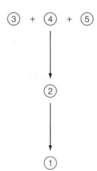

13. ① *When, in ordinary . . . of light*
② *But the other . . . real.*
③ *To avoid favouritism . . . colour.*

15. Not an argument

17. ① *The idea of solidity is . . . and distinct
existence.*
② *Solidity, . . . this separate and distinct
existence.*

19. ① *If we leave . . . stimulate.*
② *A community . . . at first glance.*
③ *Selection . . . vote.*
④ *Only a panel . . . public money.*

Chapter 2

Exercise 2.3A

1. Deductively valid. It must be that Max takes organic chem because all chem majors must and he's a chem major.

3. Not deductively valid. Given that drinking coffee does stunt one's growth and that Max's growth is stunted, it can still be denied that Max drinks coffee. Something else may be responsible.

5. Not deductively valid. Given the premises, it can still be denied that you will get better. After all, the first premise says that patients almost always get better.

7. Not deductively valid. It does not follow necessarily that Redford lives in Hollywood, since, while Redford is a movie star and only movie stars live in Hollywood, it may be true that he does not.

9. Deductively valid. Given these premises, it follows with necessity that Redford lives in Hollywood.

11. Deductively valid. It follows necessarily that you are right to be suspicious of Harold. He thinks he doesn't need to abide by the rules, and you are right to be suspicious of someone who does not think he needs to abide by the rules.

13. Deductively valid. If a right to life does not give one a right to whatever one needs to live, then the kidney patient's right to life does not give him or her a right to what he needs either.

15. Deductively valid. It has to follow that they are not the same because they do not have the same properties and things are the same only if they have the same properties.

Exercise 2.3B

1. Inductively strong. Since most religions include a belief in god, it is likely that Buddhism, a religion, contains such a belief, too.

3. Inductively weak. One instance of a faulty transmission doesn't make it likely that the next Galaxy will have a faulty transmission. Maybe Lauren is hard on the transmission!

5. Inductively strong. Given the premises, it seems wise to take an antibiotic. Otherwise, there's a good chance of an infection.

7. Inductively strong. Those premises, if true, give good reason for thinking that tax cuts are a good thing for the economy.

9. Inductively strong. There is a good chance that two of them have birthdays on the same month.

11. Inductively weak. The conclusion that vitamin C can prevent the onset of colds is not made likely given that the vitamin could reduce symptomatic days from 7.8 to 7.1.

13. Inductively strong. The conclusion is probable given the premises that most people majoring in the humanities, teach them and, ultimately, experience a labor of love.

15. Inductively strong. Given that infections in hospitals affect nurses more so than such infections occur in the outside community, it seems to follow that the pathogens strengthen in the hospital environment, a phenomenon called "cycling."

Exercise 2.4A
1. *Modus ponens.* Valid.   3. Barbara. Valid.   5. Fallacy of undistributed middle. Invalid.
7. Fallacy of denying the antecedent. Invalid.   9. *Modus ponens.* Valid.   11. Fallacy of affirming the consequent. Invalid.   13. Fallacy of denying the antecedent. Invalid.   15. *Modus ponens.* Valid.

Exercise 2.4B
1. Barbara is the theme of this argument. If you were to rewrite the statements with the term 'All' and the appropriate changes, and substitute the letters 'A', 'B', 'C', 'D', etc. for the content terms, you would see a pattern reminiscent of Barbara.

3. This has the form of *modus tollens*. The second premise implies the denial of the consequent of the conditional in the first premise. The argument concludes with a statement that implies that people do not get what they need in order to function as citizens. Therefore, we have an argument that exhibits *modus tollens*.

5. The argument abbreviated shows Barbara in statements (2), (3), and (4):
   1. A damaged bone undergoes a series of changes before stabilizing.
   2. Mr. Fuller's bone tissue exhibits that process of changes.
   3. The bone's process of changes takes generally five years.
   4. Therefore, Mr. Fuller's injury is at least five years old.

Exercise 2.5
1. (a) These statements are all true.   (b) Deductively invalid because it is the fallacy of undistributed middle.   (c) Not good because the conclusion follows neither with deductive validity nor with inductive strength.

3. (a) Statements (2) and (3) are not clearly true. Hang gliding is less dangerous than driving.
(b) This is deductively invalid; fallacy of affirming the consequent.   (c) The argument has a false premise and does not follow either necessarily or with probability.

5. (a) Statement (1) is true. Statements (2), (3), and (4) are very controversial. Some people argue that (2) is false. Many would deny (3) on the ground that some acts of killing persons are morally justified.
(b) The argument is deductively valid.   (c) It is not a good argument because its premises are dubious.

7. (a) All true statements.   (b) Invalid; fallacy of undistributed middle.   (c) Not good because the conclusion does not follow, either with deductive validity or inductive strength.

Chapter 3

Exercise 3.3A
1. Subject: astronomers
Predicate: trained in mathematics
Form: A
Quality: affirmative
Quantity: universal

3. Subject: past presidents
Predicate: invited to a luncheon on Friday
Form: A
Quality: affirmative
Quantity: universal

5. Subject: traffic monitors
Predicate: well-trained people
Form: O
Quality: negative
Quantity: particular

7. Subject: football fans
Predicate: fanatics
Form: A
Quality: affirmative
Quantity: universal

9. Subject: members of the Kiwanis Club
Predicate: active supporters of the right-to-life movement
Form: I
Quality: affirmative
Quantity: particular

Exercise 3.3B

1. No piranhas are vicious fish.   **3.** Some sailboats are not equipped with outboard motors.
5. No good investments are tax-free investments.   **7.** No bartenders are licensed in this state.
9. Some wheelwrights are not still in business.

Exercise 3.3C

1. Some happy people are happy in the same way.   **3.** Some specimens from the site are not ready for examination.   **5.** All vicious fish are piranhas.   **7.** Some bartenders are not licensed in this state.
9. No chess players are grand masters.

Exercise 3.4A

1. Form E; negative; universal

eucalyptus   natives of Cal.
trees

3. Form A; affirmative; universal

machines   products of
intelligence

5. Form I; affirmative; particular

lawyers   people
whom we
can respect

7. Form E; negative; universal

persons   persons
wanting
to be harmed

9. Form A; affirmative; universal

logicians   lovers of
Venn diagrams

11. Form E; negative; universal

male   sopranos
vocalists   at Met

13. Form A; affirmative; universal

members of   persons who
student council   must maintain
a 3.0 average

15. Form E; negative; universal

computers   things capable
of thought

17. Form A; affirmative; universal

animal   persons
lovers   who will
appreciate

19. Form I; affirmative; particular

teas   things
containing
caffeine

Exercise 3.4B

1. Some congresspersons are not muskrats. **3.** Some singers are not dancers. Some singers are dancers. **5.** All plants are living things.

Exercise 3.5

1. *1. No modern sculptors are better than Henry Moore.*   TRUE E

    2. So, it's false that some are better than Moore.   FALSE I

5. *1. It is false that all great chess players are foreigners.*   FALSE A

    2. Thus, no great chess players are foreigners.   TRUE E

9. *1. All logicians are cold and heartless.*   TRUE A

    2. Thus, it's false that no logicians are cold and heartless.   FALSE E

3. *1. Some senators voted for the tax cut.*   TRUE I

    2. Therefore, it's false that no senators voted for it.   FALSE E

7. *1. It's not true that all people like logic.*   FALSE A

    2. Thus, no people like logic.   TRUE E

Exercise 3.6A

1. Valid

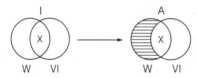

3. Valid

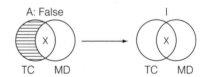

5. Invalid

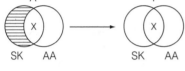

7. Valid

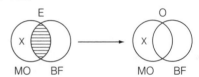

9. Valid

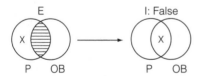

11. Invalid

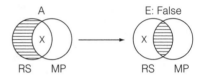

13. Invalid

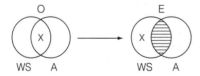

15. Invalid

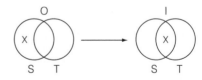

1. Valid

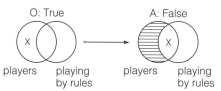

O: True → A: False

players / playing by rules   players / playing by rules

3. Valid

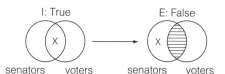

I: True → E: False

senators / voters   senators / voters

5. Valid

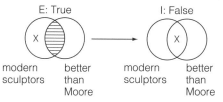

E: True → I: False

modern sculptors / better than Moore   modern sculptors / better than Moore

7. Valid

A: True → O: False

philanthropists / benefactors   philanthropists / benefactors

9. Invalid

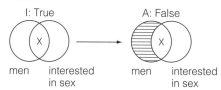

I: True → A: False

men / interested in sex   men / interested in sex

Exercise 3.6C

1. (a) The A-form is false; **(b)** The I-form is false; **(c)** The O-form is true.

3. No inference can be made. I does not imply A.

5. No inference can be made. O does not imply I.

7. No inference can be made. I does not imply O.

9. The claim is true because a false O implies that the A-form is true.

Exercise 3.6D

1. Invalid

3. Invalid

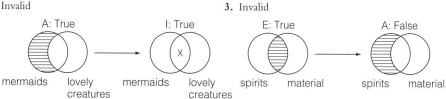

A: True → I: True

mermaids / lovely creatures   mermaids / lovely creatures

E: True → A: False

spirits / material   spirits / material

5. Valid

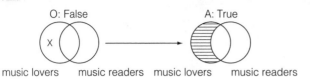

music lovers   music readers   music lovers   music readers

7. Invalid

9. Invalid

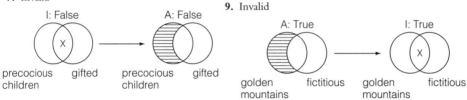

precocious   gifted   precocious   gifted
children   children

golden   fictitious   golden   fictitious
mountains   mountains

Exercise 3.7A

1. All scientists are researchers. All researchers are scientists.

scientists   researchers   scientists   researchers

3. No artists are wealthy persons.   No nonwealthy persons are nonartists.

5. All trees are plants. No trees are nonplants.

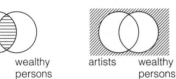

trees   plants   trees   plants

artists   wealthy   artists   wealthy
persons   persons

7. Some buyers are market managers.   Some non–market managers are nonbuyers.

9. No gypsies are loiterers.   All gypsies are nonloiterers.

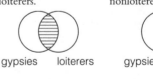

buyers   market   buyers   market
managers   managers

gypsies   loiterers   gypsies   loiterers

11. Some citrus growers are not nonunion supporters. Some citrus growers are union supporters.

citrus   nonunion   citrus   nonunion
growers   supporters   growers   supporters

13. Some retired servicepeople are nonbeneficiaries. Some nonbeneficiaries are retired servicepeople.

retired service people   nonbeneficiaries   retired service people   nonbeneficiaries

15. Some sociopaths are not nonmoral people. Some sociopaths are moral people.

sociopaths   nonmoral people   sociopaths   nonmoral people

Exercise 3.7B
1. Quality changes; predicate is negated. Obversion.
3. Subject and predicate change places. Conversion.
5. Subject and predicate change places and each is negated. Contraposition.
7. First, subject and predicate change places. Conversion. Then quality changes; predicate is negated. Obversion.
9. Subject and predicate change places. Conversion.
11. Quality changes; predicate is negated. Obversion.
13. Quality changes; predicate is negated. Obversion.
15. Subject and predicate change places and each is negated. Contraposition.

Exercise 3.7C
1. No patriots are traitors. Therefore, all patriots are nontraitors.

patriots   traitors   patriots   traitors
Obverse; valid

3. All revolutionaries are radicals. So no revolutionaries are nonradicals.

revolutionaries   radicals   revolutionaries   radicals
Obverse; valid

5. Some people are not friendly, so some people are unfriendly.

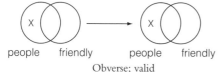

people   friendly   people   friendly
Obverse; valid

7. Some metals are liquids. Therefore, some liquids are not nonmetals. Some liquids are metals.

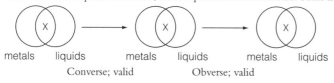

metals   liquids   metals   liquids   metals   liquids
Converse; valid   Obverse; valid

9. No senators are infants. Therefore, no noninfants are nonsenators.

senators   infants   senators   infants

Contrapositive; invalid

Exercise 3.7D

1. Some comatose patients are conscious. By obversion.

3. Some professors are not moral people. By contraposition.

5. All alien spaceships are identified flying objects. By obversion.

7. All educated persons are enlightened persons. By contraposition.

9. Some business people are not moral people. By contraposition.

Chapter 4

Exercise 4.2A

1. Some phones are things off the hook.

3. All times we have a picnic are times it rains.

5. Some historians are good writers. Some historians are not good writers.

7. All persons who go to war are young persons.

9. No faculty members are persons permitted to cancel classes.

11. All things logic develops are things identical to the mind.

15. All persons identical to Aristotle are persons who developed the doctrine of the golden mean.

17. All major African religions are religions that contain the idea of a supreme god.

19. All cases in which consumer spending increases are cases in which interest rates will decline.

21. All persons are persons who need regular exercise.

23. All things identical to the whole of science are things that are nothing more than a refinement of everyday thinking.

25. All things identical to religion are things that are an illusion.

Exercise 4.2B

1. All sound arguments are good arguments. All good arguments are sound arguments.

sound arguments   good arguments

3. Some singers are successful singers. Some singers are not successful singers.

singers   successful singers

5. All medical doctors are persons who have earned an M.D. degree. All persons who have earned an M.D. degree are medical doctors.

medical doctors   earned M.D. degree

7. No emperor—North American geese are regular visitors to Missouri. All non–emperor—North American geese are regular visitors to Missouri.

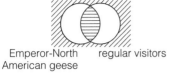

Emperor-North   regular visitors
American geese

NOTE: Next is a solution using three categories. The advantage of this solution is that it makes explicit the assertion that all North American geese that are not emperor geese are visitors.

No emperor geese are regular visitors to Missouri. All non–emperor–North American geese are regular visitors to Missouri.

North American geese

emperor geese   regular visitors

9. All persons who can order a drink here are persons who are at least twenty-one.

persons who can order   persons who are at least 21

Exercise 4.4A

1.   members

athletes   professionals

3.   arguments with four premises

valid syllogisms   arguments unprovable

5.   reptiles

cold-blooded creatures   good pets

7.   chess players

grand masters   checkers players

9. elected officials

Palestinians   freedom fighters

Exercise 4.4B

1. Yes   **3.** Yes   **5.** Yes   **7.** No   **9.** No   **11.** No

Exercise 4.4C

1. *1. All dancers are vegetarians.*
2. No dentists are dancers.
─────────────────────────────
3. No dentists are vegetarians.

dancers

Invalid

dentists   vegetarians

3. *1. No conservationists are advocates of nuclear energy.*
2. All farmers are conservationists.
─────────────────────────────
3. No farmers are advocates of nuclear energy.

conservationists

Valid

farmers   advocates

5. *1. All books are books worth reading.*
2. Some books are novels.
─────────────────────────────
3. Some novels are books worth reading.

books

Valid

novels   books worth reading

7. *1. Some females are not women.*
2. All mothers are females.
─────────────────────────────
3. Some mothers are not women.

females

Invalid

mothers   women

9. *1. All Egyptians are North Africans.*
2. No Egyptians are Asians.
─────────────────────────────
3. Some North Africans are not Asians.
NOTE: Valid only by existential assumption of premise (1).

Egyptians

North Africans   Asians

11. *1. Some emotions are sensations caused by thought.*
2. Some sensations caused by thought are neurotic states.
─────────────────────────────
3. Some emotions are neurotic states.

sensations caused

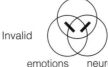

Invalid

emotions   neurotic states

13. *1. All cameramen are photographers.*
2. Some photographers are not artists.

    3. Some cameramen are not artists.

photographers

Invalid

cameramen   artists

15. *1. Some Japanese watches are digital watches.*
2. No analog watches are digital watches.

    3. Some analog watches are not Japanese watches.

digital watches

Invalid

analog watches   Japanese watches

Exercise 4.5A

1. *1. Some bankers are voters for the new tax structure.*
2. Some bankers are not voters for the new tax structure.
3. All voters for the new tax structure are capitalists.

    4. Some bankers are not capitalists.

voters

Invalid

bankers   capitalists

3. *1. All forecasters who can predict the heat wave are good weather reporters.*
2. All good weather reporters are persons trained in meteorology.

    3. All forecasters who can predict the heat wave are persons trained in meteorology.

good weather reporters

Valid

forecasters   persons trained in. . .

5. *1. All things capable of thought are things capable of meaningful speech.*
2. All humans are things capable of meaningful speech.

    3. All humans are things capable of thought.

capable of meaningful speech

Invalid

humans   capable of thought

7. *1. All poisonous snakes are things to avoid.*
2. Some snakes are nonpoisonous. = Some snakes are not poisonous snakes. (Obversion)

    3. Some snakes are not things to avoid.

poisonous snakes

Invalid

snakes   things to avoid

9. *1. All Iranians are Persians.*
2. All Persians are Iranians.
3. No Iraqis are Persians.

    4. No Iranians are Iraqis.

Persians

Valid

Iranians   Iraqis

Exercise 4.5B
1. All X are Y.
All Y are Z.

Therefore, * all X are Z.
* All X are Z.
All Z are T.

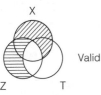

Valid

Therefore, all X are T.

3. No A are non-D = all A are D
(obversion)
Some A are B.

Therefore, * some B are D.
* Some B are D.
All B are C.

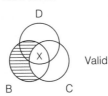

Valid

Therefore, some C are D.

5. Some humans are mortals.
Some mortals are Romans.

Invalid

7. All sailors are recruits.
No volunteers are recruits.

Therefore, * no sailors are volunteers.
* No sailors are volunteers.
All officers are volunteers.

sailors

officers   volunteers

Therefore, * no sailors are officers.
* No sailors are officers.
All veterans are officers.

sailors

veterans   officers
Valid

Therefore, no sailors are veterans.

9. All computer programmers are people
proficient in BASIC.
No people proficient in BASIC are computer illiterates.

programmers

proficient in BASIC   illiterates

Therefore, * no computer programmers are
computer illiterates.
* No computer programmers are computer
illiterates.
No computer illiterates are
mathematicians.

programmers

Invalid

illiterates   mathematicians

11. All artisans are woodworkers.
All carpenters are artisans.

woodworkers

carpenters   artisans

Therefore, * all carpenters are woodworkers.
* All carpenters are woodworkers.
Some carpenters are journeymen.

woodworkers

carpenters   journeymen
       Valid

Therefore, some journeymen are
woodworkers.

Chapter 5

Exercise 5.4
1. R ⊃ C conditional   **3.** J ⊃ I conditional   **5.** −A negation   **7.** T-F symbolization permits two possible interpretations: "It is not the case that pizza and beer are recommended for people with ulcers," −(P + B) negation; "Pizza is not recommended for people with ulcers and beer is not recommended for people with ulcers," −P + −B conjunction   **9.** T + −O conjunction   **11.** P + A conjunction   **13.** M ≡ V biconditional   **15.** −L ∨ S disjunction   **17.** A ⊃ S conditional
19. S + G conjunction

Exercise 5.5
1. − (M ⊃ H) negation   **3.** −T ∨ I disjunction   **5.** J ⊃ (T + R) conditional   **7.** (B + A) + −S *or* B + (A + −S) conjunction   **9.** L ⊃ (T + P) conditional   **11.** (L ∨ T) ⊃ P conditional
13. (L ∨ T) ⊃ P conditional   **15.** T ∨ (C ⊃ −S) disjunction   **17.** −(P ⊃ F) ⊃ −(B ⊃ G) conditional   **19.** [(T + D) ∨ I] ⊃ B conditional
20. Let statements be symbolized as follows, for example:

     T = Each taxpayer must file an income tax report
     C = Each taxpayer must complete a statement of earnings
     A = An authorized tax preparer must file an income tax report
     S = An authorized tax preparer must complete a statement of earnings

Then T-F symbolization permits two interpretations:

                 (T + C) ∨ (A + S) disjunction

According to this interpretation either the taxpayer files the tax report and completes the statement of earnings or the authorized tax preparer does both.

                 (T ∨ A) + (C ∨ S) conjunction

According to this interpretation either the taxpayer or the tax preparer must file the income tax report and either the taxpayer or the tax preparer must complete the statement of earnings.

Notice that according to T-F logic either interpretation correctly symbolizes the given compound statement. If one interpretation is preferable to the other, then it must be so for non−truth-functional considerations. For example, perhaps you might argue that, given the way tax preparation typically works—tax preparers usually do both tasks—the more plausible interpretation is the first.

21. −A negation   **23.** I ⊃ (C + A) conditional

Exercise 5.6
1. −(S + M)   **3.** C ⊃ D   **5.** S ⊃ D   **7.** H ∨ −F   **9.** H ∨ C   **11.** P ⊃ C
13. −(C ∨ P) or −C + −P   **15. (a)** (M ∨ F) + −(M + F)   **(b)** −(M + F)   **17.** (L + J) ⊃ U   **19.** −(C ∨ R) or −C + −R   **21.** −(D ∨ R) or −D + −R   **23.** (−S + −I) ⊃ B
25. H + (−S + −Y) or H + −(S ∨ Y)   **27.** (S + T) ⊃ C   **29.** N ⊃ C   **31.** F ⊃ [C + (B + W)]

Exercise 5.8A

1.
```
 −  p
F | T
T | F
```

3.
```
p ∨ q
T T T
F T T
T T F
F F F
```

5.
```
p ≡ q
T T T
F F T
T F F
F T F
```

Exercise 5.8B

1.
```
R + −S
T F FT
F F FT
T T TF
F F TF
```

3.
```
P ∨ (Q ⊃ R)
T T T T T
F T T T T
T T F T T
F T F T T
T T T F F
F F T F F
T T F T F
F T F T F
```

5.
```
Q ⊃ (P + Q)
T T T T T
F T T F F
T F F F T
F T F F F
```

7.
```
− (P + R)
F T T T
T F F T
T T F F
T F F F
```

9.
```
− (P ∨ Q)
F T T T
F F T T
F T T F
T F F F
```

11.
```
R ≡ (S ⊃ T)
T T T T T
F F T T T
T T F T T
F F F T T
T F T F F
F T T F F
T T F T F
F F F T F
```

Exercise 5.8C

1.
```
S ⊃ −R
T F FT
F T FT
T T TF
F T TF
```

3.
```
(−T + S) ⊃ (M ∨ C)
FT F T  T  T T T
TF T T  T  T T T
FT F F  T  T T T
TF F F  T  T T T
FT F T  T  F T T
TF T T  T  F T T
FT F F  T  F T T
TF F F  T  F T T
FT F T  T  T T F
TF T T  T  T T F
FT F F  T  T T F
TF F F  T  T T F
FT F T  T  F F F
TF T T  F  F F F
FT F F  T  F F F
TF F F  T  F F F
```

5.
```
I ⊃ L
T T T
F T T
T F F
F T F
```

7. L + (J ⊃ B)

```
T  [T]  T T T
F  [F]  T T T
T  [T]  F T T
F  [F]  F T T
T  [F]  T F F
F  [F]  T F F
T  [T]  F T F
F  [F]  F T F
```

9. − (S v G)

```
[F]  T T T
[F]  F T T
[F]  T T F
[T]  F F F
```

11. O ≡ (S + M)

```
T  [T]  T T T
F  [F]  T T T
T  [F]  F F T
F  [T]  F F T
T  [F]  T F F
F  [T]  T F F
T  [F]  F F F
F  [T]  F F F
```

13. (S v −S) + −(S + −S)

```
T  T  FT  [T]  TT  F  FT
F  T  TF  [T]  TF  F  TF
```

15. S ⊃ (−N + −W)

```
T  [F]  FT  F  FT
F  [T]  FT  F  FT
T  [F]  TF  F  FT
F  [T]  TF  F  FT
T  [F]  FT  F  TF
F  [T]  FT  F  TF
T  [T]  TF  T  TF
F  [T]  TF  T  TF
```

17. I ⊃ (L v D)

```
T  [T]  T T T
F  [T]  T T T
T  [T]  F T T
F  [T]  F T T
T  [T]  T T F
F  [T]  T T F
T  [F]  F F F
F  [T]  F F F
```

19. (R + M) v (−L ⊃ C)

```
T T T  [T]  FT T T
F F T  [T]  FT T T
T F F  [T]  FT T T
F F F  [T]  FT T T
T T T  [T]  TF T T
F F T  [T]  TF T T
T F F  [T]  TF T T
F F F  [T]  TF T T
T T T  [T]  FT T F
F F T  [T]  FT T F
T F F  [T]  FT T F
F F F  [T]  FT T F
T T T  [T]  TF F F
F F T  [F]  TF F F
T F F  [F]  TF F F
F F F  [F]  TF F F
```

21. −C + −P

```
FT  [F]  FT
TF  [F]  FT
FT  [F]  TF
TF  [T]  TF
```

23. − D v (M + E)

```
F T  [T]  T T T
T F  [T]  T T T
F T  [F]  F F T
T F  [T]  F F T
F T  [F]  T F F
T F  [T]  T F F
F T  [F]  F F F
T F  [T]  F F F
```

25.

```
[(P  v  T) +  V]  ⊃  (W  +  L)
 T  T  T  T  T   [T]  T  T  T
 F  T  T  T  T   [T]  T  T  T
 T  T  F  T  T   [T]  T  T  T
 F  F  F  F  T   [T]  T  T  T
 T  T  T  F  F   [T]  T  T  T
 F  T  T  F  F   [T]  T  T  T
 T  T  F  F  F   [T]  T  T  T
 F  F  F  F  F   [T]  T  T  T
 T  T  T  T  T   [F]  F  F  T
row 10
 F  T  T  T  T   [F]  F  F  T
 T  T  F  T  T   [F]  F  F  T
 F  F  F  F  T   [T]  F  F  T
 T  T  T  F  F   [T]  F  F  T
 F  T  T  F  F   [T]  F  F  T
 T  T  F  F  F   [T]  F  F  T
 F  F  F  F  F   [T]  F  F  T
```

```
[(P  v  T) +  V]  ⊃  (W  +  L)
 T  T  T  T  T   [F]  T  F  F
 F  T  T  T  T   [F]  T  F  F
 T  T  F  T  T   [F]  T  F  F
row 20
 F  F  F  F  T   [T]  T  F  F
 T  T  T  F  F   [T]  T  F  F
 F  T  T  F  F   [T]  T  F  F
 T  T  F  F  F   [T]  T  F  F
 F  F  F  F  F   [T]  T  F  F
 T  T  T  T  T   [F]  F  F  F
 F  T  T  T  T   [F]  F  F  F
 T  T  F  T  T   [F]  F  F  F
 F  F  F  F  T   [T]  F  F  F
 T  T  T  F  F   [T]  F  F  F
row 30
 F  T  T  F  F   [T]  F  F  F
 T  T  F  F  F   [T]  F  F  F
 F  F  F  F  F   [T]  F  F  F
```

Exercise 5.8D

1. It snows or it rains.

3. If the temperature is above freezing and there is precipitation, then it rains.

5. If it rains and the temperature is not above freezing, then the maintenance crews are salting the roads.

7. The maintenance crews are salting the roads or, if the temperature is above freezing, then classes must be canceled.

Chapter 6

Exercise 6.1

1.
```
K ⊃ D    -K  ∴  -D
T T T    FT      FT
F(T)T   (T)F    (F)T
T F F    FT      TF
F T F    TF      TF     Invalid
```

3.
```
- (G + E)    -E  ∴  G
F T T T      FT      T
T F F T      FT      F
T T F F      TF      T
(T)F F F    (T)F   (F)   Invalid
```

5.
```
C ⊃ (S v M)    -M  ∴  C ⊃ S
T T T T T      FT      T T T
F T T T T      FT      F T T
T T F T T      FT      T F F
F T F T T      FT      F T F
T T T T F      TF      T T T
F T T T F      TF      F T T
T F F F F      TF      T F F
F T F F F      TF      F T F    Valid
```

7.
```
S ⊃ [E v (D + H)]    -S  ∴  -E
T T T T T T T        FT      FT
F(T)T T T T T       (T)F    (F)T
T T F T T T T        FT      TF
F T F T T T T        TF      TF
T T T T F F T        FT      FT
F T T T F F T        TF      FT
T F F F F F T        FT      TF
F T F F F F T        TF      TF
T T T T T F F        FT      FT
F T T T T F F        TF      FT
T F F F T F F        FT      TF
F T F F T F F        TF      TF
T T T T F F F        FT      FT
F T T T F F F        TF      FT
T F F F F F F        FT      TF
F T F F F F F        TF      TF    Invalid
```

9.
```
M ⊃ P    P ⊃ S    -P  ∴  -M + -S
T T T    T T T    FT      FT F FT
F T T    T T T    FT      TF F FT
T F F    F T T    TF      FT F FT
F(T)F   F(T)T    (T)F     TF (F) FT
T T T    T F F    FT      FT F TF
F T T    T F F    FT      TF T TF
T F F    F T F    TF      FT F TF
F T F    F T F    TF      TF T TF    Invalid
```

11.

```
V ⊃ −M      − −M  ∴  −V
T F FT      TFT        FT
F T FT      TFT        TF
T T TF      FTF        FT
F T TF      FTF        TF      Valid
```

13.

```
L ⊃ M  ∴  −L ⊃ −M
T T T      FT T FT
F ⊤ T      TF Ⓕ FT
T F F      FT T TF
F T F      FT T TF      Invalid
```

15.

```
S ⊃ M      M ⊃ J  ∴  S ⊃ J
T T T      T T T      T T T
F T T      T T T      F T T
T F F      F T T      T T T
F T F      F T T      F T T
T T T      T F F      T F F
F T T      T F F      F T F
T F F      F T F      T F F
F T F      F T F      F T F      Valid
```

17.

```
P ⊃ C      −C  ∴  −P
T T T      FT       FT
F T T      FT       TF
T F F      TF       FT
F T F      TF       TF      Valid
```

19.

```
        (T + −U) ⊃ F      (T + L) ⊃ [G + (W + K)]      −K  ∴  −T v −L
        T F FT T T        T T T T T T T T T            FT      FT F FT
        F F FT T T        F F T T T T T T T            FT      TF T FT
        T T TF T T        T T T T T T T T T            FT      FT F FT
        F F TF T T        F F T T T T T T T            FT      TF T FT
        T F FT T F        T T T T T T T T T            FT      FT F FT
        F F FT T F        F F T T T T T T T            FT      TF T FT
        T T TF F F        T T T T T T T T T            FT      FT F FT
        F F TF T F        F F T T T T T T T            FT      TF T FT
        T F FT T T        T F F T T T T T T            FT      FT T TF
row 10  F F FT T T        F F F T T T T T T            FT      TF T TF
        T T TF T T        T F F T T T T T T            FT      FT T TF
        F F TF T T        F F F T T T T T T            FT      TF T TF
        T F FT T F        T F F T T T T T T            FT      FT T TF
        F F FT T F        F F F T T T T T T            FT      TF T TF
        T T TF F F        T F F T T T T T T            FT      FT T TF
        F F TF T F        F F F T T T T T T            FT      TF T TF
        T F FT T T        T T T F F F T T T            FT      FT F FT
        F F FT T T        F F T T F F T T T            FT      TF T FT
        T T TF T T        T T T F F T T T T            FT      FT F FT
row 20  F F TF T T        F F T T F F T T T            FT      TF T FT
        T F FT T F        T T T F F F T T T            FT      FT F FT
        F F FT T F        F F T T F F T T T            FT      TF T FT
        T T TF F F        T T T F F F T T T            FT      FT F FT
        F F TF T F        F F T T F F T T T            FT      TF T FT
        T F FT T T        T F F T F F T T T            FT      FT T TF
        F F FT T T        F F F T F F T T T            FT      TF T TF
        T T TF T T        T F F T F F T T T            FT      FT T TF
        F F TF T T        F F F T F F T T T            FT      TF T TF
        T F FT T T        T F F T F F T T T            FT      FT T TF
row 30  F F FT T F        F F F T F F T T T            FT      TF T TF
        T T TF F F        T F F T F F T T T            FT      FT T TF
        F F TF T F        F F F T F F T T T            FT      TF T TF
        T F FT T T        T T T F T F F F T            FT      FT F FT
        F F FT T T        F F T T T F F F T            FT      TF T FT
        T T TF T T        T T T F T F F F T            FT      FT F FT
        F F TF T T        F F T T T F F F T            FT      TF T FT
        T F FT T F        T T T F T F F F T            FT      FT F FT
        F F FT T F        F F T T T F F F T            FT      TF T FT
        T T TF F F        T T T F T F F F T            FT      FT F FT
```

```
row 40   F  F  TF  T  F      F  F  T  T  T  F  F  F  T      FT      TF  T  FT
         T  F  FT  T  T      T  F  F  T  T  F  F  F  T      FT      FT  T  TF
         F  F  FT  T  T      F  F  F  T  T  F  F  F  T      FT      TF  T  TF
         T  T  TF  T  T      T  F  F  T  T  F  F  F  T      FT      FT  T  TF
         F  F  TF  T  T      F  F  F  T  T  F  F  F  T      FT      TF  T  TF
         T  F  FT  T  F      T  F  F  T  T  F  F  F  T      FT      FT  T  TF
         F  F  FT  T  F      F  F  F  T  T  F  F  F  T      FT      TF  T  TF
         T  T  TF  F  F      T  F  F  T  T  F  F  F  T      FT      FT  T  TF
         F  F  TF  T  F      F  F  F  T  T  F  F  F  T      FT      TF  T  TF
         T  F  FT  T  T      T  T  T  F  F  F  F  F  T      FT      FT  F  FT
row 50   F  F  FT  T  T      F  F  T  T  F  F  F  F  T      FT      TF  T  FT
         T  T  TF  T  T      T  T  T  F  F  F  F  F  T      FT      FT  F  FT
         F  F  TF  T  T      F  F  T  T  F  F  F  F  T      FT      TF  T  FT
         T  F  FT  T  F      T  T  T  F  F  F  F  F  T      FT      FT  F  FT
         F  F  FT  T  F      F  F  T  T  F  F  F  F  T      FT      TF  T  FT
         T  T  TF  F  F      T  T  T  F  F  F  F  F  T      FT      FT  F  FT
         F  F  TF  T  F      F  F  T  T  F  F  F  F  T      FT      TF  T  FT
         T  F  FT  T  T      T  F  F  T  F  F  F  F  T      FT      FT  T  TF
         F  F  FT  T  T      F  F  F  T  F  F  F  F  T      FT      TF  T  TF
         T  T  TF  T  T      T  F  F  T  F  F  F  F  T      FT      FT  T  TF
row 60   F  F  TF  T  T      F  F  F  T  F  F  F  F  T      FT      TF  T  TF
         T  F  FT  T  F      T  F  F  T  F  F  F  F  T      FT      FT  T  TF
         F  F  FT  T  F      F  F  F  T  F  F  F  F  T      FT      TF  T  TF
         T  T  TF  F  F      T  F  F  T  F  F  F  F  T      FT      FT  T  TF
         F  F  TF  T  F      F  F  F  T  F  F  F  F  T      FT      TF  T  TF
         T  F  FT  T  T      T  T  T  F  T  F  T  F  F      TF      FT  F  FT
         F  F  FT  T  T      F  F  T  T  T  F  T  F  F      TF      TF  T  FT
         T  T  TF  T  T      T  T  T  F  T  F  T  F  F      TF      FT  F  FT
         F  F  TF  T  T      F  F  T  T  T  F  T  F  F      TF      TF  T  FT
         T  F  FT  T  F      T  T  T  F  T  F  T  F  F      TF      FT  F  FT
row 70   F  F  FT  T  F      F  F  T  T  T  F  T  F  F      TF      TF  T  FT
         T  T  TF  F  F      T  T  T  F  T  F  T  F  F      TF      FT  F  FT
         F  F  TF  T  F      F  F  T  T  T  F  T  F  F      TF      TF  T  FT
         T  F  FT  T  T      T  F  F  T  T  F  T  F  F      TF      FT  T  TF
         F  F  FT  T  T      F  F  F  T  T  F  T  F  F      TF      TF  T  TF
         T  T  TF  T  T      T  F  F  T  T  F  T  F  F      TF      FT  T  TF
         F  F  TF  T  T      F  F  F  T  T  F  T  F  F      TF      TF  T  TF
         T  F  FT  T  F      T  F  F  T  T  F  T  F  F      TF      FT  T  TF
         F  F  FT  T  F      F  F  F  T  T  F  T  F  F      TF      TF  T  TF
         T  T  TF  F  F      T  F  F  T  T  F  T  F  F      TF      FT  T  TF
row 80   F  F  TF  T  F      F  F  F  T  T  F  T  F  F      TF      TF  T  TF
         T  F  FT  T  T      T  T  T  F  F  F  T  F  F      TF      FT  F  FT
         F  F  FT  T  T      F  F  T  T  F  F  T  F  F      TF      TF  T  FT
         T  T  TF  T  T      T  T  T  F  F  F  T  F  F      TF      FT  F  FT
         F  F  TF  T  T      F  F  T  T  F  F  T  F  F      TF      TF  T  FT
         T  F  FT  T  F      T  T  T  F  F  F  T  F  F      TF      FT  F  FT
         F  F  FT  T  F      F  F  T  T  F  F  T  F  F      TF      TF  T  FT
         T  T  TF  F  F      T  T  T  F  F  F  T  F  F      TF      FT  F  FT
         F  F  TF  T  F      F  F  T  T  F  F  T  F  F      TF      TF  T  FT
         T  F  FT  T  T      T  F  F  T  F  F  T  F  F      TF      FT  T  TF
row 90   F  F  FT  T  T      F  F  F  T  F  F  T  F  F      TF      TF  T  TF
         T  T  TF  T  T      T  F  F  T  F  F  T  F  F      TF      FT  T  TF
         F  F  TF  T  T      F  F  F  T  F  F  T  F  F      TF      TF  T  TF
         T  F  FT  T  F      T  F  F  T  F  F  T  F  F      TF      FT  T  TF
         F  F  FT  T  F      F  F  F  T  F  F  T  F  F      TF      TF  T  TF
         T  T  TF  F  F      T  F  F  T  F  F  T  F  F      TF      FT  T  TF
         F  F  TF  T  F      F  F  F  T  T  F  F  F  F      TF      TF  T  TF
         T  F  FT  T  T      T  T  T  F  T  F  F  F  F      TF      FT  F  FT
         F  F  FT  T  T      F  F  T  T  T  F  F  F  F      TF      TF  T  FT
         T  T  TF  T  T      T  T  T  F  T  F  F  F  F      TF      FT  F  FT
```

row 100	F	F	TF	T	T		F	F	T	T	T	F	F	F	F	TF	TF	T	FT
	T	F	FT	T	F		T	T	T	F	T	F	F	F	F	TF	FT	F	FT
	F	F	FT	T	F		F	F	T	T	T	F	F	F	F	TF	TF	T	FT
	T	T	TF	F	F		T	T	T	F	T	F	F	F	F	TF	FT	F	FT
	F	F	TF	T	F		F	F	T	T	T	F	F	F	F	TF	TF	T	FT
	T	F	FT	T	T		T	F	F	T	T	F	F	F	F	TF	FT	T	TF
	F	F	FT	T	T		F	F	F	T	T	F	F	F	F	TF	TF	T	TF
	T	T	TF	T	T		T	F	F	T	T	F	F	F	F	TF	FT	T	TF
	F	F	TF	T	T		F	F	F	T	T	F	F	F	F	TF	TF	T	TF
	T	F	FT	T	F		T	F	F	T	T	F	F	F	F	TF	FT	T	TF
row 110	F	F	FT	T	F		F	F	F	T	T	F	F	F	F	TF	TF	T	TF
	T	T	TF	F	F		T	F	F	T	T	F	F	F	F	TF	FT	T	TF
	F	F	TF	T	F		F	F	F	T	T	F	F	F	F	TF	TF	T	TF
	T	F	FT	T	T		T	T	T	F	F	F	F	F	F	TF	FT	F	FT
	F	F	FT	T	T		F	F	T	T	F	F	F	F	F	TF	TF	T	FT
	T	T	TF	T	T		T	T	T	F	F	F	F	F	F	TF	FT	F	FT
	F	F	TF	T	T		F	F	T	T	F	F	F	F	F	TF	TF	T	FT
	T	F	FT	T	F		T	T	T	F	F	F	F	F	F	TF	FT	F	FT
	F	F	FT	T	F		F	F	T	T	F	F	F	F	F	TF	TF	T	FT
row 120	F	F	TF	T	F		F	F	T	T	F	F	F	F	F	TF	TF	T	FT
	T	F	FT	T	T		T	F	F	T	F	F	F	F	F	TF	FT	T	TF
	F	F	FT	T	T		F	F	F	T	F	F	F	F	F	TF	TF	T	TF
	T	T	TF	T	T		T	F	F	T	F	F	F	F	F	TF	FT	T	TF
	F	F	TF	T	T		F	F	F	T	F	F	F	F	F	TF	TF	T	TF
	T	F	FT	T	F		T	F	F	T	F	F	F	F	F	TF	FT	T	TF
	F	F	FT	T	F		F	F	F	T	F	F	F	F	F	TF	TF	T	TF
	T	T	TF	F	F		T	F	F	T	F	F	F	F	F	TF	FT	T	TF
row 128	F	F	TF	T	F		F	F	F	T	F	F	F	F	F	TF	TF	T	TF	Valid

21.

−	(A	v	B)	⊃	D		C	+	−D		∴	A	v	B	
F	T	T	T	T	T		T	F	FT			T	T	T	
F	F	T	T	T	T		T	F	FT			F	T	T	
F	T	T	F	T	T		T	F	FT			T	T	F	
T	F	F	F	T	T		T	F	FT			F	F	F	
F	T	T	T	T	F		T	T	TF			T	T	T	
F	F	T	T	T	F		T	T	TF			F	T	T	
F	T	T	F	T	F		T	T	TF			T	T	F	
T	F	F	F	F	F		T	T	TF			F	F	F	
F	T	T	T	T	T		F	F	FT			T	T	T	
F	F	T	T	T	T		F	F	FT			F	T	T	
F	T	T	F	T	T		F	F	FT			T	T	F	
T	F	F	F	T	T		F	F	FT			F	F	F	
F	T	T	T	T	F		F	F	TF			T	T	T	
F	F	T	T	T	F		F	F	TF			F	T	T	
F	T	T	F	T	F		F	F	TF			T	T	F	
T	F	F	F	F	F		F	F	TF		Valid	F	F	F	

23.

−	(P	+	Q)		P	∴	−Q	
F	T	T	T		T		FT	
T	F	F	T		F		FT	
T	T	F	F		T		TF	
T	F	F	F		F		TF	Valid

25.

T	⊃	W		−W	∴	−T	
T	T	T		FT		FT	
F	T	T		FT		TF	
T	F	F		TF		FT	
F	T	F		TF		TF	Valid

Exercise 6.2

1.
   T   F
W + S ∴ S ∨ M   Valid
| | | |
T Ⓣ   Ⓕ F

3.
    T   T   T   F
  G   H   N   −D   (H + C) ⊃ D ∴ N ⊃ −G
  | | | | | | | | |
  T   T   T   TF   T   F   F   T   FT
                            \   /
                            F
                        T   Invalid

5.
   T   Ⓣ   F
S ⊃ M   M ⊃ J ∴ S ⊃ J
| | | | | |
T   T   T   F   T   F   Valid
            \   /
             Ⓕ

7.
     T   T   T   F
(T + −U) ⊃ F   (T + L) ⊃ [G + (W + K)]   −K ∴ −T ∨ −L
| | | | | | | | | | | |
T   TF   T   T T   T   T T Ⓣ   TⒻ   FT FT
     \   /   \   /   \   /
       T   T   Valid   F

9.
  T   T   F
I ≡ (T + F)   F ∴ I
| | | | |
F   F   T   Invalid
| \ /
| F
\   /
 T

11.
  T   T   F
T ∨ O   T ⊃ O ∴ O ⊃ −T
| | | | | |
T   T   T   T   T   FT   Invalid

13.
   T   T   Ⓣ   F
M + N   −M ∨ L   −P ⊃ −L ∴ P + N
| | | | | | | |
T   T   FT T   TF   FT   F   T
                     \   /
                     Ⓕ   Valid

15.
  T   Ⓣ   T   F
P ⊃ Q   Q ⊃ (S ∨ F)   −S + −F ∴ −P
| | | | | | |
T   T   T   F   F   TF   TF   T
           \   \   /
                F
            Ⓕ   Valid

17.
    T   T   F
(E + F) + L   (F ∨ G) + −(F + G) ∴ −G
| | | | | | | | |
T   T   T   T   T   F T   T   T
                   \   /   \   /
                   Ⓕ   T   Valid

19.
       T   F
−(I + O) ∨ T ∴ I ⊃ T
  | | | | |
T T   F   F   T   F
  \ /
   F   Invalid

Exercise 6.3A

1. P ⊃ (P v Q)

P		P	v	Q
T	T	T	T	T
F	T	F	T	T
T	T	T	T	F
F	T	F	F	F

Tautology

3. −P + (P + Q)

FT	F	T	T	T
TF	F	F	F	T
FT	F	T	F	F
TF	F	F	F	F

Self-contradiction

5. (P ⊃ −Q) ≡ (P + Q)

T	F	FT	F	T	T	T
F	T	FT	F	F	F	T
T	T	TF	F	T	F	F
F	T	TF	F	F	F	F

Self-contradiction

7. (P v Q) v −Q

T	T	T	T	FT
F	T	T	T	FT
T	T	F	T	TF
F	F	F	T	TF

Tautology

Exercise 6.3B

1. P ⊃ Q   − (P + −Q)

T	T	T		T	T	F	FT
F	T	T		T	F	F	FT
T	F	F		F	T	T	TF
F	T	F		T	F	F	TF

Equivalences

3. − (P + −Q) v S   (−P v Q) v S

T	T	F	FT	T	T		FT	T	T	T	T	T
T	F	F	FT	T	T		TF	T	T	T	T	T
F	T	T	TF	T	T		FT	T	F	F	T	T
T	F	F	TF	T	T		TF	T	F	T	T	T
T	T	F	FT	T	F		FT	T	T	T	T	F
T	F	F	FT	T	F		TF	T	T	T	T	F
F	T	T	TF	F	F		FT	F	F	F	F	F
T	F	F	TF	T	F		TF	T	F	T	T	F

Equivalences

5. P ≡ Q   (P ⊃ Q) + (Q ⊃ P)

T	T	T		T	T	T	T	T	T	T
F	F	T		F	T	T	F	T	F	F
T	F	F		T	F	F	F	F	T	T
F	T	F		F	T	F	T	F	T	F

Equivalences

7. − (P + Q)   −P v −Q

F	T	T	T		FT	F	FT
T	F	F	T		TF	T	FT
T	T	F	F		FT	T	TF
T	F	F	F		TF	T	TF

Equivalences

9. −P ⊃ Q   P v Q

FT	T	T		T	T	T
TF	T	T		F	T	T
FT	T	F		T	T	F
TF	F	F		F	F	F

Equivalences

11. P ⊃ Q   Q ⊃ P

T	T	T		T	T	T
F	T	T		T	F	F
T	F	F		F	T	T
F	T	F		F	T	F

Neither

Chapter 7

Exercise 7.2A

1. Simplification

p	+	q	∴	p
T	T	T		T
F	F	T		F
T	F	F		T
F	F	F		F

p	+	q	∴	q
T	T	T		T
F	F	T		T
T	F	F		F
F	F	F		F

3. *Modus tollens*

p	⊃	q	−q	∴	−p
T	T	T	F T		F T
F	T	T	F T		T F
T	F	F	T F		F T
F	T	F	T F		T F

Exercise 7.2B

1. 1. F + G   premise / ∴ G
    2. G   1, Simp

5. 1. A ⊃ S   premise
    2. −S   premise / ∴ A
    3. −A   1, 2, MT

9. 1. K ∨ N   premise
    2. −K + O   premise / ∴ N
    3. −K   2, Simp
    4. N   1, 3, DS

3. 1. Z ∨ T   premise
    2. −T   premise / ∴ Z
    3. Z   1, 2, DS

7. 1. G ⊃ P   premise
    2. S + −P   premise / ∴ −G
    3. −P   2, Simp
    4. −G   1, 3, MT

Exercise 7.3A

1. Hypothetical syllogism

p	⊃	q	q	⊃	r	∴	p	⊃	r
T	T	T	T	T	T		T	T	T
F	T	T	T	T	T		F	T	T
T	F	F	F	T	T		T	T	T
F	T	F	F	T	T		F	T	T
T	T	T	T	F	F		T	F	F
F	T	T	T	F	F		F	T	F
T	F	F	F	T	F		T	F	F
F	T	F	F	T	F		F	T	F

3. Conjunction

p	q	∴	p	+	q
T	T		T	T	T
F	T		F	F	T
T	F		T	F	F
F	F		F	F	F

Exercise 7.3B

1. DS   **3.** MT   **5.** MP   **7.** MP   **9.** MT
11. Simp   **13.** DS   **15.** Simp   **17.** Con   **19.** DS
    Simp   MT   DS   MP   MP

Exercise 7.3C

1. 1. K ⊃ P   premise
    2. −P ∨ D   premise
    3. −D   premise / ∴ −K
    4. −P   2, 3, DS
    5. −K   1, 4, MT

3. 1. S ⊃ P   premise
    2. −P + −A   premise / ∴ −S
    3. −P   2, Simp
    4. −S   1, 3, MT

5. 1. H + −T   premise
    2. T ∨ (A + J)   premise / ∴ J
    3. −T   1, Simp
    4. A + J   2, 3, DS
    5. J   4, Simp

7. 1. [(A ∨ B) + C] ⊃ (T ∨ A)   premise
    2. −(T ∨ A)   premise / ∴ −[(A ∨ B) + C]
    3. −[(A ∨ B) + C]   1, 2, MT

9. 1. −L   premise
    2. −L ⊃ (T + A)   premise / ∴ T
    3. T + A   1, 2, MP
    4. T   3, Simp

11. 1. (R ∨ T) ⊃ (T ⊃ L)   premise
    2. (T ⊃ L) ⊃ S   premise / ∴ (R ∨ T) ⊃ S
    3. (R ∨ T) ⊃ S   1, 2, HS

13.
1. (S + A) ∨ (P + M)   premise
2. (S + A) ⊃ R   premise
3. −R   premise / ∴ P + M
4. −(S + A)   2, 3, MT
5. P + M   1, 4, DS

17.
1. T   premise
2. (T + R) ⊃ S   premise
3. R   premise / ∴ S
4. T + R   1, 3, Con
5. S   2, 4, MP

15.
1. (T ⊃ Q) + (S ⊃ P)   premise
2. T   premise / ∴ Q ∨ P
3. T ∨ S   2, Add
4. Q ∨ P   1, 3, CD

Exercise 7.4A

1.
1. A ⊃ B   premise / ∴ −A ∨ B
2. −A ∨ B   1, Impl

5.
1. −A   premise / ∴ A ⊃ B
2. −A ∨ B   1, Add
3. A ⊃ B   2, Impl

9.
1. P ∨ −Q   premise / ∴ −P ⊃ −Q
2. −−P ∨ −Q   1, DN
3. −P ⊃ −Q   2, Impl

13.
1. A ∨ C   premise / ∴ −A ⊃ C
2. −−A ∨ C   1, DN
3. −A ⊃ C   2, Impl

17.
1. −(R + S) ∨ T   premise / ∴ (R ⊃ −S) ∨ T
2. (−R ∨ −S) ∨ T   1, DeM
3. (R ⊃ −S) ∨ T   2, Impl

21.
1. A   premise
2. B   premise / ∴ A + (B ∨ C)
3. B ∨ C   2, Add
4. A + (B ∨ C)   1, 3, Con

3.
1. −E   premise / ∴ −(E + D)
2. −E ∨ −D   1, Add
3. −(E + D)   2, DeM

7.
1. −(A ∨ B)   premise / ∴ −B
2. −A + −B   1, DeM
3. −B   2, Simp

11.
1. −P ∨ (−R ∨ S)   premise / ∴ P ⊃ (R ⊃ S)
2. −P ∨ (R ⊃ S)   1, Impl
3. P ⊃ (R ⊃ S)   2, Impl

15.
1. −S ∨ −(R + P)   premise / ∴ S ⊃ −(R + P)
2. S ⊃ −(R + P)   1, Impl

19.
1. −(S + R)   premise / ∴ S ⊃ −R
2. −S ∨ −R   1, DeM
3. S ⊃ −R   2, Impl

23.
1. A ⊃ B   premise
2. S + A   premise / ∴ B + S
3. A   2, Simp
4. B   1, 3, MP
5. S   2, Simp
6. B + S   4, 5, Con

Exercise 7.4B

1.
1. −P ∨ Q   premise
2. (P ⊃ Q) ⊃ R   premise / ∴ R
3. P ⊃ Q   1, Impl
4. R   2, 3, MP

5.
1. (L + P) ⊃ Q   premise
2. −Q   premise / ∴ −L ∨ −P
3. −(L + P)   1, 2, MT
4. −L ∨ −P   3, DeM

3.
1. −P   premise
2. (P + R) ∨ S   premise / ∴ S
3. S ∨ (P + R)   2, Com
4. (S ∨ P) + (S ∨ R)   3, Dist
5. S ∨ P   4, Simp
6. S   1, 5, DS

7.
1. −(P + Q)   premise
2. Q   premise / ∴ −P
3. −P ∨ −Q   1, DeM
4. −−Q   2, DN
5. −P   3, 4, DS

9. 1. R ∨ (P + S) premise / ∴ R ∨ S
   2. (R ∨ P) + (R ∨ S) 1, Dist
   3. R ∨ S 2, Simp

13. 1. A ≡ −C premise
   2. −A premise / ∴ C
   3. (A ⊃ −C) + (−C ⊃ A) 1, Equiv
   4. −C ⊃ A 3, Simp
   5. − −C 2, 4, MT
   6. C 5, DN

17. 1. C ⊃ D premise
   2. D ⊃ G premise
   3. F ⊃ N premise
   4. C ∨ F premise / ∴ G ∨ N
   5. C ⊃ G 1, 2, HS
   6. (C ⊃ G) + (F ⊃ N) 3, 5, Con
   7. G ∨ N 4, 6, CD

11. 1. −(P ∨ T) premise / ∴ −T
   2. −P + −T 1, DeM
   3. −T 2, Simp

15. 1. −(A + B) premise
   2. B premise
   3. D ⊃ A premise / ∴ −D
   4. −A ∨ −B 1, DeM
   5. − −B 2, DN
   6. −A 4, 5, DS
   7. −D 3, 6, MT

19. 1. (A ⊃ B) + (C ⊃ D) premise
   2. A ∨ C premise
   3. D ⊃ −S premise
   4. A + S premise / ∴ F ⊃ B
   5. A ⊃ B 1, Simp
   6. A 4, Simp
   7. B 5, 6, MP
   8. B ∨ −F 7, Add
   9. −F ∨ B 8, Com
   10. F ⊃ B 9, Impl

21. 1. P ⊃ (A ⊃ B) premise
   2. D ∨ −B premise
   3. −D + A premise / ∴ −P
   4. −D 3, Simp
   5. −B 2, 4, DS
   6. A 3, Simp
   7. A + −B 5, 6, Con
   8. − −A + −B 7, DN
   9. −(−A ∨ B) 8, DeM
   10. −(A ⊃ B) 9, Impl
   11. −P 1, 10, MT

Exercise 7.4C

1. 1. J ⊃ (C ∨ N) premise
   2. P ⊃ J premise
   3. P + −C premise / ∴ N
   4. P 3, Simp
   5. J 2, 4, MP
   6. C ∨ N 1, 5, MP
   7. −C 3, Simp
   8. N 6, 7, DS

3. 1. C ⊃ L premise
   2. L ⊃ (−S + −M) premise
   3. −M ⊃ E premise
   4. −E premise / ∴ −C
   5. − −M 3, 4, MT
   6. M 5, DN
   7. S ∨ M 6, Add
   8. − −S ∨ − −M 7, DN
   9. −(−S + −M) 8, DeM
   10. −L 2, 9, MT
   11. −C 1, 10, MT

5.	1. $-F \supset S$	premise		7.	1. $(P + E) \supset (M + L)$	premise
	2. $-S$	premise			2. $(M + L) \supset T$	premise / $\therefore$ $-P \vee (E \supset T)$
	3. $F \supset (-G + -K)$	premise / $\therefore$ $-G$			3. $(P + E) \supset T$	1, 2, HS
	4. $--F$	1, 2, MT			4. $-(P + E) \vee T$	3, Impl
	5. F	4, DN			5. $-(P \vee -E) \vee T$	4, DeM
	6. $-G + -K$	3, 5, MP			6. $-P \vee (-E \vee T)$	5, Assoc
	7. $-G$	6, Simp			7. $-P \vee (E \supset T)$	6, Impl
9.	1. $(P \supset F) + P$	premise / $\therefore$ $--F$		11.	1. $(D \vee I) + -(D + I)$	premise
	2. P	1, Simp			2. D	premise / $\therefore$ $-I$
	3. $P \supset F$	1, Simp			3. $-(D + I)$	1, Simp
	4. F	2, 3, MP			4. $-D \vee -I$	3, DeM
	5. $--F$	4, DN			5. $--D$	2, DN
					6. $-I$	4, 5, DS
13.	1. $M \supset P$	premise		15.	1. I	premise
	2. $-P + -A$	premise / $\therefore$ $-M$			2. N	premise / $\therefore$ $I + (N \vee C)$
	3. $-P$	2, Simp			3. $N \vee C$	2, Add
	4. $-M$	1, 3, MT			4. $I + (N \vee C)$	1, 3, Con

Chapter 8

Exercise 8.2A

1. 1. *From a one-gallon jar filled with 1,000 variously colored gumballs, Teddy grabbed five handfuls for a total of 157.*
 2. *Sixty-three out of the 157 gumballs were red.*

 3. *Therefore, almost fifty percent of all the gumballs are red.*

 (a) *Sample: 157 gumballs*
 (b) *Population: jar of 1,000 colored gumballs*
 (c) *Target: color of gumballs*

3. 1. *Pat has been counseling families for ten years and has never yet seen a family that does not exhibit some form of dysfunction.*

 2. *No families are functional.*

 (a) *Sample: Pat's observations over ten years of counseling*
 (b) *Population: all families*
 (c) *Target: whether families are functional*

5. 1. *About one-third of freshmen nursing students have dropped out for the past three years.*

 2. *Thus, the nursing department can expect an attrition rate of about one-third of all freshmen nursing students each year.*

 (a) *Sample: three years of observations of nursing students in department*
 (b) *Population: all freshmen nursing students in this department each year*
 (c) *Target: attrition rate of nursing students*

7. 1. *A study of approximately 200 Canada geese migrating through New England last year showed that 6% had a virus that causes brain damage.*

 2. *Thus, probably 6% of the 300 thousand geese who migrate through New England suffer from that viral disease.*

 (a) *Sample: 200 Canada geese migrating in New England last year*
 (b) *Population: all geese traveling through New England*
 (c) *Target: presence of virus*

9. 1. *The U.S. Air Force Space Command uses radar to track roughly 8,000 pieces of garbage in space left by hundreds of satellites and rockets.*

2. *Thus, the actual amount of debris floating in our atmosphere is easily three times as much.*

(a) *Sample: radar observations of atmosphere*
(b) *Population: all debris in atmosphere*
(c) *Target: pieces of debris picked up by radar*

Exercise 8.2B

1. 1. *In 1991 a study of a nursery ward for newborns in Chicago showed that nurses followed appropriate hand-washing guidelines about half the time; doctors in the ward followed the guidelines half as frequently as that.*

2. *Probably, the effectiveness of antibiotics in U.S. hospitals has caused generations of hospital staff to rely on antibiotics rather than on hygiene.*

(a) *Sample: 1991 study in Chicago nursery ward*
(b) *Population: hospital staff in U.S. hospitals*
(c) *Target: hand-washing*
(d) *Representativeness: This is a ten-year-old study of one ward in one hospital. More sampling is needed.*
(e) *Inductive strength: Not inductively strong because the sample is biased.*

3. 1. *Don has skied the same terrain weekly for the past five ski seasons.*
2. *He always sees at least one person skiing with reckless abandon.*

3. *Thus, there are many people who have no regard for safety.*

(a) *Sample: Don's observations of the skiers for five ski seasons.*
(b) *Population: all skiers on these slopes.*
(c) *Target: reckless behavior of skiers*
(d) *Representativeness: The sample seems to provide good evidence when you consider that Don has been skiing these slopes for five years.*
(e) *Inductive strength: Seems to be a strong generalization.*

5. 1. *A study at a large teaching hospital involving 82 physicians and 75 patients found that there were 154 cases of resuscitation.*
2. *Only 19 percent of the patients were asked for their consent prior to resuscitation being administered.*

3. *Thus, the practice at most hospitals is to administer resuscitation without first discussing it with patients.*

(a) *Sample: a study of one large teaching hospital*
(b) *Population: presumably the generalization is made about all hospitals*
(c) *Target characteristic: patients having consented to resuscitation prior to its use*
(d) *Representativeness: One large teaching hospital is not representative of the variety of hospitals across the country. Most hospitals are not large and not teaching hospitals. It is true that teaching hospitals have a reputation for higher-quality care, better-informed staff, and better facilities than nonteaching hospitals. Thus, had the arguer provided such a premise, we might be led to conclude that the incidence of consultation prior to resuscitation is even lower at most hospitals.*
(e) *Inductive strength. The results reported in the study are disturbing, but they do not provide strong evidence for a generalization about the majority of hospitals. They do, however, inspire us to investigate further.*

7. 1. *Tim has done a nonscientific survey of a two-square-mile tract of woodlands near his home to estimate this coming spring's population of gypsy moth caterpillars.*
2. *Following the same path through the woods at approximately the same time of year, Tim counted the number of egg cases on tree trunks visible*

from the path. The first count totaled 1,090 egg cases; the second year's count totaled 650.

3. Tim concluded that there will be 40 percent fewer gypsy moth caterpillars feeding on the trees this coming spring because he observed 40 percent fewer egg cases.

(a) Sample: two observations of woodlands taken a year apart.
(b) Population: number of gypsy moth caterpillars in the woods.
(c) Target characteristic: egg cases on tree trunks.
(d) Representativeness: To be representative it must be assumed that gypsy moth egg cases are randomly distributed throughout the woods, not, for example, more or less likely to be on trees near the path. Given that reasonable assumption, we can say that the likelihood of egg cases being on trees near the path is the same as egg cases being on any tree within the woods. Thus, the sample is representative of what one would find nearly anywhere in the woods.
(e) The sample shows a significant decline in the number of observed egg cases; thus, strong evidence is provided for the conclusion.

9. 1. Macro Market Research of Burlington, Vermont, conducted a phone survey of 508 Vermonters representing 0.1 percent of the total state population of approximately 500,000 people.
2. Callers were selected through random-digit dialing.
3. The number of calls within each of the state's fourteen counties was proportional to the counties' population and distributed geographically according to population.
4. For governor the survey showed that 49 percent were likely to vote for Richard Snelling, 29 percent for Peter Welch, and 21 percent were undecided. The margin of error is plus or minus 4.5 percent with a confidence level of 95 percent.

5. Therefore, based on these statistics it is nearly certain that Snelling will be the state's next governor.

(a) Sample: phone survey of 508 Vermonters
(b) Population: approximately 250 thousand Vermonters
(c) Target characteristic: voter preferences in upcoming election
(d) Representativeness of sample: The sample is representative because it is a random selection of voters stratified proportionately by county reflecting one-tenth of one percent of the state population.
(e) Inductive strength: The generalization is inductively strong, particularly given the margin of error of plus or minus 4.5 percent.

11. 1. By randomly selecting names from the phone book, surveyors for Ace Phone Company asked people whether they owned an Ace phone.
2. Out of 450 calls, 14 percent owned an Ace phone, 36 percent did not know, 2 percent hung up, and 48 percent owned another brand.

3. Marketing researcher Victor Kay concluded that 14 percent of all area phone owners have an Ace and that Ace should print its name boldly across the front of each phone it produces. He is convinced, he argued, that a large percentage of those who "did not know" were Ace owners who couldn't find the label.

(a) Sample: 450 telephone owners
(b) Population: all area telephone owners
(c) Target characteristic: ownership of an Ace phone
(d) Representativeness of sample: The sample is randomly composed, but we do not know the size of the population; nevertheless, 450 respondents may be considered a reasonable sample size for an average city. Given that assumption, a random selection of respondents does provide each phone owner an equal chance of appearing in the survey.
(e) Victor's conclusion that 14 percent of all area phone owners own an Ace is strongly supported by the sample. However, Victor's conclusion that a large percentage of those who did not know their brand were indeed Ace owners is unsupportable. His attempt at optimism lacks evidence.

Exercise 8.3A

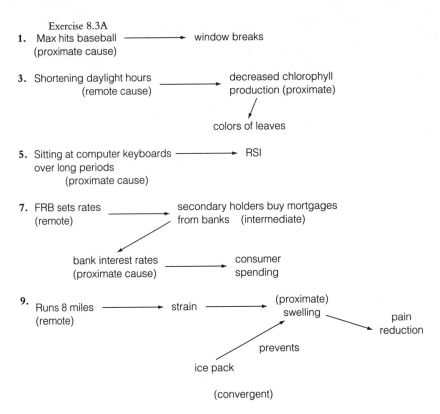

1. Max hits baseball ─────────→ window breaks
   (proximate cause)

3. Shortening daylight hours ─────────→ decreased chlorophyll
   (remote cause)   production (proximate)
                                              ╱
                                  colors of leaves

5. Sitting at computer keyboards ─────────→ RSI
   over long periods
        (proximate cause)

7. FRB sets rates ─────────→ secondary holders buy mortgages
   (remote)   from banks   (intermediate)
               ╱
   bank interest rates ─────────→ consumer
   (proximate cause)   spending

9.
   Runs 8 miles ─────────→ strain ─────────→ (proximate)
   (remote)   swelling ────→ pain
                                                              reduction
                                   ╱
                            prevents
            ice pack

            (convergent)

Exercise 8.3B

1. Max hitting the baseball as he did is a sufficient condition for the breaking of the window but not a necessary condition, since the window's breaking can occur without Max hitting the baseball.

3. If decreased production of chlorophyll occurs, then the leaves change color. Thus, decreased production of chlorophyll is a sufficient condition for color change. Conversely, if there is color change, then it must be that the leaves are producing less chlorophyll. Thus, decreased production is a necessary condition as well. Decreasing daylight seems to figure the following way: decreased daylight is a sufficient condition for decreased chlorophyll but not a necessary condition. Other factors might cause a tree to produce less chlorophyll. Thus, daylight is sufficient but not necessary for color change in leaves.

5. Sitting at a computer keyboard can produce but does not necessarily produce RSI. Furthermore, RSI may occur in the absence of long periods at the keyboard. Thus, prolonged sitting at a computer keyboard is neither a necessary nor a sufficient condition of RSI. Prolonged sitting is best described as a partial cause, a factor that increases the likelihood of RSI.

7. The causal claims are that if the FRB lowers interest rates for preferred customers, then secondary holders will buy mortgages. And if secondary holders buy mortgages, then banks will decrease interest rates on borrowing and, if so, then consumer spending increases. It is arguable that the antecedents in each conditional are causally sufficient conditions. That is, if the FRB lowers rates, then buying increases. However, since buying may increase for other reasons as well, lowering of interest rates is not a causally necessary condition.

9. Running eight miles is neither a necessary nor sufficient condition for strained tendons; others do it and are not injured. Nevertheless, the run and Evelyn's particular conditioning are jointly sufficient. The run itself is a partial cause. Packing her ankle in ice is causally sufficient for reducing swelling but not necessary, since swelling is reducible in other ways. Reducing swelling is sufficient for reducing the pain, but pain can be decreased without reducing swelling, by painkillers, for example. Thus, reducing swelling is not a necessary condition for reduction of the pain of swelling.

Exercise 8.3C

1. 1. *Improper cabin pressure in an airplane causes earache. (Causal statement)*
2. *Several passengers have complained of earache.*

3. *Thus, there is probably a problem with cabin pressure. (Causal explanation)*

5. 1. *The absorbent in disposable diapers draws moisture from the skin and reduces diaper rash. (Causal statement)*

2. *Therefore, if you are interested in protecting your infant from diaper rash, you'd be wise to use disposable diapers. (Causal prescription)*

9. 1. *Shaking a bottle filled with carbonated liquid releases the gas and increases the pressure inside the bottle. (Causal statement)*
2. *The soda bubbled out and all over when you opened it.*

3. *Therefore, you shook the bottle filled with carbonated liquid. (Missing conclusion) (Causal explanation)*

13. 1. *Shortly after the arrival of Cortez and his Conquistadores, smallpox spread like wildfire through the Indian population.*
2. *As smallpox was then prevalent in Europe, the Spaniards had probably developed immunity to it through early exposure, whereas the Indians, who had no racial experience with it, proved very susceptible.*
*3. *Exposure to smallpox, without having developed immunity, causes death. (Missing premise)(Causal statement)*

4. *By killing at least half the Indians and demoralizing them at a crucial time, the epidemic certainly played a part as important as Spanish arms and valor in bringing about the conquest of the South American continent. (Causal explanation)*

3. 1. *Whenever an orange female cat is mated with a black male, the resulting male kittens will be orange and the resulting female kittens will be tortoiseshell. (Causal statement)*
*2. *We are mating your black male and my orange female. (Missing premise)*

3. *Thus, they will probably produce no black kittens. (Causal prediction)*

7. 1. *The mammalian eye may exhibit two types of nerve receptors, cone-shaped receptors for color vision and rod-shaped receptors for low-intensity light.*
*2. *Color vision is caused by having cone-shaped receptors, and night vision is caused by having rod-shaped receptors. (Missing premise)(Causal statement)*
3. *Owls have only rods.*

4. *Therefore, owls can hardly see in daylight. (Causal explanation)*

1. *The mammalian eye may exhibit two types of nerve receptors, cone-shaped receptors for color vision and rod-shaped receptors for low-intensity light.*
*2. *Color vision is caused by having cone-shaped receptors, and night vision is caused by having rod-shaped receptors. (Missing premise)(Causal statement)*
3. *Hens have only cones.*

4. *Therefore, hens can hardly see at night. (Causal explanation)*

11. 1. *Measurable levels of stress are not correlated with complications in pregnancy.*

2. *Measurable levels of stress do not increase the likelihood of complications in pregnancy. (Causal statement)(Causal conclusion)*

15. 1. *Of 838 subjects, who had survived a previous heart attack and had cholesterol levels above 220, half modified their diets, some were given drugs, while the other half underwent a surgical procedure that reduced absorption of cholesterol.*
2. *In the surgery group, cholesterol levels dropped to an average of 96 compared with 241 in the control (nonsurgery) group.*
3. *Over a ten-year period the combined rate of second heart attacks or death from heart disease was 35 percent lower in the treated patients— and they required less than half as many cardiac operations as the controls.*

4. *Therefore, cholesterol does contribute to heart disease. (Causal statement)(Causal conclusion)*

Exercise 8.3D

1. **a.** The causal assertion is that the addition of white is what causes purple to change to lavender.
   b. The method of residue is employed. Smith believes that lavender is caused by the combination of red, blue, and white. He knows that red and blue make purple, so the remaining color, white, must account for the change of purple to lavender.

3. **a.** The causal assertion is that Bud's cat is the cause of her allergic reaction.
   b. The methods of agreement and difference are employed. By agreement she knows that her allergic reaction occurs whenever the cat is present; and by difference she knows that whenever the cat is not present, she does not have an allergic reaction. By these methods, she seems to have good evidence for her causal assertion.

5. **a.** The causal assertion is that turning the knob causes the music to change volume.
   b. The method of concomitant variation is employed. Kay-kay notices that loudness and softness vary proportionately to turning the knob one way or the other.

7. **a.** The causal assertion is that social interaction reduces the incidence of chronic ailment.
   b. The methods of agreement and difference are employed. By agreement, it is implied that jobs with a high degree of social interaction are correlated with reduced chronic ailment; whereas, by difference, jobs without a high degree of social interaction are correlated with no reduction in chronic ailment.

9. **a.** The causal assertion is that caffeine does not increase the risk of heart disease. There is also a suggestion, but not an assertion, that using decaffeinated products contributes slightly to heart disease.
   b. The methods of agreement and difference are employed. If caffeine increases the risk of heart disease, then by the method of agreement caffeine users should exhibit higher risk of heart disease, and by the method of difference, nonusers should show lower risk. However, a comparison between caffeine users and those who use neither caffeinated nor decaffeinated products showed no difference. In addition, the facts that slightly higher risk was present with users of decaffeinated products (agreement) and absent with nonusers (difference) suggest a possible causal relation between the use of decaffeinated products and heart disease.

11. **a.** The causal assertion is that the bumps in the road are causing the misfiring of the engine.
    b. The methods of agreement and difference are employed. By agreement, it is noticed that misfiring is present whenever there is a bump. By difference, it is noticed that whenever there is no bump, there is no misfiring.

13. **a.** The causal assertion is that seeing the movement of celestial objects across the sky causes birds to calibrate their innate sense of magnetic north.
    b. The study employs the methods of difference and concomitant variation. By concomitant variation, the study shows that whenever birds are shown a rotating disk of artificial stars—whether rotating on an axis at true north, east, south, or west—they calculated for what they believed would be south accordingly. On the other hand, by the method of difference, when birds were shown no disk of stars at all, there was no calculation, no adjustment, for south. They followed their innate sense of magnetic north.

15. **a.** The causal assertion is that heavy rains in West Africa are causally connected to hurricane patterns in the eastern U.S. On the basis of this and the fact that rainstorms are expected in Africa, Gray makes the prediction that there will be hurricanes on the east coast of the U.S.
    b. The study uses the methods of agreement and difference. By agreement, Gray reports, strong hurricanes are present when rain in the western Sahel region of Africa is plentiful. By difference, he reports, drought in the Sahel is correlated with fewer hurricanes on the east coast.

Exercise 8.4

1. Subject: the case of police officers using their revolvers in actual situations
   Analogue: the case of police officers using their revolvers in practice
   The argument is that, since using a revolver in practice is like using it in actual situations, if an officer does well in practice, he or she will do well in actual situations.
   Relevant analogy? Is target practice sufficiently similar to using a gun in actual situations to support the claim that officers who shoot well in practice will shoot well in actual situations? There are relevant similarities: Good marksmanship is essential for good performance in actual situations. Without it, an officer cannot be expected to shoot well. On the other hand, there are dissimilarities. Compare target practice with actual situations. There are likely to be differences in lighting and setting. There are psychological differences, for example, the element of surprise, an officer's anxiety and fear about killing and being killed, little or no information about the assailant(s), the officer's reaction to

seeing injury, and so on. The features likely in an actual situation—dissimilar to the practice setting—are likely to bear negatively on the officer's performance. Thus, there are relevant dissimilarities that weaken the analogy. This argument is inductively weak.

3. Subject: the universe
Analogue: organisms

The argument, a causal analogy, is that the universe is probably a product of natural processes because it is analogous to organisms in its organization of parts, and organisms are products of natural processes. In short, since the two things are similar in their organization, they are probably similar in their origin.

Relevant analogy? It does seem true that the universe is a highly organized system composed of dependent parts, working together, whose activities are irreversible. Are there dissimilarities between organisms and the universe? Organisms are living things; the universe is not a living thing. Most organisms generate through some form of sexual reproduction; the universe does not. Organisms die; the universe does not die because it is not an animate thing. There may be other differences as well but are these *relevant* dissimilarities? Do these differences bear negatively on the likelihood of a similar origin? The features possessed by the universe and not by organisms do not seem to bear negatively on whether the universe is also a product of natural processes. Thus, it seems reasonable to conclude that the analogy is inductively strong.

5. Subject: what Dad thinks is appropriate as a tie for the wedding
Analogue: what Dad thinks is pretty as a TV performer

The argument, an aesthetic analogy, reasons that Dad will like the tie because he liked Madonna on TV.

Relevant analogy? Both the TV program and the tie feature a picture of Madonna, and Dad thinks Madonna is pretty. That similarity is not relevant to what Dad thinks is pretty and appropriate for a tie at the wedding. Thus, the argument is inductively weak.

7. Subject: other people
Analogue: my own case

The argument is that, since people are like me and I feel pain when fire touches me, so when fire touches them, they feel pain, too.

Relevant analogy? Other people are like me in behavior and physiology. The dissimilarities between me and other people such as my particular body, personality, and locations in space and time do not seem to be relevant dissimilarities. Thus, the argument is arguably inductively strong.

9. Subject: cats
Analogue: humans

The argument is that cats do not see in color because they are like us in so many other ways, yet lack the nerve cells we know are required for color vision in humans.

Relevant analogy? The argument implies but does not assert that there are a number of physiologically relevant similarities. Most of the obvious dissimilarities between cats and humans are irrelevant to the issue of how the eyes work. But similarity in structure of the eye and brain is relevant. Thus, if their nervous system is, by assumption, like ours in many ways, yet unlike ours in the presence of cells responsible for color vision, then the analogy is inductively strong.

11. Subject: a football player's ability to tackle another player
Analogue: a football player's ability to tackle a tackling dummy

The argument is that, since the dummy is like a real player in inertia—size, weight, and shape offering resistance—a player who cannot hold onto the dummy probably cannot hold onto the real player.

Relevant analogy? The similarity in inertia between the dummy and the real player are relevant to predicting a player's ability to hold on. The typical dissimilarities between a tackling dummy—inanimate, faceless, no grasping hands—and a real player seem not to bear negatively on whether a player has the strength to hold on. Thus, the argument is inductively strong.

13. Subject: animals
Analogue: humans

The argument is that the similarity in basic nervous systems between animals and humans is a basis for concluding that animals feel pain as we do.

Relevant analogy? Our evidence about pain perception is that it is dependent on the nervous system. We have no evidence of pain perception in creatures lacking a nervous system. Thus, the similarity in nervous system between humans and animals is relevant. The dissimilarities between humans and all other animals—size, shape, appearance, and so on—probably do not bear negatively on the capacity to feel pain. Therefore, it is an inductively strong argument.

15. Subject: MacDonald's sweepstakes
Analogue: national clearinghouse sweepstakes
　　The argument is that since both sweepstakes are national games with prizes of one million dollars and the clearinghouse sweepstakes have a winning ratio of 1 in 70,000, probably so does the Mac-Donald's sweepstake.

　　Relevant analogy? The facts that the MacDonald's sweepstakes is like the other sweepstakes in having the same prize and being national do not make it more likely that the winning ratio is the same. Thus, from what we are given, the argument seems weak.

　　If, on the other hand, we were told that all national lotteries with large prizes must meet certain regulations, then we could expect winning ratios to be regulated, too. Can we assume that large games are constructed similarly? If so, that is background information that strengthens the argument.

Exercise 8.5A

1. Inductive Generalization
1. *A Price Waterhouse survey of randomly selected families that found that the average number of monthly trips to the mall has dropped from 3.7 in 1980 to 3.1 in 1998.*

2. *Thus, downtowns are winning the war against suburban malls.*

3. Causal prediction
1. *In 1900, the three top killers of Americans were all infectious diseases: pneumonia, tuberculosis, and "diarrhea, enteritis, and ulceration of the intestines."*

2. *By wiping out infectious diseases, medical science made an astounding contribution to human longevity.*

3. American Demographics *reports that a baby girl born in 1900 could be expected to live to age forty-nine; but a girl born in the year 2000 will probably live almost eighty years.*

4. *My children can expect, on average, to live half as long again as their grandparents.*

5. Causal explanation
1. *A six-year decline in murders by teenagers brought the 1999 homicide arrest rate for juveniles down 68 percent from its 1993 peak to the lowest level since 1966, the Justice Department reported.*

2. *Experts say the decline of crack cocaine and the violent gangs that peddled it, combined with big city police crackdowns on illegal guns and expanded after-school crime-prevention programs, have turned around the juvenile crime wave that pushed murder arrest rates for youths, age 10 to 17, up from 1987 to a peak in 1993.*

9. Deductively valid. *Modus tollens*
1. *If children are to develop into mature, healthy adults, then they should have consistent parental guidance.*
2. *But that is something that children do not have.*

3. *Therefore, they do not develop into mature, healthy adults.*

7. Inductive generalization
1. *The lifetime risk of depression (defined as the probability that a subject will suffer at least one episode lasting a year or more) ranged from 1.5 percent in Taiwan to 19 percent in Lebanon.*

2. *That data indicate that the risk of depression is much lower in Asia than in the Middle East.*

Exercise 8.5B

1. 1. *Ignorance causes fear.*
2. *Fear causes hatred.*
3. *Homophobia is fear and hatred of homosexuality.*
4. *Homophobia is most often caused by ignorance [lack of accurate information].*

5. *The problem of homophobia in the workplace is most effectively addressed through education.*

This is a *causal prescription:* Since ignorance causes homophobia and we want to reduce homophobia, we should address its cause, ignorance.

3. 1. *A 1990* Fortune *magazine survey of 799 of the largest U.S. industrial and service companies showed that only nineteen women—less than one-half of 1 percent—were listed among the more than 4,000 highest-paid officers and directors.*

2. *Therefore, in academe as in business, women earn less than men, are promoted more slowly, and work in less prestigious institutions. (Inductive generalization)*

5. 1. *In the last four years, 11 cases of a human form of transmissible spongiform encephalopathy, called Creutzfeldt–Jakob disease, have been diagnosed in rural western Kentucky, . . . "All of them were squirrel-brain eaters."*

2. *Within the small population of western Kentucky, the natural incidence of this disease should be one person getting it every 10 years or so. . . .*

3. *While the patients could have contracted the disease from eating beef and not squirrels, there has not been a single confirmed case of mad cow disease in the United States. . . .*

4. *Since every one of the 11 people with the disease ate squirrel brains, it seems prudent for people to avoid this practice until more is known. . . .*

Causal conclusion: Eating squirrel brains increases the risk of spongiform encephalopathy. The argument provides evidence of agreement—eating squirrel brains is a common factor in all eleven cases.

9. 1. *As every boat owner knows, equipping a boat with an engine that is twice as powerful as the original one will not make the boat go twice as fast.*

2. *In fact, if the engine tries to force the boat to go faster than its "hull speed," the craft may lower its nose and drive itself underwater.*

3. *Similarly, it is fallacious to think that if the efficiency of computers doubles (or rises a thousandfold) the whole set of industrial inputs should therefore become twice as efficient. (Argument by analogy)*

13. 1. *We want to protect our national interests.*
2. *Our current economic relationship with China is against our national interests.*

*3. Therefore, we want to remedy our economic relationship with China.
4. *Reducing the trade deficit with China will improve our economic relationship.*
*5. Increasing exports will reduce the trade deficit. The goal should be increasing American exports to China.

6. *Therefore, since we want to reduce the trade deficit, we should increase exports. (Deductively valid argument)*

7. 1. *Sexual encounters . . . have consequences that make them different from those other pursuits.*
2. *With other pursuits pleasure by itself is a sufficient justification.*

3. *With sex, pleasure is not a sufficient justification for sex. You can't just have sex because it feels good.*

4. *You need a good reason. That is, sex needs justification. (Deductively valid argument)*

11. 1. *Historically, job growth has been greatest in the occupations that new technology affects the least.*
2. *Technology tends to eliminate jobs. For example, we have become supremely efficient at growing food; that is why there are so few farmers.*
3. *In the Labor Department's list of "occupations with the largest job growth," the top five categories are cashiers, janitors and cleaners, salespeople, waiters and waitresses, and nurses.*
4. *The typical worker of the 21st century will be doing precisely the kinds of thing that you can't do over the Internet.*
*5. The economic trends of the future will be like those of the past.

*6. Therefore, it is not true that the jobs of the future will be related to the technologies of the future. . . , that we will become a society of telecommuting nerds. (Deductively valid argument)

15. 1. *Scientific knowledge is subject to revision pending new real-world evidence. Every week the* New York Times *comes out with news of some discovery that makes scientists rethink their theories. A recent* Newsweek *had a cover story about how the observations made with the Hubble telescope have forced astronomers to change their view of the universe.*
2. *Science is the opposite of faith: It is a perpetual "Show me!"*
3. *Religious belief, on the other hand, is not subject to such revision; it is not falsifiable by any real-world evidence. The existence of God cannot be disproved. Religious beliefs are "leakproof"—there's no evidence that will contradict them.*
*4. A belief system is not falsifiable.

5. *Science is not a belief system. (Deductively valid argument)*

Chapter 9

Exercise 9A

1. Appeal to force. The arguer threatens loss of job to win listeners' acceptance of the arguer's position, namely, that they should keep quiet about the funding.

3. *Ad hominem*, abusive. The argument is that since Tolstoy was unable to live as he preached, then his prescription is not worth our attention.

5. Appeal to pity. The argument is that feeling sorry for the speaker is a good reason for agreeing to go out with him.

7. Equivocation, between use and mention. The word 'love' is first used to refer to the phenomenon of love. Then it is "mentioned," that is, used to refer to the word 'love', which consists of four letters.

9. Hasty generalization. A three-day visit to Los Angeles does not provide a representative sample of the general aesthetic character of California.

11. Slippery slope. Studying philosophy, it is argued, ultimately leads by a series of steps to damnation. Becoming critical does not necessarily or even probably lead to giving up one's religion. Neither does atheism lead to immorality. Further, *some* would argue that a life of immorality does not result in damnation on the grounds that there is no such thing as damnation.

13. Red herring. Rather than addressing the issue of working conditions, the speaker diverts attention to the character of those employees who complain. The speaker, it can be said, also commits the fallacy of appeal to force.

15. Appeal to pity. It is argued that feeling sorry for the speaker is a good reason for accepting the paper late.

17. Appeal to authority. This is a fallacious appeal to authority because expertise in American literature does not make one an authority about matters of nuclear energy.

19. Appeal to force. The speaker offers a threat as a reason for accepting belief in Christ.

21. Equivocation. In the first occurrence, the word 'see' normally means "understand." In the second occurrence, the word 'see' refers to visual perception. To see what a person is saying is to understand what is said. Thus, the premise—we can see only what is visible—is not true. We can also see, in the first sense, what a person means.

23. Fallacy of composition. The argument employs the assumption that what is true of the parts (no team member can lift over 250 pounds) is true of the whole (the team cannot lift over 250 pounds). In this case we know that the lifting ability of one individual is not the same as the lifting ability of a group of individuals.

25. *Ad hominem, tu quoque*. The speaker defends his action by charging his opponent with having done the same action. In fact, the police officer's speeding is not the same kind of action as a citizen's speeding. Police officers are authorized to exceed speed limits when engaged in their duties. In such circumstances, police officers do not speed unlawfully.

27. Equivocation. The phrase "controlling his pupils" is ambiguous between controlling his students and controlling his eyeballs. A cross-eyed teacher can do the former while, perhaps, not being able to do the latter.

29. Not a fallacy. This is a legitimate appeal to authority.

31. Straw man. The arguer interprets the claims of Plato and Aristotle as meaning that all humans are rational and all humans are two-legged, respectively. The arguer claims, rightly, that neither universal statement is true and, thus, concludes that the two philosophers are wrong. However, Plato's and Aristotle's claims should not be interpreted as universal statements but rather as generalizations of the form "In general, all humans are . . ."

33. Equivocation. The phrase "making discriminations on the basis of color" is ambiguous between discriminating between colors and discriminating between people in terms of their color. The latter is racial discrimination; the former is not. The former is a legitimate part of art instruction.

35. Appeal to authority. The *National Enquirer* is not recognized as an authoritative publication regarding UFOs and extraterrestrials. Thus, this is a fallacious appeal to authority.

37. Appeal to the people. The arguer bases his disapproval of the son's actions on what he believes is commonly disapproved. The fact, if it is one, that people generally disapprove of living together is not a good reason for disapproving of the practice.

39. Equivocation. Here the phrase "we are all brothers" is ambiguous between meaning that we are all human and we are all siblings of the same parents. Only the latter meaning justifies a claim to part of the millionaire's money.

Exercise 9B

1. *Ad hominem,* abusive. The lawyer Swasey commits this fallacy by implying that, since Justice Stephen was committed as feeble-minded, his position on the importance of a speedy trial is not a good reason for denying the continuance. Justice Holmes should have replied that even the feeble-minded can say what is true.

3. Appeal to pity. The arguer attempts to win sympathy for the tobacco industry by claiming, first, that "the case against cigarette smoking has by no means been proven" and then describing a number of actions he calls "harassment."

5. Straw man. Schlafly interprets the pro-abortion position unfairly as seeking to protect the right to kill babies. She rejects this on the ground that women do not want to kill their babies. In that, she is correct. However, abortion proponents do not seek the right to kill babies; they seek the right to abortion. Abortion, proponents claim, is not the act of killing a baby.

7. Equivocation. The arguer is objecting to the claim that religion is not taught in the public schools. The arguer states that "secular humanism" is being taught in the schools and since, so he or she claims, that is a religion, it follows that religion *is* being taught in the schools. The word 'religion' is used in two different senses: (1) an organization centered around a body of beliefs involving some notion of the divine or supernatural as, for example, Christianity, Islam, or any of the world's major religions; and (2) a body of beliefs or theories that addresses major questions about human existence. The argument is as follows:

1. Secular humanism is being taught in the schools.
2. Secular humanism is a body of beliefs or theories that addresses major questions.
3. A body of beliefs or theories that addresses major questions is a religion.
4. Therefore, an organization centered around a body of beliefs involving some notion of the divine is being taught in the schools.

The laws that prohibit the endorsement of any particular religion in the public schools are aimed at religions in the proper sense, that is, (1) above. They are not aimed at the teaching of beliefs or theories that address major questions, no doubt in part because such beliefs or theories do not constitute religious views even in some stretched sense of the word as in (2) above.

9. *Ad hominem,* abusive; red herring. The writer objects to the statement by criticizing the character of the speaker, calling Farrakhan an evil and satanic man. The writer also diverts attention from Farrakhan's remark by reading into it more than is said. Although it is true that Farrakhan's remark—if accurately reported—is inflammatory, the proper response is to examine Farrakhan's reasons or, if none are given, to ignore it altogether. The issue is not advanced by attacking Farrakhan's character or attributing to him beliefs he has not expressed.

11. Begging the question; either/or fallacy. If the issue is whether corporal punishment of children is acceptable, the writer begs the question by characterizing it as abuse. The truth-functional interpretation of the writer's remark—we should take a stand against corporal punishment of our children or we will continue to abuse them—reveals reasoning that commits the either/or fallacy. If it is arguable that at least some form of corporal punishment of children is not abuse, then there is an alternative to either eliminating corporal punishment or abusing children.

13. There are a number of confusions in this letter. It is possible to find the following fallacies: Straw man. The author of this letter seems to agree with McGrory's conclusion that AIDS is not God's punishment for homosexuality but immediately goes on to characterize it as punishment, if not for homosexuality, then for disobedience to God or "an unclean, unbiblical lifestyle." The respondent seems to misunderstand McGrory's point. McGrory is not arguing about the kind of sin for which AIDS is a punishment but rather that AIDS is not a punishment at all. It is straw man to construe the issue as resting on whether homosexuality is the wrongdoing responsible for AIDS.

Inconsistency. It is inconsistent to maintain that God does not punish homosexuals and that AIDS is "what happens when a person puts his own interests and pleasures ahead of what God's will is" or because of "an unclean, unbiblical lifestyle." If (1) AIDS is "what happens" for an unbiblical lifestyle and (2) homosexuality is an unbiblical lifestyle, then (3) AIDS is a punishment for homosexuality. Is there part of this syllogism that the writer would reject? If the writer rejects (2), then the writer must explain how this is consistent with the remark that homosexuals bring AIDS upon themselves by an unbiblical lifestyle.

Inconsistency. Is it consistent to maintain that AIDS is what happens when a person disobeys God's will, that people bring it upon themselves by their unclean, unbiblical lifestyle, and that nonhomosexuals who have AIDS "pay the price for the reckless behavior of a few"? To be consistent, the writer must say that some people with AIDS bring it upon themselves and some with AIDS do not. But, of course, McGrory's point is precisely that AIDS is not a punishment because it afflicts even those who have not sinned. Had the writer followed the logic of that point, he or she would not characterize AIDS as resulting from disobedience to God.

15. Red herring. The arguer does not respond directly to the issue of the seat belt law but digresses into issues that distract the readers with the hope of winning their support.

17. Begging the question. It begs the question—is abortion morally permissible?—to describe it as murder, for, in part, the moral question is precisely whether it is or is not something akin to murder.

19. Either/or fallacy. The arguer ignores the arguably legitimate complaints about conditions in the county jail by falsely characterizing the issue as having only two alternatives: (1) poor conditions or (2) extravagant conditions. There is clearly a middle ground between such extremes. Thus, the argument does not successfully rebut the complaints about jail conditions.

21. Begging the question. Rather than asking respondents how they would characterize television programming, the survey presents choices that no reasonable person would accept. Who favors obnoxious, gratuitously violent, pornographic programming? Another possible analysis is the either/or fallacy.

23. Either/or fallacy. The arguer presents only two alternatives: Kill the suspect or "let this criminal be released after a prison term—to kill again." The latter is clearly unacceptable; therefore, the arguer concludes that it is justified to kill the suspect. The arguer overlooks other outcomes such as life imprisonment or rehabilitation.

25. Inconsistency. Younger argues that life imprisonment without the possibility of parole is not an acceptable alternative to capital punishment because, he says, there must always be "a safety valve," the right of the governor to commute a sentence. However, by the same reasoning capital punishment should be unacceptable since by putting a person to death we eliminate the "safety valve," making it impossible for the governor to exercise the right to commute a sentence. Thus, Younger implies that (1) the option to commute must always exist, yet by endorsing capital punishment he implies that (2) the option to commute need not always exist.

27. Equivocation. Cavett's humorous retort rests on taking the phrase "adjusting to homosexuality" equivocally. In the question he asks Liddy he would seem to be asking "Did you find it hard to adjust to the presence of homosexuality where you were?" Cavett construes Liddy's answer to be to a different question: "Did you find it hard to adjust to being a homosexual in prison?"

29. Straw man; false analogy. The argument is that regulation of smoking is unacceptable because, to be consistent, we must then regulate and, perhaps, prohibit all other potential health hazards, too: cough syrup, pecan pies, footballs, aspirin, automobiles, sunbathing, and so on. This argument misrepresents the requirements of consistency. Consistency does not require proponents of smoking regulation to endorse regulating all possible health hazards no matter how remotely hazardous. It requires only that they endorse regulating similarly hazardous products. This misrepresentation suggests the fallacy of straw man but it also suggests false analogy—namely, the disanalogy between the harmful effects of smoking and such things as playing football, driving a car, sunbathing, etc.

31. Inconsistency. The writer's position on abortion is inconsistent. One cannot say, on the one hand, that abortion is wrong and, on the other, that women have a right to choose abortion. If one believes an act is wrong, then one believes no one has a right to do it, and the obverse.

33. Straw man. It is a misrepresentation of the pope's position against abortion and his position regarding procreation to claim that Catholic women are "urged to produce as many children as possible." It is on the basis of that misrepresentation that the arguer characterizes the Catholic Church as a menace. The arguer further misrepresents the church's position when he or she claims that it is contrary to the tenets of Christianity to love our fellow human beings and to follow Christ.

35. False cause. The writer claims that the increase in mergers is causing the decline in quality production in the U.S. This oversimplifies matters greatly, as though if mergers ceased, the U.S. would produce quality goods at a reasonable price. The writer has identified, at best, only one factor responsible for the current quality of production.

37. The writer is accusing the editor of the *Economist* of inconsistency.

39. Schneider is being accused of the fallacy of false analogy.

41. This is an analogical argument, and a false analogy, it can be argued. Limbaugh argues that just as the crooks duped people out of their money, so the government does the same. The analogy can be disputed in virtue of the facts that (1) at least the government's intention is to serve the common good—no crook ever pretends to do so; and (2) the people have recourse—they may change the very laws that put claims on their money. There is no formal mechanism for negotiating the conduct of crooks.

43. False analogy. The writer argues against an ethical concern for the treatment of animals on the ground that they, the animals, have no such concern for their victims. If they don't care about killing other animals, why should we? Of course, there is a very good reason why the cases are not analogous: We are capable of deliberating and directing our action; animals are not. For that reason, we should not take our lead from their behavior.

45. The implication is that eating animals is permissible because they are made out of meat. If they weren't, then an argument for vegetarianism could be made, this writer implies. Apparently, anything edible is fair game for the human menu, including other humans! In a defense of carnivorism, this writer's argument begs the question. If the question is whether there are any good reasons why animals can be eaten, then to offer that they are made of meat is circular reasoning; the very issue is whether to eat meat.

Exercise 9C

Students complete the argument given by committing the fallacy requested.

Chapter 10

Exercise 10.3

1. *1. A coach cannot run the draft, make personnel decisions, draw up the game plan, dissect the salary cap, manage free agency, baby-sit the players, and choose between lasagna or turkey sandwiches for the team lunch all by himself.*

   2. Those who oppose the idea of the all-powerful coach claim that no one man can oversee everything.

5. *1. Economists across the political spectrum agree: Turning a nonunion job into a union job very likely will have a bigger effect on lifetime finances than all the advice employees will ever read about investing their 401(k) plans, buying a home, or otherwise making more of what they earn.*

   2. Over all, union workers are paid about 20 percent more than nonunion workers, and their fringe benefits are typically worth two to four times as much. . . .

   3. From a pocketbook perspective, workers are absolutely better off joining a union.

3. *1. Scientific knowledge is subject to revision pending new real-world evidence.*

   2. Science is the opposite of faith: It is a perpetual "Show me!"

   3. Religious belief, on the other hand, is not subject to such revision; it is not falsifiable by any real-world evidence.

   4. Religious beliefs are "leakproof"—there's no evidence that will contradict them.

   5. Science is not a belief system or religion.

7. *1. Natural predators have to live with their resource.*

   2. Natural predators cannot afford to exterminate their resource.

   3. They tend to range widely, exploiting one or more ecological niches, cropping individuals of abundant prey species.

   4. The domestic dog and cat have become politicized by long association with man.

   5. The instinct to kill and the territorial imperative, though largely irrelevant, have been retained and confused.

   6. Consequently, predatory pets tend to hunt the limited territory described on their owners' deeds; and the results, if the pet is a skilled killer, can be disastrous for the area's wildlife.

   7. Domestic dogs and cats are not natural predators.

9. 1. *Personality traits, abilities, values, motivations, roles, dreams, and desires: All vary across culture and history, and depend on time and place, context and situation.*
2. *The differences you may see between men and women at a particular time in history tell us nothing about what women and men are in some unvarying sense— or about what they can be.*

3. *There is nothing* essential—*that is, universal and unvarying—in the natures of women and men.*

13. 1. *Historically, it is not true that job growth tends to be greatest in the areas most changed by technology.*
2. *Rather, job growth tends to be greatest in the occupations that new technology affects the least.*
3. *In the Labor Department's list of "occupations with the largest job growth," the top five categories are cashiers, janitors and cleaners, salespeople, waiters and waitresses, and nurses.*
4. *All of these jobs involve "being there"—having face-to-face contact with the consumer. . . .*

5. *The typical worker of the 21st century will be doing precisely the kinds of thing that you can't do over the Internet.*

6. *The common assumption that the jobs of the future will be related to the technologies of the future is not true.*

11. 1. *Creationists believe in the literal word of Genesis, and if that's true, everything goes.*
2. *If the Earth really is 10,000 years old, then all astronomy is wrong, and all of cosmology is wrong, because the astronomers tell us that most of the stars are so far away that their light takes longer than 10,000 years to reach us, therefore, there's something wrong if the universe is only 10,000 years old.*
3. *All of physics and atomic theory goes, because if radioactive dating consistently gives these ancient ages for old rocks then, as it's based on the fundamental behavior of atoms, there's something wrong with that knowledge of atomic structure, if it's all a delusion and the Earth is only 10,000 years old.*

4. *So Creationism is an attack on all of science; it's an attack on all of knowledge . . . not just my narrow little field.*

15. 1. *The most basic task of science is to catalogue and describe the universe around us.*
2. *If as much as 99 percent of the universe is unseen and hidden, as recent evidence suggests, then we have barely begun to document its contents.*

3. *Therefore, we should care about dark matter.*

1. *Evidence suggests that the missing mass is intrinsically different from everyday matter.*
2. *Our understanding of the universe and its origin may be woefully biased and incomplete until we account for dark matter.*

3. *Therefore, we should care about dark matter.*

1. *The amount of missing mass is closely tied to the ultimate fate of the universe—whether cosmologists expect it to expand forever or eventually collapse into itself.*
2. *The missing mass problem thus lies at the heart of our most fundamental attempts to understand the past, present, and future state of the cosmos.*

3. *Therefore, we should care about dark matter.*

17. 1. The sadness that a loss brings has certain invariable effects: it closes down our interest in diversions and pleasures, fixes attention on what
has been lost, and saps our energy for starting
new endeavors—at least for the time being. In
short, it enforces a kind of reflective retreat from
life's busy pursuits, and leaves us in a suspended state to mourn the loss, mull over its
meaning, and finally, make the psychological
adjustments and new plans that will allow our
lives to continue.
2. Melancholy, like every other mood, has its
benefits.
3. Not all sadness should be escaped. . . .

19. 1. If quitting smoking were easy, all rational
smokers would do it.
2. You may die tomorrow in an automobile
accident. . . .
3. Living is difficult and smoking is one of your
few pleasures.
4. Cigarettes are relatively inexpensive.
5. Smoking is a good way to handle stress.
6. Smoking goes well with other important pleasures such as eating and drinking.
7. There is no good reason why you should deny
yourself the pleasure of smoking.
8. You should not bother to quit smoking.
9. If smokers were really free to smoke or not,
then they would exercise this freedom.
10. Smokers do not exercise the freedom not to
smoke.
11. There is no evidence that smokers are free to
choose whether to smoke.
12. We human beings have a great capacity for rationalizing, for creating conceptual illusions
that screen us from reality.
13. A smoker is not someone who is free to choose;
a smoker must choose to smoke.
14. A cigarette smoker is a slave to tobacco.
15. Slavery is an evil.
16. It is better to control your own life than to let a
plant control it.
17. It is better to be free from the slavery of tobacco
addiction than to be a slave to it.
18. The chief reason has nothing at all to do with
health or with pleasure: it has to do with being
out of control.

Exercise 10.4
1. 1. According to statistics reported in Harper's
Magazine, the percentage of first-year medical
students who believe a knowledge of nutrition is
important to their career is 74.
2. On the other hand, the percentage of third-year
medical students who believe this drops to 13.
3. Somewhere between the first and the third year
of medical school, students get the idea that
knowledge of their patients' diets is not
important.
4. Yet, the fact is that over 80 percent of illnesses
is caused by things people put in their mouths.
*5. Therefore, knowledge of nutrition is important
knowledge and medical students are being
taught to ignore it.

3. 1. One of the best ways to make consistently good
decisions is to try deliberately to make decisions
that you will not later regret.
2. Nothing is more regrettable than wasted
potential.
*3. Formal education enables one to make consis-
tently good decisions.
4. Furthermore, persons with more formal education are quite likely to make much more money
over the course of their lives than persons with
less formal education.
5. Everyone should get as much formal education
as possible.

5. 1. *Nonhuman animals are not capable of consider-ing the alternatives open to them or of reflecting on the ethics of their diet.*

*2. *Animals can be held responsible for what they do only if they are capable of considering the al-ternatives open to them or of reflecting on the ethics of their actions.*

3. *Hence, it is impossible to hold the animals re-sponsible for what they do, or to judge that be-cause of their killing they "deserve" to be treated in a similar way.*

9. 1. *To write a successful book on the possibilities of extraterrestrial life would require good knowl-edge in many widely separated fields, such as biology; organic and inorganic chemistry; physics concerning atmosphere, oceans, and surfaces of other planets; and astronomy.*
2. *Such a man does not exist.*

*3. *Therefore, there is no one able to write a suc-cessful book on the possibilities of extraterres-trial life.*
4. *Life is the most interesting thing in the entire universe. . . .*

5. *It is "a crying shame" that no one is suffi-ciently knowledgeable about life.*
6. *Life "deserves better treatment."*

13.*1. *If bodies were not composed of atoms, then they would not have spaces between atoms that could be compressed.*

*2. *If bodies did not have spaces that could be com-pressed, then they would not be capable of hav-ing their dimensions reduced by pressure or per-cussion without diminishing their mass.*

3. *All known bodies are capable of having their dimensions reduced by pressure or percussion without diminishing their mass.*

4. *All bodies are composed of atoms, the spaces between which may be diminished.*

7. 1. *No one knows whether death may not be the greatest good that can happen to us.*
2. *But men fear death as if they knew quite well that it was the greatest of evils.*

*3. *To fear something one does not know is to think oneself wise without really being wise.*

4. *To fear death is to think oneself wise without really being wise.*

11.*1. *If we substitute a woman's name for 'Socrates' in the famous syllogism—All men are mor-tal; Socrates is a man; therefore, Socrates is mortal—we either get a false premise, 'Alice is a man', or we get a conclusion that does not follow, 'Alice is mortal'.*

2. *Alice, being female, is in a category that is nei-ther masculine nor mortal. . . .*

*3. *The famous syllogism—All men are mortal; Socrates is a man; therefore, Socrates is mortal—works for males but not for females.*

4. *In philosophy, the centrality in thought and language of the universal male affects the ability to reason about humanity.*

15.*1. *A conservation system based wholly on eco-nomic motives recognizes only economic value.*
2. *Most members of the biotic community have no economic value.*
3. *Yet, most members of the biotic community are important to its stability.*

*4. *Therefore, a conservation system based wholly on economic motives does not recognize the value of most members of the biotic community.*
5. *Therefore, there is a basic weakness in a conser-vation system based wholly on economic motives.*

Exercise 10.5A

1. Empirical   **3.** Nonempirical   **5.** Empirical   **7.** Nonempirical   **9.** Nonempirical
11. Nonempirical   **13.** Nonempirical   **15.** Nonempirical   **17.** Nonempirical
19. Nonempirical

Exercise 10.5B

1. Nonempirical   **3.** Empirical   **5.** Nonempirical   **7.** Empirical   **9.** Empirical
11. Nonempirical   **13.** Nonempirical   **15.** Nonempirical   **17.** Empirical   **19.** Empiri-cal   **21.** Nonempirical   **23.** Empirical   **25.** Nonempirical

Exercise 10.6

1. ① Of course, human nature is fundamentally good! Why am I so sure of this? That is what I want to tell you. ② The proposition "Human nature is fundamentally good" is a logical consequence of two other propositions, both of which are as self-evident to me as any axioms, but either or both of which the reader is, of course, free to reject.

③ The first of my two axioms is that *I* am fundamentally good. This to me is so utterly obvious!④ By "fundamentally" good, I mean, of course, that I was born good. I say this because ⑤ I distinctly remember coming into the world in complete good faith, loving and trusting everybody, with good will to all and malice towards none. ⑥ I only developed hostilities, hatreds, pettinesses, envies, jealousies, etc. as a result of having been mistreated and distrusted. ⑦ Now, I haven't been all that badly treated, and that's why I'm not half bad as I now stand. ⑧ But whatever badness I have, 'tis nothing more nor less than a reaction to the badness I have experienced. ⑨ I did not bring this badness into the world when I arrived! Of this I am certain. Thus, my first axiom is unequivocably, "I am fundamentally good."

⑩ My second axiom is that it is obvious that I am no better than anyone else! Fundamentally better, I mean. ⑪ Of course, I sometimes act better than other people and sometimes worse. ⑫ But it is inconceivable to me that human natures can be so radically different that some are good and others are bad at birth! No, that is ridiculous! ⑬ So, if I am fundamentally good, then everyone is fundamentally good. ⑭ And since I *am* fundamentally good, then *everyone* is fundamentally good.

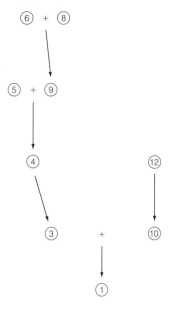

There appear to be two weaknesses in the argument. One concerns premise ⑫. Some people would argue that it is empirically false that all children are born predisposed to be good. If there is any truth to claims that there are genetic predispositions toward character, then there is no more reason to suppose that children are born good than bad. Thus, premise ⑫ is dubious. A second line of criticism is the following. Once we understand that by "fundamentally good" the author simply means "born good," this argument loses its appeal. The conclusion turns out to be rather trivial. It argues that human beings are born good. It does not claim that they are good at heart or inherently good. For all it shows, many humans lose whatever goodness they had as children and become mean people. In other words, "everyone is fundamentally good" equivocates between "everyone is inherently good" and "everyone is born good." The latter is the argument's real conclusion, and not an impressive one. What do you think?

3. In his essay "Why War Is Ignoble," Morland argues that many people romanticize war as a test of manhood, but this is no justification for war. First, war is not an ennobling experience; rather than bringing out the best in people, it brings out the worst. Second, the only legitimate justification for going to war is in defense of international law or homeland. Thus, he concludes, no American should ever be required to kill or die simply as a test of manhood. His argument is as follows:

11. *As I airlifted them from the battlefield, soldiers told me stories of killing, maiming, brutality, and shame.* ⑪–⑰
19. *The dead boys in the boxes on the airplane were testament to the truth.* ⑱–⑲
30. *As Mark Twain writes "only dead men can tell the truth in this world" and the truth is that war is horrible.* ㉖–㉚
35. *War brings out the worst in people, not the best.*

47. *War is too brutal to be used as a rite of passage.*
46. *For lethal force to have any legitimate role, we must strictly and dispassionately confine it to legitimate questions about international law and homeland defense.*
*46a. *War as a rite of passage is a defense of neither homeland nor international law.*
*46b. *War is not justified as a rite of passage.*

44. *No American should ever be required to kill or die simply as a test of manhood—particularly if that test involves some politicians' perception of manhood.*

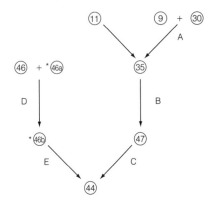

As the diagram shows, there are two lines of argument in support of the conclusion. Let's consider first that line of argument to the effect that war is too brutal to be used as a rite of passage.

Argument A: Given ⑪ and given ⑲ and ㉚, therefore ㉟, inductively strong inference. Premises ⑪, ⑲, and ㉚ provide anecdotal evidence for the claim that war brings out the worst, not the best, in people. The arguments are best construed as inductive generalizations reasoning that these anecdotes represent typical experiences for soldiers. Assuming that the people Morland talked with are representative of typical soldiers and their combat experiences, then it follows with a reasonable degree of probability that most soldiers are worse off for the experience of war. Premise ⑪, a summation of the stories Morland heard, is acceptable on basis of authority. Premises ⑲ and ㉚ might best be rewritten as asserting that the dead are evidence of the horrible deeds of war. Some might argue that the dead are not merely that but are evidence as well of the brave deeds of war. That may be true, but it is not a denial of the statement. Thus, it is an acceptable premise. Argument A is a good argument.

Argument B: Given ㉟, therefore ㊼, the conclusion does not follow deductively. The argument needs the addition of a premise such as 'A rite of passage is good for people'. Then if war brings out the worst in people and a rite of passage is good for people, then war is not suitable as a rite of passage. Given that additional premise, ㊼ follows deductively. Premise ㉟ is acceptable as supported by good argument.

Argument C: Given ㊼, therefore ㊹, deductively valid inference. If war is too brutal to be used as a rite of passage, then it follows that we should not require Americans to go to war as a rite testing their manhood. Premise ㊼ is acceptable as supported by good argument. Argument C is a good argument.

Argument D: Given ㊻ and ⸢46a⸣, therefore ⸢46b⸣, deductively valid inference. If war is justifiable only in circumstances of international law or self-defense and war as a rite of passage is neither a defense of homeland nor international law, then it must follow that war as a rite of passage is not justified. Premise ㊻ is a nonempirical claim that is not provided support within the argument and is highly controversial. Many would accept this premise for reasons they would need to provide. Others claim that some circumstances other than international law or self-defense justify going to war. In the context of this argument, this premise cannot be accepted without support. Premise ⸢46a⸣ is clearly acceptable. Argument D as written is not a good argument. However, in defense of the conclusion, one might argue that ⸢46b⸣ is true because the harm done to others by war greatly outweighs the good that may come from a rite of passage.

Argument E: Given ⑭₆ᵦ, therefore ㊹, deductively valid inference. Given that war is not justified as a rite of passage, then it follows deductively that no American should be required to go to war as a rite testing manhood. Premise ⑭₆ᵦ is acceptable as a premise that might be supported by the argument described above. Argument E is good. Morland's argument is good.

5. Patrick Macdonald, a law student at Aberdeen University, has been granted legal aid to sue his mother for the living expenses required to complete his degree. Others are already following his example.

① That a son should sue his mother . . . is more than just an offence to filial piety, it is a grotesque misuse of the legal system. ② Mr. Macdonald is within his rights under the Scottish Family Law Act of 1985 but that does not make his actions right. ③ He protests that he has to go to law because he does not wish to go into debt. ④ A proper horror of indebtedness is a decent Scots prejudice, but when it leads a man to use the blunt instrument of a writ to bludgeon money from his mother it becomes not proper prudence but ugly selfishness.

⑥ Parents, if they can, may wish to support their children at university. ⑦ Those who have the resources to do so, and choose not to, should certainly be thought the less of. ⑧ Affection should not diminish with the end of adolescence. ⑨ But enforced responsibility should. ⑩ Parents should not be expected in law to indulge their adult offspring any more than grown-up children should be forced in law to turn up for Christmas lunch.

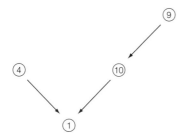

The conclusion ① is a universal statement asserting that all lawsuits brought against mothers by their sons are unethical and misuses of the legal system. It is supported, on the one hand, by premise ④ stating that it is "ugly selfishness" to sue one's mother out of fear of debt. While ④ is nonempirically acceptable, it does not seem to be sufficient evidence for the generalization in ①. Suing Mom to avoid debt may be selfish, but are all lawsuits brought against mothers by sons unethical and unjustified?

The second line of support for ① is the inference from claims ⑨ and ⑩, that parental responsibility ends with adolescence and so parents should not be legally required to support their children. Even if ⑩ is true, it just does not follow that it is always unjustified to sue one's mother. The young man's conduct may be indefensible, but this argument draws a fallacious conclusion from his example. This is not a good argument.

7. Here is a shorthand version of the argument.

1. *Gay people may be "afraid of coming out because of the hostility they hear and see in the workplace."*
2. *It takes a lot of energy to protect your life.*
*3. *Energy spent on protecting oneself means less energy available for productive work.*

4. *Gay people who have to worry about what will happen to them if they come out of the closet (acknowledge their homosexuality) generally produce at a lower level than gay people who don't worry about what will happen to them.*

The argument provides good reasons for accepting premise (2). It describes with examples the various efforts and restraints gay people may exhibit trying to disguise their private life. With the addition of the missing premise (*3), the argument is deductively valid. Premises (1) and (2) are empirically true. Therefore, it is a good argument.

9. ① All our theories of science are formulated on the assumption that space-time is smooth and nearly flat, so they break down at the big bang singularity, where the curvature of space-time is infinite.

② This means that even if there were events before the big bang, one could not use them to determine what would happen afterward, because predictability would break down at the big bang. ③ Correspondingly, if, as is the case, we know only what has happened since the big bang, we could not determine what happened beforehand. ④ As far as we are concerned, events before the big bang can have no consequences so they should not form part of a scientific model of the universe. ⑤ We should therefore cut them out of the model and say that time had a beginning at the big bang.

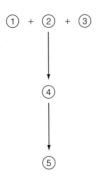

Given that, because of the big bang, we can make no predictions either from events before the big bang to events after, or vice versa, it follows with necessity that events before the big bang can form no part of our "scientific model of the universe." Therefore, the argument concludes that we should say that time begins with the big bang. It follows deductively that "we should . . . say that time had a beginning. . . ." It does not follow, however, that time does have a beginning! If we distinguish between *what is* and *what we say is*, then it is clear that the argument is about the latter. Are you willing to accept the authority of physicist Stephen Hawking? Most people would. Then, with its deductively valid inferences, it is a good argument.

11. 1. *For one, impulse is the medium of emotion; the seed of all impulse is a feeling bursting to express itself in action.*
   2. *Those who are at the mercy of impulse—who lack self-control—suffer a moral deficiency: The ability to control impulse is the base of will and character.*
   3. *By the same token, the root of altruism lies in empathy, the ability to read emotions in others; lacking a sense of another's need or despair, there is no caring.*

   4. *There is growing evidence that fundamental ethical stances in life stem from underlying emotional capacities.*
   5. *And if there are any two moral stances that our times call for, they are precisely these, self-restraint and compassion.*
   6. *These are times when the fabric of society seems to unravel at ever-greater speed, when selfishness, violence, and a meanness of spirit seem to be rotting the goodness of our communal lives.*

   This passage might be interpreted in a couple of different ways, depending on how one weighs (4), (5), and (6). In the rendition above, (6) is the overall conclusion. Beyond question, however, is that (1), (2), and (3) are evidence for (5) and probably (4) as well. Statement (6) seems to be a strongly supported conclusion, since it follows necessarily from premises (1) through (3), and they are plausible statements. If (4) is to be concluded from the same premises, then it doesn't follow necessarily, since nothing in the premises mentions growing evidence. Nevertheless, those premises do provide good reason for thinking that (4) is probably true. Now, given that ethical stances are grounded in emotional capacities and that in our times self-restraint and compassion are the two moral stances most needed, conclusion (6) does seem to follow. A pretty convincing argument, would you agree?

13. Rebuttal to criticism 1: Grading is unreliable.

   1. *A student's work is generally not judged with significant difference by different instructors.*
   2. *Two competent doctors may offer divergent diagnoses of the same condition, but their disagreement does not imply that doctors' diagnoses*

are in general biased and unreliable. Similarly, two competent art critics may offer divergent evaluations of the same work of art, but such a disagreement does not imply that a critic's evaluations are usually biased and unreliable.

3. Inevitably, experts, like all human beings, sometimes disagree about complex judgments, but we would be foolish to allow such disagreements to obscure the obvious fact that in any established field of inquiry some individuals are knowledgeable and others are not. Clearly the opinions of those who are knowledgeable are the most reliable measure of an individual's achievement in that field.

4. Of course, two competent instructors may offer divergent evaluations of the same piece of work, but it does not follow, however, that there is no such thing as expertise.

5. Thus, it is not true that the student's grade is not a reliable measure of his achievement but merely indicates the particular bias of his instructor.

Rebuttal to criticism 2: Grading traumatizes.

6. Often only by competing with others do we bring out the best in ourselves.
7. Competition fosters excellence, and without that challenge most of us would be satisfied with accomplishing far less than we are capable of.

*8. The benefits of competition are more important than the possible harmful effects.
9. The criticism that grades traumatize students by fostering competition and arousing bitterness and hostility emphasizes only the possible harmful effects of competition while overlooking beneficial effects.

*10. Therefore, the criticism based on harmful effects of grading is not plausible.

Rebuttal to criticism 3: Grading dehumanizes.

11. A grade does not measure the person; it measures the person's level of achievement.
12. It does not dehumanize a person to recognize that one person is better at some activity or skill than another.
13. Indeed, to recognize an individual's strengths and weaknesses, to know areas of expertise, areas of competence, and areas of ignorance is not to deny but to emphasize individuality.

14. It is not true that grades only dehumanize and, therefore, defeat one of the essential purposes of an education: to aid each individual in developing individuality.

15. Thus, grades do not dehumanize an individual; on the contrary, they contribute to a recognition of uniqueness and to the possible development of individual interests and abilities.

This passage consists of a series of rebuttals to three criticisms of grading: that grading is unreliable, that by creating competition it traumatizes students, and that it is dehumanizing. The first rebuttal is deductively valid, since (1) there is general agreement in grading among graders and (2) disagreement does not imply unreliability. It would be interesting to see empirical studies supporting premise (1), but it is acceptable on authority; further, premise (2) is nonempirically true.

The argument refuting the second criticism becomes deductively valid given the supplied premises. However, premises (6) and (7), which report the benefits of competition, are too important for this argument to go without evidence. Further, how do we know that (*8), the benefits outweigh the costs, is true? This is not a strong argument.

The last rebuttal claims that grading is not dehumanizing; in fact, it provides useful self-evaluation, which is important for self-knowledge. Premises (11) and (13) are probably best interpreted as nonempirical claims, telling us how we ought to view the practice of grading. Are they true? They have no support within the argument, other than the examples. Yet, it is a defensible claim that we ought to view evaluation as useful rather than demeaning. If you grant the premises, as I would, then it follows with necessity that grading does not dehumanize. These are successful defenses of grading. Agree?

15. ① That man is, in fact, only a member of a biotic community is shown by an ecological interpretation of history. ② Many historical events, hitherto explained solely in terms of human enterprise, were actually biotic interactions between people and land. ③ The characteristics of the land determined the facts quite as potently as the characteristics of the men who lived on it.

Consider, for example, the settlement of the Mississippi valley. ④ In the years following the revolution, three groups were contending for its control: the native Indian, the French and English traders, and the American settlers. Historians wonder what would have happened if the English at Detroit had thrown a little more weight into the Indian side of those tipsy scales which decided the outcome of the colonial migration into the cane-lands of Kentucky. ⑤ It is time now to ponder the fact that the cane-lands, when subjected to the particular mixture of forces represented by the cow, plow, fire, and axe of the pioneer, became bluegrass. ⑥ *If the plant succession inherent in this dark and bloody ground had, under the impact of these forces, given us some worthless sedge, shrub, or weed, it is likely that Boone and Kenton would not have held out. There might not have been any overflow into Ohio, Indiana, Illinois, and Missouri, any Louisiana Purchase, any transcontinental union of new states, or any civil war.*

⑦ We are commonly told what the human actors in this drama tried to do, but we are seldom told that their success, or the lack of it, hung in large degree on the reaction of particular soils to the impact of the particular forces exerted by their occupancy. In the case of Kentucky, we do not even know where the bluegrass came from—whether it is a native species, or a stowaway from Europe.

⑧ In short, the plant succession steered the course of history; the pioneer simply demonstrated, for good or ill, what successions inhered in the land. Is history taught in this spirit? It will be, once the concept of land as a community really penetrates our intellectual life.

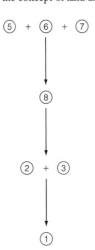

The argument is that "the plant succession steered the course of history" and, therefore, human history is at least as dependent on ecological factors as human factors. In support, the arguer speculates that the course of U.S. history might have been significantly altered were it not for the particular plant succession in Kentucky. The evidence for ⑧ does not, however, appear very strong. It seems plausible that ecological facts could have such significance, but the arguer's example is speculative. A central part of the argument, that in support of ⑧, is not good.

A Glossary of Important Terms

Affirming the consequent, Fallacy of   One of the formal fallacies; a logically invalid argument form having as its premises a conditional statement and the affirmation of the consequent, and concluding with the affirmation of the antecedent. Schematically: *If A then B; B; therefore, A.* 40

Agreement, Method of   One of Mill's Methods for identifying causal relations; in this case, we have evidence that C causes E if we know that C is the only antecedent circumstance always present when E occurs. *If two or more instances of a phenomenon E have only one antecedent circumstance in common, then probably that antecedent circumstance is the cause or a partial cause of E.* 232

Analogy, Argument from   Also called *analogical argument,* this is a type of argument in which a conclusion about one thing is drawn on the basis of a presumed analogy or similarity to something else. The rationale is that if two or more things are alike and one is known to have a certain characteristic, then probably the other does, too. Schematically, the argument form is: *given that A is like B and B is f, then probably A is also f.* (See *false analogy*) 243

Antecedent   A conditional statement asserts, schematically, *If A, then B;* for example, *If it rains, then my car is wet.* The antecedent is that part of the conditional referring to the condition A to be met if the consequent B is to occur. (See *conditional statement* and *consequent*) 40

Argument   In logic, an identifiable piece of reasoning consisting of a group of statements, one of which, called the *conclusion,* is claimed to follow from the other(s), called the *premise(s).* The word also refers to the proof, evidence, or reasons offered in support of something—*Your argument for censorship is weak*—or the debate disputants may have—*The topic of their argument is censorship*. (See *good argument*) 7

Authority, Appeal to   (*Argumentum ad Verecundiam*) A type of argument based on the testimony of someone considered an expert on the subject. The informal fallacy called *Fallacious Appeal to Authority* occurs when the person cited is not in fact an authority or for some reason should not be relied upon. 264

Barbara   A deductively valid argument form whose statements, all categorical, are of the forms: *All A are B, All B are C, therefore, All A are C*. 38

Begging the question   Often described as the fallacy of assuming the conclusion in the premises or, again, as *circular reasoning*. It involves a violation of the principle that *in order to provide reason for accepting a conclusion, a premise cannot itself depend upon the conclusion*. This violation is most blatant in the case of circular reasoning, where a premise for a conclusion is itself supported by the conclusion. Another type of begging the question is the *complex question*, a question framed in such a way that it assumes incrimination. For example, *Is this another of your stupid ideas?* assumes that your ideas are stupid. 284

Biased sample   A sample that is not representative of the population and, therefore, not reliable as evidence for an inductive generalization. The method of sampling is biased if it does not give every member of the population an equal chance to occur in the sample. (See *sample*) 214

Categorical logic   A system of logic based on the logical relationships of categorical statements. It provides a theory of *statement, argument,* and *logical inference* including rules for analysis and the determination of deductive validity. 50.

Categorical statement   In the theory of categorical logic, the preferred forms for statements are the categorical forms: *All A are B, No A are B, Some A are B,* and *Some A are not B,* where A and B stand for subjects and predicates that name categories or groups of things. 51

Categorical syllogism   The standard form of argument in categorical logic. It consists of three categorical statements—two premises and a conclusion—exactly three categories, each one occurring in exactly two of the statements. 109

Causal argument   Any of a family of arguments in which at least one causal statement occurs as premise or conclusion. Two types of causal arguments have a causal statement as premise: *causal explanation* and *causal prediction*. The causal argument ending in a *causal conclusion* is named accordingly. 220

Causal conclusion   An argument that concludes with a causal statement. This is the type of argument for which John Stuart Mill provides an evidentiary theory called *Mill's Methods*. (See *causal statement* and *Mill's methods*) 229

Causal explanation   An argument consisting of a causal generalization, an instance of an effect, and concluding that an instance of a cause has occurred. Formally, *Cs cause Es; an E occurred; probably a C occurred*. 228

Causal prediction   An argument consisting of a causal generalization, an instance of a causal circumstance, and concluding that a specific effect occurs. Formally, *Cs cause Es; a C occurs; probably, E will occur*. 228

Causal prescription   An argument consisting of a causal generalization and concluding with a prescription or recommendation for producing or preventing some effect. For example, *Since flossing reduces tooth decay, which is desired, you should floss regularly*. 228

Causal statement   Any statement that asserts or denies a causal relation, for example, *Cats make me sneeze; Novocaine deadens pain; Spanking does not cause aggression*. 220

Charity, Principle of A normative principle applicable to interpretation in logic. Given that the logical analysis of an argument may require decisions about the meaning and structure of an argument, the principle of charity advises us not to weaken an argument through interpretation but to apply the most plausible construal. 23

Concomitant variation, Method of One of Mill's Methods for identifying causal relations; in this case, we have evidence that C causes E if we know that C and E vary together. For example, the occurrence of certain kinds of cholesterol in human blood and the occurrence of coronary blockage are two phenomena that can and do change together. *Higher cholesterol is associated with higher incidence of blocked arteries.* So, according to this Method, we have evidence of a causal connection. 236

Conditional statement An extremely important kind of statement since it asserts an inferential relationship, namely, that something is the case on the condition that something else is the case. Schematically, a conditional statement is of the form *If A, then B.* 5

Conjunction A compound statement that asserts the truth of two or more statements, as in *It rains and my car is wet.* 134

Consequent A conditional statement asserts, schematically, *If A, then B.* The consequent B is that part of a conditional said to obtain if the condition A is met. (See *conditional statement* and *antecedent*) 40

Contingent statement In truth-functional logic, a statement whose truth-values include at least one T and one F. A contingent statement is neither a necessary truth nor falsehood; rather, if true, it might have been false and vice-versa. 173

Contradiction In logic, contradiction is the formal property of statements in which their truth-values are exactly opposite. If one is true, the other is false, and vice-versa. The two statements are said to be *contradictories.* For example, *Ann is a grandmother; Ann is not a grandmother.* In colloquial speech, a contradiction is less rigorously conceived. It may mean merely that one statement is the denial of another, as in "Your testimony contradicts the defendant's." (See *self-contradiction*) 173

Contraposition One of the defined operations performable on statements. In this case, to *contrapose* a statement is to negate the subject and predicate terms and switch their places as well. For example, *Some believers are Buddhists* becomes *Some non-Buddhists are nonbelievers,* where the latter is called the *contrapositive* of the former. (See *conversion* and *obversion*) 79

Contrary Two statements are contraries if only one can be true, though both may be false. *Contrariety* in logic is the formal relationship between two statements in which if one is true, then the other is false but not vice-versa. For example, *Tony was born in Vermont; Tony was born in Utah.* (See *contradiction* and *subcontrary*) 67

Conversion One of the defined operations performable on statements, in this case, that of switching the subject and predicate. For example, *All birds are flyers* is converted to *All flyers are birds,* where the latter is said to be the *converse* of the former. (See *contraposition* and *obversion*) 79

Deductive reasoning Refers to reasoning by means of *deductively valid arguments.* The study of such reasoning is called *deductive logic.* These concepts are typically defined in contrast to the concepts of *inductive reasoning* and *induction* following a traditional theory in logic in which all arguments are either deductive or inductive. That theory has been challenged in two ways: (1) the deductive/inductive distinction is not exhaustive of kinds of reasoning; and (2) the distinction ought to be made in terms of degree of inferential support rather than the structure of the argument. (See *inductive reasoning* and *deductive validity*) 31

Deductive validity That property of an argument in which, given the premises, the conclusion follows necessarily. In a deductively valid argument, it is a logical contradiction to maintain the premises and deny the conclusion. This is the highest standard of inferential strength, that is, support that premises pass to a conclusion. (See *deductive reasoning, inductively strong argument,* and *good argument*) 31

Denying the antecedent, Fallacy of A formal fallacy consisting of a conditional statement and denial of the antecedent of the conditional as premises, and concluding with a denial of the consequent. Schematically, *If A then B, not A, therefore not B.* 40

Difference, Method of One of Mill's Methods for identifying causal relations. Comparing the case in which a phenomenon E occurs with the case in which it does not occur, if antecedent circumstance C is the only difference, then probably C is causally related to E. 234

Disjunction A compound statement that asserts, usually by using the word *or,* that at least one of two or more statements is true. For example, *Tim is shopping or Todd is working late.* The statements in a disjunction are called *disjuncts.* The truth-functional definition of the disjunction is that it gets a T if at least one of its disjuncts is T otherwise it is F. The disjunction exemplifies the *inclusive* sense of the word *or:* that sense in which one or both disjuncts may be true. This is in contrast to the *exclusive* sense of *or.* (See *'or'*) 134

Disjunctive syllogism A deductively valid argument form having as its premises a disjunction and the denial of one of the *disjuncts,* and then concluding with the assertion of the remaining disjunct. Schematically, *A or B, not A, therefore B.* (See *disjunction*) 39

Either/or fallacy Reasoning fallaciously that a certain option must be accepted because there is only one alternative and it is unacceptable. The fallacy occurs in presuming that there is only one alternative. This type of argument is also called *black and white reasoning,* a helpful name connoting the failure to see the "gray," or other possibility. 274

Empirical/nonempirical statements A distinction, not uncontroversial, about how the truth-value of statements is determined. *Empirical statements* are those whose truth-value is determinable, at least in principle, by the appropriate observations or sense experiences, generally. For example, *Squirrels lay eggs* is false by observation. *Nonempirical statements*—for example, *Chemists are scientists*—are not verifiable by observation. A more complex group, the truth-value of nonempirical statements often involves analysis of terms, logical form, or mathematical calculation. 333

Enthymeme Any argument that is missing a premise or conclusion. Aside from the obvious requirements of a conclusion and at least one premise, what a specific argument needs in order to be whole may be relative to the context or to some theory of good argument form, for example, the theory of the syllogism. 17

Equivocation An informal fallacy in which the inference depends upon using a term or phrase in two or more different senses. 276

Existential assumption The assumption about a statement that members of the subject class exist. For example, if we make such an existential assumption about *All Batavians are Europeans,* then we assume that Batavians exist. It follows, then, that if Batavians do not exist, the statement is false. In categorical logic, in particular, a distinction is made between the existential and the *modern* or hypothetical interpretation of the universal statements. (See *modern square of opposition* and *traditional square of opposition*) 64

Fallacy An error in reasoning. Since the purpose of logic is to identify good reasoning, the study of fallacies is crucial. Historically, logicians have identified numerous patterns of reasoning that are, in the appropriate contexts, fallacious. An important distinction is made between those that are identifiable by form or structure, called *formal fallacies,* and those identifiable by content, *informal fallacies.* (See the specific fallacies) 263

False analogy   An informal fallacy involving reasoning by an irrelevant analogy. One way of refuting an analogical argument is to show that the purported similarity is in fact not relevant to the conclusion. That would be charging the argument with false analogy. (See *argument from analogy*) 281

False cause   An informal fallacy in which a causal claim is based on insufficient evidence. One version, called *post hoc ergo propter hoc* (literally, "after this, therefore because of this"), fallaciously concludes a causal connection because one event precedes the other. Another type of false cause, called *oversimplification,* occurs when, for example, a solution is offered that, on inspection, seems to ignore the complexity of the situation. 271

Force, Appeal to   (*Argumentum ad Baculum*) An informal fallacy in which a conclusion is based upon a threat. Rather than offering a reason relevant to the conclusion, the arguer presents a threat to the listener, attempting to compel acceptance through force, not reason. 266

Good argument   In logic, an argument with true, or at least acceptable, premises from which the conclusion follows either with necessity (called *deductive validity*) or high probability (called *inductive strength*). The requirements of a good argument are that the conclusion follows and that the premises are true. These two requirements are logically separable, giving us some arguments that lack truth and some that lack inferential strength. 29

Ignorance, Appeal to   (*Argumentum ad Ignorantiam*) The informal fallacy of taking the absence of disproof as a reason affirming a statement. For example, *There's probably life on Mars because they've not shown otherwise.* One way of understanding this fallacy is that it places the burden of proof on the wrong side of an issue. A clear example is the arguer who ignores the presumption of innocence in the law and claims that a person is guilty because *he's not been shown innocent.* 267

Inconsistency, Fallacy of   Two statements, beliefs, or positions are inconsistent if they cannot be true simultaneously. An *implicit* inconsistency occurs when beliefs carry implications that are inconsistent. The charge of the fallacy of inconsistency is that a person is defending or reasoning from inconsistent premises. 267

Inductive generalization   A major type of inductive argument in which a conclusion about a group of things, called the *population,* is based upon observations about a subset or *sample* of the group. A statistical generalization is an inductive generalization expressed statistically and based upon a statistical description of a sample. 210

Inductive logic   The name given to that part of logic devoted to the study of reasoning held to a standard of inferential strength less than deductive validity yet still persuasive. Inductively supported arguments are held to a standard of *high degree of probability* that the conclusion follows from the premises. Three types of inductive arguments are typically the subjects of the study of inductive logic: the *inductive generalization,* the *causal conclusion,* and the *argument from analogy.* (See *deductive validity* and *inductively strong argument*) 206

Inductive reasoning   Used in contrast to *deductive reasoning,* this concept refers to using or examining arguments that are not deductively valid but provide some degree of support for the conclusion. The study of such reasoning has been called *inductive logic.* Logicians have distinguished different types of inductive arguments including the *inductive generalization, causal argument,* and the *argument from analogy.* (See *inductive logic* and *inductively strong argument*) 206

Inductively strong argument   An argument that, although not meeting the high standard of deductive validity, nevertheless is good because it has premises that provide a high degree of probability for the conclusion. An *inductively weak* argument is one whose premises, if true, do not make the conclusion likely. (See *inductive logic, deductive validity* and *good argument*) 207

Inference   A step in reasoning in which one idea is thought to be a reason for another. That part of an argument referring to the connection of support between premise and conclusion. In this sense every argument contains an inference. 5

Logic   The study of the principles of good reasoning. Its purpose is to provide analysis of important concepts in reasoning—argument, statement, inference, etc.—and principles by which good reasoning may be distinguished from bad. Historically, reflection on reasoning probably began with the Egyptians, who were certainly familiar with deductions in geometry. Pre-Socratic philosophers (c. 600 B.C.E.) and Plato (c. 429-347 B.C.E.) were highly skilled theoreticians of reasoning; however, the first record of a developed theory of logic is attributed to Aristotle (384-322 B.C.E.) with his logical works called the *Organon*. Aristotelian or traditional logic, also called the logic of the *syllogism*, dominated logic until the nineteenth century. Gottlob Frege (1848-1925), a German logician and mathematician, developed the concepts that constitute modern logic, in particular the truth-functional conception of the statement and theory of inference, the predicate calculus, the quantifiers and variables. In the past century logic has undergone considerable expansion and renewed interest in ancient topics. There are specialized studies in the logic of possibility or *modal logic*, the logic of obligation or *deontic logic*, and informal logic and critical thinking. 1

Mill's Methods   A theory of evidentiary support for conclusions about cause and effect. Attributed to John Stuart Mill (1806–1873), it consists of four principles: method of agreement; method of concomitant variation; method of difference; method of residue. 232

Modern square of opposition   In categorical logic, the name for one of the representations of the set of logical relations among the four categorical forms. In contrast to the *traditional square of opposition,* the modern does not interpret the universal statements *existentially*. That is, the A and E forms are not assumed to imply the existence of members of the subject category. Thus, for example, *All deserters will be shot* does not require the existence of deserters in order to be true. (See *existential assumption*) 74

Necessary condition   With regard to a conditional statement, this is the *consequent*. If A is a necessary condition of B, then A's failure to obtain implies that B does not obtain. For example, *Mary is a female is a necessary condition of Mary's being a mother*. (See *sufficient condition*) 146

Obversion   One of the defined operations performable on statements. In this case, the *obverse* of a statement is formed by changing the quality and negating the predicate. *Changing the quality* means changing a statement from an affirmation to a denial or vice versa. An example of obversion: *All birds are flyers* is obverted to *No birds are nonflyers*. (See *conversion* and *contraposition*) 79

"Or"   This word deserves special attention because it can be used in two logically very different senses. For example, *John is six-foot tall or John is six-foot two inches tall* is best understood as asserting that only one of two states of affairs is true. Interpreted so, we say that 'or' is used in an *exclusive* sense. Colloquially, it means "one or the other but not both." However, to imply by 'or' that one or more of the states of affairs can obtain is to use the *inclusive* sense. For example, *We can go to dinner or the movies* leaves open that we might do both! *One or the other or both,* you might say. The inclusive sense is the sense captured in the truth-functional concept of the *disjunction*. (See *disjunction*) 134

Particular statement   In logic, categorical logic specifically, any statement that has as its subject at least one but not all members of a class. (See *universal statement*) 56

People, Appeal to the   (*Argumentum ad Populum*) Related to the *Fallacious Appeal to Authority*, this type of fallacy cites customary belief or popular opinion as a reason for a conclusion. 267

Pity, Appeal to   (*Argumentum ad Misericordiam*) A fallacious argument in which the arguer attempts to support a conclusion not by relevant reason but by inciting the listener's sympathy. 267

Premise   A statement offered in support of a conclusion; a reason for accepting an inference. 29

Red herring   An informal fallacy, usually advanced as a rebuttal, that consists of distracting attention from the subject at hand by raising some controversial issue. It gets its name from a prank, using a bag of dead herring to divert the hunting dogs from the scent of the fox. 287

Residue, Method of   One of Mill's Methods for identifying causal relations. In this case, we have evidence that C causes E if C is the only antecedent circumstance remaining after the other causal factors have been accounted for. 238

Sample   A subset of a group, called the *population,* that is used as the basis for an inductive generalization about the rest. A sample is considered good evidence for an inductive generalization if it is *representative* of the population. Representativeness depends upon the nature of the population and how the sample is constructed. A *simple random sample* is one in which every member of the population has an equal chance of appearing in the sample. *A stratified random sample,* on the other hand, is intentionally constructed with subsets as they are believed to occur in the population. (See *biased sample*) 211

Self-contradiction   A statement that is necessarily false in virtue of its form. *Marge is and is not wealthy.* (See *contradiction*) 173

Slippery slope   A criticism or argument against a proposal by claiming that, if undertaken, it will lead by steps to some undesirable conclusion and, for that reason, ought to be rejected. The informal fallacy called slippery slope, a version of *false cause,* occurs when there is no good evidence for such a series of events. 273

Statement   A sentence, either written or spoken, that makes an assertion that has truth-value. Statements are the building blocks of arguments and, therefore, among the fundamental elements of any system of logic. Truth-functional and categorical logic provide theories of statements and their logical relations. 3

Straw man   A fallacious response that involves distorting an opponent's argument, criticism, or position to one's advantage. A man made of straw, just like an argument that is misrepresented, is easy to knock over. Two characteristic ways by which an argument may be distorted are by oversimplifying, on the one hand—*Vegetarianism is a nice idea but we kill things all the time*—or by grossly exaggerating, on the other—*Vegetarianism is a nice idea but we have to eat something!* 285

Subalternation   That logical relationship between two statements in which the falsity of one, called the *subalternate,* implies the falsity of the other but not vice-versa. Thus, if *Ann is a mother* is false, then so also is *Ann is a grandmother* but not the converse. In categorical logic, the particular statements are *subalternates* of their respective universals. 66

Subcontrary Two statements are *subcontraries* if both can be true but only one can be false. Thus, if either is false, then the other is true. Consider the pair: *Ann is not a grandmother; Ann is not a grandfather.* 67

Sufficient condition With regard to a conditional statement, this is the *antecedent.* If A is a sufficient condition of B, then if A obtains, B obtains. For example, *Mary is a mother is a sufficient condition of Mary's being a female.* (See *necessary condition*) 146

Superalternation That logical relationship between two statements in which the truth of one, called the *superalternate,* implies the truth of the other but not vice-versa. For example, *Smith is a surgeon* implies that *Smith is a doctor* but not the reverse. In categorical logic the universal statements are *superalternates* of their respective particulars. 66

Tautology A statement that, due to its form, is a necessary truth. In truth-functional logic, a tautology is a statement whose truth-values are always and only Ts. 173

Traditional square of opposition In categorical logic, the name for the representation of the set of logical relations among the four categorical forms. In contrast to the *modern square of opposition,* the traditional interprets the universal statements *existentially.* That is, the A and E forms are assumed to imply the existence of members of the subject category. (See *existential assumption*) 64

Truth In logic, truth is a property of statements, those that assert what is the case (or deny what is not). In some philosophical theories, truth is also said to be a property of those beliefs for which we have good argument. In the evaluation of argument, truth is distinguished from *validity* and inferential support generally. We say that a good argument must have true premises and strong inferential support, where these two conditions are logically separable. 44

Truth-functional logic A system of logic based on the concept of the *truth-function:* that the *truth-value* of a compound statement is a function of the truth-values of its component statements and the logical meaning of the *operator* that forms their relationship. Standardly, there are five logical operators: *not, and, or, if . . . then . . . ,* and *. . . if and only if. . . .* It provides a theory of *statement, argument,* and *logical inference* including rules for analysis and the determination of deductive validity. 131

Truth-value That property of a statement in which it is true or false. That a sentence has a truth-value entails that it is a *statement.* 3

Undistributed middle, Fallacy of A deductively invalid argument form whose statements, all categorical, are of the forms: *All A are B, All C are B, therefore, All A are C.* For example, *All scientists are democrats; all historians are democrats; therefore, all scientists are historians.* The fallacy gets its name from the fact that the middle term—*democrats* in our example—is undistributed, that is, does not refer to all members of that category. 40

Universal statement In logic, and particularly categorical logic, any statement that has as its subject all members of a class. (See *particular statement*) 55

Index

Deduction. *See* Deductive validity; Formal deduction
Deductive argument. *See* Deductive validity
Deductive validity, 31ff., 44ff., 308
  defined, 33
  determining with indirect truth table method, 169–172
  determining with truth table method, 166ff.
  determining with Venn diagram method, 110ff.
  good argument and, 31ff.
  inductive strength and, 31, 206, 255
  invalidity, 111
  logical contradiction and, 34
  logical form and, 37ff.
  requiring existential assumption, 114–115
  truth and, 44ff.
DeMorgan's rule, 176, 196–197, 200
Denying the antecedent. *See* Fallacy of denying the antecedent
Diagrams. *See* Venn diagram
  of the operations, 87
Diagramming. *See* Venn diagram
  arguments, 12–15
Difference. *See* Method of difference
Disjunct. *See* Disjunction
Disjunction, 134–136, 144–146, 155
  exclusive "or," 135, 145
  inclusive "or," 135
  truth function for, 154, 155
  truth functional, 134, 154
  variations on, 144–146
Disjunction sign, 136
Disjunctive statement. *See* Disjunction
Disjunctive syllogism, 39, 185–188, 200, 275
  valid logical form of, 39, 41
Distribution, 199–200
Division, fallacy of, 280–281, 292
Double negation, rule of, 176, 196, 200

E-form statement, 55, 60
  Venn diagram for, 60
"Either . . . . . or." *See* Disjunction
"Either . . . . . or . . . but not both," 145
Either/or fallacy, 274–276, 291
Empirical statement, 333–336
Enthymeme, 17–19. 327–329
Equivalence, 79, 86, 175, 180. *See also* Biconditional statements; Material equivalence
  formal deduction in, 180, 195ff.

identifying with Venn diagrams, 79, 86
operations and, 86
truth functional equivalence, 175
Equivocation, 276–277, 291
Evaluating arguments, 307ff.
  procedure for, 307–308
  sample evaluations, 339–342
Examining premises, 332–336
Exclusive "or." *See* Disjunction
Existential assumption, 64ff., 74
  four categorical forms with, 66
  making an, 65ff., 114–115
Exportation, 199–200
Exposing the argument, 7ff., 308ff. *See also* Real arguments
  omitting sentences, 309–314
  paraphrasing, 318–321
  rewriting sentences, 314–318
Extended argument, 14

Fallacy, 263. *See* Formal fallacy; Informal fallacy; *specific fallacies*
Fallacy of affirming the consequent, 40–41
Fallacy of denying the antecedent, 40–41
Fallacy of undistributed middle, 40–41
False analogy, 281–283, 292. *See also* Argument from analogy
False cause, 271–273, 292
  oversimplification, 272, 292
  post hoc ergo propter hoc, 272, 292
False dichotomy. *See* Either/or fallacy
"Few," 101–102
Formal deduction, 180ff.
Formal fallacy, 263
Four categorical forms. *See* Categorical statement

Generalization. *See* Inductive generalization; Hasty generalization
Good argument, 29–33, 45, 207. *See also* Deductive validity; Inductive strength; Premise
  defined, 30, 33
Grouping and the scope of operators, 139–142

Hasty generalization, fallacy of, 214, 227–279, 291
Horseshoe, 136, 138
Hypothetical syllogism, 189, 200

I-form statement, 55, 60
  Venn diagram for, 60
"If," 135–136, 146

"if and only if," 104–105, 154. *See also*
    Biconditional statements
    categorical translation, 104–105
    truth functional translation, 135–136,
        154
"If. . . then," 104, 135–136, 146. *See also*
    Conditional statement; "Only";
    "Only if"; "The only"
    categorical translation, 104–108
    truth functional translation, 135–136,
        154
"Implies," 149
Inclusive "or." *See* Disjunction
Inconsistency, fallacy of, 288–290, 292
Independent support, 13
    distinguished from joint support, 13
Indirect truth table, 169–172
Induction. *See* Inductive strength
Inductive argument. *See* Inductive
    strength
Inductive generalization, 210–216, 255.
    See also Population; Sample;
    Statistical generalization; Target
    characteristic
    criteria of inductive strength, 215
    features of, 211
    summary of, 215–216
Inductive logic, 206ff.
Inductive strength, 31, 207–210, 255. *See*
    also Argument from analogy; Causal
    conclusion; Inductive generalization
    criteria, summarized, 255
    deductive validity and, 31–33, 206–
        207
    defined, 208
    good argument and, 31–33, 206–208
    probability, mathematically described,
        208–209
Inductive weakness, 208
Inference, 5, 7, 63
    deductively valid. *See* Deductive
        validity
    inductively strong. *See* Inductive
        strength
    inferential relationship, 7, 44
    inferential support, 30–33, 207–208
    valid rules of. *See* Equivalences; Rules
        of inference
Inferred feature, in argument from anal-
    ogy, 244, 252
Informal fallacy, 263. *See also specific*
    fallacies
    summarized, 291–292
Invalid deductive argument. *See* Deductive
    validity

Invalid logical form, 40–41. *See also* Fal-
    lacy of affirming the consequent;
    Fallacy of denying the antecedent;
    Fallacy of undistributed middle
Invalidity. *See* Deductive validity

Joint support, 13
    distinguished from joint support, 13

Logic,
    basic concepts summarized, 26–27.
        See also Categorical logic; Truth
        functional
    defined, 1, 26
    inductive. *See* Inductive logic
    psychology and, 2
    system of. *See* Logical systems
Logical equivalence, 79, 85–86. *See also*
    Equivalence
Logical form, 37. *See also* Invalid logical
    form; Valid logical form
    summarized, 41
Logical operator, 132ff.
    symbols for, 136
    truth functions for. *See specific operators*
Logical system,
    practical use of, 50
    purpose of, 51

"Many," 101–102
Material equivalence, 198–199, 200
Material implication, 175, 198, 200
Megarians, 131
Method of agreement, 232–234, 240
    modified, 234
Method of concomitant variation, 236–
    238, 240
Method of difference, 234–235, 240
Method of residue, 238–239, 240
Mill, John Stuart, 232
Mill's methods, 232ff. *See also* Method of
    agreement; Method of concomitant
    variation; Method of difference;
    Method of residue
    summary, 239–240
Missing premise and conclusion. *See* Sup-
    plying missing parts
Modern square of opposition, 64, 74–78
Modus ponens, 39, 41,183, 187, 200
Modus tollens, 39, 41, 184, 187, 200
"Most," 101–102

Names. *See* Proper names
Necessary condition, 146ff., 149, 222. *See*
    also Causally necessary condition